SHILOH

and the Western Campaign of 1862

O. Edward Cunningham

Edited by
Gary D. Joiner and Timothy B. Smith

SB

Savas Beatie

New York and California

ISBN 10: 1-932714-27-8
ISBN 13: 978-1-932714-27-2

Published by
Savas Beatie LLC
521 Fifth Avenue, Suite 3400
New York, NY 10175

Editorial Offices:

Savas Beatie LLC
P.O. Box 4527
El Dorado Hills, CA 95762

Book Club Edition

For T. Harry Williams

Contents

Contents (continued)

List of Illustrations

A Confederate photo gallery begins after page 68

A Union photo gallery begins after page 114

List of Maps

List of Maps (continued)

List of Maps (continued)

MAP KEY

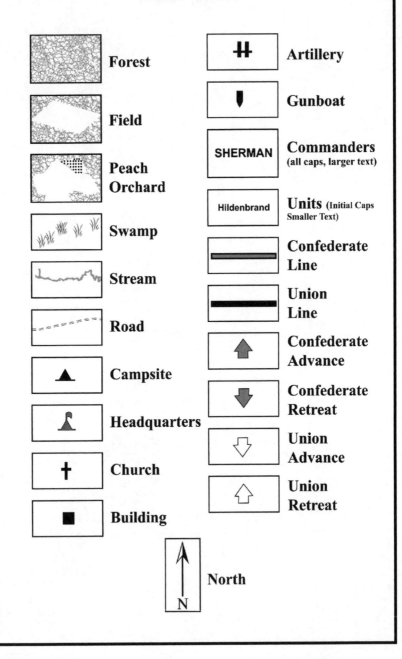

Forest

Field

Peach
Orchard

Swamp

Stream

Road

Campsite

Headquarters

Church

Building

Artillery

Gunboat

SHERMAN — Commanders (all caps, larger text)

Hildenbrand — Units (Initial Caps Smaller Text)

Confederate
Line

Union
Line

Confederate
Advance

Confederate
Retreat

Union
Advance

Union
Retreat

North
N

Acknowledgments

THE ASSISTANCE OF MANY persons made this project possible, but the person who conceived and directed this dissertation is Professor T. Harry Williams. Without his guidance, this work would never have been started, let alone brought to fruition.

Mrs. Hilda B. Cunningham, my mother, performed many secretarial duties connected with this work. Mr. Jerry L. Schober, Supervisory Park Historian at Shiloh National Military Park, helped me locate many disputed locations, while Mr. Edwin Bearss, Park Historian of Vicksburg National Military Park, Mr. Fred Benton, Jr. and Mr. Charles East, of Baton Rouge, courteously allowed me to use valuable materials. Mr. Ray Smith of the Chicago Industrial Institute generously permitted me to use his index to the *Confederate Veteran*. The staffs of numerous archival depositories aided me in my research work, but Mr. E. L. Bedsole of the Department of Archives, Louisiana State University, was especially helpful. Mr. Maurice duQuesnay read the manuscript, making many valuable suggestions. To all these people I wish to extend my heartfelt thanks for their aid.

Edward Cunningham

In addition to Dr. Cunningham's 1966 acknowledgments, we the editors would like to thank a few people who have aided in the process of publishing this book. Chief among them is Dr. Cunningham's family, especially Mrs. Iris Cunningham and Vicki Gully.

The good people at Savas Beatie LLC worked hard to make this book a reality. Managing Director Theodore P. Savas warmed immediately to the idea of publishing this dissertation and shepherded the book through the complicated publishing process. Lee Merideth helped lay out the book and produced its index.

The staff of Precision Cartographics in Shreveport, Louisiana, aided greatly with the map work. We would also like to thank Karen Peters for her able assistance in converting the battlefield maps for publication.

The staff at Shiloh National Military Park, particularly Stacy Allen and Bjorn Skaptason, offered insights into some of Dr. Cunningham's conclusions and minor errors.

Last but certainly not least, our wives, Marilyn and Kelly, supported and loved us through the entire process. We thank them for making life so much more pleasurable—just by their presence in our lives.

Gary D. Joiner and Timothy B. Smith

CIVIL WAR BOOKS CONTINUE to be published at an astounding clip on nearly every topic imaginable. Campaign and battle studies, especially those eschewing social history and take a more traditional military approach, remain very popular with students of the war. Some combats, like the fighting at Gettysburg in the summer of 1863, attract hundreds of writers on every imaginable aspect of the fighting. Others, like the horrific early-war battle of Shiloh, catch the attention of far fewer scribes. Given the latter battle's complexity, fascinating cast of characters, and obvious importance to the course of the war, it is difficult to account fully for this lopsided disparity.

Some readers will likely inquire (and with some justification) what makes the publication of a forty-year-old dissertation on the subject of Shiloh worthwhile? And what could possibly be inside a decades-old document that can be touted as new material?

There are good reasons behind the decision to publish Dr. Cunningham's *Shiloh and the Western Campaign of 1862*. For starters, Shiloh is the exception to the rule mentioned above. It has been the recipient of only four scholarly book-length battle studies. Only three of these are academically "modern": Wiley Swords' *Shiloh: Bloody April* (1974), James Lee McDonough's *Shiloh—In Hell Before Night* (1977), and Larry J. Daniel's *Shiloh: The Battle That Changed the Civil War* (1997). The fourth entry to this rather exclusive group was the first to appear in print more than a century ago, David W. Reed's *The Battle of Shiloh and the Organizations Engaged* (1902). There is definitely plenty of elbow room available for another book on the subject.

We also firmly believe Dr. Cunningham's work is the best overall account of the Shiloh battle. Reed's study has an early familiarity with the subject seldom seen elsewhere, but it is in no way comprehensive. Sword's book is the best tactical study of the four. McDonough's account makes for good reading, but offers little tactical detail. Daniel's work breaks ground with his "new military history" slant. Each of these books has its strengths and weaknesses, just as all books do. We believe Dr. Cunningham's dissertation offers the strengths of each of these works without their associated weaknesses—a feat he managed to accomplish before three of these authors ever put pen to paper.

Writing in 1989, revered and long-time Shiloh Chief Ranger George Reaves observed that Cunningham's unpublished dissertation "is the most detailed analysis of the campaign and the battle." It is also an extremely well written piece of scholarship (which is not the case with the vast majority of dissertations). His work might be described as a significantly expanded and in-depth version of McDonough's work. Cunningham, however, finished his study more than a decade before McDonough's book appeared.[1]

Perhaps most important, Dr. Cunningham's dissertation deserves publication because the passage of forty years has not, as some might initially believe, dated his efforts. Indeed, readers will quickly discover it is still a fresh and vivid player in Shiloh historiography.

Dr. Cunningham espoused in his 1960s-era dissertation many new ideas about the fighting that were not widely accepted (or even seriously considered) until very recently. *Shiloh and the Western Campaign of 1862* was forty years (an eternity in Civil War historiography) ahead of its time. It is not, therefore, simply an older treatment of the battle dusted off and repackaged for a wider audience. Shiloh historiography is just now catching up with Cunningham.

Historical writing on Shiloh falls into four distinct schools of thought. The first school, post-battle to the late 1880s, is comprised of a recounting of the battle by its participants. The second school of thought—which is the dominant school even today—began with the establishment of the park in 1894. With access to published reports, accounts penned by the veterans, and the battlefield itself, this school

---

1 Joseph Allen Frank and George A. Reaves, *"Seeing the Elephant": Raw Recruits at the Battle of Shiloh* (Westport: Greenwood Press, 1989), 15.

insisted that the keys to the battle were the Hornet's Nest and Sunken Road. A more recent third school argued it was Albert Sidney Johnston's death—and not the struggle in the Hornet's Nest—that determined the fate of the battle. The fourth and final school, which is just emerging and quite revisionist in nature, takes a new and almost radical approach to understanding the combat at Shiloh. This school argues that neither the Hornet's Nest nor Johnston's death was the key to the battle. Rather, it was a misunderstanding of the enemy's positions, deployment, and a failure to understand the battlefield's geography that resulted in the Confederate defeat; simply put, Johnston, et. al., fought the battle incorrectly.[2]

The first school of Shiloh historiography, the Veterans' School, spanned three decades and consisted of hundreds of works. Large numbers of soldiers, from privates to general officers, wrote about their experiences in the battle. Newspapers ran weekly serials, as did *Century* magazine and several others. Old soldiers like Confederate Sam Watkins put their memories on paper for distribution, while more famous personages like U. S. Grant, William T. Sherman, and P. G. T. Beauregard received large sums of money for their recollections. Veterans' organizations such as army societies published many reminiscences, as did state historical societies. The flood of information that emerged during these thirty-plus years following the war was simply immense.[3]

David W. Reed, a Shiloh veteran of the Union Army of the Tennessee and Shiloh National Military Park's first historian, dominated

2 Much of the following material is adapted from Timothy B. Smith, "Historians and the Battle of Shiloh: One Hundred and Forty Years of Controversy" *Tennessee Historical Quarterly* 63 (Winter 2003): 332-353. This article was also reprinted in Timothy B. Smith, *The Untold Story of Shiloh: The Battle and the Battlefield* (Knoxville: University of Tennessee Press, 2006), 1-19.

3 For a good example of these works, see Robert Underwood Johnson and Clarence Clough Buel, eds., *Battles and Leaders of the Civil War, Being For the Most Part Contributions By Union and Confederate Officers: Based upon "The Century" War Series*, 4 vols. (New York: Century Company, 1884-1887).

the next period called the Reed School. Appointed in 1895 by Secretary of War Daniel S. Lamont, Reed became the chief historian of the battle. His efforts at marking the field, writing about the battle, and interpreting the events of April 1862 combined to produce a major school of thought that has dominated Shiloh historiography to this day. Reed's findings became manifest on the battlefield, in newspaper accounts, in journal articles, and in two books.

The first volume reflecting this was a history of his regiment, the Twelfth Iowa Infantry. The book emphasized the regiment's activities in the battle, with the Hornet's Nest and Sunken Road playing the major role. With the second book, *The Battle of Shiloh and the Organizations Engaged*, Reed produced the first volume dealing specifically with the battle itself. Published for the Shiloh commission by the Government Printing Office in 1902, Reed's study contained a general overview of the campaign as well as detailed actions of each unit down to the brigade level. He also included orders of battle and casualty tables. Veterans received a free copy, and when the supply was exhausted by 1909, a new edition was produced. The 1909 version incorporated new knowledge and corrected errors in the first edition. When that supply dwindled, the commission reprinted the 1909 edition four years later.[4]

After the National Park Service took control of the battlefield in 1933, the agency's historians helped institutionalize Reed's thesis. In a 1950s handbook written by park historian Albert Dillahunty, the Hornet's Nest message gained further widespread attention. Sold at Shiloh, these small books gave a short overview of the battle in which the Hornet's Nest was emphasized over other sectors of the battlefield. Likewise, the park's 1956 film, *Shiloh: Portrait of a Battle,* heavily concentrated on the Hornet's Nest, leaving other actions relatively untouched. This film has been shown to millions of visitors throughout

---

4 David W. Reed, *Campaigns and Battles of the Twelfth Regiment Iowa Veteran Volunteer Infantry: From Organization, September, 1861, to Muster-Out, January 20, 1866* (np: np, nd); David W. Reed, *The Battle of Shiloh and the Organizations Engaged* (Washington, DC: Government Printing Office, 1902); David W. Reed, *The Battle of Shiloh and the Organizations Engaged,* 2nd edition.(Washington, DC: Government Printing Office, 1909).

the decades, and was still being shown at the visitor center when this book went to press.[5]

It was not until the late 1970s that an academic historian published a book on the battle. A professor at David Lipscomb College in Nashville, James Lee McDonough produced *Shiloh: In Hell Before Night* (1977). McDonough's entertainingly written book utilized primary and secondary sources and was well received by the Civil War reading community. Although it is not deep on tactical detail, it is laced with human-interest stories and remains useful to the study of the battle. Its appearance played a major role in the perpetuation of the Reed School. Reed developed the idea and the park service interpreted it; McDonough's work reinforced and carried the Reed thesis to scholars and public alike.[6]

Paralleling the academic emergence of the Hornet's Nest thesis was a smaller yet equally important school of thought centering on Albert Sidney Johnston's death at Shiloh. One of the few major books on the battle is Wiley Sword's *Shiloh: Bloody April*, which first appeared in 1974 (with a revised 2001 edition). Sword argued that Johnston's death at Shiloh was the key factor in determining ultimate victory and defeat. Although the impact of what has been called the Sword School has not been as significant on popular opinion as the Reed thesis, Sword's *Shiloh* has played an important role in determining how others interpret the battle.[7]

The Johnston death thesis propounded by Sword appeared earlier in the Veterans' School, most notably in the writings of Johnston's son, William Preston Johnston. The thesis gained scholarly credence when the first academic biography of Johnston appeared. In 1964, Charles P.

---

5 Albert Dillahunty, *Shiloh National Military Park, Tennessee* (Washington, DC: National Park Service, 1955); *Shiloh: Portrait of a Battle* (Shiloh: Shiloh National Military Park, 1954).

6 James Lee McDonough, *Shiloh: In Hell Before Night* (Knoxville: University of Tennessee Press, 1977).

7 Wiley Sword, *Shiloh: Bloody April* (New York: William Marrow and Co., 1974); Wiley Sword, *Shiloh: Bloody April*, Revised Edition (Dayton, Ohio: Morningside Bookshop, 2001).

Roland published *Albert Sidney Johnston: Soldier of Three Republics*. This respected work portrayed Johnston's life in an objective and clearly presented manner. Roland did not excuse Johnston's mistakes, but he did emphasize that other commanders new to war made similar mistakes. They lived to learn from their sins, a luxury Johnston did not enjoy. Roland argued that if Johnston had lived, he might have provided the Confederacy with an equal to Robert E. Lee in the Western Theater. Sword's major 1974 battle study reinforced the Johnston "mystique."[8]

An emerging revisionist school of thought incorporates within it the arguments about the Hornet's Nest and Johnston's fatal wounding, but reaches new conclusions about the meaning and significance of these events. This line of thinking is the first to use the battlefield as a major source. The battlefield holds the key to understanding what happened at Shiloh, not only because of the relatively undisturbed terrain but also because of the vast array of troop position monuments and tablets erected by the veterans themselves. Thus, in many ways the field itself provides historians with as much or more insight into the action than simple reports, letters, and diaries. Indeed, most of these revisionist works cite battlefield tablets and monuments in their footnotes.

The revisionist school is also the first to challenge former schools in both matter of interpretation and questions of fact. This school explores, for example, the number of charges launched against the Hornet's Nest, the number of artillery pieces in Confederate Brigadier General Daniel Ruggles' line, and the effects of terrain on the outcome of the battle.

Finally, the recent revisionist manner in examining Shiloh is the first to attempt to place the battle in the complete context of Civil War history. Former schools dealt only with the tactical and strategic context of Shiloh. This school also looks at the political as well as the postwar Civil War memory of the nation as a whole. The result is a fresh, if not yet completely coherent, interpretation of the battle.

Readers well versed in Shiloh literature will be familiar with the revisionist works of Larry Daniel, Stacy Allen, and Timothy B. Smith. Daniel broke new ground when he published *Shiloh: The Battle that*

---

8 Charles P. Roland, *Albert Sidney Johnston: Soldier of Three Republics* (Austin: University of Texas Press, 1964).

Changed the Civil War (1997). Most important, Daniel incorporated Washington's and Richmond's views of the operations in his coverage of the preliminary strategic campaign leading up to the tactical action. In addition to the political context, Daniel also evaluated the battle from the viewpoint of other eyes, such as those in major cities like New Orleans and Chicago, and even those watching from afar in foreign nations. Daniel's study capably placed the battle in its correct political and social light. [9]

Also in 1997, Shiloh's Chief Ranger Stacy D. Allen published a revisionist account of Shiloh in two widely-circulated issues of *Blue and Gray Magazine*. These issues also contained fresh interpretations of the battle. Allen was able to document only seven attacks in five hours against the Hornet's Nest position. He noted also that these charges were made in the least populated area of the battlefield. When most of the attacks took place, he explained, the "vast majority of the brigades [Confederate and Union] were actively engaged on either the left or the right flank." As far as Allen is concerned, for the majority of the day the Hornet's Nest was *not* the critical point on the battlefield. Allen also reached the conclusion that the Confederate command authority (most notably Johnston) misread the Union deployment at Pittsburg Landing in the context of the geography of the site. [10]

Timothy B. Smith has written two revisionist books that carry on the earlier work of this school. *This Great Battlefield of Shiloh: History, Memory, and the Establishment of a Civil War National Military Park* (2004) looked at the establishment of the battlefield park and how that effort shaped how modern historians and readers alike view the battle of Shiloh. In a memory study, a field that is becoming quite popular, Smith argued that David W. Reed's work in building the park created the dominant school of thought centering on the importance of the Hornet's Nest. Smith's next book, *The Untold Story of Shiloh: The Battle and the Battlefield* (2006), was a collection of essays delving into a variety of

9 Larry J. Daniel, *Shiloh: The Battle That Changed the Civil War* (New York: Simon and Shuster, 1997).

10 Stacy D. Allen, "Shiloh! The Campaign and First Day's Battle," *Blue and Gray* 14 (Winter 1997), 54.

topics, including myths of Shiloh and the historiography of the battle. Both works continued the emerging revisionist treatment of the battle.[11]

The foundations for this nascent revisionist school were poured several decades ago. In 1966, Otis Edward Cunningham graduated from Louisiana State University with a Ph.D. in history. Working under Dr. T. Harry Williams, Cunningham wrote his dissertation "Shiloh and the Western Campaign of 1862," a detailed study that focused largely on the battle itself.[12]

Although Cunningham's excellent work predated both McDonough and Sword, his dissertation laden with original interpretations was universally ignored by historians in the 1970s. Neither McDonough nor Sword cited Cunningham in their bibliographies. As a result, the revisionist school launched by Cunningham in the 1960s took a thirty-year sabbatical. It would not be resuscitated until the 1990s, when historians Daniel, Allen, and Smith began taking a serious interest in this groundbreaking dissertation and incorporating it into their own research.[13]

Dr. Cunningham examined the old stories related by Reed and the veterans and invigorated them with a unique freshness not found anywhere else. He located previously untapped sources rich with personal anecdotes and peppered his narrative with them to enliven his work. His study also made positive historiographical advances in the study of Shiloh. Unlike many historians, Cunningham was never content to merely accept the standard version of events. Instead, he carefully studied the sources and analyzed what they revealed. For example, he was the first historian to question the existence of sixty-two Confederate cannon in Ruggles' artillery-studded line. By carefully examining battery reports and other documentation, Cunningham was able to

---

11 Timothy B. Smith, *This Great Battlefield of Shiloh: History, Memory, and the Establishment of a Civil War National Military Park* (Knoxville: University of Tennessee Press, 2004); see also Smith, *The Untold Story of Shiloh.*

12 O. E. Cunningham, "Shiloh and the Western Campaign of 1862" (Ph.D. diss., Louisiana State University, 1966).

13 *Ibid.*

account for and confirm only fifty-one artillery pieces in the line. Apparently, Reed had not taken into consideration the losses suffered by some of the Confederate batteries earlier in the day.[14]

Another of Dr. Cunningham's contributions was the manner in which he dealt with the Hornet's Nest thesis, which by this time was deeply ingrained in the American consciousness. He was the first historian to publicly challenge the idea that the Sunken Road was sunken. He did so by quoting extensively from the participants' own letters and diaries and concluded that the nature of the road was not what gave the Union forces a decided advantage. He believed it was the open fields of fire on the flanks and the impenetrable thicket at the Hornet's Nest that made the Sunken Road position almost impregnable. Moreover, where the Reed School counted as many as twelve or thirteen different charges against the Sunken Road line, Cunningham documented only seven (and perhaps eight), a calculation with which most modern historians agree.[15]

Unlike most historians writing before and after him, Cunningham's study is a much more contextual look at the battle. He emphasized places other than the handful of famous sites like the Hornet's Nest, Peach Orchard, and Bloody Pond. The fighting around the Crossroads (where the Hamburg-Purdy and Corinth-Pittsburg roads intersect) offers a prime example.

Today's readers of the Civil War are the most informed in history, and yet even most diehard Civil War buffs will draw a blank when asked if they know anything about the fighting at the Crossroads on the Shiloh battlefield. Cunningham spent fully as much ink on the western side of the battlefield around the Crossroads (an entire chapter) as he did on any other part of the field. He detailed the fighting in that sector and gave it the attention it deserved. The combat waged there is now recognized as more important to the outcome of the battle than previously believed. It should be kept in mind that Cunningham was emphasizing that area of the battlefield forty years ago.

Dr. Cunningham's treatment of the second day at Shiloh, while not as in-depth as his first day's narrative, was in the 1960s the most detailed

14   *Ibid.*, 397-398.

15   *Ibid.*, 331-362.

anyone had written on the April 7 fighting. His unique east-to-west divisional organization methodology is in our view easier to understand than other treatments of the fighting.

Once the combat wrapped up on the Shiloh battlefield, Cunningham refused to end his study there, as most historians have done. Instead, he followed the armies south into Mississippi, treating the siege of Corinth for what it was: a vital part of the Shiloh operation. His decision to do so provides readers with a much broader and richer context of the Shiloh operation.

The footnotes in Cunningham's dissertation explain the uniqueness of his early methodology. He delved deeply into the battle reports, soldiers' letters, newspapers, and postwar reminiscences, but he also walked the field and documented action and troop positions by using the monuments and markers on the battlefield. Few other historians, before or since, have made such an effort. Even Reed, who placed the monuments and tablets, became mired in the detail and was unable to completely see the larger picture.

It should now be clear why Dr. Cunningham's dissertation, important though overlooked in its time, is worthy of publication today. With the new revisionist school less than a decade old and just emerging into the academic world, Cunningham still has much to share with interested readers. His work is not forty years dated; rather, it was four decades ahead of its time, and Shiloh historiography has just begun to catch up with his path-breaking work.

*   *   *

Edward Cunningham was one of the bright young scholars of the mid-1960s. He was born Otis Edward Cunningham in McComb City, Mississippi, on July 20, 1940. He received his elementary and secondary education in the public schools of Pike County, Mississippi, and Tangipahoa Parish, Louisiana.

In 1957, he entered Southwest Mississippi Junior College before transferring to Southeastern Louisiana College in Hammond, Louisiana, the following year, where he completed work on his B.A. degree in 1960. In September of that year he was admitted to Louisiana State University's Department of History graduate program and received his Master's degree in 1962. From 1962-1964 he was a graduate assistant at LSU, working toward his Ph.D. in American History. In September 1964, even while he was laboring to complete his dissertation, he joined the faculty of the University of Tennessee at Martin (UTM) in Martin, Tennessee, as an assistant professor of history. Whenever he could spare the time, he made the trip two hours south to visit the battlefield at Shiloh.

Dr. Cunningham taught at several schools across the nation, including Tulane University, and taught overseas to military men stationed abroad. He published only one book, *The Port Hudson Campaign, 1862-1863* (LSU, 1963). Unfortunately, Dr. Cunningham's career and life came to a premature end with his death on March 2, 1997.[16]

*   *   *

Shiloh and the Western Campaign of 1862 is valuable in its original form because it provides a snapshot of what Dr. Cunningham was thinking and how he wrote in 1966. The overriding principle we followed in preparing this study for publication was to let Cunningham's pen tell the story. It is inappropriate to attempt to speak for someone who can no longer speak for himself. Thus, with a few very minor exceptions (discussed at length below), what you are about to read was entirely written by Dr. Cunningham, who was an exceptionally fine researcher and writer (which made our job much easier). Light stylistic alterations were made in the main text to correct slight irregularities and minor issues of grammar and style (changing the designation of Sherman's Division to lower case, for example). We left his entire set of footnotes intact, but we have added new material that has come to light over the years.

Our additions to the footnotes are clearly designated by the use of the following symbol: || Everything written after || is entirely our own work (the editors); anything before || was from the original dissertation. Any changes made to the original footnotes were purely stylistic in nature (changing roman numerals to Arabic, for example).

16 Edward Cunningham, *The Port Hudson Campaign, 1862-1863* (Baton Rouge: Louisiana State University Press, 1963).

Some additional changes were made to the main text, and these require some explanation. The most basic changes came in the form of misspellings, which we simply changed without noting any difference. For example, Dr. Cunningham consistently spelled Lloyd Tilghman as Tilgham. He likewise spelled Charles Whittlesey as Whittlessley, and Fraley Field as Farley Field. These corrections needed to be made, and we saw no need to alert the reader in a footnote each time we did so.

Dr. Cunningham also made a few errors of fact. For example, he referenced William "Bull" Nelson as Samuel Nelson, confused Cairo for Paducah as the city at the confluence of the Tennessee and Ohio rivers, and accidently promoted 6th Iowa Captain Daniel Iseminger to the rank of colonel. On a few occasions, he also misstated some of the regimental numbers. None of these minor errors could be allowed to stand, but we did not believe each occurrence warranted an explanation in a footnote.

On some occasions, Dr. Cunningham did not include first names for some of the characters in his human interest stories. This is understandable, because finding the names of some of these men in 1966 would have been a monumental research task. Today, however, it is quite easy with the National Park Service's "Civil War Soldier and Sailor System" on the Internet. With that tool we found most, but not all, of the missing first names and simply inserted them into the text.

Dr. Cunningham made several statements of interpretation, some of which we agree with and some with which we do not. For instance, we believe Cunningham was on firm ground when he argued that General P. G. T. Beauregard could not have taken Grant's last line on the evening of April 6, but do not necessarily agree with his claim that Lew Wallace would have been better off had he continued on his original march and suddenly appeared behind enemy lines. Whether we agree with his analysis and interpretation, of course, is not the issue. These are not facts that can be disputed, but issues over which many historians can and do disagree. On matters of this sort we left his original interpretation but indicated what we believe in the footnotes, usually including what more recent Shiloh scholars have to say on the matter.

There were, however, some errors we could not allow to pass that required more extensive treatment in the footnotes. For example, Dr. Cunningham asserted that Colonel Everett Peabody's patrol (led by Major James Powell) marched out the Corinth-Pittsburg Landing Road toward Fraley Field. We now know with certainty that Powell led his patrol along what is today called Reconnoitering Road. We changed the text and alerted the reader in the footnote. Dr. Cunningham's claim that Julius Raith's brigade moved all the way forward to the 53rd Ohio camp in Rhea Field was incorrect, as were his conclusions that James Veatch's first battle position was 200 yards behind John McClernand's line at the Crossroads and that the Confederates penetrated Ralph Buckland's first line at Shiloh Church. In each of these instances we corrected the text and alerted the reader in a footnote, complete with citations that support our position and usually with additional information about what other recent historians have said about the issue. However, mistakes like these were few and far between. Dr. Cunningham knew his subject extremely well.

Only one major alteration was performed on the original dissertation. In his chapter dealing with the Peach Orchard fighting, Dr. Cunningham inserted an unusual paragraph just two or three sentences long that completely unraveled the time line of the action he was describing. Its removal did not delete any material of significance. It is possible the paragraph was a holdover from an earlier draft and overlooked. Regardless, its removal is fully noted in the appropriate footnote.

In discussing Dr. Cunningham's study, the late George Reaves, one of the all-time authorities on the battle of Shiloh, together with co-author Joseph Allen Frank, wrote: "[W]e believe this dissertation deserves a better fate than remaining a manuscript on microfilm." We obviously agree.

We hope our goal of presenting Edward Cunningham's work on Shiloh to the general public will please readers, spark ongoing vigorous debate, and broaden the knowledge of this great but terrible battle that is so special in the hearts of many people.[17]

Gary D. Joiner,
Shreveport, Louisiana

Timothy B. Smith,
Adamsville, Tennessee

17 Frank and Reaves, *"Seeing the Elephant,"* 15.

Chapter 1

Along the Rivers

A POET MIGHT DESCRIBE them as arrows running though the heart of the Confederacy, but to the military and political leaders of the North and South back in 1861, the Cumberland, Tennessee, and Mississippi rivers represented something much more prosaic, yet vital: the probable difference between victory and defeat in the American Civil War. Besides serving as a major peacetime avenue of trade for the western states, these rivers dissected and divided much of the richest area of the South. With its tremendously greater industrial resources, the North could easily utilize these rivers as avenues of invasion into the heartland of the South, striking at the population centers of Tennessee, at the railroad lines connecting the Confederacy, and at the industrial centers that were beginning to bud, notably Chattanooga, Nashville, and Atlanta. The Confederacy, lacking the industrial facilities to build a powerful river fleet, would be forced to utilize river fortifications as a defense against a Northern push down the lines of these rivers.

One of the prizes in the war in this heartland region was the all important border states, Kentucky and Missouri. Not only for their geographical locations, but also as a fertile field for recruiting and obtaining munitions, these states were of the utmost importance to both sides.

The geographical features of this heartland region, where the war was slowly developing, were significant. The two great rivers, the Tennessee and Cumberland, intersected the region, and would be of great use as a means of moving troops and supplies with minimum cost. The Tennessee was navigable from its mouth, through Western Kentucky and Tennessee, and into the northern part of Alabama as far as Mussel Shoals,

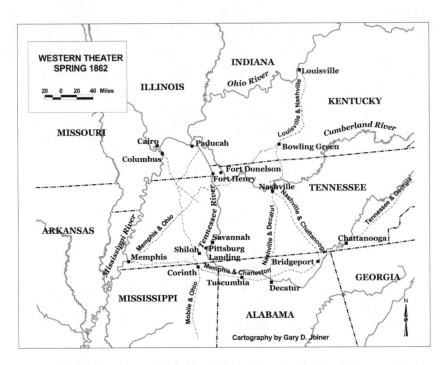

while the Cumberland could be navigated far up beyond Nashville. In the eastern region were the Cumberland Mountains which could be crossed at certain passes, the most important of which was Cumberland Gap, if the Union forces could develop a strong enough army with a secure logistics base to immediately advance and drive out the comparatively small Confederate force in the area. The Tennessee and Georgia Railway ran up the valley of these mountains into Virginia, making it one of the main lines of communications between the Southern armies operating in that region and the Gulf States. At the city of Chattanooga, in East Tennessee, Unionist territory, this railway connected with the Georgia Central Railroad, which led into the heart of Georgia, and with the Memphis and Charleston, which passed into northern Alabama and Mississippi and Memphis, Tennessee. From Louisville, Kentucky, the Louisville and Nashville line ran southward through Bowling Green a hundred miles and to Nashville, seventy miles farther.

From General Albert Sidney Johnston's base at Bowling Green, the Memphis and Ohio passed through Clarksville, Paris, and Humboldt, Tennessee, and to Memphis, two hundred and forty miles away. Running from Paris, Tennessee, there was a branch through to Columbus, which was about a hundred and seventy miles by rail from Bowling Green, the center of the Confederate line. There was a double line of railroads directly from Humboldt into the state of Mississippi. From Nashville, Tennessee, the Nashville-Decatur line ran southward into Alabama, while the Nashville and Chattanooga connected Nashville with the Confederate railroad center at Chattanooga. As long as General Johnston could hold the line from Bowling Green to Columbus, he not only plugged off the Cumberland, Tennessee, and Mississippi rivers against a Unionist advance, but he also protected this powerful and important railway system. An advance overland by either army was apt to be an extremely difficult proposition, for the roads in Kentucky and Tennessee were usually of the ordinary country type, which was passable in the summer, but was very difficult to move over when the rains came in winter and spring.[1]

Besides the transportation system, there were other pressing reasons why the South had to defend this heartland region. By retaining control of the region, Southern authorities could eventually draw large numbers of conscripts and drafted troops. If the Union army could occupy this region, then persons of lukewarm sympathy could be drafted into the Federal army. Also, mines in the extreme southeastern part of Tennessee, at Ducktown, furnished 90 percent of the copper mined in the Confederacy. Furthermore, Tennessee, with seventeen furnaces smelting twenty-two hundred tons of iron ore annually in 1860, was the largest producer of pig iron in the South.[2] The Kentucky-Tennessee region was also tremendously important for the large quantities of food stuffs produced. In 1860, Kentucky produced almost seven and one-half million bushels of wheat, six times that of Alabama, while Tennessee produced five and one-half million bushels as compared to less than six hundred thousand raised in Mississippi. In the same year, Kentucky

---

1 Matthew F. Steele, *American Campaigns* (Washington: Combat Press, 1951), 73, 74. || For more on the importance of railroads in the Civil War, see George Edgar Turner, *Victory Rode the Rails: The Strategic Place of the Railroads in the Civil War* (New York: Bobbs Merrill, 1963), or the more recent John E. Clark, *Railroads In The Civil War: The Impact Of Management On Victory And Defeat* (Baton Rouge: Louisiana State University Press, 2004).

2 Clement Eaton, *History of the Southern Confederacy* (New York: The McMillan Company, 1954), 135, 136.

produced sixty-four million bushels of corn, and Tennessee produced fifty-two million as against twenty-nine million for Mississippi and thirty-three million for Alabama. This meant the Kentucky-Tennessee region not only produced adequate supplies for its own use, but enough to export, potentially, to other regions of the Confederacy, both for military and civil use. This region was also vastly important for livestock. In 1860, Kentucky was listed in the census records as possessing three hundred and fifty-five thousand horses, one hundred and seventeen thousand mules and asses, and more than a third of a million sheep, while Tennessee followed only slightly behind with two hundred and ninety thousand horses, one hundred and twenty-six thousand mules and asses, and three quarters of a million sheep. At this same time Alabama only had a hundred and twenty-seven thousand horses, one hundred and eleven thousand mules and asses, and three hundred and seventy thousand sheep, while Mississippi followed with one hundred and seventeen thousand, one hundred and ten thousand, and three hundred and fifty-two thousand, respectively. Thus not only was this region a bread basket, but it also would be extremely useful for supplying remounts for Confederate cavalry and work animals for Confederate ordnance and commissary depots.[3] Tennessee also supplied more than a quarter of the scant leather supply that would be available in the Southern Confederacy.[4] Economics as well as strategy dictated that the Confederacy must hold the line in Kentucky and Tennessee.[5]

It naturally followed that whoever could gain control would be in a much better position both militarily and politically. The governors of Tennessee and Kentucky both tended to be pro-secessionist, but at the outbreak of war the legislators tended to either favor a policy of neutrality

3 United States Bureau of the Census, *Eighth Census of the United States: 1860* (Washington, 1864).

4 A. L. Conger, "Fort Donelson," *The Military Historian and Economist* 1 (January 1916): 57-59.

5 || See Benjamin F. Cooling, *Fort Donelson's Legacy: War and Society in Kentucky and Tennessee, 1862-1863* (Knoxville: University of Tennessee Press, 1997), for more information on the region's importance to the Confederacy.

or were in favor of remaining within the framework of the Union. Using illegal or extra legal means, pro-Unionist forces quickly gained control of the Missouri state government, seized most of the large stocks of munitions lying within the state, and launched an offensive to clear out pro-Confederate forces from the state. After a preliminary engagement at Boonville, Missouri, Unionist forces led by Brigadier General Nathaniel Lyon began a move southward.

Brigadier General Franz Sigel was defeated in a minor action at Carthage, Missouri, but managed to link up with Lyon in time to attack the Confederate army in Missouri, which was led by Brigadier General Ben McCullough, and the Missouri State Confederate Guard, commanded by Brigadier General Sterling "Pap" Price. Lyon was killed in battle at Wilson's Creek, Missouri, on August 10, 1861, and his numerically smaller army was forced to retreat in one of the bloodiest actions for its size in the entire war. The following month, in September, Price succeeded in capturing Lexington, Missouri, after a two weeks' siege, but lack of equipment and numbers forced the pro-secessionist forces to withdraw southward.

In Kentucky, the situation was even more complex. Brigadier General Simon Bolivar Buckner commanded the Kentucky State Guard, a well-trained and organized military force of about twelve thousand men, largely pro-Confederate in sympathy. Buckner, the soul of honor, refused to use his position to advance the cause of the Confederacy and entered into an agreement with Major General George B. McClellan to maintain Kentucky's neutrality. Both sides immediately began raising troops from this state. The Confederates, who were theoretically at least in the eyes of most Northerners, Rebels, unfortunately insisted on acting in the most legal and officious manner possible, while their Northern foe, who supposedly represented the forces of good order and legality, acted with almost true revolutionary zeal. Arms and munitions were brought into Kentucky from Northern arsenals, and several bodies of pro-Union Kentucky troops were soon organized, the most important at Camp Dick Robinson, in Northern Kentucky, commanded by one of the most interesting figures of the war, Brigadier General William Nelson, a naval officer turned soldier in the emergency.

The Confederates drew troops from the state, but they set up their camps across the Kentucky line in the friendly state of Tennessee, which had seceded in June. The Kentucky situation finally exploded on

September 3, 1861, when Major General Leonidas Polk led Confederate force across the state line and occupied Columbus, which he immediately began fortifying into one of the strongest Confederate positions in the West. In retaliation for the act, Brigadier General U. S. Grant led a small Union force south, occupying Paducah on the following day. Polk's act was militarily important because it did give the Confederates a good base of operations for their left flank in Kentucky, but it was politically unfortunate because it put on the South the stain of first invading a neutral state and alienated many Kentuckians, who might otherwise have been more sympathetic to the Southern position. The line of Confederate forces in Kentucky was soon stabilized, running from Bowling Green in the center, left to Polk's newly acquired position at Columbus, and to the right roughly to the vicinity of Cumberland Gap. Confederate headquarters were at Bowling Green, on the south bank of the Barren River, where the railroad from Nashville to Louisville crosses. This position also enabled the Southerners to use the Mobile and Ohio Railroad, which crossed over into Tennessee, enabling the Confederates to use rail communications between their center and their left. Across the Mississippi River, the Confederates occupied and began fortifying New Madrid, Missouri, as well as Island No. 10, which actually was an island at a point between the Tennessee and Missouri shores.[6]

Even before Tennessee seceded Union authorities had already begun work on building a fleet capable of potentially dominating this heartland region. At Cairo, Mound City, and St. Louis, Union ironclad warships, as well as wooden gunboats, were quickly constructed and outfitted. Across half a dozen states Confederate and Union generals raised troops, collected munitions, and tried frantically to put their forces together in some reasonable state of preparation for the fighting that sooner or later would break out. At this early stage in the war, both sides were handicapped by the lack of practical experience, as well as sufficient quantities of supplies and weapons. The South naturally suffered most in this department, lacking funds to buy materials in Europe and resources

---

6 || See Larry J. Daniel and Lynn Bock, *Island No. 10: Struggle for the Mississippi Valley* (Tuscaloosa: University of Alabama Press, 1996); See Joseph H. Parks, *General Leonidas Polk C.S.A.: The Fighting Bishop* (Baton Rouge: Louisiana State University Press, 1962), for Polk.

at home with which to build war equipment, but even the Union forces were often inadequately equipped in the first days of the war. Neither side was prepared to launch any kind of major offensive operation at this time, and most Union leaders were too happy to retain control of Missouri and Kentucky.

After the fall of Fort Sumter, Major Robert Anderson, Kentucky-born but loyal to the Union, achieved the status of a national hero even though he had been forced to yield his position, after a two day bombardment, to Brigadier General Pierre Gustave Toutant Beauregard. Because of his Kentucky connections, Lincoln and other Washington officials thought it would be politically expedient to send him to command in Kentucky once Union and Confederate forces had moved into the state. Anderson was in ill health, and he soon asked to be relieved after a little more than a month in service. On October 7, the hero of Fort Sumter was formally relieved of his command by Brigadier General William Tecumseh Sherman, who after his services at the Battle of First Manassas had been appointed to command an infantry brigade at Lexington, Kentucky. Sherman held this command for a little more than a week before he became involved in his famous discussion with Secretary of War Simon Cameron over just how many troops would be needed to suppress the rebellion and crush the Rebels in the Mississippi and Tennessee valleys. The following month Sherman was replaced by Brigadier General Don Carlos Buell as head of the Department of the Ohio. Sherman was shunted off for a short rest, and was out of the main-stream of events for some weeks while he recovered control of his nerves.[7]

With Buell in command in central and eastern Kentucky and the adjacent Northern states and Major General Henry W. Halleck in command of the Department of the West across the river and the district of western Kentucky, it would seem that the Union army was suffering from a serious error in divided command. Actually the division of the West in the various departments was the product of the thinking of the

---

7 || See John F. Marszalek, *Sherman: A Soldier's Passion for Order* (New York: Free Press, 1993), for a modern biography of Sherman. For a modern treatment of Buell, see Stephen D. Engle, *Don Carlos Buell: Most Promising of All* (Chapel Hill: The University of North Carolina Press, 1999).

new General-in-Chief of the Union Army, George Brinton McClellan. On November 9, just eight days after McClellan assumed his new position as head of the Union army, he divided the extensive Western Department into the Department of Kansas and Missouri. The latter included not only Missouri but the Western states of Iowa, Wisconsin, Illinois, Arkansas, and the segment of Kentucky lying west of the Cumberland River. Lincoln's home state of Illinois had been in the Western Department since the third of July, but all of Kentucky, with Tennessee, had comprised the old Department of the Cumberland, though forces from the Western Department had been stationed at Paducah and Cairo.

With a large but motley collection of half-trained armies scattered on both sides of the Mississippi River, the stage was practically set for the opening of the real war for the Mississippi and Tennessee valleys. But if the stage were set, the casting of the roles of the leading actors was not complete. Most of the characters were on hand, but no one had been picked to direct the play. Major General John Charles Fremont, the famous Pathfinder of Western exploration fame, was appointed to command in Missouri and the adjacent territory on July 9, but his tenure of office was extremely stormy. Politically protected by his wife, a member of the Thomas Hart Benton family, and by tie-ups with Frank Blair, a leading Missourian pro-Unionist politician, Fremont enjoyed great renown for his first few weeks in command, but his failure to adequately support General Lyon, and still later, his lack of action during the siege of Lexington, caused the administration to lose faith in him and worse, he succeeded in alienating the influential Blair family by his arrogance and conceit. The Pathfinder was finally officially relieved of his command on November 2, 1861, and Brigadier General David Hunter, Virginia-born but a strong abolitionist and Union sympathizer, was picked to temporarily succeed him until a new department commander could be brought out from Washington.[8]

---

8 || See also Tom Chaffin, *Pathfinder: John Charles Fremont and the Course of American Empire* (New York: Hill and Wang, 2002). Although Dr. Cunningham did not mention it, Fremont's policy regarding slaves was a major reason for his removal.

On November 19, Major General Henry Wager Halleck arrived at St. Louis to relieve Hunter of his temporary post and to assume the direction of the Department of the Missouri, which also included Kentucky.[9] Hunter was shunted off to a lesser command in Kansas, while Halleck declined to take to the active field against the local Confederate forces, preferring to act as a war director. Brigadier generals Samuel Curtis and John Pope were given the task of clearing northern and southern Missouri of Confederate irregulars and driving General Sterling Price out of the state.

Across the river in eastern Kentucky the command system was even more confused, if that were possible. By placing both banks of the Mississippi below its junction with the Ohio and the lower part of the Tennessee River under a single central system, McClellan directly paved the way for the operations that would follow during the winter. This led to the elimination of the Department of the Cumberland and the formation of the Department of the Ohio, which would be General Buell's command, consisting of Kentucky, cast of the Cumberland River, all of Tennessee (occupied by the Confederate army), plus Michigan, Indiana, and Ohio. It can be seen from this arrangement that the Tennessee and Cumberland rivers changed departments as they crossed the Kentucky state line, but at the moment this made little difference, since Tennessee was controlled by Confederate forces. It was a complicated arrangement once offensive operations south began, but for the moment it was adequate.[10]

If Generals Buell and Halleck could work together, coordinated by McClellan as General-in-Chief and the good offices of the Secretary of

---

9 Stephen E. Ambrose, *Halleck: Lincoln's Chief of Staff* (Baton Rouge: Louisiana State University Press, 1962), 13. || See John F. Marszalek, *Commander of All Lincoln's Armies: A Life of General Henry W. Halleck* (Cambridge: Belknap Press, 2004), for a modern biography of Halleck.

10 *The War of the Rebellion: A Compilation of the Official Records of the Union and Confederate Armies*, 128 vols. (Washington: Government Printing Office, 1890-1901), Series 1, Volume 13, 567; 4, 349. Hereinafter cited as *OR*, with all references to Series 1 unless otherwise stated. The citation will normally read *OR* 10 (volume number), pt. 1 (part number), 212 (page number).

War and the President, then the command system in the West could be made to work without too much friction.

South, in Confederate territory, the command system was considerably more simplified. The original Confederate commander, Polk, had been replaced with the arrival of one of the South's greatest wartime heroes, General Albert S. Johnston. The Kentucky-born Confederate leader reached Nashville on September 14,[11] and assumed command of Department No. 2 on the following day. The text of the order giving Johnston his command, issued five days earlier, assigned him to direct military operations in Tennessee, Arkansas, that part of Mississippi lying west of the New Orleans, Jackson, and Great Northern and Central Railroad, Kentucky, Missouri, and the Indian country to the west of Missouri and Arkansas. Johnston was the senior officer in the Confederate army, after the Adjutant General, Samuel Cooper, who was too infirm to engage in active field operations. The appointment of a man of Johnston's prestige and repute to command the West demonstrated the force of President Jefferson Davis' feelings in regard to the importance of the theater, but the wisdom of giving such a large command to one man, since everyone assumed that Johnston would also lead the main Confederate field army in battle, is possibly debatable. An old military axiom says that a general should never have to lead one army in person while directing the operations of others at the same time. Whether Johnston could act as soldier and as a master theater strategist would remain to be seen, but at least the Confederate forces in the West would have a certain unity of command that their Bluecoated foes would lack, at least for the time being.[12]

If General Johnston possessed a national reputation, his foes to the north of the Bowling Green-Columbus line were of a lesser known quality. None of the leaders who would fight for the Union cause had achieved any spectacular peacetime prominence. Brigadier General U. S. Grant had indeed lived in mediocrity for most of his thirty-nine years. Of

11   Charles P. Roland, *Albert Sidney Johnston: Soldier of Three Republics* (Austin: University of Texas Press, 1964), 261.

12   William Preston Johnston, *The Life of Gen. Albert Sidney Johnston* (New York: D. Appleton and Company, 1878), 292.

distant Scottish ancestry, Grant's family had originally come from Scotland to Massachusetts in May 1630, and later one ancestor fought in the American Revolution. Born on April 27, 1822, Grant, baptized Hiram Ulysses, lived the routine life of a small town Ohio boy, studying in the local subscription schools of Point Pleasant. Not a terribly capable scholar, Grant worked steadily and doggedly, prodded by his father, who had ambitions for his male child. In the winter of 1838-39, Jessie Grant decided his young son, Ulysses, needed a higher education, and without consulting him asked United States Senator Thomas Morris to get the boy an appointment to the Military Academy at West Point, New York. Young Ulysses' reaction when informed by his father that he was going to the Academy was a prompt, "But I won't go."[13] He went, however. Grant's stay at the Academy was not particularly pleasant, for he always lacked enthusiasm for the routine life of the soldier or cadet. Still he managed to graduate twenty-first out of a class of thirty-nine.[14] His classmates included William B. Franklin, who won top honors in the class of 1843, Roswell S. Ripley, John J. Peck, J. J. Reynolds, C. C. Augur, Frederick Steele, Rufas Ingalls, and a young New York-born cadet, Franklin Gardner, who would oppose Grant in battle just nineteen years later.[15]

Assigned to the Fourth Infantry, Grant was stationed at Jefferson Barracks, near St. Louis, Missouri. Still lacking enthusiasm for a military career, the young second lieutenant began an intensive study in mathematics, the only subject in which he had shown special aptitude at the Point, hoping to get an assistant professorship at the Academy. One of Lieutenant Grant's former cadet friends, Fred Dent, was a native of St.

---

13 Ulysses S. Grant, *Personal Memoirs of U. S. Grant*, (ed.) E. B. Long, (Cleveland: World Publishing Company, 1952), 1-11. Hereinafter cited as Grant, *Memoirs.*

14 Ezra Warner, *Generals in Blue: Lives of the Union Commanders* (Baton Rouge: Louisiana State University Press, 1964), 184.

15 Ezra Warner, *Generals in Gray: Lives of the Confederate Commanders* (Baton Rouge: Louisiana State University Press, 1959), 97. || See Brooks D. Simpson, *Ulysses S. Grant: Triumph Over Adversity, 1822-1865* (Boston: Houghton Mifflin, 2000), for the best modern biography of Grant.

Louis, and he invited the Ohio boy to his home, where he met the Dent sisters. Six year old Emmy was strongly attracted to the nattily uniformed army officer, but it was her seventeen year old sister, Julia, who won Grant's heart. The young couple decided they were in love, but unfortunately the Mexican crisis had taken a turn for the worse and the War Department ordered the Fourth to Fort Jesup, Louisiana.[16] More than four years were to pass before the two were finally married on August 22, 1848, after Lieutenant Grant's return from the war.[17]

Hostile to the idea of warfare with Mexico and convinced that Southern annexationists were behind all the trouble, Grant loyally obeyed orders, accompanying General Zachary Taylor's army to Louisiana and then to Texas. At Corpus Christi the army almost lost a new second lieutenant when Grant fell off the transport *Suviah* into the Gulf of Mexico. Fished out of the water without a scratch, the soggy lieutenant went through a lot of joking and remarks about his clumsiness before his fellow officers let him forget the incident.[18]

Surviving the bloody battles of Palo Alto, Resaca de la Palma, and Monterrey, Grant was eventually transferred to General Winfield Scott's army, taking part in many of the battles from Vera Cruz to the capture of Mexico City. Although most of the time a regimental quartermaster, he managed to participate in many of the battles as a combat soldier.[19] In the storming of the Mexican capitol, the Fourth Infantry was part of William Jenkins Worth's division, and Lieutenant Grant helped drag up the army's little mountain howitzers, aiding in hoisting them to the roofs of the stone houses from where they could be used to blast out the Mexican defenders. A young naval officer, Raphael Semmes, assisted Grant in moving the guns up. Only a few hundred yards away, P. G. T. Beauregard, Earl Van Dorn, and Adley Gladden, all of whom would again meet Grant in battle, but under a different flag, fell wounded from

---

16 W. E. Woodward, *Meet General Grant* (New York: Literary Guild of America, 1928), 57-62.

17 Grant, *Memoirs*, 19, 21, 97; Woodward, *Meet General Grant*, 101, 57-61.

18 Grant, *Memoirs*, 27, 28.

19 Warner, *Generals in Blue,* 184.

Mexican gunfire. Grant's brigade commander reported that the young Ohioan "acquitted himself most nobly," and General Worth sent an aide, Lieutenant John C. Pemberton, to bring Grant to divisional headquarters. Just sixteen years later, on a hot, sticky day, these two men would meet again, and Grant would receive the surrender of his old war comrade at Vicksburg, Mississippi, following a grim and merciless forty-seven day siege.[20]

With the end of hostilities and with his marriage to Julia, Grant settled down to the routine peacetime army life, serving at Sacketts Harbor and Detroit. Then the Fourth was ordered to the Pacific Coast, and Julia returned to St. Louis to stay with her family. On the West Coast Grant lived the dreary life of a bachelor officer. Never particularly enamored with military life and bored by the deadly, dull routine of the isolated outposts at which he was stationed, Grant began drinking.

In 1854, possibly to avoid a court-martial, Grant, holding the permanent rank of captain, submitted his resignation to Secretary of War Jefferson Davis. The future Confederate President accepted the resignation, and Grant found himself a civilian once more. Short of funds, the ex-army captain succeeded in getting passage to New York, where he arrived penniless. Staying at a hotel in the city, U. S. Grant attempted to collect an old debt, but without success. His hotel bill began running up, and the hotel manager seized his baggage and ordered him out. At this time Captain Simon Bolivar Buckner, an old army comrade, happened to run into Grant, and upon discovering the situation went to the hotel manager and agreed to be responsible for the Ohioan's debt. Grant was allowed to stay in the hotel upon Buckner's promise. Buckner did not loan any money to Grant, as some stories current during the Civil War claimed, and Grant was soon able to settle his own accounts with the aid of his father.

The next six and one-half years of Grant's life was a period of mediocrity and failure. As a businessman and farmer, he did not prosper in the little Illinois town of Galena. With the outbreak of hostilities in April 1861, he became involved in local military activities, holding a

---

20 Woodward, *Meet General Grant*, 96; R. S. Henry, *The Story of the Mexican War* (New York: Frederick Ungar Publishing Company, 1961), 365.

number of minor military positions in recruiting troops. Weeks passed, and then Governor Dick Yates offered the West Pointer the command of the Twenty-first Illinois Infantry Regiment. This job was no sinecure. The first commander of the regiment was Colonel Simon Goode, a handsome, swashbuckling Kentuckian who had served in the Mexican War, the Lopez-Cuba expedition, and the Kansas border wars. Goode, although brave, was extremely incompetent, and he had the habit of calling his sentinels from their posts to drink whiskey with him. The troops began getting out of hand, and some of the regiment's officers went to Governor Yates to ask for a new colonel. Someone suggested Captain Grant, and Yates promptly agreed that it should be Grant.

Grant arrived at the regiment's camp in civilian clothes, his elbows sticking out through the holes in his worn coat sleeves, and wearing a very battered hat. Used to the more magnificent appearance of Colonel Goode, the soldiers made fun of him, and one soldier even pushed him in the back. Later Grant wrote of the incident, "I found it very hard work for a few days to bring all the men into anything like subordination, but by the application of a little regular army punishment all were reduced to as good discipline as one could ask."[21]

For the next few months Grant was in eastern Missouri, unsuccessfully chasing parties of Confederate guerrillas. Almost a thousand miles away, at the home of Senator Lyman Trumbull on Eighth Street, Washington, D. C., Illinois congressmen and senators met to vote on placing in nomination for promotion a number of Illinois soldiers. The name of U. S. Grant was first on the list and when the appointments were presented to President Lincoln and Congress, the nomination of Grant as brigadier general was approved. Grant first heard of his promotion in a St. Louis newspaper, and he remarked to a chaplain standing nearby, "I had no suspicion of it. It never came from any request of mine. It must be some of Washburne's work."[22]

In September Brigadier General Grant led an invasion of Kentucky, occupying Paducah on the 4th. For the next two months he was busy

---

21 Woodward, *Meet General Grant*, 185; Grant, *Memoirs*, 124.

22 Albert D. Richardson, *A Personal History of Ulysses S. Grant* (Hartford: M.A. Winter and Hatch, 1885), 180.

raising and organizing an army around Paducah and in threatening the Confederate base at Columbus, Kentucky. On November 7, Grant drew blood for the first time in a strike at the small Confederate garrison at Belmont, Missouri. Ferried over by the navy, Grant routed the small Confederate army, but Southern reinforcements arrived and the newly appointed brigadier was forced to abandon the Confederate camp, load his army on the navy transports, and with naval gunfire covering him, retire to Paducah. Union and Confederate armies both claimed the victory at Belmont. Union losses were 607 men against 641 Confederate casualties. The first real battle in the West since Wilson's Creek, the engagement attracted great publicity and made U. S. Grant the rising star of the Union army in that theater. It was not so much that Belmont was a great victory for the North, but rather that Grant had bothered to fight at all, while dozens of other Union generals sat around training troops, bragging to newspapers, or causing trouble for the administration in Washington.[23]

The man who would become one of Grant's closest friends and most loyal supporter came from a background in many ways similar to Grant's. William Tecumseh Sherman, although of Ohio-birth, was two years older than the man who would become his trusted superior, and who with him would make up one of the deadliest fighting teams in military history. The death of his father when the boy was nine caused young Tecumseh to be brought up by United States Senator Thomas Ewing, a friend and fellow citizen of his father. The Ewing family was influential in middle Western politics, which gave Sherman something of an edge over Grant in seeking public advancement. As a lad Sherman received a sound education in the local academy at Lancaster, but in 1836, Ewing secured an appointment for him at West Point. Always something of a rebel, the young Ohioan did not particularly excel at the Academy, disdaining the strict conformity to rules which was expected

---

23 Woodward, *Meet General Grant*, 160-192, 209-211. || See William Garrett Piston and Richard W. Hatcher, III, *Wilson's Creek: The Second Battle of the Civil War and the Men Who Fought It* (Chapel Hill: The University of North Carolina Press, 2000), for Wilson's Creek. For Belmont, see Nathaniel C. Hughes, *The Battle of Belmont: Grant Strikes South* (Chapel Hill: The University of North Carolina Press, 1991).

of the cadets. Even so, at the isolated post amid the highlands of the Hudson River Valley, young Sherman survived the grueling grind to eventually graduate in the same year that a young plebe from Ohio, U. S. Grant, entered. Sherman's grades were fairly good, although his records show a respectable collection of demerits, and after graduation he was commissioned with the Fifth Infantry Regiment.[24] After service in various military posts Sherman eventually was sent to California, where he left the army to go into business. Still later, he migrated to Louisiana, where he became superintendent of what later became Louisiana State University, at Alexandria, from 1860-1861.[25]

At the age of forty-one Sherman re-entered the United States army. The first forty-one years of his life had been a record of frustrated ambitions and minor successes. At the Battle of First Manassas he led a brigade with considerable success, but it was only with his transfer from the Army of the Potomac to the Western theater that Sherman began to exhibit any unusual or outstanding characteristics. Unfortunately those characteristics he first demonstrated were those of emotional instability, and possibly even derangement. Sherman always had a sense of the dramatic and tended to see things in an extremely pessimistic light on some occasions. The responsibilities of a major command tended to overly upset him and led to his eventual removal from command in Kentucky. After a short spell of duty in Missouri, where he helped create a panic by insisting that Confederate forces under General Price were advancing on him, he was eventually shifted away to avoid embarrassment.

A few weeks of rest and the redoubtable Tecumseh was ready for a field command again; this time it would be an infantry division under his fellow Ohioan, General U. S. Grant. Somehow these two men hit it off.

---

24   B. H. Liddell Hart, *Sherman: Soldier, Realist, American* (New York: Dodd, Meade, and Company, 1930), 1-11; William T. Sherman, *Memoirs of General William T. Sherman by Himself* (Bloomington: Indiana University Press, 1957), 9-165.

25   Liddell Hart, *Sherman*, 11-71. || See Charles Bracelen Flood, *Grant and Sherman: The Friendship That Won the Civil War* (New York: Farrar, Straus and Giroux, 2005), for a modern account of the relationship between Grant and Sherman.

Possibly it was because neither of them had ever achieved any particular success, and this helped create some sort of bond between them, not so much a recognition of mediocrity, but rather, a sense of feeling they could achieve something if only given the opportunity, or perhaps it was simply that the men liked each other. Anyway, they would work together as corps commander and army commander to help create the military victory that would preserve the American Union.[26]

The third member of the military group that would dominate military affairs in the West at this time was Don Carlos Buell, major general of United States Volunteers. Born on March 23, 1818, and of Welch descent, Buell, like Sherman and Grant, was an Ohioan. His father died when he was very young, and he was reared by an uncle, George P. Buell of Lawrenceburg, Indiana. After the usual education for a member of the rough and semi-frontier society, young Buell entered West Point, and upon graduating was assigned to service with the Third Infantry Regiment. After service in the Seminole War he joined Taylor in Texas, and was brevetted captain for meritorious service at the Battle of Monterrey on September 23, 1846. Much later, in the double battle of Contreras and Churubusco, Don Carlos Buell was brevetted again for gallant conduct.

His peacetime service was honorable, but not particularly distinguished, and in April 1861, Buell was a lieutenant colonel in the adjutant general's office. Promoted to major general, he helped organize and train troops for the Army of the Potomac, where his services were apparently extremely creditable. Buell and McClellan, his superior at the time, seemed to work well together, and apparently there was a close, friendly relationship between the two men, something like that existing between Fritz John Porter and the young general-in-chief.[27]

26 T. Harry Williams, *McClellan, Sherman, and Grant* (New Brunswick: Rutgers University Press, 1962), 53-59.

27 "Campaigns in Kentucky and Tennessee Including the Battle of Chickamauga 1862-1864," *Papers of the Military Historical Society of Massachusetts* (Boston: 1908), 7: 17; T. Harry Williams, *Lincoln and His Generals* (New York: Grosset and Dunlap, 1952), 47, 48.

In November, Buell arrived in Kentucky to take command of the Army of the Ohio (sometimes known as the Army of the Cumberland).[28] Basically his job was to secure the Union left flank in the West and eventually invade Eastern Tennessee. A lack of combat experience and practical experience in handling troops in the field was not particularly a handicap, as there was virtually no one in either army—Union or Confederate—with such a background. Buell seems to have been thought of favorably by most of his contemporaries at this time. Of medium stature, Buell wore a full beard and possessed an extremely stern appearance.[29] The only person who seems to have registered any criticism of Buell at this time was a young officer serving under Grant, who wrote in a letter that Buell "is too cautious." Only time would tell whether Buell would have the necessary aggressiveness and skill to command a field army.

Fourth of the major Union army officers, but certainly not least, was Henry Wager Halleck. One of the most controversial figures of the war, Halleck at one time or the other was condemned by just about every major figure is the entire Union army. William T. Sherman was one of the very few who seemed to always favor Halleck and respect him for his undoubted administrative ability.[30] Halleck's tragedy was that he was called on to perform the functions of a daring, dashing field commander, while basically at heart he was simply a bookkeeping bureaucratic official.[31]

If Halleck was a little lacking in the abilities necessary for an aggressive field commander, he was fortunate in that his subordinates

---

28 ‖ For the Army of the Ohio, see Gerald K. Prokopowicz, *All for the Regiment: The Army of the Ohio, 1861-1862* (Chapel Hill: University of North Carolina Press, 2001) and Larry J. Daniel, *Days of Glory: The Army of the Cumberland, 1861-1865* (Baton Rouge: Louisiana State University Press, 2004).

29 Dumas Malone (ed.), *Dictionary of American Biography* (New York: Scribners, 1935), 3: 241. Hereinafter cited as *D. A. B.*

30 John H. Brinton, *Personal Memoirs of John H. Brinton* (New York: The Neale Publishing Company, 1944), 144.

31 Ambrose, *Halleck*, 3-21.

had these qualities. One of his most able men was Brigadier General Charles Ferguson Smith, a man whose untimely death cut short possibly a brilliant career, perhaps even the supreme command of Union armed forces. Smith, a native of Philadelphia, Pennsylvania, entered West Point in 1820, at the age of thirteen, graduating five years later. After holding various field positions, he returned to West Point in 1829 as an instructor, which post he held for thirteen years under Syvanus Thayer, then head of the school. It was the Mexican War that gave Smith his great opportunity, and he took full advantage of it. Captain Smith led the advance of General Zachary Taylor's army across the Salt Lagoon at Arroyo, Colorado, in March 1846. Just days later he scouted the position of the Mexican army at Resaca de Guerrera. As a measure of trust in him General Taylor assigned Smith the duty of taking a force of artillery and Texas cavalry and assaulting the Mexican army's position on the redoubt at the western end of the summit of Federation Hill at Monterrey during the bloody battle of that city. Transferred to General Winfield Scott's command, Smith, now a lieutenant colonel, took part in the advance on Mexico City, missing out on the final bloody assault only through illness. Once the city actually fell, such was the measure of Scott's confidence in the young officer, he was assigned the difficult and dangerous task of policing the city with a special force of five hundred military police recruited from the most reliable volunteers and regulars.[32]

After the Treaty of Guadeloupe Hidalgo ended hostilities, Smith returned to the routine life of peacetime soldiering, taking part in an expedition to the Red River country and later in the famous Utah expedition under Colonel, later Confederate General, Albert Sidney Johnston. On the outbreak of the Civil War, Smith was promoted to brigadier general and eventually was placed under the command of Brigadier General U. S. Grant, a former student at West Point.[33]

There was much discontent in the Union army that General Smith, who had put in thirty-seven years soldiering, should be placed under the

---

32 Henry, *Story of the Mexican War*, 147, 353, 368.

33 || For Smith, see Benjamin Franklin Cooling, "The Reliable First Team: Grant and Charles Ferguson Smith," in Steven E. Woodworth (ed.), *Grant's Lieutenants: From Cairo to Vicksburg* (Lawrence: University Press of Kansas, 2001), 43-61.

command of a man not only his junior in years but in military experience. Fortunately for the cause of the Union, Smith completely subordinated himself to the general welfare of the Union and willingly and loyally served under his former student. Smith had not forgotten Grant from academy days, and he particularly remembered Grant as a modest young man, a fine horseman, and a very efficient student in mathematics.[34]

General Halleck was among those who felt that Smith had not been fairly treated, and Grant, himself, was embarrassed by the relationship. In conversation with a junior officer, Grant remarked that he did not like to think of having to give General Smith orders, "which don't seem just right to me, for this veteran officer was a commandant at West Point when I was a cadet and all the school regarded him as one of the very ablest officers of his age in the army."[35] Smith was described as being "every inch a soldier, and a true disciplinarian." He was tall, over six feet three inches in height, "slender, well proportioned and upright with a remarkably fine face, and a long twisted white mustache . . . the very beau-ideal of a soldier."[36] General Lew Wallace once called Smith "by all odds the handsomest, stateliest, most commanding figure I have ever seen,"[37] and many of the regular officers felt him the best all around soldier in the United States Army.[38]

Geographical conditions in the Eastern or Atlantic theater of war made the army dominant, but in the West the location of the great waterways made it apparent from the beginning that the navy would play a major role in military operations. The man selected to lead the Union navy was Captain Andrew Hull Foote. Originally Foote entered West

34 Bruce Catton, *Grant Moves South* (Boston: Little, Brown and Company, 1960), 50.

35 Augustus Chetlain, *Recollections of Seventy Years* (Galena: The Gazette Publishing Company, 1899), 81-83.

36 Brinton, *Personal Memoirs*, 121, 122.

37 Lew Wallace, *An Autobiography*, 2 vols. (New York: Harper, 1906), 1: 339.

38 Mark Mayo Boatner, *Civil War Dictionary* (New York: David McKay Company, 1959), 769; Wallace, *An Autobiography*, 1: 338, 339; Chetlain, *Recollections of Seventy Years*, 81-83.

Point, but after a six month stay at the Academy he left to join the navy as a young midshipman. Just sixteen years old, Foote was fortunate to serve with some of the United States Navy's best officers, notably Commodore David Porter. In 1827, the twenty-one year old officer, while serving on the U.S.S. *Natchez,* was converted to Christianity, and for the rest of his life he attempted to gain more converts. In 1849, while skipper of the brig *Perry*, Foote gained much renown for his services in suppressing the slave trade on the African coast. One of his most notable contributions to the American navy was his work for temperance, of which he was a violent advocate.[39] As skipper of the *Cumberland*, he was successful in making her the first temperance ship in the navy.[40]

Of a crusading temperament, Foote set down certain of his ideas and experiences in a book entitled *Africa and the American Flag*. Possibly the most spectacular of his duties entailed the famous attack on the Canton barrier forts. In 1856, Chinese military authorities failed to give proper protection to American merchants, and even fired on a naval vessel, killing one American sailor. With the permission of Commodore Samuel Armstrong, Commander of the American East Indies Squadron, Foote, supported by the U.S.S. *Portsmouth* and the *Levant*, attacked the forts guarding the approaches to Canton. With a combination of naval gunfire, and employing a detachment of 287 marines and sailors as a landing party, he took four powerful forts mounting 168 cannon, some of them 8.5-inch caliber. Some five thousand Chinese troops were defeated, many of them killed or wounded, in exchange for a loss of only seven American sailors and marines killed and twenty-two wounded. The vigorous retaliatory action was responsible for forcing the imperial government to apologize for firing on the American flag, and it paved the way for peaceful American mercantile activities in China for many years.[41]

39 Clarence C. Buel and Robert U. Johnson (eds.) *Battles and Leaders of the Civil War,* 4 vols. (New York: Century Company, 1887-1888), 1: 359, 360.

40 || For Foote, see Spencer C. Tucker, *Andrew Foote: Civil War Admiral on Western Waters* (Annapolis: Naval Institute Press, 2000).

41 Clyde H. Metcalf, *A History of the United States Marine Corps* (New York: G.P. Putnams Sons, 1939), 173-176.

Popular with the sailors, who often sang of him, "He increased our pay ten cents a day, and stopped our rum forever," Foote was a stern disciplinarian. With a strong sense of duty, he was always willing to do his duty to God, country, and the temperance movement.[42] Commodore C. R. P. Rogers once said of him that "Foote had more of the bulldog than any man I ever knew."[43] Slow thinking but steady and completely reliable, and popular with his fellow officers, Foote was probably the perfect man for the difficult task of organizing and commanding a fleet in Western waters. Only the closest and most exacting army-navy cooperation would be adequate to give the Union victory in the heartland region.

It remained to be seen if these men from diverse backgrounds would be able to cooperate to the necessary degree for this.

---

42   Brinton, *Personal Memoirs*, 118.

43   James M. Hoppin, *Life of Andrew Hull Foote, Rear-Admiral United States Navy* (New York: Harper and Brothers Publishers, 1874), 404.

Chapter 2

Lincoln Takes a Hand

NO ONE KNOWS FOR certain who first conceived of the idea of a great Union push down the lines of the Mississippi and Tennessee rivers. Perhaps many men thought of the plan in its broadest outlines at the same time. It was certainly evident to anyone who looked at a map that such an offensive utilizing the rivers as avenues of transportation and invasion would be the easiest way to conquer this region in the South, by splitting the Confederacy in two.

In April 1861, while yet an officer of the Ohio militia, young George McClellan proposed to General Winfield Scott, the fat and aging General-in-Chief of the United States Army, that one possible plan of action would be to "cross the Ohio at Cincinnati or Louisville with 80,000 men, march straight on Nashville, and act according to circumstances," with the ultimate aim of advancing on "Pensacola, Mobile and New Orleans."[1] Just days later, Scott presented his own famous Anaconda plan. This proposed a "complete blockade of the Atlantic and Gulf ports . . . in connection with such blockades," proposing a mighty "movement down the Mississippi to the ocean, with a cordon of posts at proper points . . . the object being to clear out and keep open this great line of communication in connection with the strict blockade of the seaboard, so as to envelop the insurgent states," and crush them with the minimum amount of bloodshed. Scott went on to say in a letter to McClellan that twelve to twenty steam gunboats would be

---

1 Charles Elliott, *Winfield Scott: The Soldier and the Man* (New York: The Macmillan Company, 1937), 721.

needed, besides transports to carry 60,000 men who would be inducted in the army.[2] Scott's plan did not allow for the difficulties that would be set forward in an invasion, and he underestimated the forces needed, but at least he offered a beginning for Union strategy in the West.

Nor were the Southerners unaware of the strategic possibilities inherent in the situation. Work continued on developing fortifications to protect the Mississippi, Cumberland, and Tennessee, while the Confederates were making all efforts possible to mass troops and equipment in the West. A young Southern ordnance officer, Captain W. R. Hunt, in a letter containing recommendations to Major General Polk, written on August 12, pointed out succinctly that "if the war should unfortunately be prolonged, the Valley of the Mississippi must ultimately become its great theater, for the enemy now working to subjugate the South knows the value of our great artery of commerce and of the prominent cities upon it too well for us to doubt that he will bend all his energies to control them."[3] Captain Hunt's fears were well founded, for just a few hundred miles north, various Union officers were already beginning to mull over ideas for a drive down the river line. One of the first high ranking officers to bring up the matter was Colonel Charles Whittlesey, a graduate of West Point in 1831 and the chief of Brigadier General Ormsby M. Mitchel's engineers. In a dispatch dated November 20, Whittlesey wrote General Halleck suggesting the propriety "of a great movement by land and water up the Cumberland and Tennessee Rivers."[4] His idea was that this would allow the army to operate along the water lines half way to Nashville without endangering the supply line, which would be vulnerable to attack by cavalry if operating overland along the crude road system. This would also make possible, even probable, the Confederate evacuation of Columbus, since it would have the effect of threatening their railway communications. Further, it was in Colonel Whittlesey's opinion the most passable route into Tennessee.[5]

2   *OR* 1, pt. 3, 177, 178, 250.

3   *Ibid.*, 4, 385-387.

4   *Ibid.*, 7, 444.

5   *Ibid.*

Only a week later General Buell, commanding in eastern and central Kentucky, on the suggestion of an engineer officer on his staff, recommended to General McClellan the feasibility of an advance along the line of the Cumberland and Tennessee rivers toward Nashville. McClellan, or "Little Mac," as he was called, objected as President Abraham Lincoln did. The President's objection was based more on political than on strategic grounds, for he was deeply interested in the possibility of a thrust in eastern Tennessee to relieve the supposedly suppressed and downtrodden Unionists living in that section. In a paper which McClellan and other Federal officers read with interest, Lincoln in late September or early October developed a plan of action calling for a movement into eastern Tennessee by the Union army. Apparently Lincoln's initial military objective in this was to seize a point on the strategic Virginia-Tennessee Railroad "near the Mountain pass called Cumberland Gap." It was not a bad idea for an amateur soldier, but the president failed to make any provisions in his plan for any operations on the Mississippi River or any other rivers in the area. At least Lincoln was thinking in terms of an offensive movement, though possibly in the wrong direction.[6]

In the mountainous regions of the state, notably in the eastern third, there was strong evidence of pro-Unionist support, and the vote had been more than four to one against secession in June when Governor Isham Harris had put it up to the people to decide one way or the other. (Actually the vote made very little difference as Tennessee was already firmly committed to the Confederate cause, but it was a shrewd political move on the governor's part to try and rally popular support.) Through the entire war this would be a scene of true civil strife, with brother against brother and noted bushwhackers and jayhawkers roaming about murdering and torturing with the greatest of enthusiasm.[7]

6 Kenneth P. Williams, *Lincoln Finds A General* (New York: The Macmillan Company, 1952), 3: 109-112.

7 || See Steven V. Ash, *When the Yankees Came: Conflict and Chaos in the Occupied South, 1861-1865* (Chapel Hill: University of North Carolina Press, 1995).

Sporadically the East Tennessee Unionists engaged in guerrilla warfare and sabotage against the Confederate administration. Knoxville was the center for pro-Unionist activities, but the surrounding counties contained many citizens who bore no great love for the South, or at least President Jefferson Davis' government. The most notable of these Rebels was Andrew Johnson, who would eventually become military governor of Tennessee and United States President, but there were many others such as William "Parson" Brownlow, a fire-eating fanatic, who would spread death and destruction upon his pro-Confederate enemies at the least provocation and sometimes without any.

During the fall of the year hundreds of East Tennessee Unionists had begun drifting north, slipping through the thinly held Confederate lines into Unionist Kentucky. Some of them enlisted in ordinary Union army regiments, but others banned together, eventually forming an East Tennessee brigade headed by acting Brigadier General Samuel P. Carter, which set up base at Camp Calvert, near London, Kentucky.[8] At the same time those Unionists who did not bother to leave the state to get into the war started a campaign of sabotage against the Confederate railroad system running through their segment of the state. Bridges were burned and Confederate transportation, both military and civilian, considerably disrupted.

The New York *Tribune* on November 6 carried the story that the East Tennessee loyalists had fought a great battle at Morristown. This was vastly exaggerated, but there had been open resistance to the Confederates and many were arrested, notably "Parson" Brownlow.

It was natural that for political reasons President Lincoln and many of his officials should be interested in seizing control of eastern Tennessee and restoring a civil administration favorable to the North. East Tennessee could then be cited as an example to show that the people of the South were basically in sympathy with the Union and that they had been merely led astray by their wicked and treasonable leaders. This would make good grist for the Northern propaganda mill. It is also extremely probable that Lincoln personally felt great sympathy for the

---

8 *OR* 7, 440, 441; Roy P. Basler (ed.), *The Collected Works of Abraham Lincoln* (New Brunswick: Rutgers University Press, 1953), 5: 54.

East Tennesseans and simply wanted to relieve them of their sufferings, even though those sufferings might be considerably exaggerated. For humanitarian and for political reasons it was necessary, Lincoln thought, to intervene in this region.

Located strategically, astride the Confederate railroad system and in position to outflank many important Confederate population and munitions centers, eastern Tennessee was destined to become a major battlefield. In this area the slaveholding and propertied classes tended to support the Confederate cause, while the common people, basically yeoman farmers or mountaineers, tended to be pro-Unionist in sympathy. In eastern Tennessee, as well as in some of the other mountainous regions of the South, the secessionist crisis tended to take on some of the characteristics of a class struggle.[9]

At first many of the East Tennesseans, like their brothers in Kentucky, preferred to occupy a neutral position, but events soon showed that this was impossible. The strategic value of the region rendered it inevitable that military operations would take place in the area. The Richmond *Inquirer* called it the "Keystone of the Southern arch." Not only did its passes afford avenues for invasion or counter-invasions, but it was also potentially a great stockpile of salt and bacon, essential to the Confederate armies in particular.

President Lincoln was scarcely in the White House before United States Senator Andrew Johnson and his associate, Horace Maynard, requested assistance for the loyalists of the area.[10] A Southern sympathizer wrote to Confederate President Jefferson Davis in November that the East Tennesseans "look for the establishment of Federal authority with as much confidence as the Jews look for the

---

9 Thomas W. Humes, *The Loyal Mountaineers of Tennessee* (Knoxville: Ogden Brothers and Company, 1888), 60.

10 James Welch Patton, *Unionism and Reconstruction in Tennessee, 1860-1869* (Chapel Hill: University of North Carolina Press, 1934), 1. In October William Blount Carter wrote to General Thomas that "whoever is the leader of a successful expedition into East Tennessee will receive from these grateful people a crown of glory of which anyone might be well proud." *OR* 4, 320.

coming of the Messiah," and that it was impossible to change their feelings, no matter what pressures might be adopted.[11]

With Lincoln in sympathy with plans for the relief of East Tennessee, it was only natural that many of the Union military leaders should at least be impressed with the idea of cooperating in this movement, even though some of them might doubt the military feasibility of a straight thrust into East Tennessee. Brigadier General George Thomas, then a subordinate commander in the Eastern district of Kentucky, helped make arrangements to send supplies and munitions into the region in June.[12]

Buell, who took command of the region in November, felt that an excursion into this region was premature. Johnson and Maynard telegraphed him that "our people are oppressed and pursued as beasts of the forest; the government must come to their relief."[13] But Buell remained inactive.

During this same time the Confederates were strengthening their hold on the region. In August, Brownlow's Knoxville *Whig* carried an address by Brigadier General Felix K. Zollicoffer, commanding the area, in which he assured the people that Confederate authorities were here "only to insure peace to their homes, by repelling invasion and preventing the horrors of civil war. Treason to the state government cannot, will not, be tolerated."[14]

The famous East Tennessee bridge burning on November 8 triggered off the real crisis in that region. The execution of the attempt was carried out by the Reverend William Blount Carter after a consultation with President Lincoln, Secretary of State William Seward, and General McClellan. He planned to burn at the same time nine bridges between Stevenson, Alabama, and Bristol, Tennessee, thus crippling 265 miles of railway and impeding the transportation of troops and supplies to the battlefields of Northern Virginia. Five bridges were actually burned, and

11 A. C. Graham to Jeff Davis, in Goodspeed's *History of Tennessee* (Nashville: Goodspeed Publishing Company, 1886), 485.

12 *OR* 52, pt. 2, 115.

13 *Ibid.*, 7, 480.

14 The Knoxville *Whig*, August 10, 1861.

Carter escaped; however, five of his associates were hanged under the instructions of Judah P. Benjamin, then Confederate Secretary of War.[15] Confederate authorities retaliated, ordering Unionist sympathizers to be imprisoned. The Knoxville *Whig* was finally suppressed and Brownlow committed to prison.[16]

Whether for military or political reasons, General McClellan was at least partly in sympathy with Lincoln's desire to aid the beleaguered loyalists, and on December 3 ordered General Buell to send troops to help protect the newly formed East Tennessee brigade from Confederate attack and, presumably, to pave the way eventually for some kind of Union advance. McClellan informed Buell that he could rely on his full support in the liberation of East Tennessee.[17]

Advancing in this area would mean a difficult supply problem for the Union army, while a drive down either the Cumberland or Tennessee River, or one overland following the line of the Louisville and Nashville Railroad, would be easier to supply. Buell continued to maintain his preference for action in central Tennessee, partly due to the influence of James Gerpy, president of the Louisville and Nashville line, and a most trusted advisor. Gerpy was strongly in favor of driving south, straight along the line of the railroad, with a subsidiary movement down the Tennessee and Cumberland rivers timed to coincide.

15 *OR* 4, 230, 251; Edward Younger (ed.), *Inside the Confederate Government: The Diary of Robert Garlick Hill Kean* (New York: Oxford University Press, 1957), 17, 18. Carter was a Presbyterian minister living in Elizabethtown. He received twenty thousand dollars from the federal government for his activity in arranging the scheme for burning the bridges.

16 For further details of these events see William Brownlow, *Sketches of the Rise, Progress, and Decline of Secession, With A Narrative of Personal Adventures Among the Rebels* (Philadelphia: G.W. Childs Publishers, 1862), 311, 312; Oliver Temple, *East Tennessee and the Civil War* (Cincinnati: The R. Clarke Company, 1899); Humes, *The Loyal Mountaineers of Tennessee*, 60. Brownlow could have escaped going to jail if he had been willing to take the Oath of Allegiance to the Confederacy, but he refused to do so. Unionist feeling continued in this region as the result of Confederate attempts to suppress Union sympathizers.

17 *OR* 7, 468.

Lincoln was not unaware of the difficulties inherent in advancing without the use of either the rivers or railroad as a logistics support, and in his message to Congress in December 1861, he urged upon that body the advisability of constructing a railroad at government expense from one of two railroad terminals in central Kentucky to either the Tennessee state line near Knoxville, the heart of loyalist territory, or to Cumberland Gap.[18] The plan for Lincoln's railroad, although never carried out, was eventually approved.

When Thomas Scott arrived in Louisville, acting more or less as a personal agent of Secretary of War Simon Cameron and President Lincoln, Generals Buell and Anderson attempted to influence him in favor of an advance down the Cumberland-Tennessee toward Nashville. Scott was duly impressed, and he wrote to Edwin Stanton, the recently appointed Secretary of War, that the proposed railroad into East Tennessee was not "wanted at all to meet the enemy or to secure Tennessee."[19] Scott even went so far as to recommend that Stanton transfer forty or fifty thousand men from the Army of the Potomac and add them to Buell's force for an advance on Nashville, although this plan was never executed.

One important reform carried out by the Union army at this time that would have a strong effect on the forthcoming campaign was the linking together of the American Telegraph Company and the Western Union Company lines with the headquarters of General McClellan. This placed "Little Mac" in direct communication with Halleck at St. Louis, Missouri, Commodore Foote at Cairo, Illinois, and Buell at Louisville, Kentucky.[20] Even before the telegraph was complete, plans for a movement into Confederate territory were underfoot. In the middle of the month of December, at the Planter's Hotel in St. Louis, Missouri, the subject of a push came up during a conversation between Generals Sherman, Halleck, and the latter's chief of staff, Brigadier General George Cullum. Many people had urged an advance down the

18   Samuel R. Kamm, *The Civil War Career of Thomas A. Scott* (Philadelphia: University of Pennsylvania Press, 1940), 94.

19   *Ibid.*, 95.

20   *Ibid.*, 95, 96.

Mississippi River, but the main objection to this was the strong Confederate concentration at Columbus, Kentucky, about eighteen miles below Cairo.

General Halleck had a map on his table and a large pencil in his hand. He asked the other officers in his presence, "Where is the Rebel line?" General Cullum took a pencil and drew a line running through Bowling Green, Forts Henry and Donelson, and Columbus. Halleck then said, "That is their line. Now where is the proper place to break it?" Generals Sherman and Cullum both replied, "Naturally the center." Halleck drew a line perpendicular to the other near its middle, and it coincided nearly with the general course of the Tennessee River. "That's the true line of operations," Halleck said.[21]

Just days later orders came through from General McClellan for the opening of a demonstration against Johnston's forces in Kentucky. One object of the demonstration was to make a diversion in favor of General Buell, who was confronting Brigadier General Simon Bolivar Buckner with a large Confederate force at Bowling Green. General Grant was supposed to move in order to pin down Confederate forces and to prevent the sending of reinforcements to Buckner. Grant instructed C. F. Smith to send a force up the west bank of the Tennessee to threaten Forts Heiman and Henry, while McClernand was detailed with six thousand men into western Kentucky, threatening Columbus with one column and the Tennessee River with another. General Grant personally accompanied McClernand's force and gained much information concerning the countryside from the move. For more than a week Union soldiers tramped about in the mud and muck of the winter, the men suffering considerably from the weather. As a result of the expedition, Smith suggested in a report that an assault on Fort Heiman was practical. This confirmed Grant's idea that the proper line of operations was along the Cumberland and Tennessee rivers.

On January 6, before undertaking this demonstration against the Confederates, Grant asked for permission from Halleck for a conference in St. Louis, whereby he wished to lay out a plan of campaign before the latter. With the confirmation of his ideas by General C. F. Smith, Grant

21 Sherman, *Memoirs*, 219, 220.

again requested to meet with General Halleck. Relations between the two men were not the most cordial, but Halleck consented. The meeting was not a success, according to Grant in his *Memoirs*.[22] Halleck cut short the plan as being preposterous, being most unfavorable in his opinion.

Grant's account of this meeting does not support Halleck's previously stated views on the subject, and it may be that the department commander simply did not understand what his subordinate was requesting, for Grant at times was a very poor speaker,[23] or it may simply have been that Grant was not trusted to fulfill such an important operation, in view of the near disaster at Belmont.

One view of this matter is that Halleck, although appreciating the need for an offensive in Kentucky and Tennessee, was reluctant to move until his right flank in Missouri was completely secured, feeling that he did not have enough troops to start two separate movements. Launching two attacks at one time would be a violation of the theories on warfare that Halleck held, since it would mean a divided effort instead of concentrating the resources of movement at a time.[24] Once the Missouri campaign began, Halleck told McClellan, when his present plans were executed he would turn on Tennessee.[25]

Buell, however, kept after Halleck to launch some kind of an advance as a diversion for an effort by him. The commander of the Army of the Ohio said that if Halleck would cut the Memphis and Nashville Railroad, he would assault and capture Bowling Green. President Lincoln, who naturally was interested in the eastern Tennessee Unionists, asked Halleck his opinion on the matter.[26] General Halleck quickly replied that it would be sheer madness, since troops could not be withdrawn from Missouri without risking the loss of the state, and also that there were not enough men available at Cairo, and that he knew the Confederates had no intentions of pulling troops from Columbus whether or not Buell ever

22 Grant, *Memoirs,* 146, 147.

23 Wallace, *An Autobiography*, 1: 353.

24 Ambrose, *Halleck*, 19.

25 *OR* 7, 463.

26 *Ibid.*, 450, 524.

advanced.[27] Lincoln finally ended up by telling Halleck to contact Buell in regard to some kind of movement on January 1. "I am not ready to cooperate with him. Too much haste will ruin everything," was Halleck's peremptory reply.[28]

Events in eastern Kentucky came to a head, with results that could have been foreseen by few, if any, of the participants. As early as October 22, fighting had broken out between the Confederates in eastern Kentucky and Tennessee by troops commanded by General Felix Kirk Zollicoffer and Federal forces commanded by General George "Pappy" Thomas. Zollicoffer's men were repulsed after a sharp but brief action. Wrote one Federal soldier, "The loss among the Rebels is said to be awful."[29] The Confederates probably had four thousand men in action, but their casualties amounted to only a few dozen in reality. Attacking on the following day, Zollicoffer suffered additional casualties, and thereby decided to call it off, falling back to Cumberland Gap. General George Thomas would have preferred to take the offensive and pursue the retreating Confederate general, but General Sherman, who was in command in Kentucky at this time, felt that it would be wisest to remain on the defensive.[30]

Eventually in December, the fiery Tennessee-born Confederate general began a slow forward movement against Thomas' command. The Union commander passed the word along to Buell of the Southern advance, and it was agreed that Thomas could advance to the Cumberland, but should not cross the river "unless absolutely necessary." Zollicoffer saved General Thomas any worry about this by making his camp on the northern bank of the river at a point about eighteen miles southwest of Colonel Albin Schoepf's position at Somerset, Kentucky. Camping on the Union side of the river was not a

---

27 *Ibid.*, 532.

28 *Ibid.*, 526

29 Cincinnati *Daily Gazette*, October 25, 1861.

30 See Freeman Cleaves, *Rock of Chickamauga: The Life of General George H. Thomas* (Norman: University of Oklahoma Press, 1948), 89-91, for details of this operation.

particularly good idea, and Major General George B. Crittenden was detached from General Johnston's army to proceed to the assistance of Zollicoffer. By the time he reached the Confederate general's army, however, it was too late to make any change. Thomas advanced on the position known as Logan's Crossroads or Mill Springs, Kentucky, reaching it on January 18. Generals Crittenden and Zollicoffer prepared to launch a surprise attack, hoping to shatter the Virginia-born Thomas before he could unite with Schoepf. The two Confederate generals led six Tennessee regiments, the Fifteenth Mississippi, and the Fifteenth Alabama, along with an artillery company and a battalion of cavalry, probably around four thousand troops, out on a night march through one of the worst experiences of the war.[31]

A blinding rain made the roads almost impassable while adding to the misery of the soldiers as they slogged along wearily, drenched to the skin and half-frozen from the low temperature.[32] About 6:30 a.m. on January 19, troops from the First Kentucky Cavalry, U. S., signaled the main force that the Southerners were advancing. Firing soon broke out, but visibility was so poor from the daybreak mist and the smoke from the guns which so thickened the air that it was hard to distinguish friend from foe. General Zollicoffer, mistaking enemy for friend, rode out too far in front of his men, approaching Colonel Speed S. Fry, Fourth Kentucky Infantry. The general told Fry, "We must not fire on our own men," and nodding his head to the left, remarked, "Those are our men." Colonel Fry answered, "Of course not. I would not do so intentionally." Fry began moving toward his regiment, and suddenly he saw another man ride up and join Zollicoffer. The new arrival opened fire with a revolver, hitting Fry's horse. The Fourth Kentucky's colonel at once opened with his own revolver at the man. A figure fell off a horse. Thus Zollicoffer died, a bullet through his breast, a victim of the poor visibility and his own recklessness.[33]

31 || For Mill Springs, see Raymond E. Myers, *The Zollie Tree: General Felix K. Zollicoffer and the Battle of Mill Springs* (Louisville: Filson Club, 1964).

32   *Battles and Leaders*, 1: 383.

33   Private Henry Doak, Nineteenth Tennessee, who participated in the action, said Fry's story of shooting Zollicoffer with a revolver was a lie, and that the

This was the beginning of the end for the Confederacy in the battle. Within a few minutes the Southerners were in full retreat. The foul weather rendered most of the Confederate troops incapable of fighting, not so much from morale as from the fact that their flintlock muskets simply would not function in the dampness. The total Union loss in the action was 40 killed, 207 wounded, and 15 captured or missing while the Southerners had 125 killed, 309 wounded, and 99 captured or missing. Confederate losses were almost twice as heavy, the most serious loss being the death of General Zollicoffer.[34]

Crittenden took over the Confederate command and helped make some kind of a retreat, although it was widely alleged that the politician turned soldier had been under the influence of alcohol at the time. He was largely discredited by these events and nevermore would hold important Confederate command. News of the defeat lowered Confederate morale drastically. A Confederate War Department official commented in his personal diary that the battle was a complete disaster.[35]

The dead Zollicoffer was hailed throughout the South as a fallen hero. Forty-nine years old and one of the leading political powers in Tennessee, the dead general had been the most important and most popular secessionist leader in the entire state. A long time member of the Whig party and a newspaperman, he had helped make and unmake governors, senators, and presidents. In 1852, Zollicoffer fought his famous duel with John Leake Marling, editor of the Democratic Oriented Nashville *Union*, who had called him a liar. Aside from a year as an officer in the Seminole War, this duel was Zollicoffer's only military experience. In exchange for a bullet through his hand, he put a shot

---

general was shot by a Union soldier with a musket. Henry M. Doak, "The Nineteenth Tennessee," Confederate Collection, Tennessee Department of Archives and History; *Battles and Leaders*, 1: 383. For a fuller discussion of the matter see Raymond Myers, *The Zollie Tree* (Louisville: c. 1964), 119-125.

34 Cleaves, *Rock of Chickamauga*, 94-99; Williams, *Lincoln Finds A General*, 3: 172-175.

35 Younger, *Diary of Robert Garlick Hill Kean*, 24.

through his duelist opponent's head, badly wounding him, although the two political rivals later became reconciled.[36]

The defeat at Fishing Creek, or Logan's Crossroads, or Mill Springs, or whatever the battle might be called, was the first significant step in the Union's conquest of the Confederate heartland. The practical result of the victory, besides a heavy Confederate casualty list and the great loss of supplies and materials, was the complete collapse of the Confederate right wing. Henceforth the way was open for a Union invasion of East Tennessee or a thrust through the eastern Tennessee region against the flank of General Albert Sidney Johnston's communications, specifically the line to Bowling Green.

On January 4, President Lincoln telegraphed Buell at Louisville asking if weapons and munitions had been forwarded to East Tennessee and requesting a progress report of movement in that direction.[37] Buell's answer was that he had been organizing two columns with reference to the movement, but that he had no real belief or faith in its feasibility, and he expressed the view that an attack upon Nashville, Tennessee, was preferable, which was not well received by the chief executive. On January 6, Lincoln wrote to Buell, suggesting an advance on the railroad at some point south of Cumberland Gap, since this would have the effect of cutting "a great artery of the enemy's communication, which Nashville does not have, and secondly because it is in the midst of loyal people, who would rally around it, which Nashville is not." Lincoln went on to tell Buell that he could not see why "the movement in east Tennessee would not be a diversion in your favor." Lincoln's humanitarian feeling showed through in his expression of concern for the fate of the loyalists in East Tennessee, who were being strongly suppressed by Confederate authorities.[38] The following day President Lincoln wired Buell again, ordering him to "please name as early a day as you safely can, on or before which you can be ready to move southward

36 Myers, *The Zollie Tree*, 13-42; *D. A. B.*, 20: 20.

37 Basler, *Collected Works of Abraham Lincoln*, 5: 90.

38 *Ibid.*, 91.

in concert with Gen. Halleck. Delay is ruining us; and it is indispensable for me to have something definite. I send a like dispatch to Halleck."[39]

Lincoln's patience was beginning to run short, although it is probable that he would really have been willing to settle for some kind of offensive, and would not have insisted on the East Tennessee campaign; but politically, militarily, economically, and from all other standpoints, the time had come for a Union offensive, somehow, somewhere, something.

On January 13, President Lincoln again wrote to Buell and Halleck, urging them into action. The President stated that his general idea of "this war to be that we have the greater numbers, and the enemy has the greater facility of concentrating forces upon points of collision." He went on to say that the Union cause would fail, "unless we can find some way of making our advantage an overmatch for his," and that this only could be done by "menacing him with superior forces at different points, at the same time," in order to attack "one or both, if he makes no change; and if he weakens one to strengthen the other, forbear to attack the strengthened one," but the point was to "seize, and hold the weakened one," gaining very much. In a nutshell this was military strategy as Lincoln saw it, and he was perfectly correct. The President elaborated that his idea was that Halleck should menace Columbus and downriver generally while Buell should harass Bowling Green and East Tennessee. If the Confederates should concentrate at Bowling Green, then Buell should not retire from its front but should avoid engaging "him," and if possible to occupy Columbus and East Tennessee, one or both, since the Confederates would have concentrated their main forces at Bowling Green and would be unable to defend them.[40]

The success of the Grant-McClernand-Smith reconnaissance in force, and probably the effect of Lincoln's obvious desire for an offensive, brought forth from Henry Halleck one of his more unusual and interesting plans of operations. In a letter to McClellan on January 20, Halleck found fault with politics and politicians interfering in the war, and he charged that the past lack of success of the Union army was

---

39 *Ibid.*

40 Basler, *Collected Works of Abraham Lincoln,* 5: 98, 99.

"attributable to the politicians rather than the generals." He seemed confused in regard to many issues of the war, but he did maintain that moving down the Mississippi River using the navy as a carrier would be "impracticable, or at least premature." He added, "It is not a proper line of operations, at least now. A much more feasible plan is to move up the Cumberland and Tennessee, making Nashville the first objective point." In flat words and terse language, Halleck positively and definitely committed himself to the general-in-chief in favor of a drive down the river lines, and not a push into eastern Tennessee.[41] Buell had suggested this plan way back on November 27 and again on December 29 to General McClernand, and on January 3 to General Halleck.[42]

Not daunted by the failure of his conference with General Halleck in St. Louis, Grant, on the 24th of January, forwarded a report to "Little Mac" of General C. F. Smith's reconnaissance on the Fort Henry bastion. Conferring with Commodore Foote, Grant and the naval officer wired Halleck in St. Louis, on the 28th, that Fort Henry could be captured.[43]

The weeks and months of delays, confusion, and sometimes downright chaos were about to come to an end. It is impossible to escape the conclusion, however, that many of the leading figures in the Union armed forces at this time were somewhat overcome with the gravity of the situation. Men like Halleck, Buell, and to some extent Grant simply lacked experience in handling large bodies of troops. At the same time they could appreciate the gravity of the situation they were involved in.

On receipt of the Foote-Grant report, Halleck finally decided to take action. Probably he was also influenced by the arrival of a report from McCullum stating that General P. G. T. Beauregard and fifteen Confederate regiments were *en route* to Kentucky. In any event Halleck promptly ordered General Grant to assault Fort Henry.[44] General Halleck immediately followed the order to attack Fort Henry with a second

---

41 *OR* 7, 120, 121.

42 *Ibid.*, 451, 521, 528, 529.

43 J. F. C. Fuller, *The Generalship of Ulysses S. Grant* (New York: Dodd, Meade and Company, 1929), 79; *OR* 7, 120, 121.

44 *Ibid.*, 121, 571, 572.

dispatch, dated the same day, January 30, 1862, containing many more details than instructions.

Grant was ordered to mass all possible troops from Paducah, Smithland, Cairo, Fort Holt, Birdspoint, and other places, but at the same time to leave sufficient garrisons to protect those places in case the Confederates at Columbus should launch an offensive. Remarking on the impassable condition of the local roads, Halleck ordered Grant to make as much use of Foote's transports as possible. Additional artillery units were promised to Grant, and Lieutenant Colonel James B. McPherson of the United States Engineers was promised as chief engineer of the expedition. Halleck reported all the details he knew of Fort Henry, and he cautioned Grant to cooperate closely with the navy.[45]

Grant quickly set out to launch his invasion. Because of the closing of the Mississippi River to Union traffic, there were a large number of steamships[46] tied up in Cairo for lack of employment. Grant immediately began rounding up these ships and their crews, but was not able to find enough transports to haul all of his command at one time. When all of the available boats were loaded, with about one-half of the seventeen thousand Federal soldiers, Grant ordered the expedition to proceed on up the Tennessee River under Brigadier General John McClernand. Rounding up some additional transports from another source, Grant soon followed with more of his army.[47]

Grant caught up with his advance force two days later, on the morning of February 4, but he did not approve of the landing site McClernand had selected because it was too far away from Fort Henry. The steamers then carried the force to a new disembarkation point about four miles from the Confederate position. The troops were landed and the steamers unloaded and turned about to Paducah to pick up General C. F.

---

45 *Ibid.*, 121, 122.

46 || Dr. Cunningham uses the terms "steamships" and "ships" throughout the dissertation. These vessels are properly termed "steamboats" and "boats" since none of them were ocean-going vessels. We have left the terms intact throughout the document.

47 Grant, *Memoirs*, 148.

Smith's infantry division, Grant personally going along to insure that everything went off right.[48]

February 5 was spent in making reconnaissances of the Confederate position while waiting for the rest of the army to show up. Grant's unofficial chief-of-staff, Colonel J. D. Webster, and several members of McClernand's staff accompanied a party of Federal cavalry on a reconnaissance of the Southern bastion. A short skirmish developed in which one Union cavalryman was killed and at least two others wounded, besides an undetermined number of Southern casualties. But the Federals were able to get a pretty good idea of the principle features of the terrain on the northern side of Fort Henry.[49]

On the afternoon of the 5th, very late, the transports returned from Paducah with Smith's soldiers, General Smith, and General Grant. About dusk Grant, Smith, and McClernand went on board the flagship of Commodore Foote, the *Cincinnati*, to arrange the program for an assault on Fort Henry, scheduled the following day. While the officers were engaged in their final conference, the Union gunboat *Conestoga* returned from a patrol up the river, during which it had checked to see if the channel was clear of obstructions. The *Conestoga* pulled alongside the *Cincinnati*, transferring a huge Confederate naval mine or torpedo, which it had picked up in the channel. The ship's crew quickly congregated about the sinister looking iron cylinder, and as the conference in Foote's cabin ended and the officers came outside, their attention was attracted to the torpedo.

Examining the five foot long iron cylinder, the curious Grant expressed a desire to see the interior mechanism of the device. The ship's armorer, armed with monkey wrench, hammer, and chisel, promptly opened the thing up. As he did so a quantity of gas came squirting out. Two of Grant's army officers, believing the contraption was about to explode, flung themselves face down on the deck. With the agility of a young tomcat, Foote flew up the ship's ladder, followed by the equally light-footed Grant. Reaching the top and realizing that the torpedo was

---

48   *OR* 7, 127; Grant, *Memoirs*, 148.

49   A. L. Conger, *The Rise of U. S. Grant* (New York: Century Press, 1931), 156.

not going to explode, Foote calmed down; and turning to face Grant, who was just reaching the top of the ladder, he smilingly remarked, "General, why this haste?" to which General Grant with equal presence of mind quickly replied, "That the navy may not get ahead of us." The whole crew broke out laughing, and the army officers soon scattered to their respective commands on shore.[50]

Whatever the humor of the occasion, Foote and Grant soon had more pressing thoughts on their minds, for the morrow was the appointed date for the assault on Fort Henry. Foote and his seven warships would hit the Confederates from the river side while Grant and his regiments moved in to isolate the Southerners on the landward side. It was obvious the forthcoming day was going to be one to long remember.

---

50 H. Allen Gosnell, *Guns on the Western Waters: The Story of River Gunboats in the Civil War* (Baton Rouge: Louisiana State University Press, 1949), 47, 48.

Adapted from the OR Atlas Plate XI

TENNESSEE RIVER

ROAD TO DOVER

ABATI

FORT
HENRY

SWAMP

Chapter 3

Breaking the River Barriers

AS PART OF THEIR line of defense, the Confederates erected fortifications at a series of strategic points stretching across Tennessee, Missouri, and Kentucky. The extreme left of the Confederate works was located at two points: New Madrid in the extreme southern portion of Missouri, and the second series of works at Island No. 10, in the Mississippi River, lying geographically south of New Madrid, but actually due to the river's taking a sharp bend, in a more advanced position along the Tennessee-Kentucky state line. At Columbus, on the Mississippi River, just across the state line, was perhaps the strongest of the many works erected by the Southerners.

More than a hundred heavy guns, some accounts say one hundred and fifty, guarded the "Gibraltar of the West." Farther east lay the vital Tennessee and Cumberland rivers. These two important waterways ran almost parallel to each other across the state of Kentucky and down into Tennessee, where they gradually split. At one point these waterways were within three miles of each other, but at the beginning of hostilities Kentucky had not been occupied by the Confederate army and the Southerners had chosen to erect their fortifications within the Tennessee state line, thus respecting Kentucky's neutrality. Works had been started at points on the two rivers approximately twelve miles apart just across the state line. These works were Fort Henry and Fort Heiman on the Tennessee, and to the right, Fort Donelson on the Cumberland.[1]

---

1 || Much has been written on Forts Henry and Donelson since Cunningham's dissertation appeared in 1966. The two best accounts are Benjamin F. Cooling,

At Bowling Green, Kentucky, General Johnston's main base of operations, the Southerners also erected some field fortifications. However, it was not necessary to erect river batteries, simply because there was no river running in that area. The only other fortifications in the region of any real importance were constructed at Fort Pillow along the Mississippi River, which had been set up to defend Memphis from attack.[2]

With the Confederate extreme right collapsed as a result of the Fishing Creek debacle, the positions at Fort Henry, Fort Heiman, and Fort Donelson took on increased importance. If Union naval and army forces could take these places, it would not only open up the Cumberland and Tennessee rivers to the Union, but it would also have the effect of outflanking both Columbus and Bowling Green, since Union forces would be south of them and in position to cut their communications with the Gulf region.

Even before Tennessee joined the Confederacy, Governor Isham Harris ordered Major Bushrod Johnson to lay out fortifications at some suitable point on the Tennessee River to protect the state from invasion along the route. The spot chosen was Fort Henry. It was not a terribly good choice, but probably the best under the circumstances, since work had to be begun at once and could not wait until Kentucky was occupied. Eventually seventeen guns were mounted in a fortified position on the east bank of the river. Eleven cannon commanded the river, while six were inside the works to help defend the landward side. To protect the fort from army assault, a line of trenches was dug some four hundred yards from the fort and some twelve thousand yards in length. Isolated rifle pits were scattered around the length of the works. The guns were a 10-inch Columbiad, two 42-pounders on barbette mounts, seven

---

Forts Henry and Donelson: The Key to the Confederate Heartland (Knoxville: University of Tennessee Press, 1987), and Kendall D. Gott, *Where the South Lost the War: An Analysis of the Fort Henry-Fort Donelson Campaign, February 1862* (Mechanicsburg: Stackpole Books, 2003).

2 || For Fort Pillow, see John Cimprich, *Fort Pillow, A Civil War Massacre, And Public Memory* (Baton Rouge: Louisiana State University Press, 2005).

32-pounders on barbette mounts, a 24-pound rifle, and six smaller pieces.[3]

Although of some use in disputing control of the river, the fort was weakened since it was on low terrain and was commanded by high ground on both sides of the river. Hence it would be readily possible for enemy forces to occupy the higher ground and shell the fort into submission. As a means of partly alleviating this situation, the Southerners began work on a smaller secondary work on the west side of the river. It was named Fort Heiman, in honor of Colonel Adolphus Heiman, a German-American who had served in the armed forces in a German state and had also acted as a lieutenant in a Tennessee regiment of volunteers in the Mexican War.[4]

The worst feature of Fort Henry was not the exposure to enemy attack but the exposure to the elements of nature, notably the waters of the Tennessee River. Captain Jesse Taylor of the garrison ascertained that at high water the highest point within the fort would be inundated by two feet. He related this fact to Tennessee state authorities, and was told to report to Major General Leonidas Polk with this news. Taylor checked with that Southern leader, who referred him to General A. S. Johnston, who dispatched an engineer, Major, later Colonel, Jeremy F. Gilmer, to investigate the situation, and it was he, who in an attempt to remedy it, began fortifying the heights of the west bank, Fort Heiman.[5]

Described by one of the authorities as a "bastioned earthwork of irregular trace," Fort Donelson represented a somewhat different proposition. Located on a high bluff, the guns of the fort could shoot down, dropping projectiles with a plunging effect on enemy ships

---

3 Conger, "Fort Donelson," 39. Conger said that one 32-pounder was rifled, but gave no source for this. According to Captain J. Taylor, Confederate artillery, Fort Henry had eight 32-pound guns, two 42-pound guns, one 128-pound Columbiad, five 18-pound siege guns which were smoothbores, one 6-inch rifle, and six 12-pounders, which were defective, and two which exploded the first time they were tested. This was his February 1st report. *Battles and Leaders*, 1: 369.

4 Conger, "Fort Donelson," 47.

5 *Battles and Leaders*, 1: 369.

attempting to approach up the river. The fort was armed with ten 32-pound guns, two of them old carronades that would only be effective at practically point blank range, one 128-pound Columbiad, one 128-pound rifled gun, plus two 9-pound field pieces, presumably smoothbores.

Actually the term "fort" is a misnomer, for Donelson was rather a fortified encampment or position. On the slope of the ridge, which faced downstream from the position, the Confederates excavated two water batteries. Here the guns were protected on all sides by dirt works, thus it was virtually impossible to enfilade them with gunfire. The lower battery was about twenty feet above the river, and it was armed with the 10-inch smoothbore and eight of the 32-pounders. The other battery was perhaps fifty feet above the level of the water and had the one rifled 128-pounder and the two 32-pound carronades. Inside the fort itself, or what was known as the fort, was a bombproof, a nineteenth century bomb shelter where troops not actually required to man the guns could take shelter during enemy fire. This was connected with the batteries by a covered way, a sort of deep trench, similar to the communication trench of World War I.[6]

At the time fighting began in February, the fort covered an area of about sixty acres. The walls or parapets occupied a ridge conforming to the bank of the river for some distance, and then diverging southward, then east, and finally again north to the place where it began. Donelson was not a regular oblong square but was arranged following the contours of the ground in a kind of jagged zigzag. The ridge on which the parapets were located extended around Donelson, except at the southeast corner where the entrance was located.

The walls of the fort varied in height, conforming to the topography of the ridge, running from about eight feet to a little more than twenty, inside measure. The outside walls were naturally higher because the dirt from which they were constructed formed a deep ditch. Confederate soldiers had driven stakes and woven brush near the interior top of the

6 Walter J. Buttgenbach, "Coast Defense in the Civil War," *Journal of the United States Artillery* 39 (March-April 1913): 210-216.

wall, forming a platform for the men to stand on. On the various angles of the wall were located gun platforms.[7]

As of January 18, Donelson was provided with 904 rounds of 32-pound ammunition, 165 rounds of 12-pound cannon ammunition, a hundred rounds of 10-inch, 250 rounds of 12-pound howitzer, and 190 rounds of 6-pounders. The smaller caliber ammunition presumably referred to the presence of some field pieces at the fort. Besides the river batteries and the series of dirt works that formed the so-called fort, there was around and about it a series of rifle pits and gun positions. These pits were simply trenches with the dirt thrown up in the front to give the men protection from frontal fire, but not enfilading or flanking fire. There were provisions or positions for the establishment of eight field batteries in nine positions about the perimeter.[8]

Fort Donelson was begun later than Fort Henry, but it was reasonably complete by the time the fighting began at that point. It was actually not until late in the fall of 1861, after General Johnston had taken command, that work was begun. Some four hundred log cabins or crude barracks were constructed to house the soldiers, and preparations were complete or reasonably complete by February 5.

The Confederate commander was Brigadier General Lloyd Tilghman, a forty-six year old native of Baltimore, Maryland. A graduate of West Point, class of 1836, Tilghman left the army soon after graduation, spending the next quarter of a century employed as a construction engineer in the South. During the Mexican War Tilghman entered the army for a short while, serving as an officer in the Maryland

7 The foregoing description of the main fortifications is taken from B. F. Thomas, *Soldier Life: A Narrative of the Civil War*. This work was privately printed March 6, 1907, for the use of the author's immediate family, and the only copy I know of is in Shiloh National Military Park Library. There are no page numbers. Thomas' account was based on his personal daily diary, and due to the unusual accuracy of his account, I have basically paraphrased his description of Donelson. For additional description of the fort, see Jefferson Davis, *The Rise and Fall of the Confederate Government* (New York: D. Appleton and Company, 1881), 28, 29. Davis said the enclosed area was about "one hundred yards."

8 Buttgenbach, "Coast Defense in the Civil War," 211-213.

and District of Columbia Battalion of Volunteers.[9] Commander Henry Walke, who met Tilghman after the fall of Fort Henry, described him as "a soldierly-looking man, a little above medium height, with piercing black eyes."[10] Personally unenthusiastic at being assigned to command what he considered a virtually hopeless position, Tilghman still determined to hold Fort Henry as long as possible.[11]

With only about two thousand five hundred men, Tilghman decided to abandon the incomplete Fort Heiman, trusting the bad terrain on the west side of the river would hinder a Federal advance from over there. On the night of February 4, the Confederates, excluding a simple force of cavalry left behind to act as scouts and skirmishers, evacuated the west side of the river, concentrating in and around Fort Henry. Unfortunately inside the fort the situation was rapidly deteriorating. The level of the Tennessee River rose constantly, flooding much of the fort and the surrounding countryside. The base of the fort's flagstaff stood in two feet of water.[12] All day during the 5th, Tilghman and his officers nervously observed the movements of the enemy regiments and gunboats, but no land action developed, except the one with Webster's reconnoitering party.

During the day the ironclad *Essex* steamed up towards the fort, firing a few rounds into the Confederates. The Southerners held their fire until the *Essex* completed her little mission and was heading back toward the rest of the fleet. Then the Confederate gunners fired a round from their single big rifle. The shot passed harmlessly overhead, but a second round

9   Warner, *Generals in Gray*, 306.

10   *Battles and Leaders*, 1: 366.

11   *OR* 7, 139. || For Tilghman, see James W. Rabb, *Confederate General Lloyd Tilghman: A Biography* (Jefferson: McFarland and Company, 2006).

12   Steele, *American Campaigns*, 75. Tilghman's soldiers were poorly trained and worse armed. Most of them had shotguns and fowling pieces. His best equipped regiment, the Tenth Tennessee, was armed with flintlock muskets, originally used by Andrew Johnson's militia in the War of 1812. Stanley F. Horn, *The Army of the Tennessee: A Military History* (New York: The Bobbs Merrill Company, 1941), 82; *Tennessee in the Civil War* (Nashville: Civil War Centennial Commission, 1964), 1: 194; *Battles and Leaders*, 1: 370.

struck the *Essex* damaging the captain's cabin, "cutting the feet from a pair of his socks," although fortunately the captain's feet were not in the socks at the time.[13] A few more shots were exchanged later in the day, both sides cautiously feeling the other out, but darkness caused an end to these activities. Sunrise the following morning brought only increasing gloom to Tilghman, who finally made a decision—evacuate the infantry and other personnel, all except the gunners for the fort's big pieces, and save the garrison for a stand at the infinitely stronger Fort Donelson.

With about eighty men, Tilghman quietly awaited the Federal onslaught. Along the west bank of the river one of C. F. Smith's brigades slowly sloshed across the flooded land toward the abandoned Fort Heiman. On the east bank Grant and the rest of the Union army painfully struggled to make their way around behind Tilghman's position, but the advance was much slower than planned because of the flooded condition of the terrain, heightened by a heavy rainfall the night before.[14]

At 11:00 a.m., Foote's seven warships, the *Essex*, *St. Louis*, *Cincinnati*, and *Carondolet* leading, with the wooden gunboats *Tyler*, *Lexington*, and *Conestoga* close behind, began steaming toward the Confederate position. About one mile from the fort the warships opened fire, the flagship discharging her bow guns first. Slowly steaming onward, the Federals maintained a steady and accurate fire, Tilghman's little band of gunners, flooded fort and all, pouring it right back. For almost forty-five minutes the Union and Confederate gunners exchanged shots, and then Tilghman's big rifle exploded, killing or injuring all of his crew. Just minutes later the big 10-inch Columbiad was accidentally jammed, putting it out of action. A Federal shell passed through an open embrasure, exploding against one of the 32-pounders, killing or mangling the gun crew. Shells and solid shot spattered all over the Confederate position, adding to the confusion. Tilghman personally

13   Gosnell, *Guns on the Western Waters*, 49.

14   Conger, "Fort Donelson," 57; Richardson, *Personal History of Ulysses S. Grant*, 210; Brinton, *Personal Memoirs*, 114; Comte de Paris, *History of the Civil War in America* (Philadelphia: Joseph H. Coates and Company, 1875), 1: 483, 484.

helped work one of the remaining guns. An officer suggested surrender, but Tilghman replied, "I shall not give up the work."[15]

The fight was not all one-sided, for a cannon shot tore through the *Essex*'s boiler, disabling her and scalding thirty-eight officers and men, including Commander W. D. Porter.[16] The six remaining warships continued to fight until after 1:00 p.m. Finally Tilghman, who was by this time reduced to two workable guns, decided further resistance was useless. Lieutenant Colonel Milton Haynes asked him if he was going to surrender. He replied, "Yes, we cannot hold out five minutes longer; our men are disabled, and we have not enough to man the two guns."[17]

At 1:50 p.m., the Confederate commander grabbed up a flag of truce and began waving it from the parapet, and just minutes later the captain and crew of the gunboat *Cincinnati* accepted the fort's surrender.[18] Besides the *Essex*'s casualties there was also one man killed and nine wounded on board the *Cincinnati*.[19]

Sailors from the *St. Louis* were the first to land and enter the fort, followed in a few minutes by the personnel from the other warships. About 3:00 p.m., a somewhat muddy General Grant and his staff rode into the fort and assumed command. Foote, Grant, and the senior army and navy officers walked around inspecting the battle area. Some of the Confederate army barracks in the rear of the fort were still smoking, Foote's sailors having put out the flames only minutes earlier. The natural feeling of exaltation on the part of Grant and his officers was considerably lessened by the sight of the carnage inside the fort. Some of the Confederate gunners had been buried alive by the tremendous debris thrown up by Northern naval gunfire.[20] Confederate losses, according to

---

15   *OR* 7, 134.

16   *Official Records of the Union and Confederate Navies in the War of the Rebellion* (Washington: 1894-1922), 22, 540. Hereinafter this will be cited as *ORN.*

17   *OR* 7, 146.

18   *OR N* 22, 559, 538.

19   *Ibid.*, 539.

20   Gosnell, *Guns on the Western Waters*, 54, 55; *Battles and Leaders*, 1: 367.

Commander Henry Walke of the *Carondolet*, were five killed, eleven wounded, five missing, and a total of ninety-four prisoners, including the sick and wounded.[21]

While Grant and the others inspected their prize, Federal cavalry was busy pursuing Tilghman's retreating soldiers. Late in the afternoon the Northern troops caught up with the tail of the retiring Confederate column, killing one man and capturing thirty-eight others. With the Yanks on their heels, the Rebels abandoned six field pieces in the mud (Captain Jacob Culbertson's Battery), plus a considerable quantity of other supplies. Darkness brought an end to Federal pursuit, and the Confederates soon straggled into Fort Donelson, wet, filthy, and disheartened.[22]

Even while his cavalry was chasing the fleeing Confederates, General Grant dictated a short victory notice to General Halleck, proclaiming that "Fort Henry is ours. The gunboats silenced the batteries before the investment was completed."[23]

Back at army headquarters Halleck, who had been anxiously awaiting news, probably breathed a great sigh of relief as he read the first two sentences of Grant's victory message, but as his eyes scanned down the missive, his cautious heart must have given a big jump, for Grant casually remarked, "I shall take and destroy Fort Donelson on the 8th and return to Fort Henry."[24] Nervous or not, Halleck quickly wired a bombastic message to General McClellan, in Washington, telling him of the capture, and saying that "the flag of the Union is re-established on the soil of Tennessee. It will never be removed."[25]

With his superiors propitiated, Halleck decided to let Grant have his lead in regard to the Donelson matter, and he ordered Foote to send gunboats up the river to cut up the various railroad bridges and interfere

---

21 *OR* 7, 142.

22 *Ibid.*, 129, 147.

23 *Ibid.*, 124.

24 *Ibid.*

25 *Ibid.*, 590.

with Confederate communications.[26] On the same day, February 7, Halleck began sending out urgent pleas for reinforcements to bolster Grant's army and make possible more extended operations once Donelson was under the Union flag.[27]

But Grant did not wish to wait for any reinforcements. He wanted to immediately advance and assault Donelson before the Confederates regrouped after the Fort Henry debacle. Unfortunately the program of capturing the second Confederate strongpoint on the eighth was completely unrealistic. For one thing, by his own orders, the Union regiments were limited to four wagons per unit, a manifestly inadequate amount of transportation to launch an overland invasion. Furthermore there was a paucity of information concerning the exact state of the Confederate defenses. The only reliable information on Fort Donelson was that obtained by Lieutenant Ledyard Phelps on his reconnaissances toward Donelson with his gunboat *Conestoga*, and the last of these had been made on January 3.[28]

General Grant seems to have forgotten or overlooked conferring with Foote about the proposed expedition. Foote was simply not in a position to support an attack on Donelson on the eighth. In order to get at the second Confederate position the Federal warships had to proceed back up the Tennessee River to Paducah, and then ascend the Cumberland. In any event the *Essex* and the other warships also needed some time to repair the damage worked by Tilghman's gunners.

Foote also had to execute General Halleck's order to destroy the Confederate Tennessee River bridges. The *Lexington*, *Tyler*, and *Conestoga* were sent on a rampage along the river, ripping up bridges and burning Confederate steamers. The Federals captured the half-completed Confederate gunboat *Eastport* in Hardin County, Tennessee, and then proceeded all the way up to Florence, Alabama, before returning to Fort Henry on February 10 without meeting any opposition, save an

---

26   *Ibid.*, 591.

27   *Ibid.*, 592-594.

28   *ORN* 22, 461, 485, 486.

occasional burst of buck and ball from behind trees along the path of advance and retreat.[29]

To add to General Grant's difficulties, any hope of "taking Donelson on the 8th" was dispelled by the bad weather and subsequent high water. On the very day he had told General Halleck he would capture Donelson, Grant found himself writing his superior that "we are perfectly locked in by high water and bad roads, and prevented from acting offensively as I should like to do."[30]

But if a big push were out of question, Grant decided to use the delay to obtain vitally needed information about a workable route to Fort Donelson. His chief engineer officer, Lieutenant Colonel James B. McPherson, personally led a force of cavalry to within a mile of the Confederate stronghold, driving in the Confederate pickets in the process.[31] Aboard his headquarters ship *Tigress*, tied up at Fort Henry, Grant and his staff worked on plans for a new target date, February 12, one which would fit in with Foote's operations.[32]

* * *

29 *Ibid.*, 570-573.

30 *OR* 7, 596; Richardson, *Personal History of Ulysses S. Grant*, 211. Grant's failure to appreciate the reality of the possibility of such an advance can be seen in a conversation between the general and correspondent Albert Richardson on February 7. The reporter stopped by briefly to tell Grant he was leaving for New York, and the general promptly remarked, "You had better wait a day or two." "Why?" asked Richardson. "I am going to attack Fort Donelson tomorrow." Richardson asked, "Do you know how strong it is?" "Not exactly; but I think we can take it; at all events, we can try." *Ibid.*

31 *OR* 7, 596, 597. In his *Memoirs* Grant says he personally accompanied this reconnaissance force. Grant, *Memoirs*, 150, 151. A. L. Conger says Grant actually accompanied a second reconnaissance party, which explored the route on February 9. Conger, *The Rise of U. S. Grant*, 164. General Gideon Pillow reported a cavalry skirmish on February 9 near Fort Donelson, which would tend to confirm Conger's account of the reconnaissance. *OR* 7, 370.

32 Brinton, *Personal Memoirs*, 115; Wallace, *Autobiography*, 1: 376; *OR* 7, 600. General Lew Wallace wrote of attending a staff conference on board the *Tigress*, at which Generals Smith and McClernand both advocated as quickly as possible. Wallace, *Autobiography*, 376, 377.

Receiving word of the fall of Fort Henry, General Johnston immediately ordered newly appointed forty-four year old Brigadier General Bushrod Rust Johnson to assume command of Fort Donelson, replacing Tilghman, now a prisoner of war.[33] The fall of Fort Henry punctured a deep hole in the entire Confederate defensive arrangement in the West. With only about forty-five thousand men available in Kentucky and Tennessee, and with his position now sliced in two, Albert S. Johnston's entire defensive system threatened to collapse.[34]

On the morning following Fort Henry's fall, General Johnston called a top level military conference at the Covington House in Bowling Green, Kentucky. Major General Hardee was there, as was the newly arrived hero of Sumter and Manassas, P. G. T. Beauregard. As a result of this meeting it was decided to adopt a new plan of strategy for the future. Realizing that the Kentucky-Tennessee line could no longer be held, General Johnston decided to withdraw all Confederate forces south of the Cumberland River. Fort Donelson, Bowling Green, and Columbus were to be evacuated; and if it proved impossible to organize adequate defensive works at Nashville, then even that prime center was to be abandoned. The two separate wings of the Confederate forces in Kentucky were to operate independently under Generals Polk and Hardee until they could be united at some undetermined spot southward. The eastern portion was to fall back on Nashville and if necessary to take the Nashville and Chattanooga Railroad to Stevenson, Alabama. The western force was to withdraw to Humboldt, Tennessee, and then to Grand Junction in order to cover Memphis. Confederate naval forces,

---

33 Horn, *The Army of the Tennessee*, 83; Alfred Roman, *The Military Operations of General Beauregard in the War Between the States* (New York: Harper, 1884), 1: 225.

34 Johnston had about fourteen thousand men at Bowling Green under his personal direction, about five thousand at Fort Donelson, including the survivors of the Fort Henry affair now under General Bushrod Johnson, about eight thousand at Clarksville, Tennessee, under General John B. Floyd, and about fifteen thousand partially organized and partially equipped fellows in the Columbus area under General Leonidas Polk. Roman, *Beauregard*, 1: 214; Horn, *The Army of the Tennessee*, 61, 62; Thomas Jordan, "The Campaign and Battle of Shiloh," *The United Service: A Monthly Review of Military and Naval Affairs* 12 (March 1885): 264.

under George N. Hollins, were to cooperate in a series of rear guard actions at Columbus, Island No. 10, Fort Pillow, and at Memphis if necessary.[35]

Johnston's decision was a bold one. Its execution would mean the loss of Kentucky and much of Tennessee, besides the terrible morale effect of the withdrawal on the North and South. The most controversial part of the decision concerned the evacuation of Columbus. General Polk argued that a holding force of five or six thousand men should be left to garrison the fortress and stand a siege if necessary. Polk reasoned that the tremendous fire power of Columbus could delay a Union advance for an extended period of time, but Johnston and Beauregard wanted to save the garrison. The guns from Columbus were transferred to Island No. 10 and New Madrid, which were appreciably weaker positions than the Kentucky fort. In the long run the South lost an even larger garrison when the two latter points fell, while not obtaining any particular strategic advantage. The decision was Johnston's and he overruled Polk's objections. On February 11, the Confederate army at Bowling Green began its withdrawal.[36] Having made his decision to withdraw, General Johnston almost immediately began nullifying it.

On February 7, General Johnston ordered Brigadier General Gideon Pillow to take his command and proceed to Fort Donelson. Lacking faith in Donelson as an impregnable bastion, the Confederate commander told Pillow to hold it as long as possible and then fall back to Charlotte and finally to Nashville. Arriving at the fort on the 9th, Pillow energetically went to work propping up the only partially completed defenses and attempting to restore the morale of the garrison.[37]

Pillow, a graduate of the University of Nashville, was fifty-five years of age. Entering into a law partnership with James K. Polk in Columbus, Tennessee, Pillow eventually played a very important role in both state

---

35 *OR* 7, 861, 862; Roman, *Beauregard*, 219-223.

36 Horn, *The Army of the Tennessee*, 109, 110; Roland, *Albert Sidney Johnston*, 290.

37 Horn, *The Army of the Tennessee*, 83; *OR* 7, 867, 868; Thomas D. Duncan, *Recollections of Thomas D. Duncan, A Confederate Soldier* (Nashville: McQuiddy Printing Company, 1922), 26.

and national politics. He claimed the major responsibility for Polk's nomination for the presidency of the United States in 1844, and in 1852, played a significant role in the nomination negotiations which resulted in Franklin Pierce's nomination for the presidency. In 1846, he was appointed a brigadier general of volunteers, and during the Mexican War fought at Vera Cruz, Cerro Gordo, Contreras, and Chapultepec, being twice wounded. After bitterly quarreling with General Winfield Scott, the testy Tennessean was whitewashed by an investigating group. When Tennessee seceded, Pillow was appointed senior major general of state forces, and later a brigadier general in the Confederate army. He fought at the Battle of Belmont, where he achieved a sort of drawn battle with General Ulysses S. Grant. Although Pillow's military career had been checkered and highly controversial, at least he had the virtue of combat experience in the field.[38]

Brigadier General John B. Floyd was ordered to concentrate his command at Clarksville, and then to reinforce the Donelson garrison. From Clarksville Floyd moved to Cumberland City on the river sixteen miles south of Fort Donelson. Here he conceived the idea of making a defensive stand. Pillow objected and appealed to General Johnston, who ordered Floyd to proceed to Donelson with his own command and that of Brigadier General Simon Bolivar Buckner. Arriving at the Fort on February 13, Floyd took command as senior officer. As General Johnston later wrote President Jefferson Davis, "I determined to fight for Nashville at Donelson, and gave the best part of my army to do it."[39]

The reversal of the original plan to retreat was not necessarily a bad idea, for by concentrating Confederate forces against Grant there existed a good chance for victory. Unfortunately President Davis' old friend committed two glaring errors: he failed to order the other troops of his command to go to Donelson for an all out effort, but worst of all, he failed

---

38 || For Pillow, see Nathaniel Cheairs Hughes, Jr. and Roy P. Stonesifer, Jr., *The Life and Wars of Gideon J. Pillow* (Knoxville: University of North Carolina Press, 1993).

39   Horn, *The Army of the Tennessee*, 83; *OR* 7, 383, 865; Roland, *Albert Sidney Johnston*, 291.

to take personal charge of the operation, as putting General Floyd in charge of an army of any size was merely inviting disaster.

Fifty-five year old Floyd's military experience, aside from his controversial three and one-half years as Secretary of War to President James Buchanan, consisted of a short spell in the unhappy West Virginia operations of the summer and fall of 1861. Even the violent and petulant Pillow was a better choice for a commanding officer, but the Virginian's commission in the Confederate army dated from May 23, 1861, while Pillow's only went back to July 9.[40]

The third of the Donelson generals, Simon B. Buckner, was even more junior, being appointed brigadier general on September 14, 1861. Under the law, Floyd's seniority ranked him above the vastly more experienced Buckner and Pillow. Only by General Johnston's coming out in person could the command of the Donelson army be placed in the hands of someone acquainted with military matters. Instead General Johnston foolishly chose to stay with Hardee's wing of the army in the retreat from Bowling Green.[41]

With Foote's warships heading for Fort Donelson *via* the Tennessee, Ohio, and Cumberland rivers, followed by strong infantry units on transports, Grant's army of fifteen thousand men and eight artillery batteries began making final preparations for the advance on Donelson on the evening of February 11. Indeed, McClernand's First Division started out on the journey late in the afternoon, moving about five miles before the Democratic general from Illinois ordered a halt.[42] On the

---

40 One Union officer described the Confederate military leadership this way: "General Floyd, the most worthless officer in the Confederate camp, had command of their forces. Next in rank was their next most worthless officer, Gen. Pillow. Buckner and Bushrod Johnson were next, both educated and practiced military men." Charles Whitlesey, *War Memoranda: Cheat River to the Tennessee, 1861-1862* (Cleveland: William Walker, 1884), 33. || For Floyd, see Charles Pinnegar, *Brand of Infamy: A Biography of John Buchanan Floyd* (Westport: Greenwood Press, 2002).

41 || For Buckner, see Arndt Stickles, *Simon Bolivar Buckner: Borderland Knight* (Chapel Hill: University of North Carolina Press, 2001).

42 Grant, *Memoirs*, 152; *OR* 7, 170.

following day the entire army advanced forward, moving along both of the roads running from Fort Henry to Fort Donelson.

As the expedition began Dr. John H. Brinton, of General Grant's staff, found it hard to control his high-spirited mount and the animal kept pushing in front of Grant and the others. Mounted on his favorite stallion, Jack, Grant spurred his horse forward. Passing Brinton, the general humorously remarked, "Doctor, I believe I command this army, and I think I'll go first."[43]

Lieutenant Colonel Nathan Bedford Forrest and a small force of Confederate cavalry skirmished with Grant's advance elements, but before nightfall the Federals reached the Donelson area and began to surround it.[44]

While the Federal soldiers slogged along the muddy roads toward Fort Donelson, the first of Foote's warships, the *Carondolet*, appeared within sight of the Confederate strongpoint. Commander Walke arrived opposite the fort about 11:20 a.m., but could see nothing of any Federal troops in the area. To feel out the Confederate defenses and to let General Grant know the navy had arrived, Walke shelled the fort briefly before retiring down the river a short distance to await the arrival of the Union army.[45]

On Thursday morning, February 13, Grant continued deploying his army to cut off Donelson from outside succor; but before the ringing of the fort could be completed General Floyd arrived with the remainder of his command, slipping into Donelson without incident. Grant's officers had strict orders to stand on the defensive and not to bring on any kind of general engagement, for he hoped Foote's gunboats could pound the Southerners into submission without an expensive army action. But events ruled otherwise. The Confederates also stood on the defensive, but their skirmishers and artillery soon began to harass the investing foe.

---

43 Brinton, *Personal Memoirs*, 115.

44 *OR* 7, 384; Grant, *Memoirs*, 152, 153. ‖ For a modern assessment of Forrest, see Brian Steel Wills, *A Battle from the Start: The Life of Nathan Bedford Forrest* (New York: Harper Collins, 1992).

45 *ORN* 22, 587, 588; Gosnell, *Guns on the Western Waters*, 59, 60.

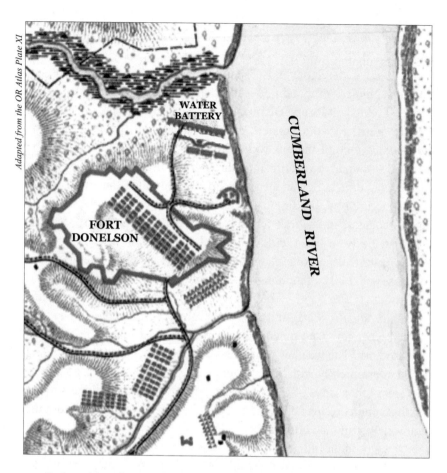

Irritated by the Confederate activity and believing he had spotted a weak point in the Rebel works, General John A. McClernand ordered an assault by four of his regiments, the Seventeenth, Forty-fifth, Forty-eighth, and Forty-ninth Illinois Infantry. Colonel William Morrison was badly wounded and the Illinois infantry was repulsed with heavy casualties.[46] General Floyd made no real effort to counter-attack, and simply waited docilely inside the fortifications, completely and foolishly surrendering the initiative to Grant.

Early on Thursday morning Walke received a dispatch from General Grant, requesting him to commence bombarding Fort Donelson. At 9:00

---

46 Grant, *Memoirs*, 153; *OR* 7, 172, 173.

a.m., the *Carondolet* slowly steamed up toward the Confederate works and opened fire. General Floyd's gunners quickly returned the compliment with vigor, and a sharp exchange of projectiles ensued. Walke's gunners dropped 139 shells on the fort, killing an engineer officer, Lieutenant Joseph Dixon, and disabling the carriage of one of the Rebels' guns. Floyd's gunners did almost as well, twice hitting the *Carondolet*. One of the hits was from the 10-inch Columbiad, and the heavy 128-pound projectile tore through the ironclad's insides with spectacular effect. Seven men were badly wounded, and five others slightly injured by this single shot. Walke withdrew from the action to repair damages, and he transferred his wounded to an auxiliary steamer, the *Alps*. Early in the afternoon, with the ship again in fighting trim, Walke resumed the contest, trading shots with the Confederates until darkness and a lack of ammunition intervened.[47]

About 11:30 p.m., Foote arrived with the ironclads *St. Louis*, *Louisville*, and *Pittsburg*, and the wooden gunboats *Lexington*, *Tyler*, and *Conestoga*. They were much welcomed by Grant because he needed a quick victory. The weather had turned cold, and the Federals were being pelted intermittently with freezing rain and snow. During the march from Fort Henry thousands of Union soldiers, deceived by the mildness of the weather, dumped their blankets to get rid of their weight, and now the men were paying the bitter price.[48]

Dawn brought little relief to the Federal soldiers, but General Grant anxiously awaited the naval assault. About 3:00 p.m., the *Carondolet* having been resupplied with ammunition and with all other preparations completed, Foote gave the order to attack. The *Louisville* approached along the west bank of the river, with Foote on the *St. Louis*, moving up toward the center of the channel. The *Pittsburg* and *Carondolet* advanced near the east bank of the river. The *Lexington*, *Conestoga*, and *Tyler* followed about half a mile to the rear. At 3:30, Confederate gunners opened fire, and within ten minutes the Federal warships began returning

---

47 Gosnell, *Guns on the Western Waters*, 60, 61; *ORN* 22, 588.

48 *Ibid.*, 61; Conger, *The Rise of U. S. Grant*, 165; Grant, *Memoirs*, 153; de Paris, *Civil War in America*, 1: 488, 489.

the fire. At first the Rebel fire was largely ineffective, while the Yankee tars were hitting the Donelson batteries with a fair degree of accuracy.[49]

To Confederate Nathan Bedford Forrest, who viewed the attack as a spectator near the battery, it seemed as though nothing could stop the irrepressible surge of the oncoming ironclads. Turning to one of his officers, the Reverend Major D. C. Kelly, he cried, "Parson, for God's sake pray! Nothing but God Almighty can save that fort."[50]

But Foote made the mistake of approaching too close in range, actually to within a quarter of a mile from Donelson. At the shortened distance the Confederates were able to use even their 32-pounders with considerable effect, since they were able to make plunging shots onto the ironclads. One of the Southerners' guns was accidentally disabled by an inept gunner, but the other pieces pumped shot after shot at the enemy ironclads. A 10-inch shot smashed the *Carondolet*'s heavy iron anchor. A small projectile shattered the pilot house, mortally wounding one of the pilots. Other cannon balls tore away all of the ironclad's boats. One of Walke's bow rifles suddenly burst, wounding a dozen men and adding to the general pandemonium. All of the ironclads were repeatedly struck. In the excitement the *Pittsburg* collided with the *Carondolet*'s stern, shattering her starboard rudder. The *St. Louis'* pilot house was shattered, killing the pilot and wounding Foote in the foot. Gradually the *Pittsburg*, *St. Louis*, and *Louisville* were obliged to withdraw out of range, leaving the *Carondolet* to continue the duel. Two 32-pound shots tore through the *Carondolet*'s underwater hull, and the ship was rapidly becoming unmanageable. His vessel struck at least thirty-five times by enemy shots, the courageous Walke was finally convinced that it was time to retreat. By 5:00, or a few minutes past the hour, the battle was over. The damaged Federal gunboats were all withdrawn beyond the range of Donelson's batteries.[51] Federal naval losses in the attack were eight

49 Gosnell, *Guns on the Western Waters*, 61, 62.

50 John Wyeth, *That Devil Forrest: Life of General Nathan Bedford Forrest* (New York: Harper and Brothers, 1959), 40.

51 Gosnell, *Guns on the Western Waters*, 61, 62; *ORN* 22, 585-594; *OR* 7, 262, 263.

killed and forty-seven wounded; Confederate losses numbered not a single casualty.[52]

The failure of Foote's attack completely disrupted General Grant's plan. Counting on the warships to crush Donelson as easily as they had Fort Henry, the Union commander had made no real preparations for the fight, and the Friday repulse left him with the problem of using his army to capture the place. But Grant's problem was eased a little by the arrival of heavy troop reinforcements.

The first of these reinforcements was Brigadier General Lew Wallace, who had originally been left behind to protect Forts Heiman and Henry. The Indianan brought the Eleventh Indiana, Eighth Missouri, and a battery of field artillery with him. Reaching General Grant's headquarters in the Crisp House near Dover, General Wallace received quite a surprise when Grant ordered him to relinquish command of his two regiments, directing them to report to General Charles F. Smith's command. The army commander then informed Wallace that he was to assume command of a newly formed Third Division, consisting of regiments even then arriving by transports. Wallace was directed to take these units and hold the Union center, while General McClernand's command protected the right, and General Smith's the left.[53]

Although a little uncertain in his mind as to what to do, General Grant was gradually tightening his hold on Fort Donelson. One thought continued to pervade his mind, and it was that the Southerners would never take the offensive. Grant had fallen into the dangerous error of thinking that the enemy would do exactly what he wanted them to do.[54]

Friday night was as bad as Thursday, the Bluecoats suffering fiercely from the inclement weather.[55] Just before daylight a messenger from

---

52 *ORN* 22, 586, 587; *OR* 7, 263.

53 Wallace, *Autobiography*, 1: 382, 389.

54 Brinton, *Personal Memoirs*, 117, 118; Wallace, *Autobiography*, 1: 392.

55 The Confederate soldiers were probably suffering a good bit more than General Grant's men because of their hopelessly inadequate clothing. J. B. Paisley to his cousin, Jane, February 23, 1862, William A. McLean Papers, Illinois State Historical Library. The Confederate soldiers' morale was up; however those inside Fort Donelson were in terrible shape clothing wise. Their

Foote reached the Crisp House and handed the worried, sleepless general a message mentioning the wound received in the Friday action and requesting Grant to come to the *St. Louis* for an immediate conference. General Grant quickly started for the conference, riding across the solidly frozen ground. He soon reached the river, where a small boat carried him out to the flagship. Foote explained that his warships had to return to Mound City, Illinois, for repairs, but added that he could return in about ten days. General Grant agreed, and bidding the crusty old seadog goodbye, quickly was rowed ashore.

In his mind the commanding general was rapidly coming to the conclusion that a formal siege was the next order of business. Reaching the shore, General Grant received a bad shock. A very white-faced Captain William Hillyer, of his staff, was waiting to notify him that the army was under heavy assault.[56]

Before Foote's gunboats began the bombardment on Friday, General Floyd called a council of war. The Southerners knew Grant was receiving reinforcements exaggeratedly estimated at thirty thousand to fifty thousand, and it was decided to evacuate Fort Donelson. The plan decided upon was to attack the extreme Union right (McClernand's First Division) and to seize the road leading to Charlotte, Tennessee. Pillow's Division was to make the assault, while Buckner's Division was to cover the withdrawal to Nashville. But by the time all preparations were complete, it was decided that it was too late to make any such movement at this time.[57]

Friday night General Floyd again called his senior officers in to council. Although Foote's attack had been repulsed, the Virginian was still determined to break out and head for Nashville. The Charlotte Road plan was again broached, and the officers immediately began making

---

garments were "thin and ragged, gray and butternut predominating, but all the colors of Joseph's coat were to be seen. For blankets they carried square pieces of carpet, comforters and coverlets." Thomas M. Stevenson, *History of the 78th Ohio Veteran Volunteer Infantry, From Its "Muster' in" to its "Muster' Out"* (Zaneville, Ohio: Hugh Dunne, 1865), 38.

56 Grant, *Memoirs*, 155, 156; Brinton, *Personal Memoirs*, 119, 120.

57 *OR* 7, 330; Horn, *The Army of the Tennessee*, 91.

preparations that night for the Saturday dawn assault.[58] During the bitter cold hours of darkness, General Floyd had Buckner withdraw all of his troops from the entrenchments on the right, leaving but a single regiment (450 men) to cover that sector of the defense. Both armies were suffering heavily from the cold, and somehow Grant's soldiers failed to notice or pay any attention to the sounds of movement coming from within the Confederate works.[59]

About 6:00 Saturday morning, Pillow's men launched their attack. McClernand's men were awake and in battle formation, and had even thrown up a few simple earthworks. A wild melee developed, with the Southerners pressing recklessly onward and endeavoring to get close enough to use their shotguns and antiquated muskets. Forrest's cavalry charged on Pillow's left, and after the first hour or so, Buckner's men joined in on the Tennessean's right. Finally McClernand was forced back, losing control of the Charlotte Road. By noon the Confederates had not only driven General McClernand backward and secured control of the desired line of communications, but they had also ripped open the Union army.[60]

Instead of throwing every man into the battle and attempting to finish the destruction of Grant's army, or at least simply evacuating Fort Donelson, the Confederates procrastinated and wound up being trapped. A wild and confused action followed with Pillow sending Buckner back to try and hold the Confederate right, which was being attacked by General Smith's command. The white haired general led the advance, yelling at his men, "Come on, you volunteers, come on. This is your chance. You volunteered to be killed for love of country, and now you can be . . . I'm only a soldier, and don't want to be killed, but you came to be killed and now you can be."[61]

58   *Ibid.*, 263.

59   Steele, *American Campaigns*, 77.

60   R. S. Henry, *"First With The Most,"* Forrest (Indianapolis: Bobbs Merrill Company, 1944), 54, 55; *OR* 7, 175; Wyeth, *That Devil Forrest*, 45, 46.

61   Brinton, *Personal Memoirs*, 121.

General Smith's men overwhelmed the single Confederate regiment at that point and broke inside the Donelson defenses; but General Buckner arrived, and another wild fight promptly developed.[62] Some of Smith's men began to falter, and the Second Division's commander gently chided them, saying, "Damn you gentlemen, I see skulkers, I'll have none here."[63] Despite the crusty old general's tirades, his division was finally stopped in its advance.

Deploying his artillery on a hill overlooking Smith's division, Buckner began pounding the Federals with shot and shell.[64] McClernand and Lew Wallace reoccupied most of the ground lost in the first Confederate onslaught, however, with the exception of one road. The road nearest the river from Dover to Nashville remained unoccupied by the Bluecoats.[65] Although informed of this last escape route late in the afternoon, General Floyd, who was by now in a deep funk, decided against trying to use it on the grounds that his men were simply physically too weak.[66]

Saturday night the Confederate high command gathered in Floyd's headquarters in the Dover Inn to discuss a future course of action. Buckner and Floyd pessimistically favored surrender, but Pillow argued for some kind of an attack. In the end it was decided to surrender. No one wanted to take on his shoulders the actual humiliation of yielding, but finally Buckner agreed to take charge.

At daybreak Sunday morning, the steamer *General Anderson* arrived with four hundred men, and Floyd promptly requisitioned the vessel, escaping with his Virginia brigade. General Pillow, with his staff and a few others, escaped across the river in an old scow.

---

62 Steele, *American Campaigns*, 78.

63 Brinton, *Personal Memoirs*, 121.

64 Horn, *The Army of the Tennessee*, 93; John T. Bell, *Tramps and Triumphs of the Second Iowa Infantry* (Des Moines: Valley Bank and Trust Company, 1961), 10.

65 Wyeth, *That Devil Forrest*, 50.

66 *OR* 7, 273.

But while Buckner was negotiating with Grant, Nathan Bedford Forrest was acting.[67] When General Buckner assumed command of the post, Forrest had promptly spoken up at the meeting, saying, "I did not come here for the purpose of surrendering my command, and I will not do it if they will follow me out," and then Forrest addressed General Pillow saying, "General Pillow, what shall I do?"

"Cut your way out," was the Tennessean's reply.[68]

Forrest, with his command, plus numerous personnel from other units, did just that, escaping over the one remaining open road.

Dawn brought the surrender of the post without further resistance. General Buckner made no further attempt on Grant's army, nor did he try to transfer, as he could easily have done, any of the troops by steamer. Fort Donelson was simply surrendered.

The loss of Donelson was one of the worst disasters to befall the Confederacy in the entire war. The loss of the post was certainly bad enough in itself, but what was infinitely worse was the loss of the garrison. These men were literally irreplaceable.

What were the Confederate losses at Fort Donelson? The records are completely contradictory, but it appears that about two thousand Confederate soldiers were killed or wounded, and between twelve to fifteen thousand were captured, out of a total of nineteen to twenty-one thousand Rebel participants. Grant's losses were five hundred killed, 2,108 wounded, and 224 captured by the Confederates and carted off to captivity with Floyd.[69]

The news of the fall of Forts Henry and Donelson, especially the latter, plunged the South into a desperate state of depression. Not only

67 Henry, *Forrest*, 57, 58; Horn, *The Army of the Tennessee*, 95, 96.

68 Henry, *Forrest*, 57, 59; *OR* 7, 288.

69 Williams, *Lincoln Finds a General,* 3: 258; Horn, *The Army of the Tennessee*, 97. Horn has a slightly different set of figures. J. F. C. Fuller gives the number of prisoners as 11,500. Fuller, *The Generalship of Ulysses S. Grant*, 89. Union accounts tend to place the number considerably higher. Reverend Thomas M. Stevenson, *History of the 78th Ohio*, 132; Francis H. Bruce to his mother, February 18, 1862, Francis H. Bruce Papers, Illinois State Historical Library; Payson Z. Shumway to wife, Hattie, March 2, 1862, Payson Z. Shumway Papers, Illinois State Historical Library; *OR* 7, 169.

General Johnston's men, but Confederate soldiers in other armies were profoundly disappointed by the severe reverses in Tennessee. Southern morale dropped to a dangerously low ebb.[70] As soon as the first shock of the news passed, Southerners, military and civilian alike, broke out in a wave of condemnation of General A. S. Johnston.[71] A delegation of prominent Tennesseans even went to Richmond to ask President Jefferson Davis to replace the commanding general in the West. Irritated by this request, President Davis dismissed the men saying, "If Sidney Johnston is not a general, we had better give up the war for we have no general."[72]

Outwardly undisturbed by the clamor against him, the Kentuckian calmly continued overseeing the retreat of the Confederate army from Bowling Green. On February 17, General Johnston withdrew from Nashville, leaving behind only a token force to maintain order and protect government property. With the main force of the army, the Kentuckian marched toward Murfreesboro. Many of his troops wept at leaving the Tennessee capital to her fate. Some soldiers bitterly protested that the army ought to stay and fight.[73]

70 W. H. Stevenson and Edwin A. Davis, "The Civil War Diary of Willie Micajah Barrow September 23, 1861-July 13, 1862," *Louisiana Historical Quarterly* 17 (July-October 1934): 22; Younger, *Diary of Robert Garlick Hill Kean*, 24, 25; John Q. Anderson (ed.), *Brokenburn: The Journal of Kate Stone, 1861-1868* (Baton Rouge: Louisiana State University Press, 1955), 90; J. B. Jones, *A Rebel War Clerk's Diary At The Confederate States Capitol* (Philadelphia: J.B. Lippincott and Company, 1866), 1: 111; Douglas S. Freeman, *R. E. Lee* (New York: Scribners, 1934), 1: 625. Lee said of this affair that "the news is not favorable." *Ibid.*

71 Basil Duke, *A History of Morgan's Cavalry* (Bloomington: Indiana University Press, 1960), 118, 119; Cecil Holland, *Morgan and His Raiders: A Biography of the Confederate General* (New York: Macmillan Company, 1943), 65.

72 Horn, *The Army of the Tennessee*, 105; Roland, *Albert Sidney Johnston*, 299.

73 Jefferson Davis to A. S. Johnston, addressed to General Johnston as "My Dear General," Mrs. Mason Barret Papers, Albert Sidney Johnston Collection, Howard-Tilton Memorial Library, Tulane University; Frank Peak, "A

Arriving at the little Tennessee town, the army remained until February 23, by which time several small Confederate commands that had been scattered throughout the theater had arrived, along with the rear guard from Nashville. Reorganizing the army into three divisions under Generals Hardee, George B. Crittenden, and Pillow, General Johnston pulled out of Murfreesboro on February 28, heading for Moorsville, Alabama.[74]

This was the start of the eventful concentration of Confederate forces at Corinth, Mississippi—the prelude to the Battle of Shiloh.

Southern Soldier's View of the Civil War," Frank Peak Papers, Louisiana State University Archives; Captain S. Ridgeway Letter, February 24, 1862, S.P. Ridgeway Papers, University of Tennessee Library.

74 Peak, "A Southern Soldier's View of the Civil War," Frank Peak Papers, Louisiana State University Archives; Roland, *Albert Sidney Johnston*, 301, 302; A. D. Kirwan (ed.), *Johnny Green of the Orphan Brigade* (Lexington: University of Kentucky Press, 1956), 17, 18.

The Confederate Leaders

Unless otherwise credited, all photos are courtesy of *Generals in Gray: Lives of the Confederate Commanders*

Col. Wirt Adams

Col. Daniel W. Adams

Brig. Gen. James Patton Anderson

Col. Henry W. Allen

Col. William B. Bate

Gen. P. G. T. Beauregard

Brig. Gen. John S. Bowen

Maj. Gen. Braxton Bragg

Brig. Gen. James R. Chalmers

Brig. Gen. John C. Breckinridge

Brig. Gen. Charles Clark

Maj. Gen. Benjamin F. Cheatham

Brig. Gen. Patrick R. Cleburne

Col. Zach C. Deas

Col. Nathan B. Forrest

Col. Randall L. Gibson

Maj. Gen. William J. Hardee

Brig. Gen. Adley H. Gladden

Brig. Gen. John K. Jackson

Brig. Gen. Thomas C. Hindman

Brig. Gen. Bushrod R. Johnson

Gen. Albert Sidney Johnston

Col. George Maney

Col. John S. Marmaduke

Col. John H. Morgan

Col. John C. Moore

Col. William Preston

Maj. Gen. Leonidas Polk

Brig. Gen. Daniel Ruggles

Col. Preston Smith

Brig. Gen. Alexander P. Stewart

Lieut. Col. Otho F. Strahl

Col. John A. Wharton

Col. Alfred J. Vaughan, Jr.

Brig. Gen. Sterling A.M. Wood

Brig. Gen. Jones M. Withers

Chapter 4

General Halleck Intervenes

WHILE GENERAL U. S. GRANT battled the Southerners for Fort Donelson, General Henry W. Halleck remained in St. Louis, anxiously worrying over his subordinate and frantically trying to scrounge up some help for him. To aid Grant, Halleck appealed to General Don Carlos Buell for some kind of demonstration against Bowling Green to divert the Southerners' attention from Fort Donelson. To General George McClellan Halleck sent an urgent plea for reinforcements.[1] But on February 16, General Halleck's worries changed to joy as he received word that Fort Donelson had fallen.[2] The Union elements in St. Louis went mad with joy at the news, and Halleck, forgetting his lawyer's dignity, joined right in.

Puffing vigorously on a cigar, Halleck ordered a clerk to distribute two dozen baskets of champagne for the crowd that gathered outside his headquarters at the Planter's House. The general told the clerk to "give public notice that I shall suspect the loyalty of any male resident of St. Louis who can be found sober enough to walk or speak within the next half hour."[3]

---

1 *OR* 7, 609, 617.

2 *Ibid.*, 156.

3 Ambrose, *Halleck*, 33; Richardson, *Personal History of U. S. Grant*, 229. According to Richardson, a war correspondent, Halleck made the following remark: "Humph! If Grant's a drunkard and can win such victories, I shall issue

With his military ability publicly vindicated by the victories in Tennessee, Halleck launched a strong onslaught for a promotion. "Make Buell, Grant and Pope major-generals of volunteers," he wrote to General McClellan, "and give me command in the West. I ask this in return for Forts Henry and Donelson."[4] Although General McClellan failed to grant Halleck's request for sole command in the West, Halleck was not discouraged, and he began preparations for new offensive moves in his theater. On February 18, Halleck began corresponding with his subordinate, General John Pope, about the feasibility of an offensive down the Mississippi River. Within a few days the somewhat outspoken Pope was moving southward with a strong army-navy force, investing the Confederate stronghold of New Madrid, Missouri, on March 1.[5]

For several days after the surrender of Fort Donelson, Grant was busy with the usual post-battle loose ends. There were wounded to be taken care of and prisoners to be moved northward.

Promoted to major general of volunteers for his victory, Grant busily managed affairs at Henry and Donelson while endeavoring to persuade Halleck to launch some sort of new offensive in the direction of Clarksville and Nashville, Tennessee. Grant seemed to think that Halleck was warmly in favor of a vigorous push southward,[6] but actually, though unknown to himself, relations with headquarters at St. Louis were slowly deteriorating. Grant began discussing the question of an offensive with the wounded naval officer, Foote. The naval commander was all for pushing on to Nashville, and actually began making preparations with his subordinate officers when General Halleck telegraphed Grant not to let the gunboats advance beyond Clarksville.[7]

---

an order that any man found sober in St. Louis tonight, be punished by fine and imprisonment." *Ibid.*

4 *OR* 7, 628.

5 Ambrose, *Halleck*, 36.

6 U. S. Grant to wife, Julia, February 24, 1862, *U. S. Grant Papers, 1844-1880*, Illinois State Historical Library.

7 *ORN* 22, 622. Foote wrote his wife that he thought Halleck's order was based on jealousy on the part of Halleck and McClellan. He told her he was

On Sunday, February 23, General Halleck suddenly changed his mind and decided to let Foote and Grant go on up the Cumberland River to Nashville, possibly as a means of aiding General Buell, or perhaps to deprive the latter of all the credit for taking the city.[8] Whatever his motives were, Halleck changed his mind again on Tuesday upon learning that Buell was almost in the city.[9]

Unfortunately for the cause of Union high echelon unity, there was a bad communications foul-up between Grant and Halleck, because of the great distance involved and the comparative inexperience of their respective staffs. On Monday, Grant had directed Brigadier General William Nelson's division (of Buell's army, but ordered to reinforce Grant for the Donelson campaign) to proceed by transport and occupy Nashville.[10] Buell, who had reached Edgefield, on the opposite side of the river from Nashville, was furious at General Nelson's arrival, fearing that General Albert Sidney Johnston might wheel around from Murfreesboro and assault the isolated division before the rest of the army could be ferried over. Buell requested Brigadier General C. F. Smith's division to come to Nashville at once as insurance against an attack by Johnston, and Grant, who had not yet received Halleck's Tuesday order rescinding the Sunday Cumberland advance order, sent Smith to Nashville on the 26th, and then went there himself to confer with Buell.[11]

Back in St. Louis Halleck was becoming increasingly frustrated over a persistent lack of information from Tennessee. He demanded of General George Cullum, commanding at Cairo, as to "who sent Smith's division to Nashville?" He continued:

> I ordered them across to the Tennessee, where they are wanted immediately. Order them back. What is the reason that no one down

---

going to report the matter to the navy, and predicted there would be a "row" over the matter. *Ibid.*, 626.

8 *OR* 7, 7, 655.

9 *Ibid.*, 677.

10 *Ibid.*, 622; Grant, *Memoirs*, 163, 164.

11 *OR* 7, 944; Grant, *Memoirs*, 164.

there can obey my orders? Send all spare transports to General Grant up the Tennessee.[12]

Cullum forwarded Halleck's message to Grant, who immediately ordered most of his troops back to Fort Henry.[13] On March 3, Halleck learned from Cullum that Grant had "just returned from Nashville," on February 28.[14]

Halleck promptly blew up, writing McClellan that he had had no communications with Grant for more than a week. Charging that Grant had absented himself from his command without authority, going on a pertinacious trip to Nashville, Halleck, from the vantage point of his comfortable headquarters in St. Louis, claimed that Grant's army "seems to be as much demoralized by the victory of Fort Donelson as was that of the Potomac by the defeat of Bull Run."[15]

Halleck went on to make his famous stab in the back:

> It is hard to censure a successful general immediately after a victory, but I think he richly deserves it. I can get no returns, nor reports, no information of any kind from him. Satisfied with his victory, he sits down and enjoys it without any regard to the future. I am worn-out and tired with this neglect and inefficiency. C. F. Smith is almost the only officer equal to the urgency.[16]

Receiving Halleck's bitter missive, Grant's old comrade from Regular Army days, McClellan,[17] replied to Halleck:

> The future success of our cause demands that proceedings such as Grant's should at once be checked. Generals must observe

---

12 *OR* 7, 674.

13 *Ibid.*, 677, 678.

14 *Ibid.*, 676.

15 *Ibid.*, 679.

16 *Ibid.*; Conger, *Rise of U. S. Grant*, 205.

17 Charles King, *The True Ulysses S. Grant* (Philadelphia: J.B. Lippincott, 1914), 144.

discipline as well as private soldiers. Do not hesitate to arrest him at once if the good of the service requires it, and place C.F. Smith in command. You are at liberty to regard this as a positive order if it will smooth your way.[18]

By the following morning, March 4, Halleck had another bee for McClellan's ears. He informed his superior that a rumor had reached headquarters to the effect that General Grant was drinking heavily, and that this accounted for "his neglect of my often repeated orders."[19] Going on to explain that he did not consider it advisable to arrest Grant just yet, Halleck wound up by saying he had placed General C. F. Smith in charge of the proposed expedition up the Tennessee.[20]

Confused by the whole matter, Grant wrote to Halleck in a desperate attempt to find out what was wrong. He could not understand why he was under a black cloud. For several days the ink flowed freely between the two men, with Grant increasingly convinced that he had enemies on Halleck's staff who were trying to sabotage him.[21]

Halleck, either satisfied that Grant was repentant or innocent, finally shelved the whole matter, although Grant did not immediately resume command of the Tennessee River expedition. The plan for the project started on March 1, when Halleck ordered Grant to send Smith up the river and wreck Confederate communications at Eastport and Corinth, Mississippi, and Jackson and Humboldt, Tennessee. The expedition was more in the form of a raid than an invasion, and Grant was directed not to pick a fight with anything he could not handle.[22]

18 *OR* 7, 680.

19 *Ibid.*, 682.

20 *Ibid.*

21 *Ibid.*, 10, 2: 15; 7: 21. In his *Memoirs*, Grant says most of the trouble was caused by a telegraph operator sympathetic to the Confederates. This fellow intercepted most of Grant's dispatches before deserting to the South. *Ibid.*, 167. See James Harrison Wilson, *The Life of John A. Rawlins* (New York: The Neale Publishing Company ,1916), 77.

22 *OR* 7, 674.

Five days later General Halleck changed the directive for the expedition slightly, saying the army should "encamp at Savannah [Tennessee] unless threatened by superior numbers."[23]

On March 6, Brigadier General William T. Sherman, in command at Paducah, Kentucky, notified Halleck that he had learned of the presence of a "large force of rebels ... collected at Eastport ... and also at Corinth." Sherman went on to tell Halleck that the Confederate force was "estimated at 20,000; engaged fortifying at both places."[24] On the basis of this information Halleck decided that Sherman's command should link up with General Smith's column for the Tennessee expedition.[25]

The expeditionary force formed up in the vicinity of Fort Henry. There were to be five divisions: Sherman's, McClernand's, Lew Wallace's, C. F. Smith's, and a brand new one under Brigadier General Stephen A. Hurlbut.

A political appointee, the South Carolina-born Hurlbut had been President Lincoln's special emissary to Charleston during the crisis at that place the year before.[26] Forty-six years old, Hurlbut was the son of a Massachusetts-born Unitarian minister who married a Charleston girl and made his home at that place. As a youth Hurlbut studied law and was admitted to the bar. During one of the interminable Seminole uprisings in Florida he served as adjutant of a South Carolina regiment of volunteers. In 1845, he immigrated to Belvidere, Illinois, where he eventually joined the Republican Party. Serving as a member of the state legislature when the war broke out, he was appointed brigadier general of volunteers on June 14, 1861. A rather corrupt man, Hurlbut also had a deep fondness for the whiskey bottle, which does not seem however to have handicapped his military duties.[27] Of about average height, Hurlbut had

---

23   *Ibid.*, 10, pt. 2, 7.

24   *Ibid.*, 12.

25   *Ibid.*

26   Williams, *Lincoln Finds A General*, 3: 275.

27   Warner, *Generals in Blue*, 245; Payson Shumway Diary, March 25, 1862, Payson Z. Shumway Papers, Illinois State Historical Library.

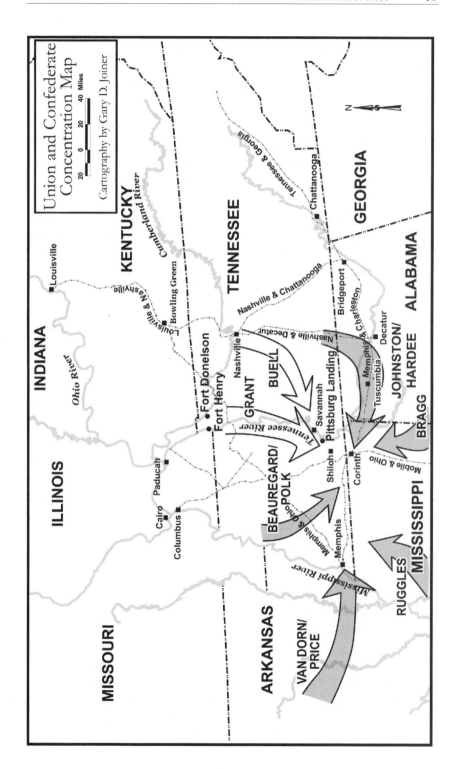

Union and Confederate
Concentration Map

Cartography by Gary D. Joiner

dark gray eyes, a short nose, a florid complexion, and close cropped chestnut hair.[28]

Of the five divisional commanders, General Sherman and General C. F. Smith were the only professional soldiers, but the other three possessed at least a little military experience, if only at the company grade level. Brigadier General Lew Wallace was the son of West Point graduate and one-time governor of Indiana, David Wallace. Even as a child Lew showed particular interest in military affairs and, at the age of fifteen, entered a militia company in Indianapolis, Indiana. At the start of the Mexican War, the nineteen year old militiaman joined the First Indiana Volunteers, rising to the rank of first lieutenant, although unable to participate in any combat activities, much to his disappointment. A jack of all trades, Wallace left the army to study politics, history, and law, finally entering the state senate in 1856. The future author of *Ben-Hur* started his varied Civil War career as state adjutant general under Indiana's famous war governor, Oliver Morton. Later commissioned colonel of the Eleventh Indiana Volunteers, the thirty-three year old Wallace took part in operations in western Virginia in the latter part of the year. He was promoted to brigadier general of volunteers on September 3, 1861, and was advanced to the rank of major general on March 21, 1862, because of his services at Fort Donelson.[29]

Brigadier General John Alexander McClernand was born in Kentucky in 1812, but grew up in Illinois. Largely self-educated, he was admitted to the bar in 1832, but took time off from his legal duties to participate in the Black Hawk War. A good party Democrat, McClernand rose rapidly in the ranks of the state organization and in 1860 was an unsuccessful candidate for the speakership of the House of Representatives. To rally Democratic support for the war effort,

28 New York *Tribune*, February 15, 1864. || For Hurlbut, see Jeffrey N. Lash, *A Politician Turned General: The Civil War Career of Stephen Augustus Hurlbut* (Kent: Kent State University Press, 2003).

29 Irving McKee, *"Ben Hur" Wallace: The Life of General Lew Wallace* (Berkley: University of California Press, 1947), 1-46. || For a modern view of Wallace, see Stacy D. Allen, "If He Had Less Rank: Lewis Wallace," in Steven E. Woodworth (ed.), *Grant's Lieutenants: From Cairo to Vicksburg* (Lawrence: University Press of Kansas, 2001), 63-89.

President Lincoln appointed McClernand a brigadier general of volunteers, ranking from May 1861. A veteran of Belmont and Fort Donelson, the Illinoisan possessed the most combat experience of any of Grant's officers; unfortunately he also possessed the greatest amount of conceit.[30]

With this choice collection of generals Grant set to work with Smith to fit out the proposed river expedition. As things worked out, Sherman's division, now numbered the Fifth, was the first to head for the heart of enemy territory. The division was embarked on its transports on March 6, 7, and 8. The First Brigade, the Fortieth Illinois and the Forty-sixth Ohio, did not bother to wait for the rest of the expedition, but departed on their own loaded on the river boats *Sallie List*, *Golden Gate*, *J. B. Adams*, and the *Lexington*.[31] The brigade, under Colonel S. G. Hicks, reached Savannah on March 8 and 9 after a speedy and quiet passage. The rest of the division, which was just then loading up, only arrived in Savannah late on March 11 and early March 12. Sherman castigated Colonel Hicks and Colonel Thomas Worthington of the Forty-sixth Ohio for going off on their own; but at least they had arrived safely.[32]

The passage of Sherman's Second, Third, and Fourth brigades were fairly uneventful, but they did, however, get a baptism of fire. A Confederate bushwhacker fired a musket shot at the Forty-eighth Ohio's steamer, and although the ball missed, there was a good deal of excitement.[33]

On March 12, General Smith arrived in Savannah with the advance elements of the rest of his army.[34] Their passage had been little more

---

30 *D. A. B.*, 2: 587, 588. || For McClernand, see Richard L. Kiper, *Major General John Alexander McClernand: Politician in Uniform* (Kent: The Kent State University Press, 1999).

31 *Campaigns in Kentucky and Tennessee*, 109; Sherman, *Memoirs*, 226.

32 *Campaigns in Kentucky and Tennessee*, 109; John Bering and Thomas Montgomery, *History of the Forty-eighth Ohio Veteran Volunteer Infantry* (Hillsboro: The Highland News Office, 1880), 15; Sherman, *Memoirs*, 226.

33 Bering and Montgomery, *History of the Forty-eighth Ohio*, 15.

34 *Campaigns in Kentucky and Tennessee*, 111.

exciting than that of Sherman's division, although there were a few eventful moments. Three members of the Forty-sixth Illinois fell overboard from their steamer and were drowned in the swollen river before anyone could help them.[35] One member of the Thirteenth Iowa fell overboard from the *Hiawatha* and sank before anyone could rescue him. The Eighth Iowa's steamer was bushwhacked a short distance from Savannah, and one soldier was killed and another wounded.[36] On board the steamer *Argyle*, the Fifty-seventh Illinois had one man wounded in the arm by a Southern partisan.[37]

The Fourteenth Iowa, on board the *Autocrat*, had a particularly trying experience. The soldiers heard a tremendous sound in the rear of their boat and confusion reigned for a moment, for the soldiers believed they were under fire. But finally the Iowans discovered that the commotion was caused by their paddle wheel becoming entangled with a tree. It took a great deal of chopping, and an even larger amount of swearing, before the civilian crew and the soldiers finally cut the tree loose.[38]

The Eighty-first Ohio shipped on board the steamer *Meteor*, one of the largest of the Mississippi River packets. A carnival atmosphere reigned on board the ship, for Governor Yates of Illinois was on board, besides numerous ladies belonging to the officers. There were horses and mules tied up on the main deck, and boxes of army supplies and fuel for the ship's engines took up the extra space. The enlisted men dined on hardtack and raw pork, drinking Tennessee River water dipped up in buckets with ropes attached. Some of the privates broke open cases packed near the bow of the ship and found they contained crackers, cheese, bologna, and other eatables, property of an army sutler. The Eighty-first had one exhilarating moment when Confederate guerrillas

---

35 Thomas Jones, *Complete History of the 46th Regiment Illinois Volunteer Infantry* (n.p., n.d.), 287.

36 Thomas, *Soldier Life*; S. M. Byers, *Iowa In War Times* (Des Moines: W. D. Condit and Company, 1888), 497. The regiment's total casualties were two killed and three wounded in the expedition. *Ibid.*

37 Adolph Engelmann to his wife, Mina, March 12, 1862, Adolph Engelmann Papers, Illinois State Historical Library.

38 Thomas, *Soldier Life*.

opened fire on the boat immediately behind them, the *Black Warrior*. No one was killed, but several enlisted men were wounded, and the Federals retaliated by spraying the banks of the Tennessee with musket balls.[39]

On board the steamer *Continental*, the Twenty-fifth Missouri had a particularly bad time, although it failed to dampen their spirits. Sparks from the ship's funnels burned the soldiers' clothing, their blankets, and even their faces and hands. Their only rations were hard bread and hog jowls, plus a little coffee made from the rather muddy and frequently polluted Tennessee River water. The diet worked havoc with their intestines, but morale remained high and these soldiers made the river ring with strains of music, "We'll hang Jeff Davis on a sour apple tree" and other patriotic ditties.[40]

By regiments, brigades, and divisions, the Army of the Tennessee gradually assembled at Savannah, and on the morning of March 14, General Smith ordered Sherman to take his command up to Eastport, Mississippi, for the purpose of destroying the railroad there. As Sherman's transports moved up the river, about eight miles from Savannah, perhaps the general's eyes noticed a burned building atop a bluff about eight miles from his destination; and if he consulted his map, he learned the place was called Pittsburg Landing. The ruined structure was the remaining evidence of a sharp skirmish that occurred at Pittsburg about two weeks earlier on March 1. This engagement was brought on by Lieutenant William Gwin, commanding a small patrol force composed of his own gunboat, the *Tyler*, and Lieutenant James Shirk of the *Lexington*.[41]

---

39 Phil Jordan and Charles Thomas (eds.), "Reminiscences of An Ohio Volunteer," *Ohio Archeological and Historical Quarterly* 43 (October 1939): 309, 310. For a complete listing of the vessels see T. M. Hurst, "Battle of Shiloh," *The American Historical Magazine and Tennessee Society Quarterly* 7 (January 1902): 31-33.

40 Charles Morton, "Opening of the Battle of Shiloh," *War Paper No. 88, Commandery of the District of Columbia, Military Order of the Loyal Legion of the United States.*

41 || For the Army of the Tennessee, see Steven E. Woodworth, *Nothing But Victory: The Army of the Tennessee* (New York: Knopf, 2005).

Having learned that the Confederates were fortifying Pittsburg, Gwin decided to launch an attack on that place, and about noon, March 1, steamed up to Pittsburg. One or more Confederate field pieces commenced firing, but the two gunboats opened up with their 32-pounders and 8-inchers; and being heavily outweighed by the gunboats' superior fire power, the Southerners soon broke off the action. For some reason Gwin decided to destroy a house on the hill near where the Confederates had fired from.[42]

Sailors and members of Company K, Thirty-second Illinois Volunteers, were quickly on board the gunboats' launches. Rowing over to the Landing, the Illinoisans quickly landed and moved out and up to the top of the bluff, where they ran into a detachment from the Eighteenth Louisiana Infantry Regiment. Gwin's sailors speedily went to work setting fire to the house, while the crew of the biggest launch opened up with shrapnel from their 12-pound boat howitzer. The gunboats continued using their big tubes to keep the Louisianans at bay, away from their landing party. Despite the artillery fire, the Louisiana soldiers swarmed over the bluff, raking the demolition party with heavy blasts of musketry. In danger of being overwhelmed, the landing party finally took to the boats and rowed vigorously back to the *Lexington* and *Tyler*. The Confederates peppered the two gunboats with strong blasts of musketry for some minutes before withdrawing. Federal losses for the brief engagement were two killed, six wounded, and three missing. Gwin established the Louisianans' losses at twenty killed and one hundred wounded, although no Confederate account of the action mentions any Southern losses.[43]

Whatever Sherman's observations were, his interest in Pittsburg greatly increased when Lieutenant Gwin gave him the full details of the March 1st affair. When the naval officer mentioned that Pittsburg was the usual landing place for the people going to Corinth, Mississippi, Sherman decided that Federal occupation of the point might be very useful.

---

42 *OR* 7, 435; *ORN* 22, 643-647.

43 *OR* 7, 453; *ORN* 22, 643-647, 833. || For more on the navy in the Shiloh Campaign, see also Smith, *The Untold Story of Shiloh*, 53-66.

Sending word back to General Smith about the desirability of posting a force at the Landing, General Sherman continued on up the river until he reached Eastport. Observing Confederate gun positions through his glasses, as well as troop movements, the general ordered his force to drop back down to Yellow Creek, several miles above the town.[44]

At 7:00 p.m. on the 14th, the Fifth Division began its disembarkation at the mouth of Yellow Creek. The plan was that part of the Fifth Ohio Cavalry, under Major E. G. Ricker, was to move overland to a point near Burnsville, Mississippi, on the Memphis and Charleston Railroad and cut the track there. The infantry and artillery was to follow on the 15th, and was to capture and destroy the Confederate railroad repair facilities in Burnsville.

The cavalry left about 11:00 p.m., amidst a heavy rainfall. About 3:00 a.m., Colonel Hicks' First Brigade moved out along the route the cavalry had taken. By 4:00 a.m., Colonel David Stuart's Second Brigade was unloaded and heading inland, while the two remaining brigades followed at daylight.

Almost immediately everything began going wrong for the Federals. The landscape was already very soggy from the heavy rainfall, and, instead of slacking off, the downpour merely increased. The temperature was below the freezing point, and horses and men alike were soon soaked through and through with icy water. The rain finally did stop for awhile, but then it began to snow. The soldiers were not only cold and miserable, but also had only the vaguest idea of what the expedition was all about.

About four and a half miles out from the landing point, the excursion was stopped by a badly flooded unnamed stream. Colonel Hicks and his men tried to put a temporary bridge across it at the shallowest point, but with little success. Then Major Ricker's cavalry showed up on the opposite side of the target, forcing them to turn back. Using the very unstable Hicks' bridge, the cavalry managed to rejoin the main body. The water was rising all around the little army, and General Sherman decided to return to the transports.

Half drowned and half frozen, the soldiers walked through three feet deep water to reach the boats. The guns of the Sixth Indiana Battery had

44 Sherman, *Memoirs*, 227.

to be disassembled and carried back to the transports piece by piece, so deep was the water. Finally by a little past noon, the whole division basked in the security and comparative warmth of the river steamers.[45]

Undismayed by the whole messy business, Sherman decided to try another landing at a point somewhere closer to Eastport, in the hope of finding higher and dryer land. The gunboats and transports moved on up the river to the mouth of Indian Creek, but the whole shore was submerged by high water. Try as he might, Sherman could find no suitable place to land.

Finally late in the afternoon of the 15th, Sherman decided to try and land at Pittsburg, but upon reaching that point he found General Hurlbut and part of the Fourth Division waiting off shore in their transports. During the night "Cump" steamed down to Savannah to report to General Smith. Having seen the river steadily rise, Smith under-stood why the expedition had failed, and he decided to try a new tact. Sherman was ordered to return to Pittsburg with his division and disembark there. Smith also issued orders for General Hurlbut to land there also. The army commander was to shortly follow in a few days, and then an advance could be made toward the enemy.[46]

Accompanied by Lieutenant Colonel McPherson, Sherman moved over to Pittsburg and began preparations to execute the railroad cutting order with his division. With the troops disembarked at the Landing, Sherman, McPherson, and a few harried staff officers rode out to Bethel, Tennessee, about three miles away. The 16th was Sunday, but there was to be little rest for Sherman and his busy staff. As soon as he returned from his personal reconnaissance to Bethel, Sherman decided to send a stronger party out to determine the local enemy strength, and if possible cut the railroad.

---

45 *OR* 10, pt. 1, 22, 23, 28, 30; Sherman, *Memoirs*, 227; Robert Flemming, "The Battle of Shiloh As A Private Saw It," *Sketches of War History 1861-1865, Papers Prepared for the Commandery of the State of Ohio, Military Order of the Loyal Legion of the United States* (Cincinnati: 1908), 6: 133; J. L. Bieler, "Shiloh," sketch in the Miscellaneous Collections at Shiloh National Military Park.

46 *OR* 10, pt. 1, 23, 24; Sherman, *Memoirs*, 228.

The Fifth Ohio Cavalry, now sturdy veterans of the soggy Eastport expedition, was again given the task of railroad bursting. About 6:00 Sunday evening, the regiment, under Lieutenant Colonel Thomas Heath, set out, to be followed about six hours later by Sherman's First Infantry Brigade, now led by its newly arrived colonel, John McDowell, brother of the ill-fated General Irvin McDowell of Manassas fame.[47] For some reason Sherman was counting on the Confederates being completely asleep. His orders were not to pick a fight with any large enemy force, and he was reluctant to take any big chances until more troops arrived.

The other brigades were supposed to follow McDowell's men, but the movement was canceled when the cavalry returned with a report that the Confederates were out in force across the proposed line of advance. At a cost of four wounded, Colonel Heath engaged Confederate pickets on the Corinth Road, capturing two enlisted men. Colonel Heath's report, coming on top of a Sunday patrol report of enemy troop movements in the area, convinced Sherman that the element of surprise was completely gone. Sherman ordered the infantry and cavalry back to the Landing area, and there directed the whole division to encamp.

On Monday, Hurlbut's division disembarked and also encamped in the Landing area.[48] Meanwhile another Union force had landed near Sherman. This was the Third Division under the Indiana-born author-general, Lew Wallace. When the army arrived at Savannah on the 13th, Smith after securing the William Cherry House as headquarters, went over to the steamer *John J. Roe*, Wallace's headquarters. Entering his subordinate's cabin, General Smith quickly got down to business, explaining that he wanted the Third Division to occupy Crump's Landing and cut the Mobile and Ohio Railroad some fifteen miles distant. When the conference was over Smith walked out of the cabin, starting to enter the small boat or yawl that had brought him to the *Roe*. It was dark, and

---

47 *Campaigns in Kentucky and Tennessee*, 109, 123; *OR* 10, pt. 1, 24. Colonel McDowell was senior to Colonel Hicks, and when his regiment, the Sixth Iowa, arrived and was assigned to the Fifth Division, he naturally took over the command of the First Brigade. Ephrain J. Hart, *History of the Fortieth Illinois Infantry* (Cincinnati: H. S. Bosworth, 1864), 81.

48 *OR* 10, pt. 1, 24, 26, 27.

the white-haired general slipped, badly skinning one of his shins. General Wallace urged him to stay on the *Roe* and have the injury tended to, but clenching his teeth against the pain, Smith groaned, "No—too much business." The boat crew rowed him away, and the two men never met again, for the slight injury to the white haired general would eventually prove fatal.[49]

Within a couple of hours the Third Division was steaming toward Crump's Landing, and by midnight most of the division was safely landed. On the following day, Thursday, General Wallace sent the Third Battalion of the Fifth Ohio Cavalry, under Major Charles Hayes, to cut the railroad. By 10:00 a.m., the fast moving cavalry reached the railroad bridge at Beach Creek, between Bethel and Brown Station. Setting to work with great enthusiasm, the Ohioans promptly demolished the fifty foot span, plus an additional fifty foot section of track on each side of the swollen creek.

A small party of Confederate cavalry showed up during the destruction work, but the Ohioans quickly chased them away, taking two prisoners in the process. This work completed, the battalion returned to Crump's, where they promptly went into camp along with the rest of the division.[50] Seemingly by a process of gravitational attraction, the Army of the Tennessee was gradually collecting near Corinth, Mississippi.

Alarmed by the news of Wallace's and Sherman's landings, the local Confederate commanders began massing their own rather pitiful strength in the Purdy-Corinth area. If the Federals chose to move out in force from the landings, the Southerners would have to fight. Fortunately for the Confederates, Halleck's orders to avoid a general engagement kept the Union army immobilized.[51]

Meanwhile the command of the expeditionary force changed hands. On Monday, March 17, General Grant arrived by steamer to assume command of the scattered Army of the Tennessee. Grant decided that although Savannah was useful as a headquarters, it would be better to move the main army to Pittsburg to expedite an advance on Corinth, once

49   Wallace, *An Autobiography*, 1: 444, 445.

50   *OR* 10, pt. 1, 10.

51   *Ibid.*, 11, 16.

Buell's army showed up.[52] In part Grant's decision to concentrate at Pittsburg was prompted by Sherman's championing of the position. Impressed with the position for its strategic location, Sherman claimed that "the ground itself admits of easy defense by a small command, and yet affords admirable camping ground for a hundred thousand men."[53]

About twenty-two miles by road from Corinth, Sherman's choice of a camp spot was indeed excellent for defensive purposes. The place formed a broad uneven triangle, or funnel, which gradually widened from the base at the landing. Bounded on the east by the Tennessee River, the position was bordered on the northwest by Snake Creek and its branch, Owl Creek, and on the south by Lick Creek and its branch, Locust Grove Creek, as well as by a fairly sharp ravine, through which part of the creek ran. The various creeks and the resulting marshy land were a perfect protection against a flanking assault. An enemy army attacking Pittsburg Landing would have to push straight in and attempt to

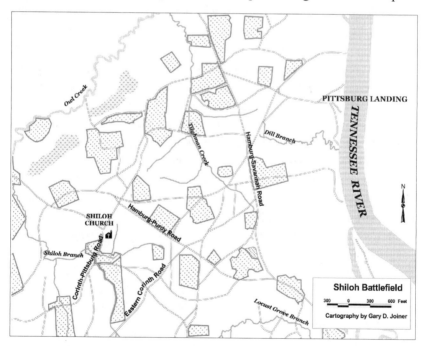

52 Grant, *Memoirs*, 169, 170.

53 *OR* 10, pt. 1, 27; Conger, *The Rise of U. S. Grant*, 218.

advance along the interior sides of the creeks in the funnel. The highest ground of the camp area was a ridge lying north of Locust Grove Creek and extending on toward the west. The extreme point of the ridge was about two hundred feet above the river at normal flood stage, and a number of Owl Creek branches zigzagged through the slopes of this ridge. Tilghman Creek was the most important of these branches, and it dissected the camp area into two main plateaus. The ground tended to be heavily wooded and uneven, except for a number of plowed cotton fields and several peach orchards.

There were several roads in the camping area, mostly running at angles roughly parallel to the Landing, making it difficult for an attacking army to maintain its communications. One was the Hamburg-Savannah or River Road, which led from Crump's Landing six miles downstream to a bridge across Snake Creek and on over to the eastern end of the ridge north of Locust Grove Creek, where it forked with the Purdy-Hamburg Road. The latter came in from Purdy by a bridge over Owl Creek, swung on in a slight southeasterly direction, crossed Lick Creek, and finally wound up in Hamburg, Tennessee. Pittsburg Landing was actually located about two-thirds of a mile below the mouth of Snake Creek. Two main roads led from the Landing, one of these, the Eastern Corinth Road, swung inland to where it joined the Bark Road, while the other ran in a more westerly direction, but parallel to the Eastern Corinth Road, and was naturally called the Western Corinth Road. Numerous other little paths and roads, including one abandoned washed out wagon trail, crisscrossed the area. There were country market roads, and they were in generally poor condition. Near the fork of the Western Corinth-Purdy Roads stood a little wooden church, the Shiloh Methodist Episcopal Church, which would give its name to the coming struggle at this peaceful place.[54]

---

54 Atwell Thompson Map of Shiloh; Steele, *American Campaigns*, 82, 83; Leander Stillwell, *The Story of A Common Soldier of Army Life in the Civil War, 1861-1865* (Kansas City: Franklin Hudson Publishing Company, 1920), 39; C. P. Searle, "War Sketches and Incidents," *War Sketches and Incidents As Related By Companions of the Iowa Commandery, Military Order of the Loyal Legion of the United States* (Des Moines: 1893), 1: 326, 327; Lucius Barber, *Army Memoirs of Lucius W. Barber, Company D, 15th Illinois Infantry*

Excepting the church, the only buildings in the camp area were a handful of simple farm structures and some sort of wooden house or store at the top of the Landing. The pattern of life in the area was exclusively rural. The climate tended to be rather humid, with an annual rainfall of more than fifty inches. Thick underbrush covered much of the area, and there was a good deal of second growth timber. Just down from the Landing there was a collection of large Indian mounds, which many of Grant's soldiers undoubtedly explored. The area was originally discovered by Colonel Joseph Hardin, but the Landing was named for Pitts, or Pittser Tucker, one of three brothers who built a small store at the point many years before the war.[55]

Following his arrival, Grant spent his time dealing with routine administrative matters, but made no effort to alter the development of the army at Pittsburg. He did write to Halleck that while it was difficult to form any idea of the exact strength of the Confederates, he felt satisfied "that they do not number 40,000 armed effective men at this time."[56] Grant went on in the same message to tell Halleck that he would visit Crump's and Pittsburg on Wednesday, and he would make any needed changes in the dispositions of the various units.[57]

Grant contemplated a quick thrust at the railroads around Corinth, but additional orders from Halleck to avoid a battle prevented any such movement.[58] Grant ordered Smith to assume personal command of the

---

(Chicago: J. M. W. Jones Stationery and Printing Company, 1894), 47. A Union observer described the church as an "exceedingly primitive" structure, "a fair type of the inertness of the people of that region at the time." Twenty-five or thirty feet on the sides, it was built of logs, and it lacked a pulpit and pews. There were crude benches for seats and the walls were not well put together. Charles C. Coffin, *The Boys of '61* (Boston: Estes and Laurit, 1881), 93, 94.

55   Gates P. Thurston, *The Antiquities of Tennessee and the Adjacent States* (Cincinnati: The Robert Clarke Company, 1897), 22-24; B. G. Brazelton, *A History of Hardin County Tennessee* (Nashville: Cumberland Presbyterian Publishing House, 1885), 6, 7.

56   *OR* 10, pt. 2, 45.

57   *Ibid.*

58   *Ibid.*, 49, 50.

army at Pittsburg, but since that officer was ill, it was necessary for General Sherman to actually continue to be in charge. McClernand was senior to Sherman, but he was embroiled in a dispute with General Smith over seniority, and Grant preferred to keep him in Savannah for the present.[59] For the moment at least the Army of the Tennessee was quietly camped in the Crump-Pittsburg-Savannah area, reasonably content, waiting for its fellow, the Army of the Ohio, to show up before resuming the advance.

Don Carlos Buell's command pulled out of Nashville on March 16 and 17. The army moved steadily, but with no particular haste. Buell saw no need for hurrying, since all the information he had from Halleck and Grant contained no hint of possible danger to the Army of the Tennessee. His soldiers were in good shape, and Buell meant to keep them that way. On March 20, the army was forced to camp after reaching the Duck River and finding the bridge at Columbia destroyed by retreating Confederate cavalry. After a week of repairing the structure, General Nelson's division finally crossed the river on March 29. Buell's plan was for the army, or at least the advance element, Nelson's division, to reach Savannah on April 7 and then cross on over to Pittsburg Landing by way of waiting steamers.

On April 1, Nelson's division marched fourteen miles, and on the following day made sixteen. On April 3, the division passed through Waynesboro, Tennessee, for a total of fifteen miles. On the following day the troops moved only ten and one-half miles because of bad roads. Finally on Saturday the division reached Savannah about noon, after having covered nine and one-half miles that day.[60]

With Grant at Savannah and Buell slowly moving forward to join him, what of the other forces under Halleck's command? For as of March 11, Halleck had been promoted to command the new Department of the Mississippi. This consisted of the old Department of the Missouri and

59 *Campaigns in Kentucky and Tennessee,* 113; John A. McClernand to U. S. Grant, March 3, 1862, John A. McClernand Papers, 1823-1896, Illinois State Historical Library.

60 Jacob Ammen, Diary, March 17-April 5, 1862, Illinois State Historical Library.

part of the Department of the Ohio. For better or for worse, Halleck became supreme commander in the Western theater. Hereafter he could answer directly to President Lincoln and Stanton without having any responsibility to McClellan. The new arrangement also meant that Buell would have to take orders from the New Yorker.

The capture of New Madrid freed General John Pope's army for a push at the Confederate position at Island No. 10.[61] Soon that position would be besieged by Pope's army and a supporting naval force under Acting Rear Admiral David Porter, effectively pinning down a small but potentially valuable Confederate army. General Halleck seemed blessed with success. His armies had overrun a third of Tennessee and were threatening Northern Mississippi. Just a little more pressure and the Confederacy might collapse in the West.

61 Roman, *Beauregard*, 1: 358, 359.

Chapter 5

The Armies Gather

THE PRINCIPLE OF CONCENTRATION of force is one of the oldest in military history. General Johnston had been forced to violate this principle in attempting to defend southern Kentucky and Tennessee, but after the fall of Fort Donelson the Southern high command rapidly began moving toward the idea of massing all available forces for one showdown attack to save the Mississippi Valley. It is impossible to say who first conceived of the idea of an all out concentration into one army in the region, but as early as February 15, Major General Braxton Bragg, writing from Mobile, Alabama, suggested to the Richmond authorities that the time had come to mass all that the South had for the struggle. In his reply three days later, Confederate Secretary of War Judah P. Benjamin maintained that the administration was contemplating an abandonment of the sea coast in order to defend the Tennessee line.[1]

Generals Johnston and Beauregard were both in favor of such a move, and in the week following the loss of Fort Donelson, the appropriate orders for such a concentration were given. Beauregard started operations by sending a confidential letter to the governors of Mississippi, Alabama, Tennessee, and Louisiana, in which he proposed a plan of strategic concentration. Each state was to send from five to ten thousand armed troops as quickly as possible, while Major General Earl Van Dorn's army in Arkansas was to cross over and link up that body of

1 *OR* 6, 826, 828. See Don Seitz, *Braxton Bragg: General of the Confederacy* (Columbia: The State Company, 1924); See also Judah P. Benjamin to R. E. Lee, February 24, 1862. *O.R.*, 6, 398.

men with General Beauregard's command. General Bragg's troops were to come up from Pensacola and Mobile, while Major General Mansfield Lovell, commanding at New Orleans, was to send as many troops as possible.[2]

The various governors' responses tended to be rather apathetic, but T. O. Moore of Louisiana did begin a vigorous campaign to raise 90-day units for General Beauregard's use. Lack of weapons and trained personnel greatly handicapped the effort, but the governor did manage to forward two battalions and one regiment, all infantry, to the Creole's army when it finally moved to Corinth, Mississippi.

Mustered in on March 6, the Crescent Regiment (Twenty-fourth Louisiana), the Orleans Guards (Thirteenth Battalion), and the Confederate Guard Response Battalion (Twelfth Louisiana Infantry Battalion) were headed north on the New Orleans, Jackson, and Great Northern almost as soon as they were formally sworn in.[3] Troops from General Lovell's command also entrained for Beauregard's temporary camp at Jackson, Tennessee. Indeed, Louisiana was very seriously weakened by the transfer of most of the best units from the state.

One of the regiments involved in this movement was the later famous Fourth Louisiana Infantry. Strung out on coastal guard duty from Berwick Bay, Louisiana, to Bay St. Louis, Mississippi, the Fourth was suddenly ordered to assemble in New Orleans, where the regiment boarded a train at 3:00 p.m. on February 25. The railroad tracks northward toward Camp Moore, Louisiana, were brightly lit up with bonfires, and crowds of civilians screamed and cheered as the train passed.

About 8:00 a.m. the following morning, the troop train halted at Canton, Mississippi, where the soldiers were told to change trains. Pausing only a few minutes to eat breakfast in town, the boys in gray dined on butter, syrup, biscuits as hard as cannon balls, and potato coffee. Within a few minutes the troops climbed on board passenger cars of the

2 Roman, *Beauregard*, 1: 240-242.

3 O. Edward Cunningham, Roster of Louisiana Units in the Confederate Army, unpublished paper prepared by the author for the Louisiana Civil War Centennial Commission, Baton Rouge: May, 1964.

Mississippi Central Railroad, which were to carry them on to Jackson, Tennessee, where the Confederates arrived about 3:00 p.m., Thursday, February 27.[4]

More troop trains quickly followed, including one carrying the Seventh Mississippi Infantry, which had also been on coast defense duty at Bay St. Louis. The regiment's train pulled out of New Orleans at dawn on February 27, with the men all in good spirits. But as the train neared Amite, Louisiana, disaster suddenly struck. Somehow a log train ran into the troop train with devastating results. Heavy timbers ripped through the wooden passenger cars, crushing and mangling soldiers right and left. Brains spattered the interior of several of the demolished coaches, while numerous legs and torsos horribly decorated the scene. Lieutenant N. B. Wilson and eleven enlisted men of Company K were killed outright, as well as ten fellows from Company H, the Pike County Dahlgren Rifles. Between twenty and forty-five men were seriously injured in the mishap. Several other companies had a few slightly injured, but the logs struck only the coaches in which Companies K and H were riding.[5] Boarding another train, the remnants of the Seventh Mississippi finally caught up with their friends in the Fourth Louisiana in Jackson, Tennessee, on March 2.[6] Altogether the New Orleans, Jackson, and Great Northern and the Mississippi Central moved up nine regiments and four artillery batteries to either Corinth, Mississippi, or Jackson, Tennessee.[7]

From Mobile and Pensacola came the regiments of General Braxton Bragg's command. Bragg's first regiment, the Ninth Mississippi Infantry, reached Iuka, Mississippi, on February 14. A number of

4 Stephenson, "Willie Micajah Barrow Diary," 179.

5 John A. Cato to wife, February 27, 1862, John A. Cato Papers, Mississippi Department of Archives and History; J. C. Rietti, *Military Annals of Mississippi* (n.p.: n.d.), 59; F. Jay Taylor (ed.), *The Secret Diary of Robert Patrick 1861-1865: The Reluctant Rebel* (Baton Rouge: Louisiana State University Press, 1959), 34.

6 Dunbar Rowland, *The Official and Statistical Register of the State of Mississippi* (Nashville: Brandon Printing Company, 1908), 568.

7 Robert C. Black, III, *Railroads of the Confederacy* (Chapel Hill: University of North Carolina Press, 1952), 142.

Mississippi and Alabama regiments followed in the next weeks, perhaps ten thousand men altogether, reaching the Johnston-Beauregard command. General Bragg's men possessed the special virtue of being well trained as a result of long months of arduous drill at the Gulf cities.[8]

Besides these commands, the Confederates also had General Polk's army, which had been stationed at Columbus, Kentucky. On the last day of February, Confederate combat units began the evacuation of the "Gibraltar of the West." Additional cavalry, artillery, and infantry units followed in the next two days in a surprisingly orderly evacuation that saw the Southerners able to carry off most of the massive array of big guns stationed at that point.[9] But there were a few mistakes in the excitement. As the Thirteenth Louisiana Infantry packed up three days rations in their haversacks on March 1, prior to moving out, the order was given to set fire to some nearby warehouses. Matches were quickly applied, and then as smoke and flame billowed from the buildings, someone suddenly remembered a store of ammunition cached inside one of the structures. Before the flames could set the powder off, Lieutenant Armond Dubroca rounded up a detail from his company, Company C, and entered the building, saving the ammunition for future use and probably preventing some casualties.

The troops from the Columbus garrison quickly reached Humboldt, Tennessee. Many were badly disorganized by the Donelson disaster and the Columbus evacuation. Confederate discipline, never very strong, began to crack. Wandering off from their units to the Humboldt bars to seek solace from alcohol, some of the men became rowdy. Private John Brannigan, Company A, Thirteenth Louisiana Infantry, was certainly no exception. Brannigan went completely berserk. Grabbing hold of Captain Stephen O'Leary, Company A, Thirteenth Louisiana Infantry,

---

8 Rowland, *The Official and Statistical Register of the State of Mississippi*, 586, 599; John P. Dyer, *"Fightin' Joe" Wheeler* (Baton Rouge: Louisiana State University Press, 1941), 27-31; Edward Crenshaw, "Diary of Captain Edward Crenshaw," *The Alabama Historical Quarterly* 1 (Fall 1930): 266.

9 Horn, *Army of Tennessee*, 111. || Dr. Cunningham's original text stated that the Confederates removed all their heavy guns. The various reports of those involved make clear the Confederates left some guns and other material. We have slightly altered the text to reflect this. See *OR* 7, 436-438.

he threw the poor Irish Confederate against a barroom window. Enraged by the attack, O'Leary's men promptly mobbed Private Brannigan, putting him in irons.[10] Temporarily, Polk's command remained at Humboldt until it was finally ordered to Corinth a few days later.

The concentration of Confederate forces for the showdown battle was shaping up fairly well, but there was one serious fly in the ointment. West of the Mississippi River, General Van Dorn declined to go along with General Beauregard's plan of concentration. Instead, Van Dorn proposed to defeat Brigadier General Samuel R. Curtis's Union army in Arkansas. This, believed Van Dorn, would create a diversion that would favor Generals Johnston and Beauregard. On February 24, he notified Johnston that the Confederate army in Arkansas was advancing on Curtis. If General Johnston made any reply to the Mississippian's message, it has not been preserved. In any event, the diversion failed, for Curtis won the ensuing battle at Pea Ridge, or Elkhorn Tavern.[11]

Once Van Dorn had been defeated, the best course of action would have been for him to cross the Mississippi and link up with Johnston and/or Beauregard. Unfortunately General Johnston neglected to issue the necessary orders to the Mississippian. On March 19, General Beauregard again appealed to Van Dorn for reinforcements, but without avail. Only after Johnston reached Corinth and closely discussed the situation with the Creole and Bragg did the Kentuckian finally order Van Dorn to join him.[12] Unfortunately the army in Arkansas would not reach Mississippi in time for the forthcoming action.

10 Frank L. Richardson, "War As I Saw It, 1861-65," *Louisiana Historical Quarterly* 6 (January 1923): 95, 96.

11 For a description of the campaign and the Battle of Pea Ridge, see Jay Monaghan, *Civil War on the Western Border, 1854-1865* (Boston: Little, Brown and Company, 1955), 233-251. || For an outstanding modern account, see William L. Shea and Earl J. Hess, *Pea Ridge: Civil War Campaign in the West* (Chapel Hill: The University of North Carolina Press, 1992). For Van Dorn, see Robert G. Hartje, *Van Dorn: The Life and Times of a Confederate General* (Nashville: Vanderbilt Univ. Press, 1967).

12 *OR* 7, 789-791; *A Soldier's Honor: With Reminiscences of Major-General Earl Van Dorn, by His Comrades* (New York: Abbey Press, 1902), 71.

Colonel St. John Liddell, of General Hardee's staff, gave a somewhat interesting account of General Van Dorn's failure to reach General A. S. Johnston in time, claiming that Governor Moore of Louisiana, who was feuding with President Jefferson Davis, would not help in providing New Orleans-based steamboats to transport General Van Dorn's army over to Mississippi.[13] But even without the Mississippian's command a considerable Confederate force was being collected in Northern Mississippi and Southwest Tennessee.

In their original correspondence on the subject of the war in the West, Generals Johnston and Beauregard had not bothered to spell out exactly where the Southerners would collect. There were several possible meeting places, including Jackson, Tennessee, Decatur, Alabama, and Chattanooga, Tennessee, but the most logical spot for troop concentration lay at the little North Mississippi town of Corinth. Located only twenty miles from the Tennessee River, Corinth was a good centrally located point for a concentration. Its value was enhanced by the town's situation on the junction of two of the South's most important railroads, the Mobile and Ohio and the Memphis and Charleston.

General Beauregard later claimed that he chose Corinth as the point of concentration, and then sent an emissary to Murfreesboro to persuade the Kentuckian to bring his troops there,[14] but it is more probable that the two ranking Confederate officers independently selected the little Mississippi town as a point of junction and then arranged the details by means of the Creole's emissary.

On March 2, General Beauregard wrote to Albert S. Johnston that the great battle of the war would be fought at or near Corinth, and in subsequent letters he pressed the supreme Confederate commander in the West to move faster.[15]

The bulk of Beauregard's own command was still in Jackson, Tennessee, and even the newly arrived Bragg was making his

---

13 Horn, *Army of Tennessee*, 112.

14 Roman, *Beauregard*, 1: 505, 506.

15 General P. G. T. Beauregard to General A. S. Johnston, March 3, 1862, Mrs. Mason Barret Papers, Albert Sidney Johnston Collections, Howard-Tilton Memorial Library, Tulane University; Roland, *Albert Sidney Johnston*, 307.

headquarters there. But on March 13, the Creole started moving his army out of the town along the Mobile and Ohio Railroad, temporarily halting part of the command at Bethel Station, Tennessee, only one day's march from Pittsburg Landing and Crump's Landing, Tennessee. After his army remained a week at Bethel, the troops were ordered to go on down to the junction at Corinth.[16]

General A. S. Johnston's army was burdened with large quantities of ammunition, provisions, and artillery. Hampered by a shortage of trained staff officers, the Kentuckian was able to move toward the junction but slowly.[17] By not abandoning his encumbrances and making a forced march to Corinth, General Johnston was actually taking a calculated risk that the Federals would not mass their forces and strike at Corinth first.

From Murfreesboro, Johnston led his column to Shelbyville, Tennessee, on the Duck River, and from there to Fayetteville, in the southern part of that state. Next the Confederates marched to Huntsville, Alabama, where they picked up the Memphis and Charleston Railroad. The army rode from Huntsville to Corinth, Mississippi, on the painfully creaking coaches and boxcars of the overworked and understaffed railroad, arriving in Corinth March 23.[18]

Arriving in Corinth on March 23, General Johnston conferred with Generals Beauregard and Bragg, and also with the other senior officers

---

16 Stephenson, "Willie Micajah Barrow Diary," 26, 27; John Cato to wife, March 20, 1862, John A. Cato Papers, Mississippi Department of Archives and History; Taylor, *Reluctant Rebel*, 34, 35.

17 General P. G. T. Beauregard to General A. S. Johnston, March 2, 1862, Barret Collection, Albert Sidney Johnston Collections, Howard-Tilton Memorial Library, Tulane University; Rowland, *The Official and Statistical Register of the State of Mississippi*, 307.

18 Henry Melville Doak, "Memoirs," Confederate Collection, Tennessee Department of Archives and History; Henry Morton Stanley, *Autobiography of Henry Morton Stanley* (Boston: Houghton Mifflin, 1906), 185; Edward Thompson, *History of the Orphan Brigade* (Louisville: Leslie Thompson, 1895), 428-431; Kirwan, *Johnny Green*, 18, 19; Frank Peak, "A Southern Soldier's View of the Civil War," Frank Peak Papers, Louisiana State University Archives; W. J. Worsham, *The Old Nineteenth Tennessee Regiment, C. S. A.* (Knoxville: Paragon Printing Company, 1902), 34, 35.

present. In a surprise move, General Johnston then offered the command of the field army to the Creole while he, the supreme commander, would continue as head of the department from headquarters at Memphis or Holly Springs, Mississippi.[19] General Beauregard declined the assignment. Albert Sidney Johnston's generous offer has caused much speculation, but the probable reason for it was that the Kentuckian felt that the army and the people no longer trusted his judgment.[20]

Once the army was collected at Corinth and the nearby railroad towns, the problem remained as to what to do with it. Generals Johnston and Beauregard, and just about everybody else, wanted to attack General Grant before Buell could link up with him, but the Confederate army, now renamed the Army of the Mississippi, was in woefully poor condition for an offensive.[21]

There were over forty thousand Southerners collected in the Confederate army, and additional individual units wandered in from day to day.[22] Thousands of soldiers had been in the ranks only a few days, or a few weeks, and they were totally lacking in training. Morale was depressed due to the recent reverses. To try and unscramble this confused mess, General Johnston authorized Beauregard to draw up a plan of organization.

The Army of the Mississippi was divided into three corps. The first corps was under Major General Leonidas Polk, the second was under Major General Braxton Bragg, and the third was under Major General William J. Hardee. A reserve division was also organized under Major General George Crittenden, who shortly afterwards was replaced by former Vice President of the United States, Brigadier General John

---

19   Roman, *Beauregard*, 1: 266; Edward Munford, "Albert Sidney Johnston," Mrs. Mason Barret Papers, Albert Sidney Johnston Collection, Howard-Tilton Memorial Library, Tulane University; T. Harry Williams, *P. G. T. Beauregard: Napoleon in Gray* (Baton Rouge: Louisiana State University Press, 1955), 125.

20   Roman, *Beauregard*, 1: 266. For fuller discussions of this matter, see Williams, *P. G. T. Beauregard*, 125; Roland, *Albert Sidney Johnston*, 311, 312.

21   Roman, *Beauregard*, 1: 267.

22   "A Sketch of Noxubee Troopers, 1st Mississippi Cavalry, Company F," T. F. Jackson Papers, Mississippi Department of Archives and History.

Cabell Breckinridge.[23] General Beauregard was named as second in command of the army, while General Bragg was appointed chief of staff, besides retaining his position as Second Corps Commander.[24]

One of the most serious problems facing the Confederate army was the lack of proper firearms. Indeed, the local blacksmiths were busily turning out pikes to arm some of the Southerners who had no guns.[25] Actually General Johnston's army possessed firearms for most of the men, but they were of a heterogeneous variety. Most of the Confederate cavalry and artillery and at least some of the infantry could only be issued shotguns, in many cases with the men's own personal weapons.[26] Many of the regiments were equipped with a varied mixture of old flintlock smoothbores and civilian squirrel rifles. The differences in caliber of these latter commercial weapons created a tremendous ammunition problem for the Confederate army, since it was impossible to issue standardized cartridges.[27]

Other Southern infantry units were equipped with military model percussion smoothbore muskets. Though obsolete and greatly inferior to

---

23 *OR* 10, pt. 1, 396; Roman, *Beauregard*, 1: 267, 268.

24 || For considered assessments of these generals, see Nathaniel Cheairs Hughes, Jr., *General William J. Hardee: Old Reliable* (Baton Rouge: Louisiana State University Press, 1965); Joseph H. Parks, *General Leonidas Polk, C.S.A.: The Fighting Bishop* (Baton Rouge: Louisiana State University Press, 1962); Grady McWhiney, *Braxton Bragg and Confederate Defeat: Vol. 1: Field Command* (New York: Columbia University Press, 1969); William C. Davis, *Breckinridge: Statesman, Soldier, Symbol* (Baton Rouge: Louisiana State University, 1974).

25 Kirwan, *Johnny Green*, 19.

26 Jackson, "A Sketch of Noxubee Troopers," T. F. Jackson Papers, Mississippi Department of Archives and History; John Cabell Breckinridge to P. G. T. Beauregard, April 1, 1862, Braxton Bragg Papers, Palmer Collection, Western Reserve Historical Collection; Claud E. Fuller and Richard D. Stewart, *Firearms of the Confederacy* (Huntington, West Virginia: Standard Publications, Inc., 1943), 289.

27 Stanley, *Autobiography*, 187; Edwin Rennolds, *A History of the Henry County Commands Which Served in the Confederate States Army* (Kennesaw: Continental Book Company,1961), 25; Henry Melville Doak, "Memoirs," 26.

the modern rifles employed by most of the Union army, they were still fairly effective at a range less than a hundred yards.[28] Still other Confederate units, such as the Eighteenth Louisiana, Third Kentucky, and Bate's Second Tennessee, possessed both modern army rifles, sporting guns, and percussion cap or flintlock smoothbores.[29] A very few infantry regiments were equipped solely with modern rifles. The Twentieth Tennessee was one such lucky group. Armed with ineffective flintlocks at the disastrous Battle of Fishing Creek, Kentucky, the regiment received a shipment of .577 caliber British Enfields while en route to Corinth, courtesy of the recent arrival of a blockade runner.[30]

If there were inadequacies in most of the Confederate soldiers' shoulder arms, this was at least slightly compensated for in the wide variety of side arms carried by even the enlisted men. Most of the officers and noncoms carried revolvers, and many of the former carried swords, and almost everyone from private to general seems to have carried some kind of knife, whether a simple Bowie or a more sophisticated Arkansas toothpick. Hundreds, perhaps thousands, of enlisted men carried revolvers or some sort of pistol stuffed in their pockets or in the waist bands of their pants.[31]

As bad as the weapon situation was in the Confederate army, the standards of training were generally even worse, excepting General Bragg's soldiers. The chief of staff described Generals Polk's and

28 Sam Watkins, *"Co. Aytch" A Side Show of the Big Show* (New York: Collier Books, 1962), 26; Henry George, *History of the 3d, 7th, 8th, and 12th Kentucky, C. S. A.* (Louisville: C. T. Dearing Printing Company, 1911), 26.

29 *Ibid.*, 19; W. E. Yeatman, "Shiloh," Confederate Collection, Tennessee State Library and Archives; Cesar Porta to J. B. Wilkinson, n.d., Louisiana Historical Association Collection, Howard-Tilton Memorial Library, Tulane University.

30 W. J. McMurray, *History of the Twentieth Tennessee Regiment Volunteer Infantry, C. S. A.* (Nashville: The Publication Committee, 1904), 84; Fuller and Stewart, *Firearms of the Confederacy*, 117. On April 1, 1862, General Hardee reported that 1,060 of his men were armed with Enfield rifles, although he was dangerously short on cartridges. *OR* 10, pt. 2, 379.

31 Stanley, *Autobiography*, 171; Stephenson, "Willie Micajah Barrow Diary," 436-440.

Breckinridge's soldiers as a "heterogeneous mass in which there was more enthusiasm than discipline, more capacity than knowledge, and more valor than instructions."[32] One of Bragg's biggest problems in trying to discipline the army lay in the lack of trained officers. Most of the senior officers were either professionals or experienced amateurs, but at the company and regimental level the bulk of officers were ex-civilians. A very few regiments had trained senior officers.

The Seventh Kentucky was very fortunate in possessing Colonel Charles Wickliffe, West Point class of 1839. Wickliffe had three years of frontier duty behind him, and he had served as a captain in the Sixteenth U. S. Infantry and major of the Fourteenth during the Mexican War. After that conflict, he left the army to enter the Kentucky legislature, later serving four years as commonwealth attorney.[33]

Colonel Joe Wheeler, Nineteenth Alabama, was another good example of the professional soldier placed in command of a volunteer regiment. A West Point graduate of 1859 and a veteran of one Indian action, the twenty-five year old Wheeler had been colonel of the Nineteenth Alabama since September of the previous year, turning it into one of the best trained organizations in Bragg's command.[34]

Colonel Jean Jacque Alexandre Alfred Mouton, Eighteenth Louisiana, was also a West Point graduate, but for ten years before the Civil War he spent his time as a railroad engineer (although he did serve as a militia officer).

John S. Marmaduke, colonel of the Third Confederate Infantry Regiment, was also a graduate of the West Point class of 1857, besides possessing four years of command experience in the peacetime U. S. Army, while Colonel John C. Moore, Second Texas, possessed the most experience of any of General Albert Sidney Johnston's regimental commanders. A member of the class of 1849 at West Point, Moore had served against the Seminoles in Florida as well as in the territory of New Mexico.

32 Braxton Bragg, "Albert Sidney Johnston," Mrs. Mason Barret Collection, Howard-Tilton Memorial Library, Tulane University.

33 George, *History of the 3d, 7th, 8th, and 12th Kentucky, C. S. A.*, 149.

34 Dyer, *"Fightin' Joe" Wheeler*, 5-19.

Twenty year old John Herbert Kelly, Ninth Arkansas Battalion, was the youngest field officer with the Army of the Mississippi. After three years at West Point, Kelly resigned to enter the Confederate Army as major of the Fourteenth Arkansas Infantry in September 1861.[35]

Excepting the West Pointers most of Johnston's regimental commanders had only service experience in the Mexican War. Colonel George Maney, First Tennessee, Colonel W. B. Bate, Second Tennessee, and Colonel John H. Clanton, First Alabama Cavalry, were all three Mexican War veterans. Colonel Robert Tyler, Fifteenth Tennessee, represented a different type of military experience. Twenty-eight years old, Tyler was a veteran of William Walker's first filibustering expedition to Nicaragua. Tyler had ably commanded his regiment at the Battle of Belmont, and this dual experience helped mark him as one of the better regimental leaders.[36]

The bulk of the regimental commanders were men of a completely civilian background, appointed colonels because of political influence or organizational ability. One of the most able of these was the commander of the Fourth Louisiana Infantry, Henry Watkins Allen, a lawyer, politician, and sometimes European traveler who originally won the election as lieutenant colonel of the regiment.[37]

Colonel John J. Thornton, Sixth Mississippi, did have several months experience as a colonel of Mississippi militia. A resident of Brandon, Mississippi, he was the one member of the state constitutional convention who refused to sign the ordinance of secession.[38]

Forty-six year old Thomas Hart Hunt of the Sixth Kentucky was a native of Lexington, a businessman, and a former officer of the state guard,[39] while of a slightly different tradition, Colonel Daniel Weisiger

35 Maud Kelly, "General John Herbert Kelly, The Boy General of the Confederacy," *The Alabama Historical Quarterly* 9 (Spring, 1947): 14-39.

36 Warner, *Generals in Gray*, 312; *OR* 3: 336.

37 Vincent Cassidy, *Henry Watkins Allen of Louisiana* (Baton Rouge: Louisiana State University Press, 1964), 3-70; Taylor, *Reluctant Rebel*, 31.

38 Rowland, *The Official and Statistical Register of the State of Mississippi*, 558.

39 Thompson, *History of the Orphan Brigade*, 429-431.

Adams, First Louisiana Infantry, had at least been under fire, although not on the battlefield. In a duel in Louisiana, the high-spirited Adams had killed a newspaper editor who had criticized his Federal judge-father.[40]

Most of the regimental commanders of the Confederacy fell into some sort of category between Adams, the duelist civilian, and the ex-militia officer John Thornton. The majority of the lower grade officers lacked any military experience, although there were a few notable exceptions such as Leon von Zinken, major of the Twentieth Louisiana. An ex-Prussian officer, von Zinken was himself the son of a Prussian general. Although he spoke only clumsy English, he was usually able to make his point to his part German, part Irish regiment.[41]

First Lieutenant William Moon, Company A, Seventeenth Alabama, had served in the Mexican War and with William Walker in Nicaragua before being elected to his position in September 1861.[42]

Some of the regimental commanders were either inept or simply completely unreliable. Colonel Thomas Hill Watts, Seventeenth Alabama, was by profession a lawyer, and he tended to carry his legal training over into his military career. Watts was persistently wrangling with General Bragg over some minor points of order. While at Corinth, he also refused to obey an order from his brigade commander, General Adley H. Gladden. The lawyer-soldier also persuaded his senior officers to join with him in his ill-conceived mutiny. The upshot of the affair was that Watts and the others were placed under arrest until they wrote an apology to General Gladden, admitting they had done wrong in refusing a lawful order from a superior officer. A few days later Watts was appointed Attorney General of the Confederate States, and upon accepting the appointment left the regiment forever, entrusting it to Lieutenant Colonel Robert C. Fariss.[43]

---

40 *D. A. B.*, 1: 55.

41 Ella Lonn, *Foreigners in the Confederacy* (Chapel Hill: University of North Carolina Press, 1940), 142, 143.

42 Crenshaw, "Diary of Captain Edward Crenshaw," 264.

43 *Ibid.*, 266, 267; W. Brewer, *Alabama: Her History, Resources, War Record, and Public Men from 1540-1872* (Montgomery: Barrett and Brown, 1872), 460, 461.

A much more serious disciplinary affair was that occurring between General Bragg and Generals George Crittenden and William Carroll. Reports circulated at Bragg's headquarters that the two latter officers were neglecting their duties and spending too much time drinking. Crittenden was already under a cloud for the Fishing Creek debacle, at which it was commonly charged that he had been drunk.[44] On General Bragg's orders, Hardee visited Crittenden's command and had the two men arrested, Crittenden for drunkenness and Carroll for the same violation, plus additional charges of neglect and incompetence.[45] For both officers it was the end as far as their military careers went. Crittenden resigned his command as major general and spent the rest of the war in various administrative capacities. Carroll resigned and went to Canada. Crittenden's loss was an especially sad one, for that officer was one of the most experienced in the Confederate army. West Point trained, he had fought in the Black Hawk War, with the Texas Republic Army, and in the Mexican War. His brother was Thomas Leonidas Crittenden, Major General, United States Volunteers.

Bragg's efforts to whip the army into shape were handicapped by the necessity to fortify Corinth in case General U. S. Grant should suddenly strike. Still, some four miles of breastworks were constructed around Corinth in late March.[46] Bragg was also handicapped by a widespread sickness among the officers and enlisted men. Corinth possessed but limited supplies of pure water, and the army, lacking knowledge of proper methods of sanitation, quickly managed to pollute most of these.[47] The continuing cold, wet weather which plagued the Southerners in Tennessee and Kentucky wreaked devastation in the ranks at Corinth. Many of the Rebels were already in poor condition from the winter's campaigning in Kentucky, and General Bragg's soldiers suffered

44 *OR* 10, pt. 2, 379; Nashville *Gazette*, January 26, 1862; Memphis *Appeal*, February 5, 1862.

45 *OR* 10, pt. 2, 379.

46 John Cato to wife, March 27, 1862, John A. Cato Papers, Mississippi Department of Archives and History; Thomas P. Richardson to Tannie, March 26, 1862, Thomas P. Richardson Papers, Louisiana State University Archives.

47 Duncan, *Recollections*, 13, 14.

severely after their stay in sunny Florida.[48] Blankets, raincoats, uniforms and even shoes were in short supply, even for officers, which added to the problems.[49] The Twentieth Tennessee was issued only thirty-three pairs of good boots, so Colonel Joel Battle decided the only fair way of distributing the foot gear was to let the men settle it with a shooting match. Firing at two hundred yard range targets, the three best shots in each company received a pair of shoes—a unique method of military supply distribution.[50]

*   *   *

Just three hours horseback ride away, General U. S. Grant's army was also undergoing a few problems. The single biggest thing wrong with the Union army was a malady which all of the men from private to general were suffering—overconfidence. On March 29, Grant wrote his beloved wife, Julia, that "a big fight may be looked for some place before a great while which it appears to me will be the last in the West." He went on to say that he was completely confident of success.[51] Three days later Grant's youngest divisional commander, Brigadier General Lew Wallace, wrote an old friend that the rebellion "is closing fast," and continuing, Wallace predicted that the Union army would have complete control of the Mississippi River before the end of April.[52]

Before the expedition started up the Tennessee River, Governor S. J. Kirkwood of Iowa visited the troops, telling them that the "backbone of the rebellion was broken," and that the war was nearly over. According to

48 Crenshaw, "Diary of Captain Edward Crenshaw," 265.

49 McMurray, *Twentieth Tennessee*, 84; Thomas P. Richardson to Tannie, March 26, 1862, Thomas P. Richardson Papers, Louisiana State University Archives; John Cato to wife, March 27, 1862, John A. Cato Papers, Mississippi Department of Archives and History.

50 McMurray, *Twentieth Tennessee*, 84.

51 U. S. Grant to wife, March 29, 1862, U. S. Grant Papers, Illinois State Historical Library.

52 *Civil War History* 8 (September 1962): 335, 336.

the governor, all of the soldiers would be home by the Fourth of July.[53] Indeed, Secretary of War Stanton was so optimistic about Union military prospects that on April 3, he issued General Order No. 33, which stated that "the recruiting service for volunteers will be discontinued in every state from this date."[54] With their military and civilian leaders in such optimistic spirits over the progress of the war, the Union rank and file could hardly be blamed for sharing the optimistic certainty.[55]

Private Enoch Colby, Jr., Battery A, First Illinois Light Artillery, wrote home that "we shall not have more than one more fight, and that will probably be at Corinth, Mississippi."[56] Lieutenant Payson Shumway, Fourteenth Illinois, wrote his wife, Hattie, that "it is generally thought that our enemy will retreat as we advance." Shumway continued, "I do not anticipate any fighting very soon, if at all."[57]

Private Elijah Shepard believed that "we have the revels [Rebels] now as it were almost in our power. They perfectly cowed down, they have lost all hope of conquering us." Shepard went on to say that many of the men were afraid to take leave or go home for fear of missing the end of the war.[58]

---

53 Bell, *Tramps and Triumphs*, 14.

54 Eugene Murdock, *Ohio's Bounty System in the Civil War* (Columbus: Ohio State).

55 John Taylor, "Reminiscences of Service as an Aide-de-Camp with General William Tecumseh Sherman," *War Talks in Kansas: A Series of Papers Read Before the Kansas Commandery of the Military Order of the Loyal Legion of the United States* (Kansas City: Franklin Publishing Company, 1906), 130, 131; John Foster, *War Stories for My Grandchildren* (Cambridge: Riverside Press, 1918), 60; Wilbur Crummer, *With Grant at Fort Donelson, Shiloh, and Vicksburg* (Oak Park: E. C. Crummer Company, 1915), 47; Lucius Barber, *Army Memoirs of Lucius W. Barber, Company D, 15th Illinois Infantry* (Chicago: J. M. W. Jones Stationery and Printing Company, 1894), 48.

56 Enoch C. Colby, Jr. to his father, April 4, 1862, Miscellaneous Collections, Shiloh National Military Park.

57 Payson Z. Shumway to wife, March 19, 1862, Payson Z. Shumway Papers, Illinois State Historical Library.

58 Elijah L. Shepard to wife, March 29, 1862, Miscellaneous Collection, Shiloh National Military Park.

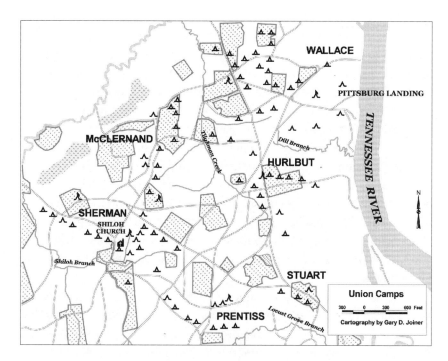

Whatever the state of the army's thinking, the men were still happy to see reinforcements arriving by steamer in a steady stream. But the new arrivals gave General Grant a number of fairly significant problems. Obviously one was a question of organization. Grant had to decide what divisions to assign the new units to. Finally the army commander handled the matter by creating a completely new division, the Sixth, to be led by Brigadier General Benjamin M. Prentiss.[59]

Forty-two year old Prentiss was born in Virginia, but grew up in Missouri and Illinois. During the Mormon troubles, he served as a junior officer in the Illinois Militia.[60] When the Mexican War broke out, Prentiss enlisted in the First Illinois. By a peculiar quirk of fate, W. H. L. Wallace served in the same company as Prentiss. Indeed, when Prentiss was promoted to company commander, Wallace replaced him as first

59 *Campaigns in Kentucky and Tennessee*, 113.

60 Warner, *Generals in Blue*, 385, 386.

lieutenant, both men participating in the Battle of Buena Vista.[61] Prentiss managed to survive the war to become a lawyer in his adopted state. On the outbreak of hostilities Prentiss was commissioned colonel of the Tenth Illinois Infantry, but was soon promoted to brigadier general of volunteers, to rank from May 7. Grant and Prentiss were not on the very best terms, but his appointment must reflect Grant's confidence in him.

Another administrative problem concerned the commander of the Second Division, Brigadier General C. F. Smith. The scratch on his leg refused to heal, and the white-haired veteran was confined to his upstairs bed in the W. H. Cherry House, unable to exercise command over his unit. The mantle of his Second Division fell upon the lean, long-faced W. H. L. Wallace. Appointed brigadier general of volunteers on March 2, 1862, William H. L. Wallace was formally directed to take charge of the Second Division on April 3.[62]

The new divisional commander was forty years old, and had served as a company grade officer in the First Illinois Infantry during the Mexican War. A capable peacetime attorney and Illinois politician, Wallace was a very devoted supporter of the Union. Although he blamed the abolitionists for starting the war, the sandy haired, gray-eyed Wallace was still ready to uphold the national flag.[63]

One of Grant's lesser difficulties was moving the First Division from Savannah to Pittsburg Landing. Most of the transports had been sent back to Kentucky to pick up reinforcements or supplies, and Grant was forced to make the switch with only two steamers, one of them a tiny vessel.

---

61   Isabel Wallace, *Life and Letters of General W. H. L. Wallace* (Chicago: R. R. Donnelley and Sons, 1909), 20-26.

62   W. H. L. Wallace to his wife, Ann, April 3, 1862, W. H. L. Wallace Papers, Illinois State Historical Library. || For a modern account of W.H.L. Wallace, see Steven E. Woodworth, "'Earned on the Field of Battle': William H. L. Wallace," in Steven E. Woodworth, ed., *Grant's Lieutenants: From Cairo to Vicksburg* (Lawrence: University Press of Kansas, 2001), 21-42.

63   Wallace, *Life and Letters of General W. H. L. Wallace*, 1-64; W. H. L. Wallace to wife, Ann, April 3, 1862, (second letter of April 3), W. H. L. Wallace Papers, Illinois State Historical Library.

The divisional transfer began on March 21 but was not completed for several days. The weather was warm and wet, but the army established a fairly rigorous program of drill. Either because he begrudged the time lost to training or simply felt it unnecessary, Grant neglected to erect the fortifications his superior Henry Halleck had directed.[64]

Training schedules were considerably handicapped by the lack of professional military training on the part of most of Grant's officers. As was the case in the Confederate army, the majority of Union officers possessed very little military background, except a stint in the militia or with the volunteers in the Mexican War.

Perhaps Colonel William Shaw, Fourteenth Iowa, was typical as any. Educated in the Maine Wesleyan Seminary, Shaw served in the Second Kentucky Infantry during the Mexican War and remained in the Southwest as an adventurer, businessman, and sometimes Indian fighter. In 1849, he was a member of the first party to cross the desolate, trackless region between Santa Fe, New Mexico, and Fort Smith, Arkansas.[65]

Colonel Joseph Woods, Twelfth Iowa, was a West Point graduate, while Colonel Marcellus Crocker, Thirteenth Iowa, had spent two years at the Military Academy before ill health forced his resignation.[66] Colonel Hugh T. Reid, Fifteenth Iowa Infantry, was fifty years old and a graduate of Bloomington, Indiana, College. Immigrating to Iowa, he practiced law, frequently serving as district attorney for almost a quarter of a century before entering the U. S. Army in 1861 as a colonel of volunteers. Major, later Secretary of War, William Belknap of the same regiment possessed only a slightly more martial background. Born at

---

64 John McClernand to U. S. Grant, March 21, 1862, John A. McClernand Papers, Illinois State Historical Library. This transfer meant McClernand became army commander at Pittsburg when Grant was absent at the Cherry House headquarters in Savannah. Ambrose, *Halleck*, 44; Grenville Dodge, "Personal Recollections of General Grant and His Campaigns in the West," *A Paper Read by Major General Grenville K. Dodge, U. S. Volunteers, October 5, 1904* (Keokuk: 1904), 353.

65 Edith McElroy, *The Undying Procession: Iowa's Civil War Regiments* (Des Moines: The Iowa Civil War Centennial Commission, n.d.), 36.

66 Mildred Throne (ed.), "Iowa and the Battle of Shiloh," *The Iowa Journal of History* 55 (July 1957): 214.

Newburgh, New York, in 1829, Belknap later was graduated from Princeton College. He later practiced law in his adopted state of Iowa. Originally a Douglas Democrat, Belknap was converted to the Republican Party on the outbreak of the Civil War. While residing in Keokuk, he entered the local militia company, the City Rifles, which he rose to command. Partly due to a martial relationship with Colonel Reid and partly to his military training and political tie-ups, Belknap was commissioned major of the Fifteenth Iowa, November 1861.[67]

The Forty-third Illinois Regiment's position was a little different. Its colonel was Julius Raith, a German-American veteran of the Mexican War, in which he had commanded a company in the Second Illinois Volunteers. When the Civil War broke out Raith helped a prominent Illinois German-American, Gustave Koerner, organize a German regiment. Koerner soon severed his relationship with the regiment and Raith was appointed colonel by the governor of Illinois.

To serve as lieutenant colonel, Julius Raith called an old friend and comrade, Adolph Engelmann, a fifty-two year old native of Bavaria. Engelmann's family immigrated to America back in 1833, but the future Civil War officer remained behind to study jurisprudence in Heidelberg, Munich, and Jena. Becoming involved in a revolutionary plot at Frankfort, Germany, Engelmann was forced to flee to France and finally to the United States. In St. Louis, Missouri, he was admitted to the bar, and he earned a living as an attorney, notary, and realtor. In 1840, Engelmann moved to the predominantly German-American settlement of Belleville, Illinois. Lawyer, circuit clerk, and deputy, Engelmann enlisted as a second lieutenant in the Second Illinois Regiment on June 16, 1846. After being wounded at Buena Vista, Lieutenant Engelmann was honorably discharged on June 18, 1847. In the years after the war, Engelmann became known as one of the most important leaders of the large German elements in Illinois and as publisher of the Belleville *Zeitung*, the first prominent German newspaper in the state of Illinois. Adolph Engelmann held various political offices before 1861. His

---

67 William Belknap, *History of the 15th Regiment Iowa Veteran Volunteer Infantry, From October, 1861, to August, 1865* (Keokuk: R. B. Ogden and Son, 1887), 15-17, 20, 21.

appointment as lieutenant colonel of the German Forty-third Illinois Infantry helped solidify pro-Unionist feelings among the extremely large group of both first and second generation Germans in the state.[68]

Officers like Shaw, Reid, Belknap, Raith, and Engelmann usually performed fairly capably, but the presence of a large number of amateur soldiers was bound to cause some trouble. Some of the field officers were incapable of maintaining discipline with their men, while others spent too much time drinking or trying to curry favor with the politicians back home. Many officers, some of whom later turned out to be capable, were put under arrest at Pittsburg.

Colonel David Moore, Twenty-first Missouri, was one of the first officers to cross swords with General Grant's Regular Army idea of discipline. Moore was placed under arrest and tried for negligence at Savannah on March 28, but the court-martial board finally cleared him.[69] Scots-born ex-militia officer, Colonel John McArthur, commanding the Second Brigade of the Second Division, ran afoul of military justice and was immediately relieved of his duties. He would, however, be restored to his command on the morning of April 6, 1862, by General W. H. L. Wallace. Wallace and the other senior officers were kept busy running back and forth to Savannah to take in the numerous court-martial proceedings which arose at this time.[70]

It was not only the colonels who were getting into trouble, but the lower grades as well. Captain Joseph Shannon, Fourteenth Iowa, drank

---

68 War Department, Adjutant General's Office, Washington, D. C., February 3, 1932, "War Record of Colonel Adolph Engelmann," Adolph Engelmann Papers, Illinois State Historical Library. See also, Adolph Engelmann to sister, October 3, 1862, Engelmann-Kirchner Papers, Illinois State Historical Library; Belleville *Daily News Democrat*, March 9, 1889, Adolph Engelmann Papers, Illinois State Historical Library.

69 *OR* 10, pt. 2, 74.

70 Marion Morrison, *A History of the Ninth Regiment Illinois Volunteer Infantry* (Monmouth: John S. Clark, 1864), 29. Army gossip had it that McArthur drank too much. It is possible this unexpected arrest was related to his drinking habits. Throne, *Cyrus Boyd Diary*, 83-86. See W. H. L. Wallace to his wife, Ann, April 1, 1862, W. H. L. Wallace Papers, Illinois State Historical Library.

too much whiskey, and he tried to improperly unload some supplies at the Landing for his regiment without waiting for his turn. An Ohio field officer, recognizing that the Iowa captain was drunk, ordered Shannon placed under arrest, but the Iowan refused to submit, exclaiming that he was officer of the day. The real officer of the day rode up, and the besotted Shannon tried to arrest him. After a few rather confused minutes, Captain Shannon wound up under arrest and headed for a fast court-martial. Colonel Shaw intervened and was finally able to get the charge dropped before the matter reached headquarters.[71]

Another bad row developed between Lieutenant Colonel F. W. Ellis, Fifteenth Illinois, and Lieutenant Colonel Markoe Cummins, Sixth Iowa. Both regimental commanders espied a good camp site and both tried to claim it. The men had a public rhubarb over the spot, but Ellis eventually won the dispute and the Fifteenth Illinois claimed his prize.[72]

Actually good camping space was not particularly scarce. There was enough cleared to provide each regiment with an abundance of room for all its facilities. Each company was assigned five or six large tents, usually of the famous Sibley variety. The enlisted men lived in these, with the officers and noncoms bunking in extra tents. With the warm weather and early spring, camping out proved fairly pleasant. The only thing particularly bad was the frequent rains. The Tennessee River continued to rise, and much of the low ground around the Landing was submerged. All of the camp area stayed muddy, making it difficult for the unlucky soldiers to keep their boots and uniforms clean and dry. For some strange reason, the whole area was alive with turkey buzzards. Thousands of these ugly creatures winged their way around the camp area, especially near the Landing.[73]

71   B. F. Thomas, *Soldier Life*; Barber, *Army Memoirs*, 47, 48.

72   *Ibid.*, 48.

73   D. L. Ambrose, *History of the Seventh Regiment Illinois Volunteer Infantry* (Springfield: Illinois Journal Company, 1868), 47; Barber, *Army Memoirs*, 48; Franklin Bailey to parents, March 27, 1862, Franklin H. Bailey Papers, Historical Collections of the University of Michigan; Payson Shumway to wife, Hattie, March 27, April 1, 1862, Payson Z. Shumway Papers, Illinois State Historical Library.

Modern methods of sanitation were still in their infancy in the Civil War, and some of Grant's regiments suffered severely from disease, usually typhoid or some other ailment brought on by permitting the water supply to become polluted.[74] If the water was often bad, at least the weather was slowly improving. Orders came through for the men to pack up their heavy clothes and send them home. The steamers that carried their winter clothing to St. Louis and Paducah returned with much welcomed mail from home and of course the usual assortment of two-week-old newspapers, which the men devoured anyway.[75]

In their off duty time the Union soldiers sat under trees or inside their tents playing euchre, sledge, poker, and for the more intellectual minded, whist or reading, with the rain pattering the roofs of the tents. When the weather permitted, or the soldiers simply decided to go outside anyway, there were the interminable ball games in addition to running, jumping, and wrestling matches for the more strenuous minded.[76]

The food was fair, at least for those units blessed with competent cooks. One cavalry battalion boasted of its fine coffee and biscuits, but other units suffered from stomach ailments caused by inexperienced cooks. The Twenty-fifth Indiana Infantry dined on fried potatoes, meat, hash, rice, beans, hominy, pies, and biscuits. For the soldiers with an extra sweet tooth it was only necessary to visit one of the numerous sutlers camped about near the Landing who sold fruits, preserves, jelly, catsup, apple butter, and a host of other delicacies, and occasionally perhaps an unofficial shot of bad whiskey.[77]

---

74 Enoch Colby, Jr., "Shiloh," Misc. Coll., Shiloh National Military Park.

75 Austin S. Andrews to his father, March 26, 1862, Austin S. Andrews Papers, Illinois State Historical Library; Foster, *War Stories*, 60; Adolph Engelmann to his wife, Mina, March 31, 1862, Adolph Engelmann Papers, Illinois State Historical Library.

76 Barber, *Army Memoirs*, 50; Stillwell, *Common Soldier*, 35; T. W. Connelly, *History of the Seventieth Ohio Regiment, From Its Organization to Its Mustering Out* (Cincinnati: Peak Brothers, 1902), 9. Even the generals found time to carry out some friendly socializing. W. H. L. Wallace to his wife, Ann, April 1, 1862, Wallace-Dickey Papers, Illinois State Historical Library.

77 Charles Dickey to his sister, Ann Wallace, April 4, 1862, Wallace-Dickey Papers, Illinois State Historical Library; Foster, *War Stories*, 59, 60.

To men on such a pleasant regime, life seemed fairly enjoyable, if a little monotonous at times. The frequent company and battalion drills were no real hardship, while the numerous reviews by General Grant and the other big brass were looked on with some favor, as it gave the ordinary soldier a chance to see what a real live general looked like. The only fly in the ointment was that some of the regimental officers occasionally became somewhat carried away with their training schedules. Instead of carrying out the routine training exercises prescribed from above, some of them added little wrinkles of their own. The farm and small town boys of the Twenty-fifth Missouri were luckier than most, for they found themselves using a large tree for target practice with their rifles. Most of the men in the regiment were experienced small game hunters, but they soon discovered that shooting a heavy army rifle was a slightly different proposition. With pure Teutonic thoroughness, Colonel Raith, Forty-third Illinois, insisted on a rigid program of training with the bayonet. General McClernand personally watched his German-Americans go through their paces and complimented them on their skill with the wicked-looking steel blades.[78]

Each warm spring day faded into the next for the Union army at Pittsburg Landing. It was a time of training and anticipation. Within a few days these soldiers would strike their tents and move southward toward the little Mississippi town of Corinth. Then there would be one more big fight that would end the war, and the Union soldiers could all go home.

78 Ambrose, *Seventh Illinois*, 47; Payson Shumway Diary, March 26-April 2, 1862, Payson Shumway Papers, Illinois State Historical Library; Engelmann to his wife, Mina, March 31, 1862, Engelmann-Kirchner Papers, Illinois State Historical Library; Morton, " Opening of the Battle of Shiloh," 10.

The Union Leaders

Unless otherwise credited, all photos are courtesy of *Generals in Blue: Lives of the Union Commanders*

Brig. Gen. Jeremiah T. Boyle

Col. Jacob Ammen

Maj. Gen. Don Carlos Buell

Col. Ralph P. Buckland

Brig. Gen. Thomas L. Crittenden

Col. Marcellus Crocker

Brig. Gen. James A. Garfield

Maj. Gen. U. S. Grant

Col. William B. Hazen

Maj. Gen. Henry W. Halleck

Brig. Gen. Jacob G. Lauman

Brig. Gen. Stephen A. Hurlbut

Brig. Gen. John McArthur

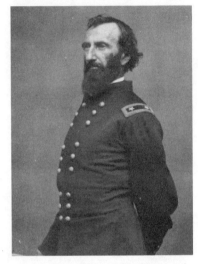

Brig. Gen. John A. McClernand

Brig. Gen. Alexander McD.
McCook

Lieut. Col. James B. McPherson

Brig. Gen. Benjamin M. Prentiss

Brig. Gen. William Nelson

Maj. Gen. William T. Sherman

Brig. Gen. Lovell H. Rousseau

Maj. Gen. Charles F. Smith

Col. Morgan L. Smith

Col. William Sooy Smith

Col. David Stuart

Col. John M. Thayer

Col. Thomas W. Sweeny

Miller's Photographic History

Col. James C. Veatch

Col. James M. Tuttle

Maj. Gen. Lew Wallace

Brig. Gen. W. H. L. Wallace

Chapter 6

The March to Shiloh

THE FIRST TWO WEEKS of the Union occupation of Pittsburg and Crump's Landing passed comparatively quietly. General U. S. Grant had orders to avoid trouble, and the Southerners were reluctant to start anything until they had enough strength available to finish it. But on the last day of March, small-scale skirmishing began. On Monday, Southern patrols applied pressure on advanced Union picket posts around Adamsville, Tennessee. General Lew Wallace sent out additional cavalry to protect his advanced posts, but Confederates abruptly attacked and routed the reinforcement party, wounding and capturing three members of the Fifth Ohio Cavalry. Lew Wallace simply wrote the affair off as a mere skirmish, but it did mark a new phase in military activities along the Union position. From now on, Confederate cavalry would increasingly take the offensive, probing Union positions and pinning down the Federal cavalry so as to deprive Grant's army of intelligence.[1]

While Lew Wallace's cavalry was being chased by the Southerners, General Grant was launching a little operation of his own. For some days, Union gunboats had been busy reconnoitering and occasionally bombarding Confederate positions near and in Eastport, Mississippi. On Monday, Grant directed General Sherman to carry out a reconnaissance in strength in the vicinity of the little Mississippi town. Two 12-pound howitzers from Captain Emil Munch's First Minnesota Battery were loaded on board the steamers *Empress* and *Tecumseh*. One hundred and fifty men of the Fifth Ohio Cavalry, under Major Elridge Ricker, and

---

1 *OR* 10, pt. 1, 78, 79.

detachments from the Fifty-seventh and Seventy-seventh Ohio Infantry Regiments also climbed on board the transports. General Sherman was eager to be off, but his orders were to wait for the gunboat *Cairo* to show up as escort. Finally about midnight, the tardy warship commanded by Lieutenant Nathaniel Bryant arrived. It was so late that Sherman decided to wait until daylight to jump off.[2]

About 6:00 a.m. Tuesday, the five vessels finally pulled out, the transports cautiously steaming about three hundred yards behind the *Lexington, Tyler,* and *Cairo*. About 1:00 p.m., the *Cairo* commenced shelling a suspected Confederate battery just above the mouth of Indian Creek. There was no return fire or any sign of activity whatever, so the expedition proceeded on up to Eastport. The *Lexington* and *Tyler* opened fire with their 8-inch and 32-pounders on the Confederate fortifications at that point. Then the *Cairo* joined in with her powerful battery of six 32-pounders, four 42-pound rifles, and three 8-inchers. Exploding shells gouged holes in the breastworks without eliciting any kind of reply. Finally it was obvious that the Southerners had abandoned the town.[3]

Sherman immediately ordered Colonel Jesse Hildebrand to disembark with the troops. The Union soldiers were quickly landed and the men deployed and moved into Eastport. Not a human being was in sight. Every man, woman, and child was gone, fled from the cannon fire. Many of the buildings were badly damaged by the effects of the bombardment, and some of Grant's soldiers noticed food and dinnerware still on the tables in several houses. Colonel Hildebrand led his force through the town and then out along the road to Iuka, Mississippi. A few hundred yards along the road, however, the Ohioans spotted a small Confederate patrol. The invaders quickly deployed for action, but the Southerners galloped off without firing to report the news of the Union landing.

---

2 || For a history of the *U.S.S. Cairo*, see Edwin C. Bearss, *Hardluck Ironclad: The Sinking and Salvage of the Cairo* (Baton Rouge: Louisiana State University Press, 1966).

3 *OR* 10, pt. 1, 83; R. R. Hancock, *Hancock's Diary or A History of the Second Tennessee Cavalry With Sketches of the First and Seventh Battalions* (Nashville: Brandon Printing Company, 1887), 138; *ORN* 22, 785.

While Colonel Hildebrand was carrying out his little reconnaissance, Sherman proceeded by transport on up to Chickasaw. Some soldiers of the Fifty-seventh Ohio were landed, but they could find no Confederates to fight. A little disgusted by the lack of resistance, General Sherman quickly ordered the landing party back to the transports and dropped back to Eastport, where he picked up Colonel Hildebrand and his force. On the whole, it was a pretty frustrating expedition, but at least it showed that the Southerners were not planning to hold either Eastport or Chickasaw. Perhaps Generals Grant and Sherman idly speculated as to where the Southern garrisons had gone, but if so, they did not seem to be worried by this minor proof of a possible build-up at Corinth.[4]

When General Sherman reported to General Grant that there were no Confederate troops in the area, the Union army commander began to think of the possibility of landing an expeditionary force near Eastport and striking inland to destroy the railroad tracks running into Corinth. Such a raid could wreck the Confederate transportation system without violating Henry Halleck's orders to avoid a battle. To discover the feasibility of such a mission, General Grant dispatched his trusted unofficial chief of staff, Colonel J. D. Webster, to personally look into the matter. On Thursday morning Webster boarded the *Tyler* for a personal reconnaissance up to the Eastport-Chickasaw area.

Returning to Savannah that afternoon, Colonel Webster reported to General Grant that the prospects for a sneak raid were not good. It was his contention that unless the Confederates were completely asleep, and it did not seem likely, an expedition to cut the Memphis and Charleston Railroad would have to fight its way through and back to accomplish its mission. Grant dropped the project. The Union army would not strike until Generals Halleck and Buell arrived. Presumably this would be only a matter of days. Telegraphic communications were already established between Savannah and Buell's army, and Nelson's division was expected in Savannah on Saturday.[5]

---

4 *OR* 10, pt. 1, 83, 84; Fleming, "The Battle of Shiloh As A Private Saw It," 134, 135.

5 *OR* 10, pt. 1, 84-86.

General Grant's only news of the enemy was from an occasional deserter. He did know they were massing at Corinth, but the natural assumption was that General Johnston was preparing to defend that place. Estimates of the Confederate strength varied from seventy-five to eighty thousand men.[6] Camp rumor at Pittsburg put the Southerners' strength at from forty-four thousand to eighty thousand men.[7]

Actually both camp rumor and General Grant's lowest estimate to General Halleck were about correct. The Confederate field army collected at Corinth and the nearby towns numbered about forty-one thousand effective troops. General Beauregard's official returns showed the army which marched out of Corinth on Thursday and Friday numbered 40,335 officers and men. There were 9,136 men in the First Army Corps, 13,589 in the Second Corps, 6,789 men in the Third Corps, with 6,439 in the Reserve Corps.[8]

Most of the Confederate army at Corinth, Mississippi, was completely green. Colonel George Maney's First Tennessee Infantry, actually only a battalion of five companies, had perhaps the most sophisticated experience of any Confederate outfit. Organized in May 1861, the regiment participated in General Robert E. Lee's Great Mountain campaign in Virginia in September. There had been no big battles, but the Tennesseans had drawn blood in a number of sanguinary skirmishes.[9] Colonel William B. Bate's Second Tennessee Infantry Regiment (Second Confederate Regiment, Walker's Legion) was mustered into the Confederate army in early May 1861. The regiment had been under Union gunfire at Aquia Creek, Virginia, on June 1, 1861.[10]

---

6   *Ibid.*, 10, pt. 2, 80, 94.

7   W. Wemple to J. D. Gillett, April, 1862, Gillett Family Papers, Illinois State Historical Library; Adolph Engelmann to his wife, Mina, March 25, 1862, Adolph Engelmann Papers, Illinois State Historical Library.

8   *OR* 10, pt. 1, 396. General Bragg's figures for the action are slightly at variance with Beauregard's. The chief of staff maintained that the army had only 39,598 officers and men as of April 3. *Ibid.*, 398.

9   Watkins, *Co. Aytch*, 20-39.

10   *OR* 2, 57-59.

Later in the month, a large number of the personnel of the regiment participated in an expedition down the Rappahannock River, resulting in the capture of the Federal vessels *Saint Nicholas*, *Halifax*, and *Mary of Virginia*. At First Manassas, the Second Tennessee was under fire, although not actively engaged. Lieutenant Colonel Calvin Venable's Fifth Tennessee Infantry had seen a small amount of action at New Madrid, Missouri, in early March 1862.[11] Five of General Johnston's regiments had been blooded at the Battle of Fishing Creek, Kentucky. These were the Fifteenth Mississippi, Sixteenth Alabama, and Nineteenth, Twentieth, and Twenty-eighth Tennessee.[12] The largest group of Confederate veterans came from the Belmont action. Colonel J. Knox Walker's Second Tennessee, along with the Twelfth, Thirteenth, Fifteenth, and One hundred and fifty-fourth Senior Tennessee had helped repulse Grant in this action. The latter unit was an old militia regiment dating back to 1854. When first organized in that year, the unit was designated Tennessee Militia 154. When Tennessee dropped the old militia system in 1859, members of the regiment took out a charter of incorporation from the state legislature which enabled them to retain their old number. Since it was the oldest Tennessee regiment in the Confederate army, Colonel Preston Smith asked for and received permission to use the word "Senior" in its official title.[13] The Thirteenth Arkansas and Eleventh Louisiana were also veterans of the desperate little Missouri battle. These were the only Confederate regiments with any kind of combat experience.

A few individual members of other regiments had taken part in raids or picket fights in Kentucky, Missouri, and Florida. Of the seventy-nine regiments and battalions in General Johnston's Army of the Mississippi, fourteen possessed at least some kind of combat experience. Personnel-wise, about fourteen per cent of the Confederate infantry could be classified as veterans. Several Confederate artillery batteries had also been engaged at Belmont or Fishing Creek, while about

11 *Tennesseans in the Civil War,* 1: 177, 185.

12 *OR* 7, 108.

13 *Tennesseans in the Civil War,* 1: 309.

one-third of the Confederate cavalry were veterans of Sacramento, Kentucky, Fort Donelson, or scattered skirmishes in the region.

Thirty of General Grant's regiments at Pittsburg Landing were veterans of the bloody Fort Donelson campaign: the Seventh, Eighth, Ninth, Eleventh, Twelfth, Seventeenth, Eighteenth, Twentieth, Twenty-ninth, Thirty-second, Forty-first, Forty-fifth, Forty-sixth, Forty-eighth, Fiftieth, Fifty-seventh, and Fifty-eighth Illinois; the Second, Twelfth, and Fourteenth Iowa; the Twenty-fifth, Thirty-first, and Forty-fourth Indiana; the Seventeenth and Twenty-fifth Kentucky; and the Thirteenth and Fourteenth Missouri. The Seventh Iowa had been not only in that action, but had won laurels at Belmont as well. The Third Iowa Infantry had taken part in the Battle of Blue Mills Landing, Missouri, on September 17, 1861, losing ninety-six casualties.[14] The Twenty-fifth Missouri had no battle stars on its flag, but most of the officers and enlisted men had fought in the siege at Lexington, Missouri, in September 1861.[15] The Seventeenth Illinois had fought not only at Donelson, but at Fredericktown, Missouri, where it suffered twenty-one killed or wounded in a fight with Confederate cavalry on October 21, 1861.[16] Several other infantry regiments had participated in skirmishes or picket fights in Missouri or Kentucky, but basically only thirty-two out of sixty-two infantry regiments at Pittsburg Landing had combat experience, or about one infantryman out of every two. About one-half of General Grant's batteries were also combat veterans, while the majority of his cavalry had been under fire at Fort Donelson or in skirmishes throughout the department. And of Grant's eleven infantry regiments stationed at Crump's Landing, seven were veterans of Donelson, and one, the Eleventh Indiana, had participated in numerous engagements in western Virginia as well as Fort Donelson.

In terms of experienced troops, General U. S. Grant possessed a considerable edge over his Southern opponents. The exact size of the Union army at Pittsburg Landing has been given as a variety of figures.

14 Byers, *Iowa in War Times*, 485.

15 Morton, "Opening of the Battle of Shiloh," 10.

16 George O. Smith, Brief History of the 17th Illinois Infantry, Manuscript, 1913, Illinois State Historical Library.

General Grant claimed he had thirty-three thousand effectives on the morning of April 6, 1862, but actually his command was considerably larger.[17] Grant's returns for April 5 show that he had 37,331 present for duty at Pittsburg. This figure included only about one-half of his field batteries. It included the Sixteenth Iowa Infantry, which was still on board a steamer tied up at the Landing.[18] But General Grant unwittingly omitted a number of infantry units which arrived at Pittsburg late Saturday night, April 5, 1862, or early Sunday morning. These units included the Fifteenth Michigan, Eighteenth Wisconsin, Fifteenth Iowa, and Twenty-third Missouri.[19]

General Grant's figures also excluded the newly arrived eight companies of the Eleventh Illinois Cavalry, the Fifth and Eighth Ohio Batteries, Batteries H and L, First Illinois Light Artillery, and B and F of the Second Illinois. The four infantry regiments were newly organized and in good shape physically, and they must have averaged at least eight hundred effectives per unit. The cavalry and batteries would have added at least a thousand more to the total, making a grand figure of about forty-two thousand effectives,[20] in addition to Lew Wallace's command, which numbered 7,564 effectives.[21] On April 6, General Grant also had at

17 Grant, *Memoirs*, 190.

18 *OR* 10, pt. 1, 112; D. W. Reed, *The Battle of Shiloh and the Organizations Engaged* (Washington, D. C.: Government Printing Office, 1902), 60.

19 *Ibid.*, 58-61; Throne, *Cyrus Boyd Diary*, 25.

20 *OR* 10, 2, 84.

21 *Ibid.*, 10, pt. 1, 112. Departmental returns show that on March 31, Grant had a total of 64,586, including Lew Wallace's command and the garrison at Savannah. He had 34,582 effectives at Pittsburg, 7,534 at Crump's, and 2,083 at Savannah. His sick list on March 31, numbered 9,459 for his entire command. It is unlikely that the ratio of sick and other absentees appreciably changed in the six days before April 6. On the morning of April 6, Grant's fighting strength was increased by the arrival of a number of personnel returning by steamer from leave at home. A considerable number of Federals on the regimental sick list gallantly rejoined their units and fought through the day. Mrs. W. H. L. Wallace to her Aunt Mag, April 29, 1862, Miscellaneous Collections, Shiloh National Military Park.

his disposal the brand new Fourteenth Wisconsin Infantry and the Forty-third Illinois Infantry, as well as detachments from several other units at Savannah.[22]

Excluding the Savannah garrison and Lew Wallace's command, Generals U. S. Grant and A. S. Johnston were just about evenly matched. Naturally the arrival of either Don Carlos Buell's or Earl Van Dorn's command would have completely changed the physical ratio.

As April opened, the Confederate army stood poised at Corinth, Mississippi. On Tuesday, April 1, General Johnston ordered the army to make preparations for an advance within twenty-four hours.[23]

For some reason, the army did not move out on the following day, and preparations were not fully carried out in most units. But sometime during Wednesday, Colonel Nathan Bedford Forrest brought the Confederate command the news that General Buell was rapidly approaching Grant's base at Savannah.[24]

Even while General Johnston was mulling over the news of Buell's movement, Brigadier General B. F. Cheatham, commanding at Bethel Station, sent an urgent dispatch to General Polk saying that part of the Union army was advancing toward Bethel. About 10:00 p.m., Polk forwarded the dispatch on to General Beauregard, who believing the enemy's force was divided, sent it on to General Johnston with the recommendation, "Now is the moment to advance, and strike the enemy at Pittsburg Landing."[25] Colonel Thomas Jordan, Adjutant General of the Army of the Mississippi, personally delivered the message, and after a few minutes discussion, General Johnston gave his authorization for the

22   Byron Abernethy (ed.), *Private Elisha Stockwell, Jr. Sees the Civil War* (Norman: The University of Oklahoma Press, 1958), 11-13; Daniel Harmon Brush to his father, April 6, 1862, Daniel Harmon Brush Papers, Illinois State Historical Library.

23   *OR* 10, pt. 2, 381. For several days at least some Confederate elements had been under order to be ready for an offensive push. A. H. Mecklin Diary, March 29, 1862, Mississippi Department of Archives and History.

24   Wyeth, *That Devil Forrest*, 60.

25   Roman, *Beauregard*, 1: 270-272.

offensive.[26] General Johnston immediately wired President Jefferson Davis of the decision to attack, saying, "General Buell is in motion, 30,000 strong, rapidly from Columbia . . . to Savannah." General Johnston went on to say that with 40,000 men, he was going "forward to offer battle near Pittsburg."[27]

To General Beauregard, General A. S. Johnston assigned the task of preparing the orders to advance. Colonel Jordan was ordered to draw up a brief notice to the corps commanders. By 1:40 a.m. Thursday morning Generals Hardee, Polk, and Bragg were all notified.[28] It was General Beauregard's idea, and General Johnston undoubtedly supported it, to cover most of the twenty-two mile march on Thursday and assault General Grant on Friday, April 4.[29]

Pittsburg Landing was about twenty-five miles from Corinth, while Generals Sherman's and Prentiss' divisions were encamped about twenty-two miles away. But many of General Johnston's units were scattered around Northern Mississippi. Cheatham's Division was at

26   Thomas Jordan and Richard Pryor, *The Campaigns of Lieut.-General N. B. Forrest, and of Forrest's Cavalry* (New Orleans: Blelock and Company, 1868), 108. In later accounts of the Battle of Shiloh, written many years after the war, Jordan intimates that General Johnston was unenthusiastic about the proposed offensive, and that it was only his strong urging to the general which resulted in the affirmative decision. Jordan was undoubtedly sincere in his belief, but he was probably reading something into Johnston's natural concern, which was simply not there. *Battles and Leaders*, 1: 594, 595; Thomas Jordan, "The Campaign of Shiloh," 270. If Johnston hesitated, it is perfectly understandable. Despite the work of the past two weeks, the army was still only partially trained and incompetently supplied with materials. J. C. Breckinridge to Braxton Bragg, April 1, 1862, William Palmer Collection, Western Reserve Historical Collection, Western Reserve Library; A. H. Mecklin Diary, March 28, 1862, Mississippi Department of Archives and History.

27   *OR* 10, pt. 2, 387.

28   Jordan, "The Campaign of Shiloh," 270, 271.

29   *OR* 10, pt. 2, 393; P. G. T. Beauregard to William Preston Johnston, March 9, 1877, Mrs. Mason Barret Papers, Howard-Tilton Memorial Library, Tulane University. Many of the accounts of the Battle of Shiloh say the Confederates planned to attack on Saturday. For a refutation of this see Williams, *P. G. T. Beauregard*, 393; Roland, *Albert Sidney Johnston*, 320.

Bethel, with part of its troops scattered as far as Purdy.[30] More of the army was located in Burnsville or scattered out in camps around Corinth. To get these scattered commands in motion toward Pittsburg Landing was a much more frustrating and difficult task than General Beauregard or Johnston at first anticipated. A year later in the war the Confederate army could have made such a concentration and march in one day, but in April 1862, the Southerners simply lacked the necessary experience. The initial Friday attack was very quickly if unofficially canceled, and the target date moved up to Saturday.

The army was to move along two narrow country roads toward Pittsburg Landing, the Ridge and Monterey roads. Both of these roads were connected together by other country roads in several places before they converged about five miles from the Landing. The Confederate army was to concentrate at Mickey's farmhouse, which lay about five miles from Shiloh Church. Cheatham's Division from Bethel was to join with Polk's Corps on the line of march, while Breckinridge's Corps would link up at Mickey's.[31]

It was a fairly simple plan of approach, but everything went wrong. General Hardee's Corps was to proceed first along the Ridge Road, followed by General Polk; but through some mix-up, the Bishop's troops and wagons became entangled in the streets of Corinth, blocking General Hardee's efforts to march out of town. It was well into Thursday afternoon before the tail end of the Third Corps finally weaved its way out of Corinth. Hardee's men bivouacked on the Ridge Road midway to Mickey's, not reaching the farmhouse until late in the morning. The Second Corps did even worse. Most of General Bragg's men were fairly well trained, but the North Carolina-born commander was inexperienced in conducting a large scale troop movement in the field. By noon Friday, the Second Corps was only at Monterey, Tennessee, only a little over half

30 J. C. Breckinridge to Braxton Bragg, April 1, 1862, William Palmer Collection, Western Reserve Historical Collection, Western Reserve Library; W. M. Polk, "Facts Connected with the Concentration of the Army of the Mississippi Before Shiloh, April, 1862," *Southern Historical Society Papers* 8 (January-December 1880): 457.

31 William Edwards, "Shiloh, The Counter Stroke That Failed," *The Quartermaster Review* 15 (No. 4 1936): 33; *OR* 10, pt. 1, 392-397.

way to the rendezvous. The Reserve Corps only pulled out of Burnsville, Mississippi, at 3:00 a.m. Friday morning.[32]

Inexperienced commanders and faulty staff work had ruined any possibility of a Friday attack. Finally, around 5:00 p.m. April 4, General Johnston met with Generals Bragg and Beauregard in a conference at Monterey. The attack was reset for Saturday morning, April 5.[33] General Albert S. Johnston's concern over the slowness of the movement was intense, but he remained rather quiet during the day. In speaking to a staff officer, he allowed his emotions to show for a moment when he said he was going "to hit Grant, and hit him hard."[34]

All of the senior officers in the Confederate army were still confident of victory, although General Beauregard did express one foreboding thought. He remarked, "In the struggle tomorrow we shall be fighting men of our own blood, Western men, who understand the use of firearms. The struggle will be a desperate one."[35]

General Johnston was accompanied by a numerous staff, many of whom lacked professional knowledge. It included Captain H. P. Brewster, Captain Nathaniel Wickliffe, Captain Theodore O'Hara, acting inspector general; Lieutenant George Baylor, and Lieutenant Thomas Jack, aide-de-camp; Colonel William Preston, acting as a volunteer aide, as did Major D. M. Hayden; Major Albert Smith, and Captain W. L. Wickham. General Johnston was also accompanied by a number of civilian aides, including Governor Isham Harris of Tennessee, Edward W. Munford, and Calhoun Benham. General Beauregard included on his staff Colonel Thomas Jordan, Captain Clifton H. Smith, and Lieutenant John M. Otley of the adjutant general's department.

---

32 Johnston, *Life of Gen. Albert Sidney Johnston*, 558, 559; Roman, *Beauregard*, 1: 272-276; Jordan, "The Campaign of Shiloh," 272. For some interesting sidelights on the Confederate quartermaster department's problems, see E. B. Carruth, "Disagreeable Experiences in War Times," *Confederate Veteran* 16 (August 1908): 408.

33 Roland, *Albert Sidney Johnston*, 319.

34 George Baylor, "With Gen. A. S. Johnston at Shiloh," *Confederate Veteran* 5 (December 1897): 609.

35 *Ibid.*

Major George W. Brent assisted General Beauregard as acting inspector general. Colonel R. B. Lee was in charge of assisting with commissary problems. General Beauregard's aide-de-camps were Lieutenant Colonel S. W. Ferguson, Lieutenant A. R. Chisolm, Colonel Jacob Thompson (former Secretary of the Interior), Major Numa Augustin, Major H. E. Peyton, Captain Albert Ferry, and Captain B. B. Waddell. Thomas Jordan and S. N. Ferguson, and a few others, had professional military backgrounds, but for the most part, the members of the two staffs were just beginning to learn about the business of war.

If the staff of the army was not working smoothly, many of the field officers were doing even worse. General Beauregard had ordered the troops to be issued five days' rations, which should have been plenty for the proposed campaign, but unfortunately there were problems connected with this. The rations had to be cooked by the troops, and some of the more inept soldiers managed to spoil all or part of their food. In the Twenty-second Alabama, most of the food did not arrive until the regiment was ready to push off. The men only had time to cook up two days' supply. The rest was loaded on board a wagon and sent off along with the unit. Unfortunately, a clumsy driver turned the wagon over in the mud, thoroughly ruining all of the food. The four hundred members of the regiment were forced to tighten their belts several extra notches. In good army fashion many of the Rebels promptly devoured their rations in the first twenty-four or thirty-six hours of the march.[36]

The roads were already thoroughly muddy from rains during the past night, but on Friday night, as the half-hungry Confederate army tried to settle down, the heavens literally seemed to burst open. Most of the soldiers lacked tents, and they were quickly soaked to the bone by the cold rain. A blistering north wind added to their misery by blowing the stinging drops of water into their faces. To add to the gloominess of the night, it suddenly began to hail. Lumps as big as musket balls pelted the

---

36 Peak, "A Southern Soldier's View of the Civil War," Frank Peak Papers, Louisiana State University Archives; A. H. Mecklin Diary, April 3, 1862, Mississippi Department of Archives and History; Roman, "Memoirs of Shiloh," Confederate Collections, Tennessee Department of Archives and History; Hugh Henry to his parents, April 10, 1862, Shiloh-Corinth Collection, Alabama Department of Archives and History.

already weary soldiers with staccato like frequency.[37] Most of the soldiers carried a blanket or even two, but they quickly became soaked. A very few officers and enlisted men owned non-regulation gum coats or water proofed tarpaulins. These were the exceptions. The weather Thursday night might have been severe, but Friday night it was even worse. By dawn most of the Confederate army was in good shape to visit a pneumonia ward.[38]

The next morning, Saturday, conditions along the line of march were chaotic. A heavy drizzle continued to harass the cold, exhausted soldiers, most of whom had not been able to get any sleep. Every step was like filing through quicksand. In General Bragg's Corps, the infantry stumbled along in foot-deep mud. Finally about midday, the rain stopped, giving the weary men a little respite.[39] General Hardee's soldiers moved as fast as they could, but it was the middle of the morning before they were drawn up in order of battle about two miles from the Union army's camp area.[40]

Discipline was pretty shaky in the Confederate army. Members of Colonel John Wharton's Eighth Texas Cavalry were riding around in the slush, firing their shotguns and revolvers at trees or stumps, or at an occasional rabbit. Many soldiers shot their guns off into the air just to see if they would still work in the dampness. A poor frightened deer suddenly

37 Micajah Wilkinson to his brother, April 16, 1862, Louisiana State University Archives; Lemuel A. Scarborough Journal, April 4, 1862, Miscellaneous Collections, Shiloh National Military Park.

38 A. H. Mecklin Diary, April 4, 1862, Mississippi Department of Archives and History; Samuel Latta to wife, April 10, 1862, Confederate Collection, Tennessee Department of Archives and History; Hugh Henry to parents, April 10, 1862, Shiloh-Corinth Collection, Alabama Department of Archives and History; Thomas Chinn Robertson to mother, April 9, 1862, Thomas C. Robertson Papers, Louisiana State University Archives.

39 Micajah Wilkinson to brother, April 16, 1862, Micajah Wilkinson Papers, Louisiana State University Archives.

40 Thomas Jordan said the last of Hardee's troops did not move into position until just before 3:00 p.m. Jordan, "The Campaign of Shiloh," 273.

ran from a thicket, and hundreds of Confederate soldiers, spying the nervous beast, let go a tremendous war whoop.[41]

About noon some troops from the First and Second Corps began to straggle into the deployment area, including many of the artillery units that had not left Corinth until Friday morning.[42] General Bragg's Corps was still not all in position. In fact a whole division was lost somewhere along the Monterey Road. At last General Johnston lost his patience with General Bragg. "This is perfectly puerile!" he exclaimed, "This is not war! Let us have our horses."[43] Accompanied by part of his staff, General Johnston rode back along the road to find that some of General Polk's wagons and artillery had blocked the missing division off. The Confederate commander and his subordinates finally managed to get the traffic jam unsnarled, but it was about 4:00 p.m. in the afternoon.[44]

There was no possibility for an offensive on Saturday. To attack with only the part of the army that was deployed was to invite disaster. Indeed it was increasingly becoming a moot question if the army should attack at all. The success of the Confederate plan depended in a large part on achieving at least strategic surprise over General Grant. If the Federals were alerted and massed behind fortifications at Pittsburg, then the Southern chances for victory were practically nil. After three days of troop movements in the field, it was quite possible that the Federals were on the alert. Even more serious was the danger that General Grant's soldiers had heard the Confederates firing their guns off and yelling. The most dangerous possibility of them all however, was that the Union army

41 Baylor, "With Gen. Albert Sidney Johnston at Shiloh;" Roland, *Albert Sidney Johnston*, 319.

42 S. H. Dent to his wife, April 9, 1862, Shiloh-Corinth Collections, Alabama Department of Archives and History; Peak, "A Southern Soldier's View of the Civil War," Frank Peak Papers, Louisiana State University Archives; Hugh Henry to his parents, April 10, 1862, Shiloh-Corinth Collection, Alabama Department of Archives and History.

43 Edward Munford, "Albert Sidney Johnston," Mrs. Mason Barret Papers, Howard-Tilton Memorial Library, Tulane University.

44 Roland, *Albert Sidney Johnston*, 320.

had been tipped off by the increasingly heavy skirmishing near the Federal camp.

Just before dawn on Thursday morning Colonel James H. Clanton's First Alabama Cavalry lost a minor argument with General Grant's cavalry. Clanton's Alabamans were placed around Pittsburg Landing to keep an eye on Northern movements. General Sherman decided on Wednesday to try and pick up some prisoners from the Confederates for the sole purpose of intelligence. Colonel William Taylor, with a force of Fifth Ohio Cavalry, was assigned the task of making the sweep. Just after midnight the Ohioans pulled out of Pittsburg. A Doctor Parkes (or Parker), who lived near the Landing, spotted Taylor's force and rode off to warn Clanton's picket post. About six miles from Pittsburg, Taylor's men stumbled upon a Confederate picket post of nine men. There was a wild exchange of shots, and the Southerners quickly mounted their horses and galloped off. The Ohioans fired pretty wildly in the murky predawn haze, but they managed to wound one Alabaman, and they bagged a Private Lammon. The raiders continued on down the Corinth Road, stumbling upon Doctor Parkes, who was busily engaged in alerting the other picket posts. With his two prisoners, Colonel Taylor broke off the expedition and returned to the Landing.[45]

The early morning skirmish of April 3 was only an opener. Early Friday morning Confederate scouts shot up a company of the Sixth Iowa Infantry on guard along the Purdy Road beyond Owl Creek. Private Charles Statton was the only Union casualty. One Johnny Reb shot Statton through the hand, and a surgeon was later forced to amputate one of his fingers. There were no more casualties on either side, as the cavalrymen quickly rode away.[46]

On April 4, General Sherman's soldiers managed to pick a pretty good firefight with the advance elements of the Confederate army. On Friday, Colonel Ralph Buckland took his Fourth Brigade out on a training exercise, in accordance with orders from his divisional commander General W. T. Sherman. The Ohio brigade marched out

45 *OR* 10, pt. 1, 86, 87.

46 Henry Wright, *A History of the Sixth Iowa Infantry*, (Iowa City: Torch Press, 1923), 76, 68.

along the Corinth Road about three or four miles. Colonel Buckland decided to give his regimental commanders a little time to drill their units before returning to camp at Shiloh Church. About 2:30 p.m., Buckland heard scattered small arms fire and yells from about where he had posted a picket post of the Seventieth Ohio. The brigade commander ordered Major LeRoy Crockett to end the training exercise and swing his Seventy-second Ohio around for a sweep in the direction of the noise. While the infantry prepared to move, Colonel Buckland galloped on ahead to find out what was going on. He found out, and the news was all bad. Lieutenant W. H. Herbert and six enlisted men of the Seventieth Ohio had been overrun and captured by Confederate cavalry, Clanton's First Alabama. The colonel ordered Lieutenant John Geer to ride back and notify General Sherman of the incident. As Geer galloped off, a courier from Major Crockett came up with the information that the Federal officer had deployed his Company B to swing way right of the picket post in the hope of engaging the enemy. Colonel Buckland sent word to Major Crockett to send Company H out to reinforce Company B.

These troop movements consumed a good bit of time, and Lieutenant Geer returned with the word that General Sherman was sending out a battalion of the Fifth Ohio Cavalry, under Major Ricker. It was Colonel Buckland's understanding that Major Crockett would return to camp as soon as he completed his swing, unless of course he ran into strong enemy opposition. There was no noise to indicate any such happening, so Colonel Buckland took the rest of his brigade on back to Shiloh Church. At the camp Buckland nervously waited for Major Crockett to show up. Eight companies of the Seventy-second came on in, but there was no sign of Crockett and Companies B and H. Long minutes passed, and then Colonel Buckland's ears began picking up the sounds of small arms fire. Rounding up a hundred men from Companies A, D, and I of the Seventy-second Ohio, he headed back to find his wayward men.[47]

A short distance beyond the Jack Chalmers' plantation Colonel Buckland encountered some soldiers from Company H, who excitedly told him that the two companies had become separated and that Major Crockett was probably captured by enemy cavalry. Stumbling through

47 *OR* 10, pt. 1, 90, 91.

the mud, the relief party moved faster toward the continuing sound of gunfire, oblivious to the heavy rainfall which had just started. Rounding a bend in the Bark Road, Colonel Buckland could see his Bluecoats engaged in a hot fire fight with a party of Confederates. Buckland's relief party raked the First Alabama with a heavy burst of musket fire. The Rebels quickly fell back to an open field where they could reform. The pugnacious Colonel Buckland started forming his own men up for a pursuit when Major Ricker and his cavalry arrived. [48]

In response to General Sherman's call, Major Ricker had reported to Fifth Division headquarters. "Cump" Sherman directed the major to take his battalion out and discover the fate of the missing Herbert and his men. Within a few minutes the major had rounded up one hundred and fifty of his troopers and was en route to the trouble spot. About 3:30, the Ohioans reached Sherman's outpost on the Corinth-Pittsburg Road. From the officer in charge, Major Ricker learned that Colonel Buckland and his relief party had passed by sometime before. Ricker could hear gunfire, and he decided to try to envelop the enemy force that was fighting with Colonel Buckland. He sent part of his force out along the Bark Road, while with half of his men he rode on a flanking movement, designed to come in at the point where the noise indicated the enemy's flank rested. The troopers found that Colonel Buckland and his infantry had the situation safely under control.

Colonel Buckland decided to attack the Southerners, and he led his command forward in a sort of slow charge. The Alabamans fell back for a quarter of a mile, to behind the brow of a hill. As Major Ricker's men followed them over the hill, they suddenly ran into stiff Confederate artillery fire.[49]

Notified that Clanton had run into an enemy force, Major General Hardee ordered Brigadier General Pat Cleburne to deploy his infantry brigade to cover the Bark Road and the approach to Mickey's. Cleburne's infantry fanned out across the road, while Captain John T. Trigg unlimbered his battery of two 6-pound smoothbores and two 12-pound howitzers. The guns were sighted in to command the top of the hill. As

48   *Ibid.*

49   *Ibid.*, 89-92.

Clanton's men frantically rode over the rise in the ground and scattered to the sides, the Arkansas gunners braced themselves. When Major Ricker's men galloped over a few yards behind them, Trigg's four guns roared. The Southerners made a bad mistake, however, in not waiting until the Ohioans' momentum carried them out into the open where they would have been an easy mark. The sudden detonation of the big guns provided a rather spectacular, if harmless, effect on the Union cavalry. Several of Major Ricker's soldiers' inexperienced mounts went completely berserk, carrying their startled riders in all directions. One unruly horse headed straight in the direction of Pat Cleburne's infantry. His gallant rider quickly drew his revolver and pistoled down a Confederate soldier. The Southern infantry instantly riddled the daring Northern trooper with a spray of musket balls. Major Ricker and the other Federal soldiers quickly rode away, rejoining Colonel Buckland to the rear. The two field officers decided to return to camp and report the situation to General Sherman. They carried back with them two badly wounded Federals and nine bewildered Confederate troopers of the First Alabama Cavalry.[50]

Back at his Shiloh Church headquarters, General Sherman heard the sound of Captain Trigg's cannon. Realizing Colonel Buckland and Major Ricker might be in trouble, he took two of his infantry regiments out along the Corinth-Pittsburg Road to the Bark Road junction, where he found his missing flock. The total losses for the Federal army were Major Crockett and Lieutenants Geer and Herbert, and nine other Federals captured, eight men wounded, and one man killed.[51]

---

50 *Ibid.*, 91-93; W. D. Pickett, *Sketch of the Military Career of William J. Hardee, Lieutenant-General, C. S. A.* (Lexington: James E. Hughes, Printer, N. d.), 8; F. A. Shoup, "The Art of War in '62—Shiloh" *United Service: A Monthly Review of Military and Naval Affairs* 11 (July 1884): 62. Some of General Cleburne's Southerners gave the dead Federal an honorable burial just off the side of the road before night fell. Pickett, *Sketch of the Military Career of William J. Hardee*, 9.

51 *OR* 10, pt. 1, 90, 91. Colonel Clanton, himself, took Major Crockett in as prisoner. Shoup, "The Art of War," 3; J. J. Geer, *Beyond the Lines: or A Yankee Prisoner Loose in Dixie* (Philadelphia: J. W. Dauyhaday, 1863), 15-28; Mildred Throne, "Letters from Shiloh," *The Iowa Journal of History* 52 (July 1954): 241.

A little past 5:00 p.m. in the afternoon, the Federal prisoners were brought into Confederate headquarters, where Generals Johnston, Beauregard, and Bragg were conferring. Lieutenant Colonel J. F. Gilmer and Colonel Thomas Jordan personally interrogated Major Crockett and the other Federals. On the basis of the information gleaned from the prisoners, Jordan and Gilmer reported to Generals Johnston and Beauregard that the enemy was apparently still completely unprepared for an attack.[52]

Over at the Union camp, the Federals still seemed unconcerned over Major Ricker's and Colonel Buckland's collision with the Confederates, although General Sherman was quite irritated with the colonel for becoming involved with the Southerners against orders.

General Grant had other things on his mind than a skirmish with the enemy. While he was riding back from investigating the Buckland and Ricker affair, just before darkness fell, the commanding general's horse lost his footing in the mud and went down, rolling over the general's leg. Grant's ankle bone was bruised so severely that it was necessary for the boot to be cut off. For the next day or so, the army commander would have to hobble around on a pair of crutches.[53]

If Generals Grant and Sherman did not seem particularly interested in what was going on at the front, some of the Federal soldiers around Pittsburg Landing were becoming a little nervous at the slowly increasing signs of enemy activity. The Twenty-fifth Missouri Infantry Regiment picked up a couple of Southern civilians prowling through the regimental camps. The two unwelcomed intruders boldly proclaimed that they were hunting cattle, but the rank and file of the Federal army insisted upon considering them as spies. After an investigation, the two fellows were finally released.[54]

---

52 Jordan, "The Campaign and Battle of Shiloh," 272, 275; Throne, "Letters from Shiloh," 241.

53 *Campaigns in Tennessee and Kentucky*, 115, 116; General W. H. L. Wallace to his wife, Ann, April 6, 1862, W. H. L. Wallace Papers, Illinois State Historical Library; Grant, *Memoirs*, 172; Jordan, "The Campaign and Battle of Shiloh," 272, 273; Throne, "Letters from Shiloh," 241.

54 Morton, "The Opening of the Battle of Shiloh," 11, 12.

On the following day, Saturday, April 5, there were more alarms in the Federal camp. A rumor was steadily circulating that General Albert Sidney Johnston was about to launch a surprise attack; however, most of the Federals simply laughed off the idea as being rather ridiculous.[55]

Apparently Major General John A. McClernand picked up some of the general nervousness floating around the Federal camps, for just after lunch, he ordered a cavalry party out to reconnoiter in the direction of Hamburg for a short distance. The troopers, however, did not go far enough or even in the right direction to find the Confederates.[56]

Out on General Sherman's picket line, Captain W. B. Mason of the Seventy-seventh Ohio, suggested to Sergeant C. J. Eagler and Private Samuel Tracey that the three might take a walk beyond the picket line to relieve the monotony. After a quarter of a mile beyond the divisional picket line, the three men reached an open field, from where they could see in the distance a strong force of Confederate infantry and artillery. Captain Mason ordered Sergeant Eagler to report to regimental headquarters what they had seen. Back at Shiloh Church, Eagler found Major D. B. Fearing and told him the news. The major told Eagler to go back to the picket post with the assurance that the matter would go to General Sherman at once. When Major Fearing informed Sherman, the general exploded. He ordered Sergeant Eagler placed under arrest for spreading a false alarm, although Captain Mason managed to protect his sergeant.[57]

The incident attracted Colonel Hildebrand, who immediately went out to find out what was going on. Mason explained that besides observing the Confederate camp he had also seen Confederate cavalry in the distance, as well as numerous rabbits and squirrels running about, aggravated by what obviously was some large scale movement. Colonel Hildebrand even saw Confederate infantry's shiny musket barrels in the

---

55   Ambrose, *History of the Seventh Illinois*, 48.

56   General John A. McClernand to General U. S. Grant, April 5, 1862, John A. McClernand Papers, Illinois State Historical Library; Morton, "The Opening of the Battle of Shiloh," 11, 12.

57   Fleming, "The Battle of Shiloh As A Private Saw It," 136, 137; *Campaigns in Kentucky and Tennessee*, 115, 116.

distance himself. The sixty-two year old ex-militia officer quickly saw the light, and he returned to Shiloh Church to inform General Sherman. Unfortunately the Fifth Division's commander refused to believe that the Confederates were anything more than a reconnoitering party.

Colonel Buckland personally visited several picket posts during the day, and he observed Confederate cavalry in the distance. Some of his soldiers on guard reported occasionally catching glimpses of enemy artillery and infantry moving in the distance. About noon a Confederate patrol probed one of Colonel Hildebrand's outposts, and Privates Sam Dillon and Dave Brown, Company A, Seventy-seventh Ohio, fired at them. The Southerners fired a few shots in reply before riding away.[58]

Colonel Jesse Appler was drilling his Fifty-third Ohio in an open field near the divisional camp when he observed a party of Southern horsemen perhaps half a mile away. He immediately dispatched a company to engage the Confederates. The Ohioans were unable to catch the troopers but followed them until they were fired upon by several Confederate infantrymen, pickets of General Hardee's Corps. None of the Yanks were hit, but when they reported to Colonel Appler what had happened, the colonel ordered Lieutenant J. W. Fulton to go tell General Sherman. In a little while Fulton returned with the general's reply, "Tell Colonel Appler to take his damned regiment to Ohio. There is no force of the enemy nearer than Corinth."[59]

Farther down the line the Sixth Division was going through a review. A rumor, later confirmed, ran through the ranks that there were Confederate cavalry watching the men drill from less than a half mile away. Colonel Everett Peabody's brigade adjutant, Captain George Donnelly, openly told the enlisted personnel and junior officers to get ready for a fight for the army was about to be attacked. The troops were told to sleep with their rifles and cartridges ready at hand.[60] Colonel Peabody was fully in accord with Captain Donnelly's opinion, and he tried to persuade General Prentiss that an attack was eminent; however, the divisional commander was skeptical.

---

58 *Ibid.*, 116, 117; Fleming, "The Battle of Shiloh As A Private Saw It," 137.

59 *Campaigns in Kentucky and Tennessee*, 116, 117.

60 Morton, "A Boy at Shiloh," 58.

Oblivious to the increasing menace, General Grant wired General Buell on Saturday that the Confederates were still in Corinth, Mississippi, and to his superior, he wrote the same day that the "main force of the enemy is at Corinth."[61] Untroubled, Sherman dropped General Grant a line in the early afternoon, commenting that "all is quiet along my lines now. . ... The enemy has cavalry in our front, and I think there are two regiments of infantry and one battery of artillery about 2 miles out."[62] Later in the day Sherman optimistically informed General Grant that he felt sure "nothing will occur to-day more than some picket firing." He claimed to have given the Southerners the worst of it Friday, maintaining that this would discourage any aggressiveness on their part. "I will not be drawn out far unless with certainty of advantage," he went on to say, "and I do not apprehend anything like an attack on our position."[63]

As darkness descended on the camp area, pickets reported to Lieutenant Colonel William H. Graves, Twelfth Michigan, that they could hear movements in the distance. The colonel promptly went to Prentiss' headquarters to report, and he was told that he "need not be at all alarmed, that everything was alright."[64]

During the day, the prisoners from the First Alabama told any and every Northerner who spoke to them that in a few hours the Union army would be destroyed, because the Confederates were about to strike. Most of the curious Federals who spoke to the prisoners passed the matter off as Rebel brag, but far more serious was the situation of one of the Alabamans, who actually was dying of his wounds. The mortally wounded Confederate was friendly with some of Colonel Hildebrand's relatives, and he expressed a desire to talk to the colonel. The dying man told Hildebrand the Union army would be attacked and surely destroyed within twelve hours. Leaving the dying Confederate, the old colonel

61 *OR* 10, pt. 2, 94.

62 *Ibid.*, 93.

63 *Ibid.*, 94.

64 John Robertson, *Michigan in the War*, (Lansing: W. S. George and Company, 1882), 325.

trudged over to General Sherman's headquarters, but the general laughed the matter off. Untroubled by any sense of danger, Sherman soon retired for the night.[65]

Crippled by his Friday accident, General Grant remained in Savannah. One unpleasant thought intruded on his relaxation, however. Although confident that Johnston would not assault Pittsburg, Grant felt that the Southerners might hazard a sudden descent on Lew Wallace's isolated Third Division at Crump's Landing. To prepare for such an eventuality, Grant ordered his Second Division to stand by to move out to Crump's in the event of a Southern onslaught.[66]

*   *   *

As Grant, Sherman, and the other Union generals settled down for the night, the Southerners were making their final preparations for their attack, which would come early Sunday morning. By late afternoon all of the Confederate army was in position across the Bark Road, the advance elements within a little more than a mile of the Union picket posts. After the confusion and delay of the march, many of the Southern soldiers considered the element of surprise gone. General Beauregard remarked, "Now they will be entrenched to the eyes."[67]

The Creole wished to cancel the attack and return to Corinth. Bragg joined in with the Louisianan, claiming the two days' delay, added to the

65 *Campaigns in Kentucky and Tennessee*, 115.

66 Grant, *Memoirs*, 172, 173; *OR* 10, pt. 2, 91; Lew Wallace to W. H. L. Wallace, April 5, 1862, W. H. L. Wallace Papers, Illinois State Historical Library; D. W. Wood, *History of the 20th Ohio Veteran Volunteer Infantry Regiment from 1861-1865*, (Columbus: Paul and Thrall Book and Job Printers, 1876), 16. Grant made no effort to re-deploy his troops at Pittsburg, as he certainly would have done if he suspicioned an attack. Sherman's and Prentiss' divisions, the two least experienced in the army, were left out in front with a gap between them, while the three comparatively veteran units remained far to the rear. One of Sherman's four brigades, the Second, under Colonel Stuart, was isolated from the division, as its camp was on the extreme left of the Union Army.

67 Roland, *Albert Sidney Johnston*, 323.

poor condition of many of the troops, were too great handicaps to be overcome by an assault now. There was some question as to the size of the Federal force. Colonel Thomas Jordan maintained it numbered less than twenty-five thousand men and twelve batteries. Other officers added comments about the situation, but General Johnston ended all discussions. Maintaining that the Federals were probably unsuspecting, he stated it would be far worse to turn back without fighting than to risk a battle. After the recent disasters in Kentucky and Tennessee, the army must recoup the situation. He added, "We shall attack at daylight tomorrow" and as he walked off, he remarked, "I would fight them if they were a million."[68]

Major General Hardee's Third Army Corps was first in the line of the night camp and in the line of battle. His left was near Owl Creek, and his right across the Bark Road. From left to right Hardee had Brigadier General Pat Cleburne's command, Brigadier General S. A. M. Wood's unit, Colonel R. G. Shaver's, and Brigadier General A. H. Gladden's brigades, the latter on temporary loan from Bragg's Corps. The Second Corps was drawn up about eight hundred yards behind Hardee. Brigadier General Jones M. Withers' Second Division was located to the right of the Bark Road, while Brigadier General Daniel Ruggles' First Division was to the left. After detaching General Gladden to reinforce Hardee's right, Withers retained brigadier generals J. R. Chalmers' and J. K. Jackson's brigades. Ruggles had the brigades of Colonels Randall Gibson and Preston Pond, Jr., and Brigadier General Patton Anderson. Polk's First Corps consisted of the brigades of Colonels R. M. Russell and W. H. Stephens and brigadier generals Alexander Stewart and Bushrod Johnson.[69]

The corps were not assigned a specific section of the Union line to shatter. Instead, Hardee and Bragg were to advance in parallel lines,

68 Confederate rumor said the Union army numbered 120,000. Jimmy Knighton to sister, April 6, 1862, Jimmy Knighton Papers, Louisiana State University Library; *OR* 10, pt. 1, 407; William Preston, Diary, April 5, 1862, Miscellaneous Collection, Shiloh National Military Park.

69 Jordan, "The Battle of Shiloh," 204. For a complete description of a breakdown into individual units, see Appendix I. The same may be found for the Union army in Appendix II.

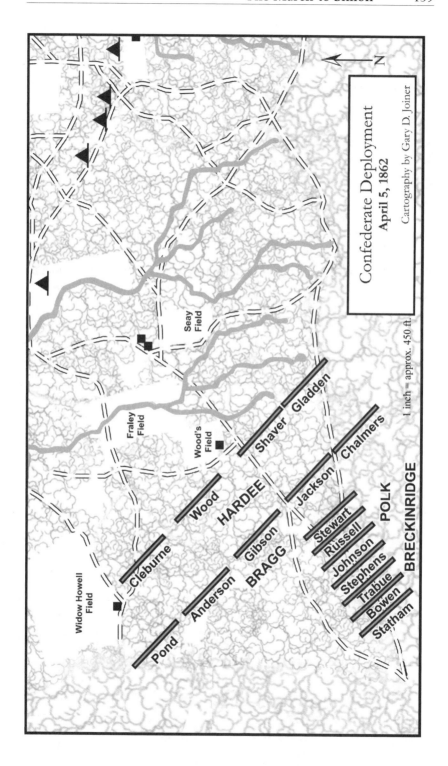

Confederate Deployment
April 5, 1862

Cartography by Gary D. Joiner

1 inch = approx. 450 ft.

N

Seay Field

Fraley Field

Wood's Field

Widow Howell Field

Pond

Cleburne

Wood

HARDEE

Anderson

Gibson

BRAGG

Shaver

Gladden

Jackson

Chalmers

Stewart

Russell

Johnson

Stephens

Trabue

Bowen

Statham

POLK

BRECKINRIDGE

stretching across a front three miles wide. This was a faulty arrangement, since it would make for confusion when the units became entangled as the battle progressed. In General Johnston's telegram to President Jefferson Davis informing him of the forthcoming battle, nothing was said about this parallel formation. Instead, the order of attack was given as Polk on the left, Hardee in the center, Bragg on the right, and Breckinridge in reserve. This plan would have been much more efficient, and it would have probably weighted the Confederate right so as to make more likely the Confederate plan of securing the Landing.

The Confederate plan was avowedly to turn the Federal left and drive the Union army away from the Landing and against Owl Creek. By seizing the Landing, the Southerners could prevent Buell's reinforcing Grant. But to accomplish this plan the greatest weight of the Confederate assault should have been concentrated on the Southerners' right instead of being dispersed all across the battlefield.[70]

As the sun went down behind the horizon, thousands of Confederate soldiers stood around the newly blossomed dogwood trees, while their muddy officers read to them General Albert Sidney Johnston's message.[71] The text of General Johnston's message read as follows:

> I have put you in motion to offer battle to the invaders of your country. With the resolution and disciplined valor becoming men fighting, as you are, for all worth living or dying for, you can but march to a decisive victory over the agrarian mercenaries sent to subjugate and despoil you of your liberties, property, and honor.

70 *OR* 10, pt. 1, 392-397; pt. 2, 387. William Preston Johnston, Jefferson Davis, and Braxton Bragg later charged that Beauregard deliberately altered Johnston's plan of attack. It is much more likely that in the confusion at the time that Johnston forgot to give Beauregard the details and the Louisianan simply acted on his own initiative, or that Johnston did give him the details and he simply forgot them. Roland, *Albert Sidney Johnston*, 321, 322. || Daniel, *Shiloh*, 120, states that Johnston acted as Beauregard's "rubber stamp" and "acquiesced to his junior." Sword, *Shiloh*, 114, argues that Johnston must carry full responsibility for orders issued in his name. McDonough, *Shiloh*, 74, states that Johnston's personality was not strong enough to control Beauregard's "colossal ego."

71 Samuel Latta to wife, April 12, 1862, Confederate Collection, Tennessee Department of Archives and History.

Remember the precious stake involved; remember the dependence of your mothers, your wives, your sisters, and your children on the result; remember the fair, broad, abounding land, the happy homes, and the ties that would be desolated by your defeat.

The eyes and the hopes of eight millions of people rest upon you. You are expected to show yourselves worthy of your race and lineage; worthy of the women of the South, whose noble devotion in this war has never been exceeded in any time. With such incentives to brave deeds and with the trust that God is with us, your generals will lead you confidently to the combat, assured of success.[72]

Strictly forbidden to light fires or make any kind of noise, forty thousand Confederate soldiers squatted, knelt, or laid down in the thick slime covering the entire area, talking quietly over General Johnston's message and mulling over Sunday's prospects. Some of the soldiers munched cold rations, but most of them went hungry. The rain had stopped during the afternoon, but most of the Confederates were still at least damp, and thick, slick brown Tennessee mud covered everything. As the soldiers tried to clean their muskets and shotguns, perhaps some of them remembered General Beauregard's order to shoot low at the enemy's legs to cause wounded men, who would have to be carried off the battlefield. It was a cheerful thought for the men to try and catch a little sleep with.

The Southerners could hear Union signal guns going off nearby. Federal bands kept the night air sparkling with their jaunty serenades. Finally there was quiet, and most of the exhausted soldiers drifted off to sleep.[73]

72 *OR* 10, pt. 2, 389.

73 A. H. Mecklin Diary, April 5, 1862, Mississippi Department of Archives and History; Richardson, "War As I Saw It;" Unidentified officer, Seventeenth Alabama Infantry Regiment, April 11, 1862, Shiloh-Corinth Collection, Alabama Department of Archives and History.

Chapter 7

_____ *Surprise*

FOR AS LONG AS there have been wars and armies, soldiers have grumbled over the prospect of early morning patrols. On that quiet Sunday morning more than a century ago, the men of the Twenty-fifth Missouri[1] and the Twelfth Michigan were no exception. Routed out of their beds sometime after midnight, the troops stumbled around, gathering up their guns, cartridge belts, overcoats, and wadding up their blankets before falling into formation. Why a patrol at this time of night? Some officer was worried about the Rebels, so the enlisted men would have it taken out on them.

The worried officer was Colonel Everett Peabody. Disturbed by the events of Saturday, he decided some kind of large scale reconnaissance was an absolute necessity. Just after midnight, scouts from the Twenty-fifth Missouri led by Major James Powell located a party of Confederate troops several miles from the Union army camped at Pittsburg Landing. Returning from the scout, Powell reported the Confederates' presence to

1 Many members of the Twenty-fifth Missouri had taken part in the siege of Lexinngton, Missouri, in September of the previous year. Everett Peabody had commanded the regiment there. *Battles and Leaders*, 1: 307-313; Monaghan, *Civil War on the Western Border*, 187-194; Charles Morton, "A Boy at Shiloh," *Personal Recollections of the War of the Rebellion: Addresses Delivered Before the Commandery of the State of New York, Military Order of the Loyal Legion of the United States,* 3rd Series, (New York: 1907), 54. Colonel Peabody was a native of Massachusetts, a Harvard graduate, and a civil engineer by profession. *Ibid.*, 53, 54; Charles Morton, "Opening of the Battle of Shiloh," 7.

Peabody. The colonel decided to send Major Powell back with a large enough detachment to ascertain exactly what the Southerners were up to and how many there were.[2]

Around 3:00 a.m., three companies from the Twenty-fifth Missouri (B, led by Captain Joseph Schmitz; E, Captain Simon F. Evans; H, Captain Hamilton Dill, a Mexican War veteran), plus a detachment from the Twelfth Michigan Infantry pulled out of their encampments and headed out along a farm road that led into the main Corinth-Pittsburg Landing Road. The patrol was Peabody's own responsibility, and as the men slipped away into the distance down the road, the colonel remarked to an aide that he would not live to see the result of it. He was nearly right—in less than four hours he lay on the battlefield, a bullet through his head.[3]

---

2   *Ibid.*

3   Joseph Ruff, "Civil War Experiences of A German Emigrant as Told by the Late Joseph Ruff of Albion," *The Michigan Magazine of History* 27 (Winter 1943): 294; Morton, "A Boy at Shiloh," 58. For years standard history works have maintained that the reconnaissance patrol under Major Powell that went out to engage the Confederates, or at least to locate them that morning, consisted of three companies of soldiers from the Twenty-fifth Missouri. This is generally based on the report of the Twenty-fifth Missouri in the *Official Records*. This, however, is incorrect. A detachment from the Twelfth Michigan went with the Missourians on the reconnaissance. Exactly why this was overlooked in the *Official Records* is not certain. Lieutenant Colonel Humphrey W. Woodyard, Twenty-first Missouri, does mention that the Twelfth Michigan had been engaged about the same time as the Twenty-first. *OR* 10, pt. 1, 283. Two members of the Twelfth Michigan specifically reported that they were engaged. Private Franklin Bailey, Company D, Twelfth Michigan, wrote a letter to his parents two days after the battle, in which he specifically stated that he and his company had taken part in this operation. Franklin H. Bailey Papers, Historical Collections of the University of Michigan. Private Charles Morton, Twenty-fifth Missouri, stated that two or three companies of the Twelfth Michigan accompanied Powell. Morton, "Opening of the Battle of Shiloh," 13. The presence of the Michigan troops with Powell's patrol was also confirmed by Edwin L. Hoburt, *The Truth About Shiloh* (Springfield: Illinois Register Publishing Company, 1909), 10; William Swinton, *The Twelve Decisive Battles of the Civil War* (New York: Dick and Fitzgerald, 1867), 105. J. G. Deuprae, "The Noxubee Squadron of the First

The night was "balmy" and "perfectly still."[4] The soldiers had only the pale light of the moon and the faint stars to guide them down the well-worn wagon road. Stumbling in the wagon ruts, and occasionally sinking in the thick layers of Tennessee mud on the "road's surface," the two hundred Union volunteers filed slowly down the road in the direction of the state line, unaware of their nearby rendezvous with destiny.[5]

Progress was slow and halting, the men frequently muttering and cursing after being bumped by the musket barrels of their comrades. Frequently the unlucky troopers straggled off the road into the darkness, or they bogged down in the mud. Upon one occasion a party of Michiganders became confused and almost shot up some of the Twenty-fifth, mistaking them for Confederates.[6] The thick clusters of trees along the farm road added to the murky darkness, shutting out what little light there was from the heavens above. Passing just beyond the edge of the Rhea field, Major Powell met Captain A. W. McCormick, of

---

Mississippi Cavalry," *Publications of the Mississippi Historical Society* (Jackson: Mississippi Historical Society (1908), 51: 30, also confirmed this. There is no regimental report for the Twelfth Michigan in the *Official Records,* and their role in the day's fighting is not specifically spelled out by any official account. Colonel Francis Quinn, who commanded the regiment, only turned in a brigade report. He said that "several companies were ordered out from the First Brigade." *OR* 10, pt. 1, 280. There is a report by Lieutenant Colonel William Graves, which does mention two companies of the Twelfth going out with the patrol. Robertson, *Michigan in the War*, 325. ‖ Despite the care taken to figure out which troops were involved, Dr. Cunningham confused the road on which the patrol marched. Today, there is no doubt that Powell's patrol took what is today known as the Reconnoitering Road, which at the time of the battle was a small field road. We have altered the original text to correct the oversight. See Reed, *The Battle of Shiloh and the Organizations Engaged*, 13, 59.

4 D. Lloyd Jones, "The Battle of Shiloh," *War Papers Read Before the Commandery of the State of Wisconsin, M. O. L. L. U. S.,* (Milwaukee: 1891), 54.

5 Ruff, "Civil War Experiences of a German Emigrant," 294, 295. ‖ Dr. Cunningham placed the patrol at 200 men, but Daniel, *Shiloh*, 143, places the number at 400 while Sword, *Shiloh*, 145, merely says "several hundred" Federals. McDonough, *Shiloh*, 87, states "less than three hundred men."

6 *Ibid.*

the Seventy-seventh Ohio, who was commanding Colonel Hildebrand's advance picket post. Telling Captain McCormick of his orders, Major Powell quickly directed his men to resume their march, heading on up the road.[7] After more than an hour of marching and cursing, the patrol had moved less than two miles.

In a million homes across America, in the strange semi-light that prevailed in the dawn, there occurred the first gradual stirrings of Sunday morning. Housewives were up, making breakfast gruel or oatmeal, while teenage sons and daughters milked the cows or took care of other household chores in preparation for dressing and making the long trip to Sunday morning services; but along the farm road no one thought of church services or hymn singing. There were no sounds of pots and pans or the gentle lowing of cattle; but, instead, the harsh tramp, tramp, slosh, slosh of men marching.[8]

Across the skyline the first vague traces of light were appearing. In this misty half-light, the advance of Major Powell's reconnaissance force suddenly stumbled upon the outpost of the Confederate army. A shot rang out, then a second, and still a third—as the men of Brewer's Alabama cavalry suddenly realized the Yankees were upon them.

Scrambling to their horses, the Alabamans quickly galloped away in the direction of Major A. B. Hardcastle's Third Mississippi Battalion on picket duty. To the advancing Federals, the Alabamans appeared to be ghost-like horsemen, moving mysteriously through the trees, a poor target along a musket sight.

Quickly forming in skirmish lines, the Michiganders and Missourians moved forward, firing. Some of the Nationals took cover behind trees, sending heavy rifle balls and slugs crashing into the underbrush after the fleeing cavalrymen. In a matter of seconds, the first action was over, with no casualties, and indeed without most of the men

---

7 Campaigns in Kentucky and Tennessee, 138. || Dr. Cunningham again mentioned the patrol marching along the Corinth Road. We have slightly altered the text to correct the statement.

8 || For a third and final time, Dr. Cunningham mentioned the patrol marching along the Corinth Road. We once again slightly altered the text to correct the statement.

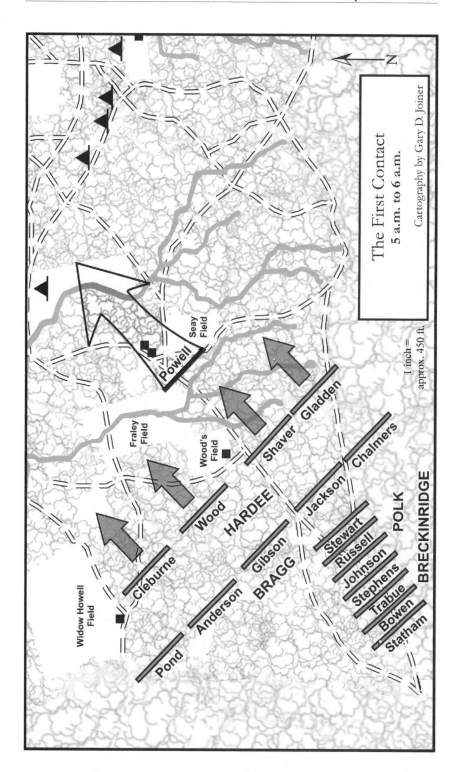

The First Contact
5 a.m. to 6 a.m.

Cartography by Gary D. Joiner

1 inch =
approx. 450 ft.

even seeing an enemy. Within moments the Union forces were again advancing, this time straight toward the waiting Mississippians.

Now deployed lengthwise over the road and in the surrounding Fraley Field, the Federals continued their somewhat stumbling advance, cautious, apprehensive, determined not to be surprised. A sudden volley of gunfire rang out as the Yanks approached within a hundred yards of Lieutenant F. W. Hammock's outpost. The seven Mississippians fired only one round before falling back on the main body of the battalion; then a second sharp volley, as Lieutenant William M. McCulty's men joined in the fray. The firing was very inaccurate due to poor visibility and the relative inexperience of the Mississippians.

Stealthily moving forward, the cautious Yanks finally collided with the main body of the Confederate advance guard. With a tremendous roar, Hardcastle's Third Mississippi Battalion unleashed a thunderous but highly inaccurate volley of bullets in the general direction of the advancing Federals.

Lieutenant Colonel J. F. Gilmer, General Albert Sidney Johnston's chief artillery officer, suddenly found himself caught up in the hazy gunfight. Reconnoitering ahead of the main body to locate suitable artillery positions, Gilmer and his small cavalry escort abruptly found themselves in the line of fire from Major Powell's patrol. Private Thomas Duncan of the escort watched a young Mississippian go down with his throat ripped open by a Northern musket ball. Then a piece of wood, torn loose by a rifle slug, caught Duncan in the left eye, while a bullet gouged his saber blade. Scurrying back to cover, Private Duncan, Colonel Gilmer, and the rest of their group escaped further damage.[9]

At two hundred yards' range, the Yankees and Rebels continued trading tremendous volleys of enthusiastic but poorly aimed gunfire as the sun slowly climbed over the horizon. For some minutes the soldiers fought it out, an occasional man dropping as he exposed himself from behind his tree or fence post. The engagement gradually rocked back and forth, with the Mississippians advancing a little and then falling back. After about an hour of sporadic firing, the Federals decided enough was

9 *OR* 10, pt. 1, 602, 603; Ruff, "Civil War Experiences of A German Emigrant," 294; Duncan, *Recollections*, 51, 52; *OR* 10, pt. 1, 405.

enough and began slowly pulling back. The continuous firing of almost five hundred men had actually produced less than thirty casualties, a pittance compared to the carnage that would be on this grim day, but it was a start.[10]

10 *Ibid.*, 602, 603; Ruff, "Civil War Experiences of A German Emigrant," 294- 296; Franklin H. Bailey to his parents, April 8, 1862, Franklin H. Bailey Papers, Historical Collections of the University of Michigan. Some dispute exists as to the exact time of the beginning of the battle. The two most frequently mentioned times are 4:55 a.m. and 5:14 a.m. Colonel Johnston, in his biography of his father, mentions the time as being 5:14, making special reference to this, saying General Johnston directed Captain Ed Munford to note the hour of the first sound of the first firing. Johnston, *Life of Gen. Albert Sidney Johnston*, 585. Colonel William Preston, on General Johnston's staff, said that at 5:30 a.m., he heard sharp volleys of musketry along the road on General Hardee's front. William Preston Diary, extract for April 6, 1862, in the Miscellaneous Collections, Shiloh National Military Park. Other works cite 4:55 a.m. as the hour, notably the extremely scholarly and detailed account of the battle by a participant, and later Shiloh National Military Park Historian, D. W. Reed. Reed, *Shiloh*, 13. Beauregard's aide-de-camp, Lieutenant Colonel S. W. Ferguson, said the firing began at 4:55. S. W. Ferguson to General Beauregard, April 9, 1862, Miscellaneous Collection, Shiloh National Military Park. Another of Beauregard's staff, Numa Augustine, confirmed this. Numa Augustine to General Beauregard, April 10, 1862, Louisiana Historical Association Collection, Howard-Tilton Memorial Library, Tulane University. Lieutenant Shumway, Fourteenth Illinois, said the battle began when "the rebs attacked about 4 A. M." Shumway to his wife, April 11, 1862, Payson Z. Shumway Papers, Illinois State Historical Library. Edwin Bearss, who performed extensive research on the subject, maintains the sun rose at 5:40 a.m. that morning, citing a letter from E. B. McGeever, Head Reference Section Science and Technical Division, Library of Congress, October 30, 1963. Edwin Bearss, "Shiloh," Miscellaneous Collection, Shiloh National Military Park. Most of the soldiers' accounts of the action said the firing began just before dawn, and that the sun rose about the time of the beginning of the skirmish between the two main bodies of troops. This would tend to lend credence to the 5:14 version. Lieutenant C. P. Searle mentioned rising from his rail bed just "as soon as it was light enough to see," and within minutes he heard the sound of heavy gunfire. Searle, "War Sketches and Incidents," 330. Lieutenant Dent, Robertson's Battery, C. S. A., said musket fire began at dawn. S. H. Dent to his wife, April 9, 1862, Shiloh-Corinth Collection, Alabama Department of Archives and History. Private Bailey, Twelfth Michigan, said the

Confederate General Johnston and his staff were just sitting down to a breakfast of cold biscuits and black coffee when the sounds of the Hardcastle-Powell fracas reached their ears. "There," said Colonel William Preston, "the first gun of the battle."[11] The command to advance was given, but to relay the order to the various brigades required many precious minutes. General Johnston briefly chatted with the still unenthusiastic General Beauregard, explaining that he planned to accompany the forward line of advance. Johnston requested that Beauregard manage things in the rear. Mounting his horse Fire-eater, Johnston set his spurs and rode forward toward the slowly but steadily increasing sound of gunfire.[12]

Several times General Johnston paused in his ride to give out friendly admonitions to the slowly advancing Confederates. To one of his officers, an old acquaintance of the Mormon campaign days back in Utah, General Johnston paused to remark, "My son, we must this day conquer or perish."[13] Perhaps the general's mind wandered for a second or two, dwelling on the beauty of the early Sunday morning, with the trees beginning to bud and the faint delicate fragrance of the peach blossoms wafting across the field.

Located on the left side of the Corinth-Pittsburg Road, Brigadier General Sterling Wood's Third Brigade moved forward in obedience to the order to attack. General Wood sent Captain William Clare to tell

---

reconnaissance party "reached the rebels camp just before day light, they were out to meet us, and began to fire into us." Franklin H. Bailey to his parents, April 8, 1862, Franklin H. Bailey Papers, Historical Collections of the University of Michigan. Private Lucius Barber, Fifteenth Illinois, said picket firing began at dawn. Barber, *Army Memoirs*, 51. Theodore Mandeville, Crescent Regiment, said the battle began about 5:30. Theodore Mandeville to Josephine Rozet, April 9, 1862, Louisiana State University Archives. || Daniel, *Shiloh*, 144, says "about 5 a.m.," while Sword, *Shiloh*, 143, sticks to Reed's 4:55 a.m. time frame. McDonough, *Shiloh*, 87, says "about five o'clock."

11 Johnston, *Life of Gen. Albert Sidney Johnston*, 585.

12 William Preston, Memoranda, Death of A. S. Johnston, Mrs. Mason Barret Papers, Albert Sidney Johnston Collection, Howard-Tilton Memorial Library, Tulane University.

13 Johnston, *Life of Gen. Albert Sidney Johnston*, 584.

Major Hardcastle to hold his position along the road until the brigade could move up in support. It was around 6:30 a.m. before the brigade reached the position of the first big skirmish.

The muddy and excited Mississippians were ordered back into line and the Eighth Arkansas Infantry and Ninth Arkansas Infantry Battalion were ordered forward to take the Mississippians' place as skirmishers. His new dispositions completed, General Wood again ordered his brigade to advance, as Colonel R. G. Shaver, acting commander of the First Brigade, moved up on his right.[14]

Pickets of the Sixteenth Wisconsin watched as Major Powell's predawn patrol passed their post. Just after dawn sounds of gunfire caused the officer of the day to direct the pickets to fall back on the reserves. Within minutes Company A was completely assembled and on the road toward the sound of firing.[15]

At divisional headquarters, reports of the firing caused General Prentiss to order the division to stand by. A little after 6:00, a courier reached Prentiss' command post with word of Powell's repulse. The Sixth Division's commander immediately ordered Colonel Peabody to reinforce the beleaguered Powell. Within minutes Colonel David Moore was moving forward with five companies of the Twenty-first Missouri. The Missourians double-quicked it up the road, bayonets and cartridge boxes wildly rattling.

14 *OR* 10, pt. 1, 591, 573. In the Confederate order of battle, Hardee had command of the Third Corps, consisting of the First Brigade, General T. C. Hindman; Second Brigade, General P. R. Cleburne; and Third Brigade, General S. A. M. Wood. To cover the interval between his right and Lick Creek, General Johnston assigned to Hardee General A. H. Gladden's First Brigade of Withers' Second Division, Second Army Corps. *OR* 10, pt. 1, 532. Sometime immediately before the battle, Hardee decided to break up his corps into two temporary divisions. He continued in overall corps command, but exercised direct tactical control over only General Gladden's and General Cleburne's brigades. General Hindman was given charge of his own brigade, now led by Colonel Shaver, and that of General Wood, but he does not appear to have given any orders to the latter unit.

15 Jones, "The Battle of Shiloh," 55-57.

Spying the lone Wisconsin company, Colonel Moore told them, "You can fall in on the right or on the left of my regiment," and the Badger State's company commander, Captain Edward Saxe, pulling off his uniform coat and throwing it on the ground in the mud, yelled, "Boys, we will fall in on the right; we will head them out."[16]

Near the Seay cotton field Colonel Moore ran into Major Powell and the remnants of his force, including a goodly number of wounded, and the colonel castigated Powell's men as cowards for retreating. Major Powell and his soldiers attempted to warn the gallant but somewhat overly enthusiastic colonel to be cautious, but with limited effect.[17] Ordering those of Powell's group who were not actually carrying wounded to join up with his command, Colonel Moore, with his collection of bits and pieces of regiments, soon moved forward in the direction of the advancing Confederates. He did take the precaution of sending Lieutenant Henry Menn to tell Lieutenant Colonel Humphrey Woodyard to bring up the remaining five companies of the regiment and join him on the road.[18]

According to General Benjamin Prentiss, Colonel Moore sent him a courier saying he had found Johnston's army and asked, "If you will send the balance of my regiment to me, by thunder, I will lick them."[19]

As soon as Woodyard, with General Prentiss' permission, arrived with the five additional companies, Colonel Moore again moved forward, but before he had gone even a quarter of a mile he found Johnston's army, or at least the advance elements of it.

Moving in columns of fours, Moore's Bluecoats reached the northwest corner of the Seay Field, when suddenly the Confederates poured a heavy fire into them. Captain Saxe and several others were

---

16 *Ibid.*; *OR* 10, pt. 1, 278, 282, 283; William T. Shaw, "The Battle of Shiloh," *War Sketches and Incidents As Related By Companions of the Iowa Commandery: Military Order of the Loyal Legion of the Union States* (Des Moines: 1893), 1: 189.

17 Ruff, "Civil War Experiences of A German Emigrant," 296.

18 *OR* 10, pt. 1, 283.

19 Benjamin Prentiss, "Reunion of Federal Veterans at Shiloh," *Confederate Veteran* 3 (February 1895): 104.

killed in the first volley, while Moore's right leg was shattered by a musket ball and he was forced to leave the field. Woodyard assumed command and deployed his men in line of battle across the brow of a slight rise in the ground in the cotton field, facing west against the fast shooting Southerners.[20]

For perhaps an hour Woodyard engaged in a sharp fire fight. Discovering the Confederates were trying to turn his right flank, he pulled his men back into the woods north of the cotton field. The pressure was heavy, but help was on the way, for three companies of the Sixteenth Wisconsin were on the way up. Somehow Captain George H. Fox, Company B, discovered the seriousness of the situation and went dashing into the camp area shouting, "Company A is fighting, and we must go and help them."[21] The company commanders soon reported to Woodyard, who directed them to take a new position east of the field, then gradually retiring on it with the rest of his men. The new position was on a slight rise in the ground, which gave the Federals a little protection from enemy gunfire. Within minutes, however, the Northerners were forced to avoid being outflanked.[22]

In the brigade area the remainder of the Twelfth Michigan and Twenty-fifth Missouri were fully equipped and drawn up in formation, ready to advance. More wounded were coming into the area as General

---

20 *OR* 10, pt. 1, 282, 283, 285; Jones, "The Battle of Shiloh," 56, 57; Shaw, "The Battle of Shiloh," 189. Doctors W. H. Gibbon and S. B. Davis amputated Moore's leg late Sunday evening on board the steamer, *Minnehaha*. Belknap, *15th Regiment Iowa*, 111. Probably the first Southerners to open fire on Moore belonged to the Seventh Arkansas, Shaver's Brigade. Wood' skirmish line also quickly became involved in this action, so the Federals were probably facing twenty-five or more companies. In his official report Moore claimed being attacked by General Daniel Ruggles, but that officer was in Bragg's Corps. Moore actually ran into Hardee's Third Corps. See Thomas J. Bryant, *Who is Responsible for the Advance of the Army of the Tennessee Towards Corinth?* (n.p.: n.p., 1885), 35; Samuel M. Howard, *Illustrated Comprehensive History of the Great Battle of Shiloh* (Kansas City: Franklin Hudson Publishing Company, 1921), 63.

21 Jones, "The Battle of Shiloh," 54.

22 *Ibid.*, 54, 55; *OR* 10, pt. 1, 284.

Prentiss came riding up to Colonel Peabody, sharply reined his horse, and with deep emotion exclaimed, "Colonel Peabody, I will hold you personally responsible for bringing on this engagement," to which, with severe dignity and ill concealed contempt, Colonel Peabody answered, "I am personally responsible for all my official acts."[23]

The brigade was immediately deployed just south of the Rhea Field. The troopers could hear gunfire from the woods in front and soon could observe bluecoated men slowly moving toward them, firing as they retreated. It was Colonel Woodyard and his men making a fighting retreat on the brigade. Peabody and the other officers soon had the new arrivals unscrambled and arranged in the line of battle.

A little after 7:30, sharp skirmishing broke out, followed by a series of rather disorganized charges delivered by the men of Wood's and Shaver's brigades. Although the firing was rapidly picking up, only Colonel Peabody's brigade was under heavy attack so far. Was this simply a Confederate reconnaissance in force—an attempt to feel out the strength and position of the Union army—or was it an all out attack? At this early hour, who could say?

There is no record that Colonel Peabody's men picked up any prisoners in these early actions, and the men's view of the battle was simply that of the enemy in the front. It is doubtful if Peabody realized what he had accomplished, for shortly he would lie dead on the field. But by his action in sending Major Powell's predawn patrol and by subsequently bringing on the engagement with Brigadier General Hindman's command, he deprived the South of complete tactical surprise and gave thousands of Union soldiers precious minutes to grab up their rifles and assemble with their regiments.[24]

Where was the Union army's commander, the man whose job it was to evaluate the significance of Colonel Peabody's action? "Sam" Grant

---

23   Morton, "A Boy at Shiloh, 60. A slightly different version has it that General Prentiss asked Colonel Peabody, "what do you mean by bringing on an engagement, when you know we are not ready?" to which Peabody replied, "I did not bring it on. It is coming without my assistance." *Campaigns of Kentucky and Tennessee*, 59.

24   ‖ See Smith, *The Untold Story of Shiloh*, 22-24, for a modern discussion of the surprise at Shiloh.

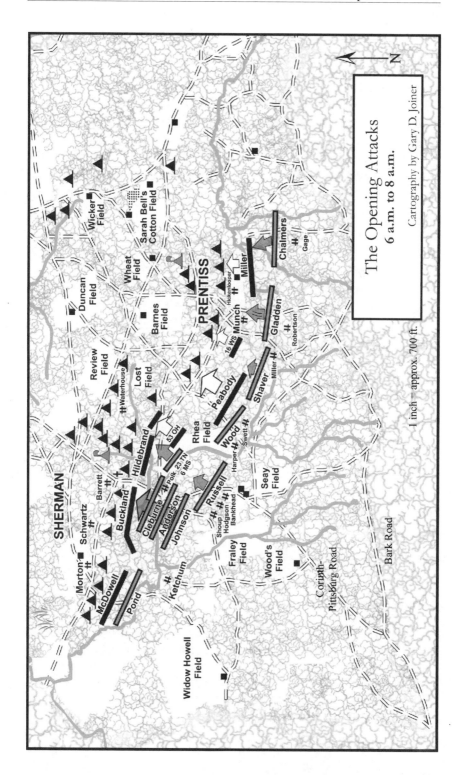

The Opening Attacks
6 a.m. to 8 a.m.

Cartography by Gary D. Joiner

1 inch = approx. 700 ft.

was on the way, stepping ashore at Pittsburg Landing a little after Peabody's entire brigade was committed. His ankle was still painfully swollen, and the general probably spent a restless night upstairs in his ornate but comfortable bed at the William Cherry House in Savannah. A little after dawn, Grant hobbled downstairs on his crutches to find that his trusted aide, John A. Rawlins, had already collected and opened the day's mail. Awakened before dawn by an orderly, Rawlins had also started the closing of headquarters at the house in preparation for the move to Pittsburg Landing as soon as General Buell arrived. Grant took the letters, which dealt with routine matters, and began browsing through them while awaiting word that breakfast was ready.

Brigadier General John Cook, just back from leave, wandered in to have breakfast and began chatting with General Grant. About 6:00 a.m., an orderly announced that breakfast was ready, and soon the dining room crackled with the sounds of hungry officers eating. Then another orderly, Private Edward N. Trembly, came in and reported there was firing up the river.[25] Coffee cups and forks were quickly pushed back on the table as Grant quietly spoke. "Gentlemen," he said, "The ball is in motion. Let's be off."[26]

25 *OR* 10, pt. 1, 184; Edward Bouton, *Events of the Civil War* (Los Angeles: n.p., n.d.), 15, 16; Los Angeles *Times*, April 6, 1912.

26 Catton, *Grant Moves South*, 223. In his report of action, written twelve months after the event, Grant's assistant adjutant general, John Rawlins, says Trembly reported hearing artillery fire. Bruce Catton also says Grant and his staff officers, seated at the breakfast table, heard sounds of cannon firing even before Trembly came in; yet the time could not have been more than 6:30 a.m., if that late. At that hour, the only fighting near Pittsburg Landing had been between comparatively small bodies of men armed with muskets. The evidence is that no field battery on either side got into action before 7:15 a.m. or 7:30. Just what did Trembly and the others hear? Presumably only musket fire, which the wind carried the nine miles to Savannah, and their imagination or memories changed into cannon fire. Colonel William Preston, on Albert Sidney Johnston's staff, said there was heavy firing on Hardee's left at 7:10 a.m., and cannon fire in woods northeast of Fraley's Field at 7:15 a.m. Extract from Colonel William Preston's Diary, April 6, 1862, in Miscellaneous Collections at Shiloh National Military Park. Captain W. Irving Hodgson, Fifth Company, Washington Artillery, reported his battery opened fire at 7:10 a.m. *OR* 10, pt. 1,

General Grant wrote two dispatches, one to Major General Buell and the other to Brigadier General Nelson, both of whom were breakfasting at the latter's headquarters, where they heard the opening sounds of the battle. To Buell, Grant wrote:

> Heavy firing is heard up the river, indicating plainly that an attack has been made upon our most advanced positions. This necessitates my joining the forces up the river instead of meeting to-day, as I had contemplated. I have directed General Nelson to move to the river with his division. He can march to opposite Pittsburg.[27]

The reference to General Nelson referred to the second note, which Grant dictated to Rawlins just before leaving the Cherry House. It informed Nelson that "An attack having been made on our forces, you will move your entire command to the river opposite Pittsburg. You can obtain a guide easily in the village."[28]

---

513. Lieutenant Colonel S. W. Ferguson, aide-de-camp to General Beauregard, reported hearing the first cannon shot of the day at 7:09 a.m. S. W. Ferguson to General Beauregard, April 9, 1862, in Miscellaneous Collections, Shiloh National Military Park. These trained observers were in error, or there was artillery firing from the general direction of General Sherman's camp. Perhaps some of Sherman's guns were being fired for purposes of signaling, or perhaps in the Third Brigade to alarm the men. Captain Samuel Barrett, of General Sherman's Battery B, First Illinois, said that he went into action about 7:40 a.m. *OR* 10, pt. 1, 276. His other two batteries did not give a definite time, but it would not have been earlier than 7:30 a.m., and probably closer to 8:00 a.m. This situation partially illustrates the difficulty of assigning definite times to definite actions, even with reliable witnesses. ‖ Daniel, *Shiloh*, 174, states Grant heard artillery around 7:00 a.m. before the orderly entered the room. Sword, *Shiloh*, 214, says Grant was first alerted by the orderly between 7:00 and 7:30 a.m. McDonough, *Shiloh*, 95, states Grant heard the guns at the breakfast table.

27 *OR* 52, pt. 1, 232.

28 *Ibid.*, pt. 2, 95. The reference to finding a guide probably referred to the strong Unionist sentiment in Savannah. A number of Savannah citizens enlisted in the Forty-sixth Ohio Infantry when it was stationed at Savannah in March. T. J. Lindsey, *Ohio At Shiloh* (Cincinnati: 1903), 18. For evidences of Unionist sympathies in Savannah and Hardin County, see Lera Durbin, "Five

The two notes finished, Grant limped aboard the waiting headquarters steamer *Tigress* as quickly as he was able and headed for the front. Ironically, even as the *Tigress* pulled away from the Savannah landing, General Buell was walking toward the Cherry House with his chief of staff, Colonel James B. Fry. Probably due to a lapse in staff work, Grant was not informed of Buell's arrival at Nelson's headquarters the night before. Because of the mistake, it would be many hours before the note would reach the general, who would be busily chasing around trying to find Grant.[29]

The missing Grant, busily steaming toward the rapidly increasing sounds of gunfire, directed the steamer's captain to pull in at Crump's Landing next to the headquarters boat of his Third Division's commander, General Lew Wallace. Wallace was on deck waiting when the *Tigress* pulled alongside, and Grant simply leaned over the railing and shouted across. His orders were to hold the division in instant readiness to move and to send patrols out to ascertain if Johnston was also moving on Crump's Landing.[30]

It was a comparatively simple order. Somehow in the next few hours, however, things would go terribly wrong, and Wallace would find himself with the opportunity of saving the day and becoming one of the nation's great heroes. But fortune would not break his way; instead, Wallace would spend the next forty-three years of his life defending his actions at Shiloh.

A few thousand yards farther Grant's steamer reached the Landing with an additional passenger on board, Ohio war correspondent Whitelaw Reid. The newspaperman had quietly slipped onto the steamer while it was tied up at Crump's Landing. Grant and his aides climbed ashore while orderlies prepared their mounts, unmindful of Reid's presence. For years thereafter, General Grant probably regretted that

---

Years of War, Manuscript History of Hardin County," Miscellaneous Collections, Shiloh National Military Park; Adolph Engelmann to his wife, Mina, March 12, 1862, Adolph Engelmann Papers, Illinois State Historical Library.

29 *Battles and Leaders,* 1: 492.

30 *OR* 10, pt. 1, 184; Wallace, *An Autobiography,* 1: 461.

neither he nor his staff had tossed the pushy reporter into the Tennessee River.[31]

It was now around 8:00 a.m. or a little after, and the Landing was still a comparatively serene spot. Some stragglers were beginning to come in with their tales of disaster, but for the most part the men standing near the Landing were on guard duty or were members of regiments waiting for orders to move up. It was with the latter that Grant began exercising his command. He ordered the Twenty-third Missouri to proceed to Prentiss' headquarters and form up with the Sixth Division. The regiment's colonel, Jacob Tindall, immediately moved out, unknowingly going forward to meet death a mere three thousand yards away.[32]

A little farther up the bluff, Grant found Colonel Hugh T. Reid and his Fifteenth Iowa. Grant immediately told Reid to draw ammunition, to form across the Landing road, to halt all stragglers, and to stand by for further orders. Colonel Reid looked very confused, as if not certain with whom he was talking. Realizing this, Grant remarked, "I am General Grant." Reid instantly caught on, and joining up with the Sixteenth Iowa, also standing by awaiting orders, he carried out his new general's instructions.[33]

Most of Grant's staff officers quickly fanned out from the Landing with orders to subordinate commanders, while others were put to work handling supply problems. One of Grant's volunteer aides, G. G. Pride, took charge of transporting ammunition from the Landing to the fighting units.[34]

---

31 Royal Cortissoz, *The Life of Whitelaw Reid*, 2 vols. (New York: Scribners, 1921), 1: 85; Wallace, *An Autobiography*, 1: 462. || For Reid's dispatches, see James G. Smart, ed., *A Radical View: The "Agate" Dispatches of Whitelaw Reid, 1861-1865*, 2 vols. (Memphis: Memphis State University Press, 1976).

32   *OR* 10, pt. 1, 278. || See Fuller, *The Generalship of Ulysses S. Grant*, 111-113, for a time line of Grant's actions once he reached Pittsburg Landing.

33 Belknap, *15th Iowa*, 289, 290; *OR* 10, pt. 1, 278, 286-288. Colonel Reid arrived with his regiment from Benton Barracks early that morning and knew Grant only by reputation. *Ibid.*, 288.

34 M. F. Force, *From Fort Henry to Corinth*, (New York: Scribners, 1881), 131.

Grant moved inland to try and find out just what the situation was. Half a mile from the river he ran into General W. H. L. Wallace and learned that this was no mere isolated attack, but a full-scale onslaught from most or all of the Southern army. Grant instantly decided that the main fight would be at Shiloh and not at Crump's Landing, and that the two widely separated segments of his army must be unified as quickly as possible.

Grant's most trusted officer and friend, Captain John Rawlins, was told to return to the *Tigress* and locate the general's district quartermaster officer, Captain A. S. Baxter. Rawlins headed for the river and soon found the quartermaster officer at the landing, whereupon he gave him Grant's oral message. Afraid that he might confuse part of it, Captain Baxter had Rawlins write it out. Within minutes the *Tigress* was headed for Crump's Landing with Captain Baxter aboard, and Rawlins started for the front to locate Grant.[35]

According to General Lew Wallace it was "exactly 11:30" when the *Tigress* arrived at Crump's and he was handed an unsigned message, purporting to be from Grant. Wallace said that his adjutant, Frederick Knefler, placed the order in his sword belt and later lost it. In his autobiography, Wallace maintained that Grant ordered him to link up with the right of the army, to form a line of battle, and to be "governed by circumstances."[36] In his report of a year later, Rawlins claimed that the order directed Lew Wallace to move to Pittsburg Landing by the River Road, to form his division in the rear of the camp of the other Wallace, W. H. L., and await instructions from Grant.[37]

---

35 *OR* 10, pt. 1, 185.

36 Wallace, *An Autobiography*, 1: 463.

37 *OR* 10, pt. 1, 185. This entire controversy is discussed fully in *Battles and Leaders*, 1: 607-610. Rawlins' version of the order has the practical merit of good sense. It is what Grant should have ordered, but in transmitting verbal orders onto paper, mistakes can happen; and in this case the mistake may have been caused by Baxter, who claimed he personally wrote the order out while Rawlins dictated it. *Ibid.*, 607. It is possible Wallace simply got confused. His only pre-Civil War service had been as a first lieutenant in the Mexican War, and although he behaved commendably at Fort Donelson, he remained basically an amateur soldier, a civilian general. Whatever the truth in the

It was fine and good that Lew Wallace would soon be arriving to help, or so Grant thought back at the battlefield; but in the meantime there were other powerful reinforcements close at hand. To Buell, whose whereabouts were still uncertain, Grant addressed a new message saying the army was under "very spirited" attack and that the "appearance of fresh troops on the field now would have a powerful effect, both by inspiring our men and disheartening the enemy." Grant suggested that Buell leave all of his baggage on the east side of the river, admitting that his speedy arrival might "save the day for us." The general did not make the mistake of underestimating the Confederate army, telling Buell their force was over one hundred thousand strong.[38]

Nelson was the next recipient of an order. The giant Kentuckian was told to "hurry up your command as fast as possible. The boats will be in readiness to transport . . . your command across the river. All looks well, but it is necessary for you to push forward as fast as possible."[39]

What thoughts ran through General Grant's mind this early in the morning with the situation in a state of flux? Did he worry about how badly scattered his five divisions were, and if there was still time to pull them together into some sort of stable battle line? Did he admit within his own mind that he and his entire army were taken by surprise and badly off balance, for this early morning's work was clearly unexpected.

General Grant's ambiguous attitude on the subject of surprise was clearly revealed in a letter that he wrote, which appeared in the New York *Herald* less than four weeks later. After criticizing some of his officers for cowardice, Grant proclaimed, "As to the talk about a surprise here, nothing could be more false. If the enemy had sent word when and how they would attack we could not have been better prepared." Yet, a few sentences later, Grant candidly announced that he "did not believe,

---

matter, Grant eventually reconciled himself to Wallace's tardiness. Grant, *Memoirs*, 182, 183. || See also Allen, "If He Had Less Rank," 63-89, for a modern account of the Wallace march controversy. Daniel, *Shiloh*, 261, believes Grant never reconciled himself to Wallace's late arrival.

38 *Battles and Leaders*, 1: 492.

39 *OR* 10, pt. 1, 95, 96.

however, that they intended to make a determined attack, but were simply making reconnaissance in force."[40]

Grant's close friend, W. T. Sherman—whose feelings for his superior are best illustrated in the remark, "I stood by him when he was drunk and he stood by me when I was crazy"—was even more bitter on the question of surprise. Writing to his United States Senator brother John Sherman, he claimed the charges of surprise were "all simply false." He went on to say, "We knew the enemy was in our front, but in what form could not tell, and I was always ready for an attack."[41] In another letter to his brother, written two weeks later, Sherman passionately denied that his division was surprised, but he ended with, "I confess I did not think Beauregard would abandon his railroad to attack us on our base."[42] In a third letter to John, "Cump" explained that "we all knew the enemy was on our front, but we had to guess at his purpose."[43]

In his autobiography, Lew Wallace noted the Union army was taken by "surprise," but he was not on the scene when the fighting began, although he was in a good position to find out what had transpired.[44]

As senior officers Grant and Sherman were naturally reluctant to admit surprise, but many of the lower ranks possessed no hesitation in expressing themselves. To William H. Chamberlain of the Eighty-first Ohio, the Union army was "entirely ignorant of the presence of an enemy" until the firing actually began.[45]

---

40 New York *Herald*, May 3, 1862. Bruce Catton says the letter was reprinted from the Cincinnati *Commercial*, which had carried articles critical of Grant's actions at Shiloh. Catton, *Grant Moves South*, 257.

41 William T. Sherman to John Sherman, April 22, 1862, in Rachel Sherman Thorndike, ed., *The Sherman Letters: Correspondence Between General and Senator Sherman From 1837 to 1891* (New York: Scribners, 1894), 143, 145.

42 William T. Sherman to John Sherman, May 7, 1862, *Ibid.*, 145, 146.

43 William T. Sherman to John Sherman, May 12, 1862, *Ibid.*, 149.

44 Wallace, *An Autobiography*, 1: 482.

45 W. H. Chamberlain, *History of the Eighty-first Regiment, Ohio Infantry Volunteers During the War of the Rebellion* (Cincinnati: Gazette Printing House, 1865), 15.

In a letter to a friend, Private John Ruckman candidly declared, "on last Sunday morning the rebels attacked us and took us on surprise and such a time I never heard of before. We were unprepared to meet them. We were not expecting them."[46]

Lieutenant Payson Shumway recorded in his diary that the attack was not expected and that "surprise was never more complete."[47]

The Fifteenth Illinois heard picket firing at dawn, but ignored it and was taken by surprise,[48] while musician John Cockerill of the Twenty-fourth Ohio first realized the battle was in progress when he heard heavy artillery fire.[49]

Peter Dobbins of the Thirteenth Iowa discovered the battle while taking a "refreshing walk and washing off in a branch not far from the camp." Before his ablutions were finished, Dobbins said he "herd firing in the front but I supposed it was gards firing there guns off so I did not mind it any but in a short time I was summoned by the long roll which told very plane what was up."[50]

Dobbins was not the only innocent who mistook the sounds of Peabody's guns. Many of the soldiers, hearing the noise from Colonel Peabody's brigade, assumed it was merely a skirmish of pickets or Federal soldiers indulging in a little target practice.[51] Private William

46 John Ruckman to John Kinsel, April 12, 1862, Miscellaneous Collections, Shiloh National Military Park.

47 Payson Shumway Diary, April 6-7, 1862, Payson Z. Shumway Papers, Illinois State Historical Library.

48 Barber, *Army Memoirs*, 51.

49 John Cockerill, "A Boy at Shiloh," *Sketches of War History 1861-1865: Papers Prepared for the Commandery of the State of Ohio, Military Order of the Loyal Legion of the United States* (Cincinnati: 1908), 6: 16.

50 Peter B. Dobbins to Robert Banta, February 6, 1864, Miscellaneous Collections, Shiloh National Military Park. See George W. Crosley, "Some Reminiscences of an Iowa Soldier," *Annals of Iowa* 10 (July 1911): 125.

51 Stillwell, *Common Soldier*, 42; Thaddeus H. Capron, "War Diary of Thaddeus H. Capron 1861-1865," *Illinois State Historical Society Papers* 12 (October 1919): 343.

Harvey of the Fifty-seventh Illinois aptly put it this way: "It was not very much of a surprise."[52]

Surprised or not, General Grant found himself with the makings of a first class disaster on his hands. At Belmont and Fort Donelson he had fought his way out of bad situations. The next few hours would show if he could repeat his feat on this violent Sunday morning.

52 William Harvey, Diary, April 18, 1862, Miscellaneous Collections, Shiloh National Military Park.

Chapter 8

Around Shiloh Church

FROM THE MAIN DECK of the sloop of war *Hornet* to the command of a regiment of Ohio volunteers was quite a step-up. In the predawn hours of that Sunday morning, thirty-year-old Colonel Jesse Appler of the Fifty-third Ohio likely wished he were back on deck of his old ship, as every owl's hoot and each frog's croak sounded like a whole division of Confederate infantry sneaking upon the regimental camp.

Finally Colonel Appler could stand it no longer. He decided to send out an extra sixteen-man picket post as additional security precaution. A few minutes later, however, these same men came running back into camp, reporting gunfire in a field to their left and the presence of Confederate troops in front of the Third Brigade position.

The already nervous colonel, who had spent quite a sleepless night in the camp area, ordered his adjutant, Lieutenant Ephraim C. Dawes, to tell Colonel Hildebrand the army was about to be attacked. Changing his mind, Appler told Dawes to wait, and he directed a private to carry the information to Hildebrand. The soldier had gone but a few yards when a member of the Twenty-fifth Missouri, Powell's patrol, came running into camp with a bullet hole in one of his arms, excitedly shouting, "Get into line; the rebels are coming."[1]

The courier private was called back, and instead Lieutenant Colonel Robert A. Fulton was sent to Colonel Hildebrand's headquarters. The

1 John Duke, *History of the Fifty-third Regiment Ohio Volunteer Infantry, During the War of the Rebellion* (Portsmouth: The Blade Printing Company, 1900), 42; *Campaigns in Kentucky and Tennessee*, 138.

regimental quartermaster, Lieutenant Joseph Warner Fulton, was ordered to report to General Sherman with the new information. Within a few minutes Lieutenant Fulton came running back, and speaking in a very low voice, told his colonel, "General Sherman says you must be badly scared over there."[2]

If General Sherman was unenthusiastic over Colonel Appler's information, Colonel Hildebrand proved more receptive and ordered two companies of the Fifty-third to establish an advance picket post as an added security measure.[3]

As the minutes passed the regiments of Sherman's division gradually began forming up, alarmed by the increasing volume and closeness of gunfire if not by Appler's report. By around 7:00 a.m., Hildebrand's picket post could observe Confederate skirmishers moving toward them slowly. This was Pat Cleburne's outfit. Sludging wearily through the mud, Cleburne's Second Brigade gradually moved toward its rendezvous with Sherman, its advance protected by a screen of skirmishers from the Fifteenth Arkansas and the Sixth Mississippi Infantry.[4]

A sharp fire fight developed as the fighting Irishman's skirmishers located Hildebrand's outpost.[5] It was becoming increasingly obvious to the officers of the Third Brigade that this was something more than a mere reconnaissance in force. General Sherman and his staff came riding up alongside the Fifty-third Ohio. Sherman took out his binoculars and began examining the surrounding area, but his vantage point was a poor one, and he was able to get but a limited view of the situation. Just then some Confederate skirmishers emerged from the thick brush along the little stream running in front and alongside the Fifty-third's camp. Lieutenant E. C. Dawes spotted the advancing Rebels and exclaimed in horror to Lieutenant Eustace H. Ball of Company E, "Ball, Sherman will

2 Duke, *History of the Fifty-third Ohio*, 42, 43.

3 *Ibid.*

4 || For a modern study of Patrick Cleburne, see Craig L. Symonds, *Stonewall of the West: Patrick Cleburne and the Civil War* (Lawrence: University Press of Kansas, 1997).

5 *OR* 10, pt. 1, 80; T. B. Cox, "Sixth Mississippi Regiment at Shiloh," *Confederate Veteran* 18 (November 1910): 509.

be shot." Just out of the sick bed, the plucky Ball ran toward Sherman, screaming at the top of his voice, "General, look to your right."[6] Sherman dropped his glasses and immediately shifted positions as a volley of musket balls sprayed the spot he had just vacated. His orderly, Private Thomas D. Holliday, fell to the ground dead, and Sherman received a buckshot in the hand, exclaiming, "My God, we are attacked."[7]

Even as Sherman was apparently convinced that this was going to be a real battle, Cleburne ordered his brigade forward against Hildebrand's drawn-up regiments just behind and along the camp area of the Fifty-third Ohio. With Trigg's Battery dropping 6-pound shot and 12-pound howitzer shells on the Ohioans, Cleburne's men moved forward only to become badly bogged down in the soft, marshy, rain-soaked ground in front of Appler's camp. Cleburne's horse became stuck and the rider fell off, forcing the usually dapper Irishman to fight the rest of the day in a muddy uniform.

The Sixth Mississippi, Colonel John Thornton, and Twenty-third Tennessee, Lieutenant Colonel James Neill, found some fairly solid ground toward the right of the Federal camp and began advancing again. From right to left the Fifth Tennessee, Colonel Benjamin Hill, the Twenty-fourth Tennessee, Lieutenant Colonel Thomas Peebles, Fifteenth Arkansas, Lieutenant Colonel Archibald Patton, and the Second Tennessee, Colonel William Bate, started moving around on less boggy ground on the left or west of the camp.[8]

---

6 Duke, *History of the Fifty-Third Ohio*, 44; Fleming, "The Battle of Shiloh As A Private Saw It," 141. Private Robert H. Fleming said Ball told him he yelled, "General, you are looking the wrong direction." *Ibid.*

7 *Ibid.*; *OR* 10, pt. 1, 249. For some reason General Prentiss did not notify General Sherman of the state of the battle. Perhaps he was too busy, although he did warn the reserve division. Liddell Hart, *Sherman*, 127. || Dr. Cunningham's original version claimed Sherman was unhurt. In fact, he was wounded in the hand by a buckshot, and most historians think it occurred here. We have slightly altered the text to reflect this interpretation. See Marszalek, *Sherman*, 178; Sword, *Shiloh*, 177; Daniel, *Shiloh*, 158.

8 *OR* 10, pt. 1, 581. The boggy area Cleburne referred to in his report was 250 or 300 yards to the southeast of the Methodist-Episcopal Church. This was an extremely rainy month and the whole area was covered with a layer of mud.

Hildebrand's right most regiment, the Seventy-seventh Ohio, began catching light artillery fire from Trigg's Battery, but most of the kneeling infantrymen, because of the large number of trees in front of their position, were unable to see the advancing Southerners. Then shots from Cleburne's men began striking all around them. Next, Captain W. A. Stevens, Company A, and the pickets, ducking from tree to tree, finally fell back on the regiment. Six-pound shot tore loose the limbs over the Ohioans' heads. More stray slugs hit, and then Private John McInerney stopped a ball just over his right eye. Blood spurted profusely as he walked over to Lieutenant Jack Henricle and remarked, "Leftenant, do you think that went in dape?" It was only a glancing wound, and McInerney, although out of the fight, managed to survive the war. Just then the volume of artillery redoubled, but the men relaxed as Major B. D. Fearing shouted at the top of his voice, "Boys, those are our guns."[9] It was a section of Captain Allen Waterhouse's James rifles opening up from a clump of woods to the right of the Fifty-third's position.[10] The Illinois gunners got off two rounds and then withdrew to the main battery position on the high ground on the northern side of Shiloh Branch, just behind and to the right of the Fifty-third,[11] where soon all six 3.5 and

---

Actually the heavy briar patches and vines alone, at this point, were probably as much of an obstruction as the soft ground. *OR* 10, pt. 1, 587, 496; Irving Buck, *Cleburne and His Command* (New York: The Neale Publishing Company, 1908), 37, 38.

9 Fleming, "The Battle of Shiloh As A Private Saw It," 139, 140.

10 *OR* 10, pt. 1, 264.

11 Duke, *Fifty-third Ohio*, 46; *OR* 10, pt. 1, 273. Ezra Taylor, Fifth Division's chief of artillery, incorrectly stated that Waterhouse's two guns were on the left bank of Owl Creek. Actually their first firing position was in the woods along Shiloh Branch. The position enabled Waterhouse to effectively cover most of the Rhea Field. It was the highest point for several hundred yards, and the battery possessed a good, clear field to fire. A slightly different version has them at the Rhea House. Reed, *Shiloh*, 55. ‖ The editors have discovered several instances of Shiloh Branch being referred to as Owl Creek. In fact, that seems to be the historic name often referenced in battle reports. See *OR* 10, pt. 1, 173, 273, 275-276. The creek was also referred to in other places as Oak Creek and Rhea Creek. See M. F. Force, *From Fort Henry to Corinth* (New

4.5-inch rifles were in action, badly punishing Trigg's Arkansas Battery.[12]

Both the Fifty-seventh and Seventy-seventh Ohio were soon busily engaged in banging away at the Sixth Mississippi and Twenty-third Tennessee, but the Fifty-third was having problems. Colonel Appler was confused by the noise and excitement, and fear was gradually taking control of his mind. The Fifty-third was isolated from the rest of the brigade by the stream and about two hundred yards of fairly open ground, basically an untenable position, and Appler was busy fouling things up worse. He first positioned the regiment facing away from Cleburne's attack, and then had to spend precious minutes completely shifting his ten shaky companies around. Finally the Fifty-third was pointing the right way and they opened fire at a party of Confederates approaching the officers' tents. The Southerners pulled back momentarily but then advanced again. Colonel Appler gave the command to fire and the Rebels pulled back a second time. Appler completely blew up, yelling, "Retreat, and save yourselves."[13]

The Fifty-third Ohio was not routed. It simply dissolved as many of its men naturally followed the example of their commanding officer. Only the left and center of the regiment actually followed Appler, for the company commanders on the right were of sterner stuff.

Even while the first Southerners were advancing on the camp, Captain W. S. Jones, Company A, told some of the other officers that he thought Colonel Appler would break as soon as the firing began, and he said, "I am not going." Captain James Percy, Company F, said he would stay with Jones. The two officers and their men did fall back a few yards

York: Charles Scribner's Sons, 1881), 127-128 and Don Carlos Buell, "Shiloh Reviewed," *Battles and Leaders of the Civil War,* 4 vols. (New York: Century Company, 1884-1887), 1: 502-503.

12 *OR* 10, pt. 1, 581.

13 Duke, *Fifty-third Ohio,* 45; Ruff, "Civil War Experiences of A German Emigrant," 296, 297. For a fuller description of this debacle, see Lieutenant Fulton's report. *OR* 10, pt. 1, 264, 265. Colonel Appler was discharged from the United States Army on April 18, 1862. *Official Roster of the Soldiers of the State of Ohio in the War of the Rebellion, 1861-1866,* 8 vols. (Cincinnati: The Ohio Valley Press, 1888), 4: 675.

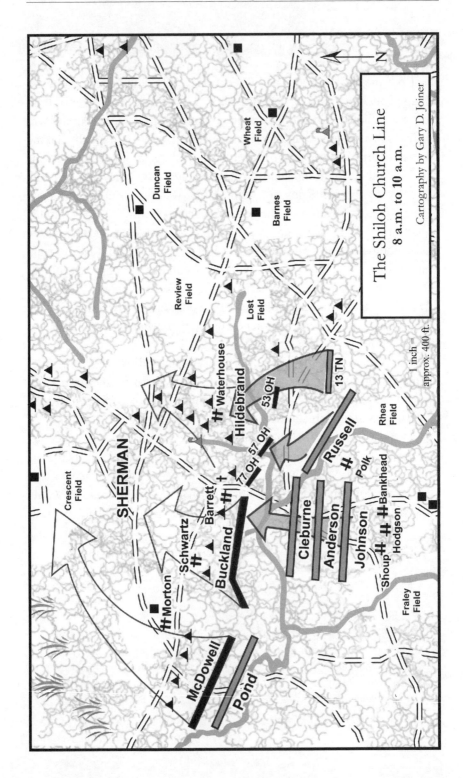

The Shiloh Church Line
8 a.m. to 10 a.m.

Cartography by Gary D. Joiner

1 inch =
approx. 400 ft.

N

Wheat
Field

Duncan
Field

Barnes
Field

Review
Field

Lost
Field

Rhea
Field

Crescent
Field

Fraley
Field

SHERMAN

Waterhouse

Hildebrand

53 OH

13 TN

57 OH

77 OH

Russell

Polk

Bankhead

Barrett

Schwartz

Buckland

Morton

Cleburne

Anderson

Johnson

Shoup

Hodgson

McDowell

Pond

when the break came, but they gallantly continued the fight, linking up with the Seventeenth Illinois when it joined in the action a little later.[14]

Lieutenant Dawes, Appler's adjutant, met a pre-battle acquaintance, Private A. C. Voris, Seventeenth Illinois, a veteran of Frederickstown and Fort Donelson. Dawes asked Voris if he would go over and talk to the remaining shaky members of his outfit. The Illinoisan said he would if his captain would allow it. The captain was agreeable, and Private Voris joined the nervous men from Ohio. First collecting some extra Enfield cartridges for the Ohioans to use, he told them that he had learned that the best way to meet the enemy was to "keep cool, shoot slow, and aim low." His parting words to the now more confident Fifty-third Ohioans were, "Why, it's just like shooting squirrels—only these squirrels have guns, that's all."[15]

The collapse of the Fifty-third endangered Sherman's left flank, but only temporarily, for General McClernand was already moving troops forward to protect the Fifth Division from being outflanked. General Sherman's right was much more secure, for Colonel Buckland's brigade, having formed up in its camp near Shiloh Church, advanced about two hundred yards just in time to meet Cleburne's overlapping left. From left to right Buckland's order of battle was the Seventieth, Forty-eighth, and Seventy-second Ohio. The Forty-eighth, carrying their not so trusty Austrian rifles, moved up first to support the picket post, already under fire from Cleburne's skirmishers. Colonel Ralph Buckland immediately advanced with the other two regiments, and just in time, for the Tennesseans opened up with a tremendous blast of musketry. The Forty-eighth began to waver as men dropped on all sides, but the regimental commander, Peter J. Sullivan, and other officers managed to steady the men. They could not, however, calm the color sergeant,

14 Duke, *Fifty-third Ohio*, 28; *OR* 10, pt. 1, 265. Jones' determined action won him promotion to full colonel on April 18, 1862. *Official Roster of the Soldiers of the State of Ohio*, 4: 676.

15 Duke, *Fifty-third Ohio*, 48. The Fifty-third Ohio monument at Shiloh National Military Park says the "regiment formed here at 8 a.m. . . . but soon fell back across the ravine in the rear." In defense of the Fifty-third Ohio, the unit was a new one, its organization completed that January, and once Colonel Appler was dismissed the regiment fought well in later actions.

Theodore D. Jones, who dropped the regimental flag and ran away at the very start of the action. Taking advantage of the cover of the trees and numerous logs, however, the Ohioans gave as good as they received.[16]

The Second Tennessee charged across the small field south of Shiloh Church, butting head on into the Forty-eighth Ohio, Colonel William Bate leading his men forward on his celebrated race horse, Blackhawk, a magnificent coal black stallion.[17] The men from Ohio promptly shot the regiment to pieces. Major W. R. Doak and Captains Joseph Tyree and Humphrey Bate were killed, while half a dozen other officers were badly wounded. Nearly a hundred privates and non-commissioned officers also littered the muddy brown earth of the field, just a short walk from the House of the Prince of Peace. Colonel Bate escaped the charge without a scratch, only to be wounded in the leg while reconnoitering the Union position a few minutes later, the wound incapacitating him for the rest of the battle.[18] Besides Captain Humphrey Bate, the colonel lost four other kinsmen either killed or wounded in this action.[19]

---

16 *OR* 10, pt. 1, 266, 270; Bering and Montgomery, *Forty-eighth Ohio*, 20. In his official report General Cleburne said the Ohioans were protected by a "breastwork of logs and bales of hay." *OR* 10, pt. 1, 581. Colonel Buckland's position was just in front of Shiloh Church, along a ridge of ground running to the east, and then turning in a slightly more southerly direction about 275 yards from the road. There was, and still is, a ravine at the point where the ridge begins turning more southward. The left of the Seventieth rested on the road by the Church, while the rest of the regiment and most of the Forty-eighth faced an unnamed field running about 200 yards down in front of the position. The rest of the Forty-eighth faced a wooded area running up the slope. The ravine was probably the dividing line between the Forty-eighth and Seventy-second. The latter's position can be seen today from Tennessee Highway 22 during the fall and winter months.

17 *Confederate Veteran* 2 (November 1894): 337.

18 *OR* 10, pt. 1, 585.

19 *D. A. B*, 2: 42. || Dr. Cunningham's original dissertation stated that Colonel Bate led his Second Tennessee across Rhea Field and hit the 48th Ohio. While conceivably correct, this interpretation provides a somewhat distorted feel to the action. An unnamed field which could have been a portion of Rhea Field did extend through a belt of fallen timber and across to the western side of the

The other attacking regiments fared no better, taking heavy losses from Buckland's fire. So devastating was the effect of the Yankees' shooting that numbers of Southerners completely broke down. Captain L. L. Dearing, Fifth Tennessee, tried to run off and hide in the rear of his regiment, but Colonel Ben Hill dragged him back under threat of shooting him. Private Perry Murrell, Company K, was the first casualty and the first man killed in the Fifth Regiment, dropping from artillery fire. As the Fifth pushed toward Buckland's position, a projectile cut the colors in the hands of the color bearer, William Sims, who managed to catch them as they fell, tying the flag back to the staff with his canteen strap. Soldier after soldier went down, killed or wounded, mostly from artillery fire, and one private, B. F. Taylor, was knocked unconscious from the concussion of a bursting shell.[20] The Fifth included at least one fifteen year old, Private John Roberts, who had his musket shattered and was twice knocked down by spent musket balls, but "displayed the courage of a veteran."[21]

The former state senator from Ohio's brigade held firm. The hard-driving Cleburne was stopped on his left, but on the right one of the defending regiments was out of the battle, and the other two were beginning to feel the pressure. Could the Mississippians recoup the attack there? With artillery support perhaps they could have made it, but General Hardee's chief of artillery, Major F. A. Shoup, ordered Trigg's Battery to pull back, thus leaving Cleburne gunless.

The Sixth Mississippi and Twenty-third Tennessee charged across the Fifty-third Ohio's camp between the rows of tents, tent pegs, tent lines, mud, Waterhouse's shells, and a heavy blast of musketry coming

---

Corinth Road. Today, the fallen timber has regrown, making the portion described by Cunningham a separate field altogether from Rhea Field. Indeed, he referred to the field as unnamed in an earlier footnote. To save confusion, we have slightly altered the original text to reflect this ambiguity.

20 *OR* 10, pt. 1, 589; Rennolds, *Henry County Commands*, 32; Thomas Head, *Campaigns and Battles of the Sixteenth Tennessee Regiment* (Nashville: Cumberland Presbyterian Publishing House, 1885), 232, 233; T. H. Peebles to wife, April 19, 1862, *Confederate Veteran* 16 (June 1908): 281.

21 *Ibid., Confederate Veteran* 25 (March 1917): 222.

from the Fifty-seventh, and possibly the Seventy-seventh. Finally they fell back, the Twenty-third in complete disorder.[22]

Most of the surviving Tennesseans took shelter in a ravine near where they had started their attack. General Cleburne went over and spoke to the men, saying, "Boys, don't be discouraged; this is not the 1st charge that was repulsed; fix bayonets and give them steel."[23]

Even with Cleburne's encouraging words, it took much time to get even part of the regiment formed up again, thus leaving it up to the Sixth Mississippi to do the job, but they were rapidly being outweighed by the arrival of reinforcements from McClernand's division.

At the request of General Sherman, McClernand directed his Third Brigade, whose nominal commander was Colonel L. F. Ross, to go to the support of the Fifth Division. Unfortunately, Ross was absent on this morning, so the command devolved on Colonel J. S. Rearden.[24] Colonel Rearden was ill, thus Lieutenant Abram H. Ryan, acting assistant adjutant of the Third Brigade, set out to find Colonel Julius Raith, letting him know that he was the senior officer present, hence, he would be in command.

Notified of his unexpected promotion, Raith soon had the brigade moving forward to support General Sherman's battered left, the Seventeenth Illinois advancing directly up to the Seventy-seventh Ohio's

22 *OR* 10, pt. 1, 581. Possibly Captain Samuel E. Barrett's Battery B, First Illinois Light Artillery, (four 6-pound smoothbores and two 12-pound howitzers) was also shelling in this attack. It went into action on Colonel Hildebrand's right about this time. *Ibid.*, 273, 139. Nispel's Light Artillery Battery, belonging to General McClernand's division, (two 6-pound smoothbores and two 12-pound howitzers) also went into action about this same time. Both batteries were veterans. Part of Nispel's Battery served at Liberty, Missouri, September 17, 1861. Battery E, Nispel's Battery, also was engaged at Fort Donelson. Battery B was engaged at Frederickstown, Missouri, October 21, 1861, and also at Belmont, Missouri, November 7, 1861.

23 J. A. Wheeler, "Cleburne's Brigade at Shiloh," *Confederate Veteran* 2 (January, 1894): 13.

24 Colonel Ross was on leave. His wife had just died, and he had not returned from leave. Adolph Engelmann to wife, April 17, 1862, Adolph Engelmann Papers, Illinois State Historical Library; *OR* 10, pt. 1, 115, 139.

camp. From left to right, he deployed the Forty-ninth Illinois, Lieutenant Colonel Phineas Pease, Forty-third Illinois, Lieutenant Colonel Adolph Engelmann, Twenty-ninth Illinois, Lieutenant Colonel Charles Ferrell, and the Seventeenth Illinois, Lieutenant Colonel Enos P. Wood.[25]

It was about this time the Sixth Mississippi made another charge on the Fifty-third's camp, so presumably the Illinoisans helped break the gallant but futile effort. The Mississippians made it into the camp area, and they raked the Federals with wicked blasts of Enfield balls. Colonel A. J. Thornton and Major Robert Lowery were both hit. (Thornton was disabled for the rest of his life.) Many others were hit, and the rest were finally forced to retreat in order to keep from being completely destroyed. Of the 425 Mississippians who jauntily moved forward to fight the Northerners only a little more than an hour earlier, 300 now lay in and around Shiloh Branch and the Ohioan's camp, dead or wounded.[26]

25 *Ibid.*; Robert W. Campbell, "Brief History of the 17th Regiment Illinois Volunteer Infantry 1861-1864," *Transactions of the Illinois State Historical Society* 2 (May 1914): 184-190; George O. Smith, "Brief History of the 17th Illinois Infantry," unpublished manuscript, Illinois State Historical Library. || Dr. Cunningham is mistaken that the 17th Illinois, or any of Raith's brigade, reached the 53rd Ohio camp. Lieutenant Colonel Enos P. Wood's report mentions only that the 17th Illinois formed "behind the encampment of an Ohio regiment." *OR* 10, pt. 1, 141. The Ohio regiment Wood mentioned was the 77th Ohio. The Shiloh Battlefield Commission placed the brigade's monuments and tablets well north of Shiloh Branch, and the modern research has confirmed this placement. We have slightly altered the text to reflect this evidence. See Shiloh Battlefield Monuments # 53 and # 57, and Tablets #36 and # 41. See also Sword, *Shiloh*, 204; Daniel, *Shiloh*, 177-178.

26 *OR* 10, pt. 1, 581; Cox, "Sixth Mississippi," 509, 510; Buck, *Cleburne and His Command*, 38. Waterhouse's Battery did most of the damage to the Mississippians. Cleburne's report bears this out. *OR* 10, pt. 1, 581. Reed, *Shiloh*, 57, said Sherman was hit by Wood and Cleburne. D. W. Reed knew more about the tactical dispositions at Shiloh than any other human being, but after hiking the battlefield, checking numerous official reports, and discussing the matter with the present Shiloh National Military Park Historian, Jerry Schober, I have come to believe that Wood's Brigade did not join in the advance until after the Fifty-third and Fifty-seventh regiments broke and were replaced by Raith's brigade around 9:00 a.m. || Dr. Cunningham's theory is interesting, but the editors believe it is only partially correct. The Shiloh

Raith soon found himself under heavy attack from Hardee and Bragg. Cleburne's Brigade was temporarily knocked out of action by the bloody repulse it had endured, but Anderson's Second Brigade quickly formed up on virtually the same ground Cleburne's men had launched their attack from. From left to right the black-bearded Anderson deployed his Twentieth Louisiana, Colonel August Reichard, Ninth Texas, Colonel W. A. Stanley, First Florida Battalion, Major T. A. McDowell, Confederate Guard Response Battalion, Major Franklin Clark, and the Seventeenth Louisiana, Lieutenant Colonel Charles Jones. The Fifth Company of the Washington Artillery set up their battery on high ground to the rear of Anderson, and they began dropping 6-pound shells and shot, along with 12-pound howitzer rounds, on Colonels Buckland's and Hildebrand's soldiers. Lieutenant George Nispel's Battery E, Second Illinois Light Artillery quickly slashed back at the men from New Orleans. Cannon balls and shells were traded with much enthusiasm but little damage to either side. Major Shoup brought two field pieces up to a position thirty or thirty-five yards from the Louisianans, and under the combined fire of the eight guns the Federal battery was forced to withdraw. Nispel left behind a disabled gun, five dead horses, one dead gunner, and he carried off three wounded cannoneers.[27]

Battlefield Commission verified Wood's Brigade with several tablets in the park. It placed the brigade in southern Rhea Field as early as 7:30 a.m., and later fighting their way through the field against Peabody on the right and taking fire from Waterhouse's Battery on the left, in the field itself, as late as 9:00 a.m. The 53rd Ohio fell back shortly after 8:00 a.m. according to their monument, Shiloh Battlefield Commission Monument # 131. Shaver did not dislodge Peabody to the east until around 9:00 a.m. See Shiloh Battlefield Commission Tablets # 211 and 215. Thus, although Dr. Cunningham is correct that Wood's Brigade did not advance through the 53rd Ohio's camp until around 9:00 a.m., the editors believe Wood's advance was as orderly and flowed at about the same speed as Shaver's, who was making no better time to the east.

27 Order Book, Fifth Washington Artillery, April 9, 1862, 45, Louisiana Historical Association Collection; *OR* 10, pt. 1, 146, 513. The two guns Shoup brought to help the Washington Artillery were from either Hubbard's Battery, Calvert's Battery, or Trigg's Battery. *Ibid.*, 146.

Bankhead's Tennessee Battery also wound up supporting Anderson's advance, firing from a position about one hundred yards from the Louisianans. With the guns pounding Sherman's position, and upon orders from General Bragg, Anderson led his brigade forward. The Twentieth Louisiana ran into the Second Tennessee, falling back after its earlier bloody encounter with the Forty-eighth Ohio, and there was some confusion as the men broke ranks and became intermingled.[28]

The two regiments were quickly unscrambled, and Prussian-born Colonel August Reichard's Twentieth was soon steadily moving toward Buckland's position again. The whole brigade somewhat clumsily straggled across Shiloh Branch or stumbled through the boggy area with a minimum of coordination. Piece by piece Anderson's units hit Sherman, some being repulsed with heavy losses, while others were able to partially penetrate Hildebrand's positions.[29]

The Seventeenth Louisiana picked up some unexpected support as one of Colonel R. M. Russell's regiments, the Eleventh Louisiana, suddenly showed up. General Bragg had directed Brigadier General Charles Clark to silence Waterhouse's Battery,[30] and the Eleventh was the closest unit at hand, so it naturally got the job. Colonel Samuel F. Marks, with General Clark standing by, launched his attack on Waterhouse's guns when the Seventeenth came wandering by. Waterhouse's James rifles had already taken a grim toll of the Eleventh. Just moments before, a bursting shell tore off Third Lieutenant John Crowley's left hand, that unfortunate officer having already lost his right arm at Belmont the previous November.[31]

---

28 *Ibid.*, 496, 507, 585, 497.

29 || Dr. Cunningham originally stated that Anderson's Brigade penetrated Buckland's and Hildebrand's lines. We have seen no evidence of Anderson or anyone else breaking Buckland's line. Anderson's extreme right regiments may have aided in pushing some of Hildebrand's units back, but they most assuredly did not drive back Buckland. Thus, we have slightly altered the text to reflect this. See *OR* 10, pt. 1, 267, 497.

30 *OR* 10, pt. 1, 414, 415.

31 *Ibid.*, 420. Later in the battle, Crowley was captured by Grant's army, and he was later exchanged near Baton Rouge, Louisiana, October 9, 1862. Andrew

The two regiments moved across the blood-spattered ground, the camp of Appler's Fifty-third Ohio, stepping over the dead and wounded Mississippians and Tennesseans. Marks and his men became entangled in the same boggy ground in which Pat Cleburne had muddied his shining uniform. The shells from Waterhouse's guns added to the confusion, and only four of Marks' companies actually got into the camp area. Having reached this point, Marks' troubles were only starting, as Federal soldiers, concealed in and behind the tents and other equipment in Appler's camp, began picking off his remaining men. Federal infantry, supporting Waterhouse, also fired into the Eleventh. One James shell burst between the legs of Lieutenant Levi S. Brown, killing him and Privates Thomas Bladon and Thomas Cameron. The Louisianans began to falter and Sergeant John Leonard, Company I, ran out in front to encourage the wavering Eleventh.[32] He received a Minie ball through his head for his trouble. The wavering turned into a rout, and the regiment wound up badly scattered, a large portion of it winding up in Stewart's Brigade.[33]

Lieutenant Colonel Charles Jones, Seventeenth Louisiana, fared a little better. Becoming entangled with a group of Tennesseans, presumably the Twenty-third, Jones spent precious minutes getting the regiment straightened out before giving the order to charge. Heading right for the Northerners, the regiment gradually slowed down and finally halted under the steady and accurate volleys of musketry coming across the stream. There was no rout; the Seventeenth simply stopped advancing, and the men began returning the enemy's fire. On both sides men began dropping, but finally the Louisianans beat a reluctant retreat.

Booth, *Records of Louisiana Confederate Soldiers and Louisiana Confederate Commands* 3 vols. (New Orleans: n.p., 1920), 2: 493; Charles Johnson to his wife, Louisia, April 11, 1862, Charles Johnson Papers, Louisiana State University Archives. In civilian life, Crowley was a mechanic. He was a private at Belmont, but was later elected lieutenant when a vacancy occurred in Company C. He was discharged from the army, but insisted on returning to his regiment on Wednesday before Shiloh. *Ibid.*

32 *OR* 10, pt. 1, 420, 421, 505; Charles James Johnson to wife, Louisia, April 11, 1862, Charles James Johnson Papers, Louisiana State University Archives.

33 *OR* 10, pt. 1, 428.

Reforming what was left of his regiment, Jones tried again, this time moving more to the left. Hit by another Federal battery, probably Barrett's, and by small arms fire, Jones was forced to fall back a second time. Two of his company commanders, R. H. Curry and W. A. Maddox, the latter just back from an extended sick leave in Claiborne Parish, Louisiana, were badly wounded in this effort.[34]

The Confederate Guards Response (Twelfth Louisiana Infantry Battalion) and the Florida Battalion fared no better in their charge on Sherman,[35] the Floridians losing their commander, T. A. McDonell.[36] In the army less than four weeks, the ninety-day volunteers from Louisiana pressed their attack home with courage, but when the troops on their right began falling back, the untrained Louisianans quickly followed them.[37] The laggard Twentieth Louisiana got into the attack also, as well as Colonel W. A. Stanley's Ninth Texas, but they were repulsed like everyone else.[38]

It was now a few minutes after 9:00 a.m. and Prentiss' division was in full retreat from its camps; the Union right, however, still held. At 9:10 a.m., General Beauregard directed General Polk to send a brigade to help break General Sherman's position.[39] The Creole then directed Polk to send Russell's brigade to help break Raith's position, not knowing that Russell was already partly engaged.[40]

Cleburne's left wing was pretty well knocked out of the fight, but the Irishman managed to collect sixty of his Mississippians and about one-half of the Twenty-third Tennessee in preparation for another charge. At the same time Anderson's individual regiments and battalions were also busy getting ready for another attempt.

---

34 *Ibid.*, 505; Booth, *Louisiana Records*, 3: 835.

35 Reed, *Shiloh*, 77.

36 *OR* 10, pt. 1, 504.

37 *Ibid.*, 510.

38 *Ibid.*, 507, 508, 510.

39 S. W. Ferguson to General Beauregard, April 9, 1862, Miscellaneous Collection, Shiloh National Military Park.

40 *OR* 10, pt. 1, 407, 408.

About 9:30 a.m., General Sherman and Colonel Raith found themselves assaulted by six separate brigades, for Sterling Wood, Bushrod Johnson, Robert M. Russell, and A. P. Stewart were also going in. (The latter was going in on orders from Bragg, although the brigade technically belonged to Polk's Corps.)[41] Partly on orders from Bragg and partly on the initiative of the individual officers, the six brigades and pieces of brigades began stumbling forward toward Sherman and Raith.

Sherman found himself being heavily pounded by Cleburne and Anderson, as well as the brand new fresh brigade of Bushrod Johnson. With his remaining tiny force, Cleburne boldly assaulted the Seventieth Ohio and the remnants of Hildebrand's Third Brigade.[42] Anderson also boldly smashed into the ridge to which Buckland still grimly clung. The Seventeenth Louisiana, making its third charge through the Fifty-third Ohio's camp, changed its direction slightly, passing to the left of the ridge. The Louisianans took a bad pounding from small arms' fire, including the loss of Lieutenant Colonel Charles Jones' sergeant major, Thuron Stone, who took a bullet through the thigh.

Reaching the top of the ridge, the Seventeenth was hit by artillery fire (probably from Nispel's new battery position near the Church).[43] The first lieutenant of Company K, Thomas O. Hynes, had his left arm blown off. Then Jones went down as an exploding shell panicked his horse, throwing the lieutenant colonel to the ground with enough force to knock him out for several minutes. Even while their commander was temporarily out of the fight, the Southerners swarmed toward Sherman's position.[44]

Supported by the fire of the Washington Artillery, the Ninth Texas and Twentieth Louisiana, along with the Confederate Guards Response

---

41 *Ibid.*, 582, 427, 416, 444.

42 *Ibid.*, 582.

43 *Ibid.*, 505, 146.

44 *Ibid.*, 506. Part of the right regiment became separated in the attack and linked up with the Confederate Guards Response Battalion and a portion of the Eleventh Louisiana. Andrew Booth maintained that Hynes was a first lieutenant in Company A. Hynes resigned from the army on July 28, 1862, presumably from his wounds. Booth, *Louisiana Records*, 3: 403.

Battalion, assaulted Buckland's position on the ridge. Screaming their wild yells, many of them in German, (three-fourths of the Twentieth were Germans by birth, and their commanding officer was the former Prussian Consul at New Orleans), the Rebels forced Buckland to fall back and entered the Seventy-seventh Ohio's camp.[45]

If Buckland was beginning to give ground, the situation on Sherman's left was even worse, for Colonel Hildebrand's brigade was disintegrating. Under heavy pressure from the troops of Johnson's and Russell's brigades, the Fifty-seventh Ohio broke and headed for the rear.[46]

From left to right, Johnson had Colonel J. K. Walker's Second Tennessee, Lieutenant Colonel R. C. Tyler's Fifteenth Tennessee, Colonel A. K. Blythe's Mississippi Battalion (subsequently known as the Forty-fourth), and Colonel Preston Smith's One hundred fifty-fourth Tennessee, plus Captain Marshall T. Polk's Tennessee Battery of four 6-pound smoothbores and two 12-pound howitzers. On orders from General Bragg, the brigade went into action, charging Sherman's left, but the Mississippians advanced around the point of the hill north of the Rhea House, attacking Waterhouse's Battery from the right flank.[47]

As the Mississippi soldiers moved up, they observed the wreckage of the earlier attack. A Private Gullick, Company H, remarked to his sergeant, "From the looks of things around here we are going to have some fun. . . . I would give a thousand dollars for a shot in my hand"—a Civil War reference to a "million dollar" wound. Meeting some wounded, who were walking and looking for a field hospital, Gullick spotted a young soldier with a smashed hand, and he laughingly made the

45 *OR* 10, pt. 1, 509-511; Charles DePetz to his wife, April 5, 1862, in Robert T. Clark, Jr., "The New Orleans German Colony in the Civil War," *Louisiana Historical Quarterly* 20 (Fall 1937): 1003. || Here again, Dr. Cunningham stated originally that the Confederates broke Buckland's line. We have found no credible evidence of this, but argue that Buckland voluntarily withdrew upon orders from Sherman. There is, however, no doubt that Anderson pushed Buckland along in the withdrawal. We have slightly altered the original text to reflect this. See *OR* 10, pt. 1, 267, 497.

46 *OR* 10, pt. 1, 249, 262, 263; Lindsey, *Ohio at Shiloh*, 31.

47 *OR* 10, pt. 1, 444, 446, 450, 451.

same remark he had made earlier to his sergeant. With tears streaming down his cheeks, the young wounded soldier replied, "Go up the hill where I have been, and the Yanks will give you one and won't charge you a cent." (Gullick was later killed in Georgia.)[48]

Many of the Mississippians suffered worse than wounded hands as they went into action. Colonel Blythe was shot dead from his horse, and within minutes his successor, Lieutenant Colonel D. L. Herron, went down mortally wounded. The regiment quickly halted, taking cover in a ravine near the battery.[49] The wounded were sent to the rear, including Private John C. Thompson, aged seventy-one, probably the oldest man on either side in the battle. The regimental surgeon took one look at Judge Thompson's scalp wound and told the elderly soldier to go ride in an ambulance. Within minutes, however, the determined Thompson, a strong secessionist, was back with his company, fighting by the side of his thirteen year old son, Flem.[50]

Johnson's two left regiments charged the remnants of the Third Brigade and the Seventy-second Ohio together. Coming under heavy fire, the Tennesseans began to falter, but Lieutenant Colonel Tyler drew his pistol and restored order. With Polk's Battery in position just behind the attacking force, the two regiments pushed steadily onward, trading shots with the Federals. Union fire wounded Colonel Tyler's horse, then the rider, forcing him to leave the field. Federal riflemen worked Polk's Battery over, breaking the doughty captain's leg and killing and wounding many men and horses. Lieutenant T. R. Smith assumed command of the battery, but its fire dropped off badly.[51]

48   J. B. Howard, "Wanted A Finger Wound," *Confederate Veteran* 7 (May 1899): 223.

49   *OR* 10, pt. 1, 444.

50   W. H. Lee, "Major John C. Thompson of Mississippi," *Confederate Veteran* 16 (November 1908): 585. Elected major, Thompson was killed at Chickamauga. Private Hugh McVey, Company D, Fourth Kentucky, a British-born veteran of Waterloo, an aggressive Confederate, was killed at Shiloh. He was over seventy years old. Thompson, *History of the Orphan Brigade*, 650.

51   *OR* 10, pt. 1, 444, 445; Edwin Bearss, "An Artillery Study Shiloh National Military Park, Project 17," Miscellaneous Collection, Shiloh National Military Park. This work will be hereafter cited as "Project 17."

Johnson's two left regiments bogged down, but his detached One hundred fifty-fourth Tennessee, charging through the Fifty-third Ohio camp and stumbling across Shiloh Branch, finally made it to Waterhouse's position just as the troops from Russell's brigade came swarming upon the Illinoisans' left flank.[52] The battery tried to withdraw, but Waterhouse was wounded and then the next officer to take over, Lieutenant Abial Abbott, also went down. Lieutenant J. A. Fitch then took charge, but by this time the Tennesseans were virtually on top of the gunners.[53] The battery personnel managed to pull back, leaving three guns behind in the hands of Company B, One hundred fifty-fourth Tennessee. Privates D. W. Collier, John C. Southerland, James W. Maury, and James Southerland were the first four to get to the cannon,[54] where they found a beautiful Irish setter guarding the body of his dead master and barking fiercely at any Southerner who approached him.[55]

52 *OR* 10, pt. 1, 446; A. J. Vaughan, *Personal Record of the Thirteenth Regiment, Tennessee Infantry* (Memphis: Press of C. S. Toof and Company, 1897), 15, 16.

53 *OR* 10, pt. 1, 276, 277; "War Experiences of George Read Lee," George Read Lee Papers, Illinois State Historical Library.

54 C. W. Robertson to D. W. Reed, May 26, 1904, Miscellaneous Collection, Shiloh National Military Park.

55 Samuel Latta to wife, April 12, 1862, Confederate Collection, Tennessee Department of Archives and History; C. W. Robertson to D. W. Reed, May 26, 1904, Miscellaneous Collection, Shiloh National Military Park. There is some dispute as to whom actually captured the guns. Both the Thirteenth and One hundred fifty-fourth Tennessee claimed them. (Copy of an interview between Colonel A. J. Vaughan and D. W. Reed, Miscellaneous Collection, Shiloh National Military Park.) Robertson claimed the One hundred fifty-fourth took them, while Vaughan did so likewise. In all probability it was a dead heat, with men from both regiments getting there about the same time. No one mentions taking Nispel's abandoned gun. It is possible some of the Tennessee soldiers scooped up this weapon, thinking it was part of Waterhouse's Battery; hence, possibly accounting for the confusion of the claims. || The Shiloh Battlefield Commission gave the 13th Tennessee the honor of capturing the position. See Battlefield Tablet #305. Subsequent authors have also given the 13th Tennessee the credit. See Daniel, *Shiloh*, 170; Sword, *Shiloh*, 197.

At this time Bushrod Johnson was severely wounded while trying to reform Walker's Second Tennessee, but his other regiments had already penetrated the Shiloh Church line.[56] The Fifth Division's position was now hopelessly compromised. The Third Brigade was either routed or shattered; Buckland's brigade front was falling back; and the entire division was cut off from Raith's Illinois brigade, which was now in danger of being overwhelmed.

Sherman's First Brigade was committed on the right of Buckland's brigade to prevent its flank from being turned by Colonel Preston Pond, Jr.'s Brigade,[57] so no reinforcements were forthcoming from that quarter. McDowell had moved his three regiments, from left to right Colonel Stephen Hicks, Fortieth Illinois, Captain Daniel Iseminger, Sixth Iowa, (Colonel McDowell was now commanding the brigade, the lieutenant colonel was under arrest, and Major J. M. Corse was absent on General John Pope's staff) and his battery, the Sixth Indiana Light Artillery, Captain Frederick Behr, into position on the ridge to cover Buckland's right about 8:00 a.m. He detached two companies of the Sixth Iowa under Captain M. W. Walden, afterwards governor of Iowa, and a 12-pound howitzer under Lieutenant William Mussman to protect the crossing at the Owl Creek Bridge.

Observing Pond's Brigade moving toward him, McDowell ordered Captain Behr to open fire with his remaining howitzer. McDowell then ordered the Fortieth Illinois to move to the left in closer support of Buckland's right.[58]

---

56 *OR* 10, pt. 1, 445.

57 Colonel Pond's Brigade advanced on orders from General Ruggles, the idea being to turn the enemy's right flank. "Ammended Report of General Ruggles," *Southern Historical Society Papers* 7 (January 1879): 38.

58 *OR* 10, pt. 1, 254, 255; Byers, *Iowa In War Times*, 138; William Salter, "Major-General John M. Corse," *Annals of Iowa* 11 (April 1895): 5. When the Sixth Iowa moved out that morning with McDowell's brigade, Lieutenant Colonel Markoe Cummins, of Muscatine, Iowa, was theoretically in command. Unfortunately he was quite drunk. After Cummins put the regiment through some strange maneuvers, McDowell placed him under arrest. Wright, *Sixteenth Iowa*, 80. In the *Official Records*, Captain John Williams is listed as commanding the Sixth. *OR* 52, pt. 1, 18. Williams turned in a report of the early

Confederate skirmishers quietly worked their way forward toward McDowell's position and commenced peppering Behr's gunners with musketry. The battery commander, formerly of the Prussian artillery, handed his binoculars to an enlisted man, J. L. Bieler, instructing him to spot the snipers. Eyes straining through the glasses, Bieler slowly searched the surrounding terrain until he finally located a group of Confederates well concealed in a far away corn crib. With this information in hand, and at Behr's order, the ponderous iron tubes were wheeled about and sighted on the crib. Shell fire raked the Confederates and the musket fire abruptly ceased.[59]

Pond's Brigade, less the Thirty-eighth Tennessee and one section of Ketchum's Battery (which was detached to cover Owl Creek Bridge), moved slowly forward. Before serious contact was made, however, McDowell received orders about 10:00 a.m. to fall back to the Purdy Road.[60]

Some of Pond's skirmishers did have a rather weird experience with Colonel Stephen Hicks' Fortieth Illinois just before the withdrawal. Still clad in their pre-war blue militia uniforms, the group of Louisianans stumbled upon the Federals. Colonel Hicks assumed that they were a party of lost Northerners, but some of the colonel's men suspected the men to be Rebels. The colonel ordered his soldiers to hold their fire, and he asked the group to identify themselves. They replied that they belonged to an Indiana regiment, and in turn asked the colonel what outfit his was. Hicks then gave the command to fall back by "right of companies to the rear into columns," and as the Federals turned around

---

part of the day's action, but it was vaguely worded, and he continually used the first person plural to describe the regiment's activities. *OR* 10, pt. 1, 256. It would seem that Iseminger was killed very early in the action, and then Williams took over until he was wounded. Later in the day Cummins sobered up and joined with the Fifteenth Iowa, fighting as a simple private soldier. Cummins was mustered out of the army on May 20, 1862. Belknap, *15th Iowa*, 83; McElroy, *Undying Procession*, 21.

59 J. L. Bieler, copy of a speech made at a reunion of the battery, Miscellaneous Collection, Shiloh National Military Park.

60 *OR* 10, pt. 1, 516, 255.

and marched off, Pond's bluecoated Confederates speeded their withdrawal by peppering the Fortieth with musketry.[61]

Sherman sent Captain J. H. Hammond of his staff to notify Buckland's regiments to pull back. He made it to the Seventieth's and Forty-eighth's commanding officers, but before he could inform the Seventy-second, Colonel Buckland, on his own initiative, ordered the regiment to retreat to the Purdy Road.[62]

After about two hours of stubborn fighting, the entire Fifth Division was falling back in some disorder. Raith's brigade was also trying to pull back, under attack by Russell, Stewart, and Wood.[63] Russell's lead regiment, the Twelfth Tennessee, had a comparatively easy advance, for by the time they attacked, the Illinoisans were already pulling back. They suffered a few casualties to rear guard fire, but managed to occupy the Fourth Illinois Cavalry camp. The Thirteenth advanced on the Twelfth's right, with Colonel Vaughan intending to turn the Illinois battery's left flank. Advancing toward Raith's brigade, the regiment began catching heavy musket fire. Private Bert Moore was hit by a spent slug, which knocked him off his feet. Men began dropping faster and faster. Sergeant John S. Scarbrough saw his brother, Lemuel, drop from a bullet, but he had only time to cry out, "Hello, Lemuel!" so swift was Vaughan's Confederates' pace.[64]

---

61 John T. Hunt, "Reminiscences of Shiloh," Miscellaneous Collection, Shiloh National Military Park. The militia uniforms worn by the Louisianans caused them much trouble all day long. As Mouton's Eighteenth Louisiana swarmed into McDowell's abandoned camps, scooping up twenty-nine stragglers, the regiment was fired into by a body of Confederate skirmishers on their right. The skirmishers simply mistook the blue uniforms of the Eighteenth for Federal outfits. One private was killed, and three privates and Captain Henry Huntington, just returned from two months sick leave, were badly wounded. *OR* 10, pt. 1, 521. The brigade was then halted and rested for several hours, excepting the Crescent Regiment, which was detached from the group to go to the aid of the Thirty-eighth Tennessee Infantry Regiment.

62 Bering and Montgomery, *Forty-eighth Ohio*, 21; *OR* 10, pt. 1, 267, 270.

63 *Ibid.*, 421; Liddell Hart, *Sherman*, 127; Roman, *Beauregard*, 1: 290.

64 *OR* 10, pt. 1, 425; Lemuel Scarborough, "Shiloh," Miscellaneous Collection, Shiloh National Military Park.

Through a mix-up in orders, Major Wingfield went wandering off to the left with four companies while Vaughan and the other six turned the corner and headed in on Waterhouse's left flank. The lost sheep became scattered and took heavy casualties, but Vaughan and the others charged the battery, which was attempting to retreat at the same time the One hundred fifty-fourth Tennessee was charging head on.[65]

Lieutenant Colonel Enos P. Wood, Seventeenth Illinois, had already fallen back about two hundred yards behind the battery's position as the Tennesseans hit it, and he could see the Southerners hoist the "Stars and Bars" above the captured pieces. Lieutenant Alexander T. Davis, Company K, grabbed a rifle from one of his wounded men and brought down the color bearer. The regiment continued falling back until it reached General McClernand and the rest of the division.[66]

Wood's and Stewart's brigades were supposed to have joined in with Russell and Johnson in this advance, but both had been delayed by some peculiar circumstances. Stewart's Second Brigade, from left to right, the Fifth Tennessee, Lieutenant Colonel C. D. Venable, Thirty-third Tennessee, Colonel A. W. Campbell, Thirteenth Arkansas, Lieutenant Colonel A. D. Grayson, and the Fourth Tennessee, Colonel Rufus Neely, formed up on the main Pittsburg Road, beginning its forward movement about 7:00 a.m. Advancing about eight hundred yards, the troops dropped their knapsacks and then resumed their march. As the Fifth Tennessee passed Fraley's Field one of Sherman's batteries opened fire on Venable and his men. One private was killed, another wounded, and the flagstaff severed.[67]

---

65 *Ibid.*; Vaughan, *Personal Record of the Thirteenth Regiment, Tennessee Infantry*, 16; Samuel Latta to his wife, April 12, 1862, Confederate Collection, Tennessee Department of Archives and History. It is not certain if Colonel Vaughan cut across, behind, or in front of the Twelfth Tennessee's advance. The Twenty-second Tennessee Infantry apparently followed along close behind Vaughan in the charge. Robert H. Wood to his father, James Wood, June 1, 1862, University of Tennessee Library, Knoxville, Tennessee.

66 *OR* 10, pt. 1, 141.

67 *Ibid.*, 433, 427. Waterhouse's Battery probably had the best shot at the Fifth, and the James rifles could have dropped a shell that far, but Venable said that a cannon ball struck the flagstaff. Perhaps it was a dud shell.

Stewart continued moving forward until General Johnston came riding up and directed him to support Bragg. The Confederate commander left, and Stewart hastened to execute his order.[68]

As his Arkansas regiment reached the camp of the Fourth Illinois, heavy fire broke out around the Trans-Mississippi soldiers. Union gunners were sporadically shelling Gibson's Brigade behind and slightly east of Stewart's unit. An exploding projectile mortally wounded a private in Company D, Thirteenth Arkansas;[69] another burst of fire killed five enlisted men in the Thirteenth Louisiana;[70] still another shell burst badly wounded Captain William A. Crawford, a member of Company E, First Arkansas.[71]

The whole brigade was getting restless and a bit nervous when suddenly Private A. V. Vertner came riding toward the Fourth Louisiana with a U. S. flag draped around his waist and a Yankee cap on his head. Vertner, a former member of Company C, Fourth Louisiana, had been detached from the company since June the previous year and was now serving as an orderly to Major General William J. Hardee. Someone yelled, "Here's your Yankee," and a hundred guns instantly were leveled at the horseman. Vertner and his horse went down, riddled with bullets before anyone recognized him.[72]

Some of the Louisianans' shots hit Stewart's Brigade, particularly the Thirteenth Arkansas. Captain H. W. Murphy, Company C, was killed and Captain R. B. Lambert, Company A, Lieutenants J. C. Hall and B. M. Hopkins, Company A, and several privates were wounded. Assuming they had been outflanked, Stewart's Arkansans returned the fire with enthusiasm. Their musket balls raked the Fourth Louisiana with deadly effect. Colonel Henry W. Allen, future governor of Louisiana, reported

---

68 *Ibid.*

69 *Ibid.*, 430.

70 Richardson, "War As I Saw It," 99.

71 *OR* 10, pt. 1, 487.

72 Thomas C. Robertson to mother, April 9, 1862, Thomas Chinn Robertson Papers, Louisiana State University Archives; Richardson, "War As I Saw It," 99.

that it was "a terrible blow to the regiment; far more terrible than any inflicted by the enemy."[73] Private Thomas Chinn Robertson reported one hundred and five members of the regiment down from the Arkansans' fire. Colonel Gibson's horse was also hit, and the brigade commander was somewhat shaken up, but he quickly ordered Colonel Allen's regiment to fall back and reform.[74] Lieutenant Colonel Grayson finally calmed his Thirteenth Arkansas, but precious minutes were lost before the unit was able to move forward again, thus the advance of the entire brigade was disrupted.[75]

Stewart soon had his men moving forward again, but Raith's Illinoisans were already falling back to link up with the rest of General McClernand's division.[76] Wood's Brigade moved up on Stewart's right, but also had trouble making contact with the Illinoisans. After resistance described as "not strong," his brigade advanced into Colonel Raith's camps.[77]

All six Confederate brigades now moved forward toward the new Union defensive arrangement established along the northern side of the Review Field at the crossroads of the Corinth-Purdy roads and on up along the Purdy Road.

73 *OR* 10, pt. 1, 489.

74 Thomas Chinn Robertson to mother, April 9, 1862, Thomas Chinn Robertson Papers, Louisiana State University Archives.

75 *OR* 10, pt. 1, 489, 430.

76 *Ibid.*, 430.

77 *Ibid.*, 597, 598, 600.

Chapter 9

The Battle Spreads

THE FEDERAL DEFENSE WAS crumbling not only on the right and center, but also on the extreme left, for Hardee was beginning to make brigade-sized attacks on Colonel Peabody's brigade. From left to right the icily-tempered Colonel Peabody placed what was left of the Sixteenth Wisconsin, Colonel Benjamin Allen, Twenty-first Missouri, Lieutenant Colonel Humphrey Woodyard, Twelfth Michigan, Colonel Francis Quinn, and the Twenty-fifth Missouri, Lieutenant Colonel Robert Van Horn.[1]

Since the forming of this position around 7:30 a.m., after its withdrawal from Seay's Field area, the Westerners had been catching fairly heavy fire from Shaver's Brigade, and, to a lesser extent, from their first foe, Wood's Brigade. For some reason the latter organization appears to have made a singularly slow advance, thus Shaver's Brigade did most of the fighting along the Rhea Field.

Captain Charles Swett's Battery opened up with its 6- and 12-pound guns as Shaver's infantry moved forward.[2] Shaver's order of advance was the Seventh Arkansas, Lieutenant Colonel John Dean, Second Arkansas, Colonel Daniel C. Govan, Sixth Arkansas, Colonel Alexander

---

1 || Dr. Cunningham originally stated that Peabody's brigade was "resting just southeast of the Bark Road, near the road touching the Rhea Field fence." We have been unable to figure out exactly what he was describing, and have removed the confusing clause for the sake of clarity.

2 *OR* 10, pt. 1, 574.

Hawthorn, and Third Confederate, Colonel John Marmaduke.[3] The Southern infantry held their fire while advancing in a tight linear formation.

Seventeen year old Private Henry Parker, Company E, Sixth Arkansas, wore some violets in his cap and naively remarked, "Perhaps the Yanks won't shoot me if they see me wearing such flowers, for they are a sign of peace." Unfortunately young Parker's idea did not work, and he ended up with a badly smashed foot.[4]

Drawn up in double lines, Peabody's soldiers had little to do but await the arrival of the enemy. Lieutenant Colonel Van Horn delayed giving an order until the Rebels were close enough to receive an effective fire. When they stepped into range, he gave the command: "Attention, battalion. Ready! Aim! Fire!" The blast of rifle fire stopped the Confederates' charge cold, with the surviving Southerners either falling back in disorder or taking cover as best they could.

But now it was the Northerners' turn to suffer, as the Confederate soldiers raked their line with musketry. Van Horn's men held, but Confederate troops turned the right of the brigade, and soon the Federals were falling back to a new position in front of their camp site. By this time Colonel Peabody was no longer alone. His left flank was protected by the rest of the division: Miller's brigade deployed along the north end of the Spain Field and two supporting artillery batteries, Munch's and Hickenlooper's.

From left to right, Miller arranged his Eighteenth Wisconsin, Colonel James Alban, Sixty-first Illinois, Colonel Jacob Fry, and the Eighteenth Missouri, Lieutenant Colonel Isaac Pratt. It was a good position, since any advancing Confederate troops would have to come up a sharp slope, while Hickenlooper's Battery, located just to the right rear

---

3 *Ibid.*, 573. The Confederate table of organization for Shiloh listed the Fifth Arkansas as part of this brigade, and it also listed the Pillow Flying Artillery as part of Shaver's Brigade. *OR* 10, pt. 1, 383. Shaver's report mentioned neither unit as being in his command during the battle. The two units are not listed in any official reports, nor in any of the sources this writer consulted. || Neither Sword nor Daniel make mention of the units either. McDonough's Order of Battle was based on the *OR*.

4 Stanley, *Autobiography*, 187, 193.

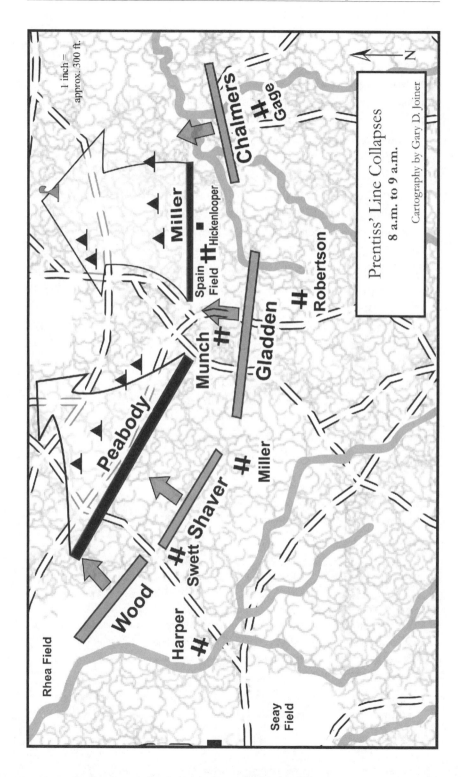

Prentiss' Line Collapses
8 a.m. to 9 a.m.

Cartography by Gary D. Joiner

1 inch =
approx. 300 ft.

of the brigade, dropped explosives on their heads. Peabody's brigade was deployed on the other side of the Eastern Corinth Road, with Munch's First Minnesota Battery immediately to their rear. There was a plowed field and a few scattered trees in front. The infantry had the protection of a slight swell in the ground along the edge of the trees.[5]

Around 8:00 a.m., Peabody's already battered men were struck again by Shaver's Brigade, which was supported by the right regiments of General Wood's outfit. At the same time Miller was hit by Gladden's First Brigade, (from left to right, the Twenty-fifth Alabama, Colonel John Loomis, Twenty-second Alabama, Colonel Zach Deas, Twenty-first Alabama, Lieutenant Colonel Stewart Cayce, First Louisiana, Colonel Daniel Adams, and the Twenty-sixth Alabama, Colonel John Coltart) advancing parallel to and on both sides of the Eastern Corinth Road, and part of Chalmers' "High Pressure" Brigade, moving up on Gladden's right, by order of General Withers.[6]

Gladden sent Robertson's Florida Battery into action to give adequate covering fire for the attack. The advancing Confederate infantry began to waver under the sharp fire from Prentiss' division, and the battery soon began catching scattered rifle fire. Lieutenant S. H. Dent and Captain Felix Robertson took the first section of the latter's Florida battery into within one hundred and fifty yards of Prentiss' line before going into action. Rifle fire chopped severely at the battery, but its fire vigorously punished Prentiss' soldiers.[7]

---

5   Arthur Walker, Jr., "Three Alabama Baptist Chaplains, 1861-1865," *The Alabama Review* 16 (July 1963): 178-179; Charles Pitts, *Chaplains in Gray: The Confederate Chaplains' Story* (Nashville: Broadman Press, 1957), 96, 97.

6   *OR* 10, pt. 1, 532. Chalmers' Brigade is usually referred to simply as the "Mississippi Brigade" or the "High Pressure" Brigade. J. C. Reitti, *History of the Mississippi Rifles, 10th Mississippi Regiment* (Glasgow: W. Anderson Fadie, n.d.), 1, 2; Rowland, *Official and Statistical Register*, 599. The Twenty-sixth Alabama was supposed to be on Gladden's left, but they were crowded out of their position by some of Shaver's men. Lieutenant William Chadwick wisely decided to quickly shift his regiment around to Gladden's right. In this new position it took part in the charge. *OR* 10, pt. 1, 545.

7   S. H. Dent to wife, April 9, 1862, Shiloh-Corinth Collection, Alabama Department of Archives and History. Bragg accompanied Gladden's Brigade

Miller's infantry permitted Gladden's hungry, muddy soldiers to advance up the slope to about one hundred yards range before squeezing their triggers. Men began to go down all around. The momentum of the attack broke down, and a stubborn fire fight quickly developed. Some of the Southerners began drifting toward the rear, but the officers went to work rallying them. One officer pointed at Robertson's guns and yelled, "Men do not disgrace yourselves by deserting those brave fellows."[8] Thanks to his initiative and the efforts of other officers, the withdrawal soon halted.

Chalmers' attack also developed some problems. From left to right his order of advance was: the Fifty-second Tennessee, Colonel Benjamin Lea, Fifth Mississippi, Colonel Albert Fant, Ninth Mississippi, Lieutenant Colonel William Rankin, Seventh Mississippi, Lieutenant Colonel Hamilton Mayson, and the Tenth Mississippi, Colonel Robert Smith, with Captain Charles Gage's Alabama Battery providing cover fire. The Mississippians advanced to within one hundred and fifty yards of the top of the slope before Chalmers ordered a halt. At his next order, the five regiments began hitting the Eighteenth Wisconsin and Sixty-first Illinois with musketry. Men dropped on both sides from cannon and rifle fire. The horse of Colonel B. J. Lea, Fifty-second Tennessee, was shot from under him, as also was the animal of the regimental major, Thomas G. Rundle.[9] After a few rounds, the order was given to fix bayonets and charge. Somehow only the Tenth Mississippi heard this command, so

---

in this attack. Reed, *Shiloh*, 73. Private Leander Stillwell, Sixty-first Illinois, commented on the exact way the Southerners advanced in "excellent order," an unknowing tribute to the excellence of Bragg's training of General Gladden's regiments. Stillwell, *Common Soldier*, 45.

8 S. H. Dent to wife, April 9, 1862, Shiloh-Corinth Collection, Alabama Department of Archives and History; Hugh W. Henry to parents, April 10, 1862, Shiloh-Corinth Collection, Alabama Department of Archives and History.

9 Colonel Lea was badly injured by his fall and carried off the battlefield. Major Rundle seems to have been injured also at this time, and Lieutenant Colonel H. S. Oliver was not present, which left Captain Andrew Wilson to assume command of the regiment. William Mosier to D. W. Reed, December 11, 1912, Miscellaneous Collection, Shiloh National Military Park.

that regiment charged toward Miller's line by itself. The Mississippians, three hundred and sixty strong, minus a few casualties in the past few minutes' firing, hit the Wisconsin regiment's line with enough force to rout the Northerners. As the Eighteenth broke, Private Micajah Wilkinson "gave it to one old blue belly about where his suspenders crossed, sending him to eternity."[10]

Colonel John Oliver and his Fifteenth Michigan arrived at the Locust Grove, to the left of the Eighteenth Wisconsin, just as Chalmers' men moved in for the charge. Oliver's regiment had landed only a couple of hours earlier and had not been issued ammunition. But he headed for the front anyway, hoping to pick up some cartridges en route. Finding himself about to be caught in Chalmers' attack, Colonel Oliver ordered his men to fix bayonets, as if to charge the approaching Mississippians, but Oliver wisely reconsidered and ordered the regiment to about face, and they returned to the Landing, where they were able to find cartridges. The Seventh and Ninth Mississippi were quickly ordered by Chalmers to follow the Tenth.[11]

Gladden's and Shaver's men were also pressing the Federals back, and the Southerners began to scent victory. Gladden gave orders for another charge and he rode forward to lead it when an aide, a Captain Scott of Mobile, Alabama, noticed the general dropped his reins. His horse moving a few steps farther, the fifty-one year old Gladden requested his aide to help him off the animal. Pointing to his left arm, he quietly remarked, "I am afraid it is a serious hurt."

Captain Scott examined the arm and found that near the shoulder it was a shattered mass of flesh and bone. An ambulance took the badly wounded commander away from the firing area. The injured limb was amputated in a field hospital a few days later by a Doctor Chappin. Unfortunately, the stump failed to heal, remaining in a "very unhealthy and dangerous state, and after a few days of suffering, gangrene

10 *OR* 10, 1: 548; Micajah Wilkinson to his brother, April 16, 1862, Micajah Wilkinson Papers, Louisiana State University Archives.

11 Captain James Sligh to his wife, April 7, 1862, James W. Sligh Papers, Michigan Historical Collection, University of Michigan; Reed, *Shiloh*, 60, 61; *OR* 10, pt. 1, 548.

supervened, and death finally relieved him of his sufferings."[12] Gladden died on April 12.

Gladden's senior officer, Colonel Daniel Adams, assumed command of the brigade. The colonel of the First Louisiana continued where Gladden left off, pressing Miller. The Union fire was destructive, and again the brigade faltered. Adams seized the battle flag from the color bearer of the First Louisiana and, with a cry for the men to follow him, galloped ahead.[13] A wild Rebel yell, wrote Andrew Hickenlooper of the Fifth Ohio Battery, caused "an involuntary thrill of terror to pass like an electric shock through even the bravest hearts" of Prentiss' men.[14]

Colonel Peabody rode up and down the line, crying out to his men, "Lexington, men! Lexington! Remember Lexington!"[15] Lieutenant Colonel Cassius Fairchild, Sixteenth Wisconsin, went down with a jagged hole in his thigh, while regimental commander Ben Allen's horse was shot from under him. Someone found Allen a second animal, but before he could mount it was killed.[16]

---

12 "The Death of General Gladden," Unsigned sketch in Miss Cottrill's Scrapbook, Alabama Department of Archives and History. According to an unidentified private in the Twenty-sixth Alabama, Gladden's last words were, "Go on my brave boys, they have hit old dad. I know you will drive every Yankee before you into the Tennessee River." "History of the 26th Alabama," Shiloh-Corinth Collection, Alabama Department of Archives and History. Gladden's arm was crushed by a cannon ball, or more probably by a large shell fragment. Colonel Deas, who ended up in command of the brigade, claimed Gladden was hit by a "cannon-ball." *OR* 10, pt. 1, 538. Adams said Gladden was hit by a cannon shot. *Ibid.*, 536. Hickenlooper's two 6-pound smoothbores fired canister, both single and double charges. The James rifles fired shrapnel. Hickenlooper, "Shiloh," 420. Munch's four rifles fired explosive shell or case shot, and his two howitzers canister. Gladden was likely hit by a shell fragment. Ezra Warner claims he was hit by a fragment. Warner, *Generals in Gray*, 107.

13 *OR* 10, pt. 1, 286.

14 Hickenlooper, "Shiloh," 415. Protected by the fire of Captain Charles Swett's Mississippi Battery, Shaver's Brigade also advanced. *OR* 10, pt. 1, 574. The Shiloh National Military Park markers indicate that the Seventh Arkansas collided head on with the Twenty-fifth Missouri on and along the road.

15 Morton, "A Boy at Shiloh," 60.

16 *OR* 10, pt. 1, 286.

Private Charles Norton, Twenty-fifth Missouri, flinched as a ricocheting slug drove wood splinters into his neck. A solid shot tore through the trees, dropping twigs and leaves on the men. A cannon shot landed in a mud hole, spattering soldiers with jagged iron splinters and clods of Tennessee dirt. The men could stand no more. What was left of the brigade began heading for the rear, Peabody's riderless horse following them, his master's lifeless body sprawled somewhere along the position that he had so gallantly defended.[17]

The remainder of Miller's brigade gave way also, and the triumphant Southerners swarmed into the Sixth Division's camp area. What little formations the Confederates retained was completely broken by the tents and wagons in the camp area, as the screaming Rebels poured through. Prentiss' headquarters were occupied, and some privates from the First Louisiana "scooped up" seven Union flags.[18] Some of the slower running Yanks were grabbed up by the charging Confederates. As he headed for the rear, Private Leander Stillwell of the Sixty-first Illinois regiment saw men in brown and gray clothing running through a camp on his right. He also saw something that sent a chill running through him—"a kind of flag I had never seen before . . . a gaudy sort of thing with red bars," not sixty yards away in the hands of a color bearer. Suddenly young Stillwell realized that for the first time in his life he had laid eyes on a Rebel battle flag.[19]

Some of the Southerners ran forward so fast that they were caught in the line of fire from their own batteries. The Twenty-sixth Alabama became entangled in the tent section of Miller's camp, losing their major, J. S. Garvin, by an exploding shell, probably fired by a Confederate battery.[20] Lieutenant S. H. Dent of Robertson's Battery was forced to order his guns to cease firing in order to keep from hitting his own men, so fast was their advance. Robertson's men quickly limbered up their battery and galloped through the camp. The wheels of one gun ran over

17   Morton, "A Boy at Shiloh," 60, 61.

18   *OR* 10, pt. 1, 537.

19   Stillwell, *Common Soldier*, 45, 46.

20   *OR* 10, pt. 1, 545.

the body of one of Miller's fallen soldiers, crushing him to a bloody pulp. Taking a new position on the northern side of the camp, the battery immediately unlimbered and reopened fire at some Yanks who were trying to rally and form a new line.[21]

Prentiss' battery commanders frantically hitched their teams to their guns, getting ten of them away safely, but the charging Rebels grabbed up two of Hickenlooper's guns.[22] This would-be Northern rally was quickly dispersed under artillery fire, and the Federals withdrew across Barnes' Field, heading in the direction of Hurlbut's division, where they were ordered to fall back by orders of General Prentiss.[23]

In the confusion of battle, Father Thomas Brady of Detroit, Michigan, Chaplain of the Fifteenth Michigan, rode around looking for his regiment. He saw a body of men close by and asked them if they could tell him where the Fifteenth Michigan was located. Unfortunately the men in question happened to be Confederates, Irishmen, probably from Adam's First Louisiana Regiment. Recognizing Brady as a priest, the soldiers politely told him they did not know where his regiment was, and they let him turn his horse around and ride safely toward the Landing and friendly troops.[24]

To the thousands of Confederate soldiers who triumphantly swarmed over the camps of Prentiss and Sherman, the battle must have seemed virtually over. Had they not seen entire regiments of Federals broken and running? Now it was time to enjoy the fruits of victory—the uniforms, boots, rifles, and most of all the food left behind by the vacating Yanks. Hundreds, perhaps thousands, of Southerners left their companies,

21 S. H. Dent to wife, April 9, 1862, Shiloh-Corinth Collection, Alabama Department of Archives and History.

22 Reed, *Shiloh*, 59. || Dr. Cunningham's original text stated that Prentiss lost four guns, two from each battery. In reality, Hickenlooper lost two guns, while Munch had two damaged and sent to the rear. One later returned to action. See Reed, *Shiloh*, 59; Shiloh Battlefield Commission Monument #111.

23 Morton, "A Boy at Shiloh," 62; *OR* 10, pt. 1, 537, 383, 284, 286; Stillwell, *Common Soldier*, 46. See Reed, *Shiloh*, for another version, 59, 60.

24 James Sligh to wife, April 17, 1862, James W. Sligh Papers, Michigan Historical Collection, University of Michigan.

battalions, and regiments, fanning out to plunder. Happy soldiers grabbed crackers, cheese, nuts, apples and biscuits, munching blissfully away while looking around for more valuable goods,[25] or souvenirs such as "belts, sashes, swords, officers' uniforms, Yankee letters, daguerreotypes of Yankee sweethearts, likenesses of Grant, Buell, Smith, Prentiss, McClellan, Lincoln," and the like.[26] One Rebel soldier found some pikes, ten to twelve feet long, with curved knife blades in the ends. Private George Bryan found a dozen sets of breastplates (body armor) in Sherman's camp.[27]

Straggling caused by the looting was terrific, and the Confederate brigade and divisional commanders found it difficult to get orders, for the initial plan of attack was rapidly collapsing. It proved impossible for Polk, Hardee, or Bragg to adequately direct their units when strung out along a three mile front. Finally Polk managed to locate Bragg, and in a quick battlefield conference the two corps commanders decided to divide up the battlefield: the Bishop took the center, Bragg took the right, and Hardee the left.[28]

After their predawn conference at army headquarters, Johnston and Beauregard were busy directing the movement of troops forward. At 6:40 a.m., Johnston left headquarters, and accompanied by his staff, rode to the front. Attaching himself to Withers' Division, Johnston helped direct that unit in its forward movement on Prentiss' camp,[29] while Beauregard remained in the rear.

25   T. H. Peebles to wife, April 17, 1862, *Confederate Veteran* 16 (June 1908): 281.

26   Charles James Johnson to wife, April 11, 1862, Charles James Johnson Papers Louisiana State University Archives.

27   George Bryan, "Handcuffs on Manassas Battlefield," *Confederate Veteran* 14 (July 1906): 304; Jordan, "The Campaign and Battle of Shiloh," 278.

28   Stanley, *Autobiography*, 191; Williams, *P. G. T. Beauregard*, 135; Comte de Paris, *History of the Civil War in America*, 1: 547; Jordan, "The Campaign and Battle of Shiloh," 278, 393.

29   S. W. Ferguson to General Beauregard, April 9, 1862, Miscellaneous Collection, Shiloh National Military Park. After the capture of Prentiss' camp, a column of Federal prisoners was led into General Johnston's presence. Many

At 9:35 a.m., with most of the army successfully moving forward, Beauregard decided to establish a new command post nearer the front. Riding forward with his staff, Beauregard established his headquarters about a quarter of a mile from the Shiloh Methodist-Episcopal Church.[30] With Johnston busy over with Withers' Division and Beauregard setting up new headquarters, the direction of the battle was largely left in the hands of subordinate officers. Despite the lack of direction, the Southerners seemed to be winning, for they were steadily pushing the Northerners back.

In part this was an illusion, for instead of turning Grant's left flank and seizing Pittsburg Landing, the Confederates were simply compressing the Federal army back closer to the Landing. If the whole Union army could be routed, then this would not matter too much, but Union resistance was beginning to stiffen as Hurlbut's division moved into action.

By 8:00 a.m. that morning, the South Carolina-born Hurlbut had his three brigades drawn up in formation, awaiting orders from someone who knew what was going on. One of General Sherman's couriers galloped over to Hurlbut's headquarters and informed the general that the Fifth Division had been "attacked in force, and heavily, upon his left." Within ten minutes Colonel J. C. Veatch's brigade was in motion with orders to "proceed to the left of General Sherman," where they were eventually attached to McClernand's command.[31] A few minutes later the commanding officer of the Fourth Division received a "pressing

---

of them were German immigrants and spoke little or no English. Some of these fellows threw themselves on the ground at Johnston's feet, begging for their lives. The general reassuringly spoke to them, saying, "Why men, you don't suppose we kill prisoners, do you? Go to the rear and you will be safe there." D. W. Yandall to William Preston Johnston, November 11, 1877, Mrs. Mason Barret Papers, Albert Sidney Johnston Collection, Howard-Tilton Memorial Library, Tulane University. The Confederates captured one very distinguished prisoner at this time, Henry Bently, war correspondent for the Philadelphia *Inquirer*. J. Cutler Andrews, *The North Reports the Civil War* (Pittsburgh: University of Pittsburgh Press, 1955), 173.

30 *Battles and Leaders*, 1: 587.

31 *OR* 10, pt. 1, 203.

request for aid from Brigadier-General Prentiss." Placing himself at the head of his two remaining brigades, Colonel N. G. Williams' First Brigade and Brigadier General J. G. Lauman's Third Brigade, Hurlbut started out on the Hamburg and Savannah Road.

As the divisional vanguard approached Wicker's Field, they encountered large numbers of panic-stricken survivors from Miller's and Peabody's brigades. One of Hurlbut's men asked a fast moving straggler what made him in such a hurry, and the soldier replied, "You go a little further out that way and you will find out what's the matter."[32] General Prentiss made desperate attempts to rally the fugitives, but most of them drifted through the lines of the Fourth Division, hunting sanctuary somewhere—anywhere.

Once past the fugitives the two brigades began deploying, Williams going to the left, forming up along the south side of the Peach Orchard Field, while Lauman's soldiers deployed to the right of Williams' men, continuing the "line with an obtuse angle" around to the west end of the field and "extending some distance into the brush and timber" near the head of Tilgham Branch.[33]

As the infantry moved into position, the divisional batteries rode up. Lieutenant Edward Brotzmann's Independent Missouri Battery (referred to as Mann's) unlimbered its two 6-pound smoothbores and two 12-pound howitzers near several log cabins adjacent to the Fifty-fourth Ohio Infantry camp. The Missourians opened fire with the howitzers, using solid shot and shell, at a body of Confederate infantry about two-thirds of a mile away (probably Chalmers' skirmishers). After firing a few rounds, Brotzmann's unit was ordered to shift to a new position in the Peach Orchard Field.

---

32 *Ibid.*; *Confederate Veteran* 3 (November 1895): 332.

33 *OR* 10, pt. 1, 203. Some of the Federals took shelter behind a wooden rail fence along the edge of the field. *Ibid.*; Seymour Thompson, *Recollections With the Third Iowa* (Cincinnati: Published by Author, 1864), 220. This whole area was comparatively flat and even. The peach trees were in full bloom, adding a touch of color and gentle fragrance to the atmosphere. W. H. L. Wallace to his wife, Ann, April 5, 1862, W. H. L. Wallace Papers, Illinois State Historical Library; Thompson, *Recollections With the Third Iowa*, 214, 219, 220.

Galloping to the right, Brotzmann unlimbered his pieces in the angle between Williams' and Lauman's brigades.[34] The cannoneers of Captain William H. Ross' Battery B, Michigan Light Artillery (Second Battery Michigan Light Artillery) emplaced their four 10-pound Parrotts and two 6-pound smoothbores in the Peach Orchard Field some distance to Brotzmann's right.[35] Captain John B. Myers' Thirteenth Ohio Light Artillery Battery was supposed to take a position to the right of Brotzmann's guns, but the Ohioans were slow in coming and Hurlbut was forced to send several aides with orders to hurry the tardy gunners. The general's orders were for Myers to "come into battery on the reverse slope of a crest of ground, where there was cover for his horses and caissons in front of the right of my infantry."[36]

Robertson's Florida Battery opened on the galloping Ohioans with solid shot from their four Napoleons. Myers and his men halted and began unlimbering their two 6-pound smoothbores and four 6-pound James rifles. A Napoleon shot crashed into one of the Ohioans' caissons, smashing it and stampeding one of the artillery teams. Myers and his gunners panicked and bolted to the rear, abandoning everything. That was the last anyone saw of the Thirteenth Ohio Battery until Myers showed up two days later asking for rations.[37]

34 *OR* 10, pt. 1, 246.

35 *Ibid.*, 245; Bearss, "Project 17," 13.

36 *OR* 10, pt. 1, 208, 209.

37 Felix H. Robertson to D. W. Reed, August 1, 1909, Miscellaneous Collection, Shiloh National Military Park. Robertson said the time was 9:30 a.m. *Ibid.*; S. H. Dent to wife, April 9, 1862, Confederate Collection, Tennessee State Library and Archives; Roman, *Beauregard*, 1: 291; *OR* 10, pt. 1, 203, 209, 245. The Thirteenth was a brand new battery, organized on February 15, at Camp Dennison, near Cincinnati, Ohio, one of the two great military cantonments set up in Ohio in the early part of the war. The battery lost one man killed and eight wounded at Shiloh, which indicates that some of the men probably joined with other commands later during the day. *Ibid.*, 103; Robert S. Harper, *Ohio Hand Book of the Civil War* (Columbus: Ohio Historical Society, 1961), 13. Myers' military career came to an abrupt end as a result of this incident.

General Hurlbut spotted the "glimmer of bayonets on the left and front" of Williams' brigade.[38] Williams' men saw the "enemy, his regiments with their red banners flashing in the morning sun marching proudly and all undisturbed through the abandoned camps of Prentiss."[39] The red banners belonged to Chalmers' "High Pressure" Brigade, fresh from its triumph over Miller's Bluecoats. After routing Peabody's men, Chalmers halted and waited for his laggard Fifth Mississippi and Fifty-second Tennessee. General Johnston rode up and ordered the brigade to fall back. Before this order was executed, however, the brigade began catching fire from Hurlbut's gunners. The pugnacious Chalmers quickly moved forward, starting his own private war with Hurlbut.[40]

The Fourth Division's riflemen opened up at four hundred yards range, delivering a noisy but inaccurate spray of slugs at the Mississippians and Tennesseans. Colonel Isaac Pugh, Forty-first Illinois, fearing that Chalmers was trying to turn his left flank, retreated a hundred yards. One of Captain Charles P. Gage's 12-pound howitzers sent a cannon ball through Colonel Williams' horse, killing the animal and crippling the rider. Williams was helped off the field, and Pugh took charge of the First Brigade, Lieutenant Colonel Ansel Tupper assuming command of the Forty-first Illinois. After two or three minutes of continued firing, Chalmers withdrew on orders from General Johnston, in preparation for a move to the right.[41]

Hurlbut's men settled down to a three-hour fight with Gladden's Brigade, now commanded by Colonel Adams. General Grant rode over to confer with Hurlbut and to find out what the situation was on his front. Wearing his sword and a buff sash and accompanied by three staff officers, Grant trotted leisurely up to Hurlbut. One of Hurlbut's officers noticed the general's face "wore an anxious look, yet bore no evidence of excitement or trepidation."[42] Grant smoked one of his beloved cigars and

---

38   *OR* 10, pt. 1, 203.

39   Thompson, *Recollections With the Third Iowa*, 213, 214.

40   *OR* 10, pt. 1, 548.

41   *Ibid.*, 203, 204, 206, 217, 548.

42   Thompson, *Recollections with the Third Iowa Regiment*, 214.

acted as nonchalantly as if he were on a routine parade ground inspection.[43] Doubtlessly reassured by what he heard and saw, the general soon rode off, but his visit inspired the soldiers.

The Confederates were badly disorganized by their capture of Prentiss' camps, and it took some time for Colonel Adams to reassemble his brigade. Some of the men were short of cartridges, and Adams was forced to send couriers to the rear to find more ammunition. All in all, Gladden's old brigade did no serious fighting for about five hours which was just as well, for if the Louisianan had led his men forward, he would have been facing General Hurlbut's two fresh brigades, plus some of Prentiss' men.[44] But Adams was not completely inactive. General Hardee, presumably on his way to the Confederate left, instructed Adams to probe Hurlbut's Peach Orchard position.[45]

While Robertson's Florida gunners traded shots with Brotzmann's and Ross' Batteries, parties of Rebel skirmishers moved out to reconnoiter the Union position. Company K, Twenty-second Alabama, worked its way toward Lauman's brigade, close enough to see the trimmings on the Federal uniforms. The Alabamans were spotted, and Hurlbut's men opened up with rifle and artillery fire, which the Southerners eagerly returned.[46]

About noon Colonel Z. C. Deas sent Companies A and B, Twenty-second Alabama, forward to clear Federal snipers out of some houses

---

43   Warren Olney, "Shiloh as Seen by A Private Soldier," *War Paper Number V, California Commandery, Military Order of the Loyal Legion of the United States* (Los Angeles: N. d.), 6.

44   *OR* 10, pt. 1, 537, 538, 542; Reed, *Shiloh*, 73. Reed said Gladden's men formed a square at Prentiss' headquarters. *Ibid.* This is partially born out by Lieutenant Hugh Henry in a letter he wrote four days later, saying, "We had formed a square, thinking their cavalry about to charge." Hugh Henry to parents, April 10, 1862, Shiloh-Corinth Collection, Alabama Department of Archives and History. In his report General Hurlbut said Prentiss "succeeded in rallying a considerable portion of his command," and went into action supporting Lauman. *OR* 10, pt. 1, 204.

45   *Ibid.*, 537.

46   S. H. Dent to wife, April 9, 1862, Shiloh-Corinth Collection, Alabama Department of Archives and History.

near the Peach Orchard. These minor operations and a few others like them were dignified by General Hurlbut with the high-sounding title of "repeated and heavy attacks."[47]

If the Fourth Division was only lightly engaged, Stuart's brigade, holding Hurlbut's left, steadily found itself increasingly sharply engaged with the rest of Withers' Division. On orders from General Johnston, Withers gradually moved to his right, pressing toward the isolated Second Brigade of Sherman's division.

After his engagement with Hurlbut in the Peach Orchard, Chalmers was ordered by Johnston to move to the right so as to turn the enemy's left flank. Guided by Lafayette Veal and moving by the right flank, the Mississippi Brigade crossed a ravine to its right, reaching the Bark Road. They moved along that avenue until the right regiments rested on the edge of the Lick Creek bottom. Here Withers halted the brigade,[48] until cavalry patrols (Clanton's Alabama Regiment) could ascertain what was in front. Chalmers' men took advantage of the break, either taking a drink of water or snatching a short nap on the ground. After half an hour the cavalry reported the way was clear, and Chalmers resumed his march, with General John Jackson's Brigade to his immediate left.

Some of Stuart's skirmishers began peppering the Fifty-second Tennessee with rifle fire. As the regiment crossed a slight rise in the ground, Captain A.N. Wilson deployed his men into two lines. The front line fired, and Wilson directed them to lie down to reload and permit the rear line to fire over their heads. Then Wilson ordered his men to fall back a few yards so a battery could engage the Federal skirmishers. Suddenly the regiment stampeded, and seized by a blind panic, the men ran wildly to the rear.[49] After repeated attempts to rally the Fifty-second failed,

47 *OR* 10, pt. 1, 542, 204.

48 *Ibid.*, 548, 549; Reed, *Shiloh*, 74.

49 William F. Mosier to D. W. Reed, December 11, 1912, Miscellaneous Collection, Shiloh Military National Park. The Fifty-second Tennessee was organized in January 1862, at Henderson Station, in what is now Chester County, Tennessee. Lea's men suffered heavily from disease, especially from measles, and he encountered great difficulty in finding arms for his men. On February 26, 1862, Lea reported that the regiment numbered 760 men, of

Chalmers ordered the brigade reshuffled to compensate for the defection of the regiment. Captain Wilson managed to rally his own unit, Company C, while Captain J. A. Russell also managed to pull together his men, Company B. Wilson attached the remnants of his band, about one hundred men, to the Fifth Mississippi.[50]

Colonel T. Kilby Smith of the Fifty-fourth Ohio was sound asleep in his tent when the regimental adjutant ran in to wake him. Slipping off his cot, Smith stumbled outside while still attempting to rub the sleep from his eyes. In a few moments he was able to make out the unfamiliar sound of heavy firing. He cried out "They are fighting!" and immediately ordered his regiment to form up.

Pickets reached Stuart's headquarters with the news of Confederate troops approaching near Locust Grove Run, and Stuart soon was busy attending to forming up his three regiments. Drawn up along the edge of their regimental camps, Stuart's men were only dimly aware of the seriousness of the situation. The firing was in the distance, and perhaps some of the men wondered if they would be involved at all. A devoted patriot, Stuart was eager for action, sensing that battle might give him a chance to redeem his reputation, tattered by his being named as correspondent in the divorce case of Mrs. Isaac Burch of Illinois.[51]

About 7:30 a.m., Stuart received word from Prentiss that the Sixth Division was under assault and, presumably, warning the colonel to be on the lookout. A little later one of Stuart's pickets ran in with news that Confederate troops were moving on the Bark Road. Just after 8:00 a.m., Stuart, looking through his binoculars into the distance, spotted the waving flag of Colonel Daniel Adams' First Louisiana fluttering above Prentiss' camp. Stuart dispatched his adjutant, Lieutenant Charles

---

whom 260 were sick, and that their only weapons were 100 double-barreled shotguns. He specifically asked Confederate headquarters to send guns, rifles, muskets, and bayonets to equip the troops. *Tennesseans in the Civil War*, 1: 291, 292; *OR* 7, 847. The regiment was poorly trained, poorly equipped, and in a very low state of morale.

50   *OR* 10, pt. 1, 549; *Tennesseans in the Civil War*, 1: 292.

51   *OR* 10, pt. 1, 565.

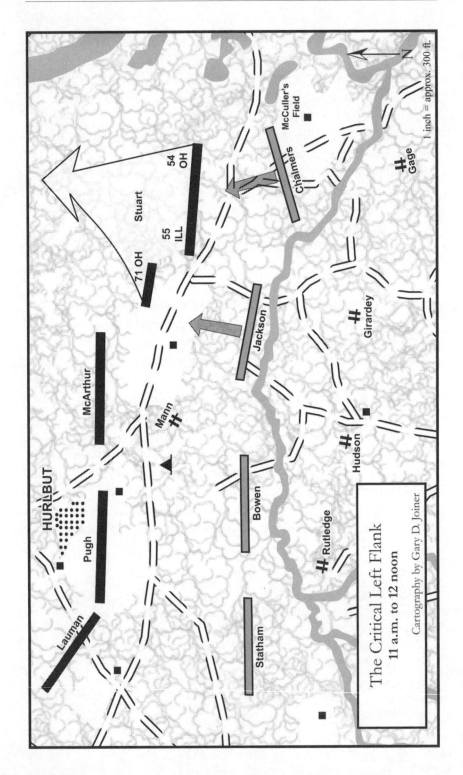

The Critical Left Flank
11 a.m. to 12 noon

Cartography by Gary D. Joiner

Loomis, to notify General Hurlbut that Prentiss was in trouble and to request support for his own brigade.[52]

As Lieutenant Loomis rode away to raise the alarm, Stuart deployed his Seventy-first Ohio, Colonel Rodney Mason, with its right resting opposite the eastern end of the camp of the Fifty-fourth Ohio. Lieutenant Colonel Oscar Malmborg was next on the left, and the Fifty-fourth Ohio, Colonel T. Kilby Smith, was just beyond facing south. Colonel Stuart sent two companies of the Fifty-fourth to slow down Withers' advance, and it was these men who routed the Fifty-second Tennessee so effectively.[53]

Chalmers deployed some of his Mississippians forward as skirmishers to cover his advance. The men "fought like Indians behind trees, logs, and lying down" on the ground. Private Joe Seals, Tenth Mississippi, picked off one of Stuart's men as the fellow carelessly stuck his head from a tree. Seals shot him between the eyes and then hit two more Yanks for good measure.[54]

Gage's Battery went into position and began dropping 3-inch and 12-pound shells on the Federal soldiers. Colonel Stuart could see the advance of Chalmers and, by moving his binoculars to the right, he was

---

52 *Campaigns in Kentucky and Tennessee*, 138; *OR* 10, pt. 1, 275. Otto Eisenschiml, in an interesting article on Shiloh, incorrectly stated that Stuart alerted General John McArthur of Hurlbut's division, who sent the Forty-first Illinois and Stone's Battery as reinforcements. Eisenschiml, "The 55th Illinois at Shiloh," 199. McArthur was in W. H. L. Wallace's division. The Forty-first Illinois was in Colonel N. G. Williams' brigade. It was not sent to support Stuart, but simply took its position on the left flank of Williams' Brigade in the Peach Orchard. From here it could give supporting fire to Stuart, and he naturally assumed this was the regiment's main function. The same applies to Stone's Battery. *OR* 10, pt. 1, 257, 203, 211, 212. After the fighting began McArthur sent a message to Stuart, saying he would assist him. Stuart said the promised help did not come. *Ibid.*, 258, 259. Actually McArthur did move over with the Ninth and Twelfth Illinois and Wood's Battery A, First Illinois, and did support Stuart's right. Reed, *Shiloh*, 50.

53 *OR* 10, pt. 1, 258.

54 Micajah Wilkinson to brother, April 16, 1862, Micajah Wilkinson Papers, Louisiana State University Archives.

able to make out Jackson's soldiers moving toward the Hamburg Road where it divided into the Purdy and Savannah segments.[55]

While swinging around to support the Mississippi brigade, Jackson's soldiers were shelled by Ross' Michigan Battery, losing two men killed and three wounded in the Seventeenth Alabama. Except for this brief firing, the brigade was still green as it moved toward Stuart's camp. The Alabamans and Texans paused to redress their lines and then swarmed into the ravine across the swampy bottom, climbing up the steep side, and moving into the camps. The Southerners fanned out among the tents, looking for Federals. One daredevil Bluecoat started a sniping campaign on the Seventeenth Alabama, firing three shots without hitting anyone. The soldiers of the Alabama regiment waited, and then the Yank made a break for it. He was immediately shot down.[56]

Colonel John Moore's Second Texas ran into a little more opposition, as Stuart's skirmishers wounded several privates and mortally wounded Captain Belvidere Brooks, who died two days later.[57] Some of the Texans fanned out to loot the Fifty-fifth Illinois camp. A large hand mirror and a silver-mounted revolver were among the prizes. One pillager found a large tin box, which when pried open proved to be filled with fresh, crisp greenbacks, ranging from one to one hundred dollars in denomination. The Southerners did not know about this new type of money, and the man who found it "gave the box a contemptuous kick and the crisp notes fluttered around as unheeded as so many autumn leaves." Another Texan secured a half gallon jug of whiskey and was sharing it with some of his buddies when Major H. G. Runnels showed up, smashing the jug and remarking that the next man who took a drink would be shot.[58]

---

55 *OR* 10, pt. 1, 549; Micajah Wilkinson to brother, April 16, 1862, Micajah Wilkinson Papers, Louisiana State University Archives; Unidentified Confederate soldier, April 11, 1862, Miss Cottrill's Scrapbook, Alabama Department of Archives and History.

56 Letter dated April 11, 1862, by an unidentified Confederate soldier, M. L. Kirkpatrick Scrapbook, Alabama Department of Archives and History.

57 *OR* 10, pt. 1, 560.

58 Sam Houston, Jr., "Shiloh Shadows," *The Southwestern Historical Quarterly* 34 (July 1930): 330.

The tempo of the fight was gradually picking up, and by 11:15 or 11:20 a.m., the first real heavy fighting commenced with a charge by the Nineteenth Alabama. After crossing the ravine, twenty-five-year old Colonel Joseph Wheeler and his Nineteenth Alabama made a determined attack on the Seventy-first Ohio. The overweight colonel of the Seventy-first, Rodney Mason, promptly defected to the rear, leaving his soldiers on their own, and many of his men naturally followed him. Wheeler's men shot the few Ohioans who tried to make a stand, killing Lieutenant Colonel Barton S. Kyle, who attempted to rally the regiment.[59] The Alabamans captured a captain and fifty enlisted men as prisoners. The Seventy-first's major led part of the men down to the Tennessee River, where they were picked up by a gunboat. Another part of the Seventy-first retired to the Landing, where they rejoined what was left of the brigade that night.[60]

Stuart reshuffled his remaining infantry to cover his now exposed right, but his raw troops began to panic. In a stentorian voice he thundered, "Halt, men, halt; halt, you cowards." Spurring his horse forward, he galloped among his fleeing men, freely using the flat of his sword to restore order. The two regiments soon were rallied with a loss of

59 *OR* 10, pt. 1, 558; Eisenschiml, "The Fifty-fifth Illinois at Shiloh," 200; *Campaigns in Kentucky and Tennessee*, 62, 64; Lindsey, *Shiloh*, 38. Mason was a combat veteran, having commanded the Second Ohio at the First Battle of Bull Run. *OR* 2, 357-360. Colonel Mason turned in a report of his conduct at Shiloh, in which he offers various extenuating explanations for the failure of the Seventy-first. *Ibid.*, 10, pt. 1, 261, 262. With tears in his eyes, he begged Grant for another chance to prove himself, and the sympathetic general listened and was convinced, so Mason continued in command of the regiment. Grant, *Memoirs*, 207. Later Mason was put in command of a Union outpost at Clarksville, Tennessee, and on August 18, 1862, he surrendered half the Seventy-first Ohio, plus a few other troops in the town, to a small force of Rebel Partisan or guerrilla troops. *Ibid.*, 16, 1: 862-870. The military governor of Tennessee and later President of the United States, Andrew Johnson, referred to Mason's conduct at Clarksville as "not only humiliating but disgraceful in the extreme." *Ibid.*, 16, 2: 388. By order of President Lincoln, Mason was "cashiered for repeated acts of cowardice in the face of the enemy." *Ibid.*, 16, 1: 865.

60 Reed, *Shiloh*, 57.

only a few hundred yards of ground.[61] Stuart stopped the rout at the price of a Rebel bullet through his shoulder, and the actual command of the brigade seems to have passed to Lieutenant Colonel Oscar Malmborg, a graduate of Stockholm Military Academy, an eight year veteran of the Swedish Army, and a twenty-one month veteran of the Mexican War.[62]

Chalmers' Mississippians and the Second Texas of Jackson's Brigade kept the pressure up on the Fifty-fourth Ohio and Fifty-fifth Illinois, but the rest of Jackson's Brigade became entangled with Hurlbut's left wing, General McArthur's two regiments, and some additional newcomers, the Fiftieth Illinois of General W. H. L. Wallace's Third Brigade.

As the battle began that morning, W. H. L. Wallace's division was going through its usual Sunday morning routine. In the Second Iowa the men were lined up for company inspection when they heard the "long roll" for the first time in the war. Within minutes Wallace's regiments were formed up and ready to march toward the sound of gunfire. Supply sergeants hurriedly issued two day's rations and sixty cartridges per man. Moving out at the double-quick, the division headed for the front, meeting hundreds of stragglers from Prentiss' division, who were heading for the rear. The scurrying stragglers passed free advice to Wallace's men, namely for the division to turn about and to go back. One frightened young fellow stood by the road waving his hands and yelling, "For God's sake don't go out there! You will all be killed. Come back! Come back!"[63]

The battle hardened veterans of the Second Division kept right on going. Meeting with Lieutenant Colonel Wills De Hass of Sherman's

---

61   *The Story of the Fifty-fifth Regiment Illinois Volunteer Infantry in the Civil War* (Clinton: Published by Author, 1887), 494, 495.

62   *OR* 10, pt. 1, 259; Eisenschiml, "The Fifty-fifth Illinois at Shiloh," 196, 197. Actually Stuart turned the command over to Colonel T. Kilby Smith, but that officer had gone wandering off searching for some of his men who had become separated from the main body, thus Malmborg ended up giving most of the orders. *OR* 10, pt. 1, 259.

63   Wills de Hass, "The Battle of Shiloh," *The Annals of the War Written by Leading Participants North and South* (Philadelphia: Times Publishing Company, 1879), 686; Reed, *Shiloh*, 48, 50.

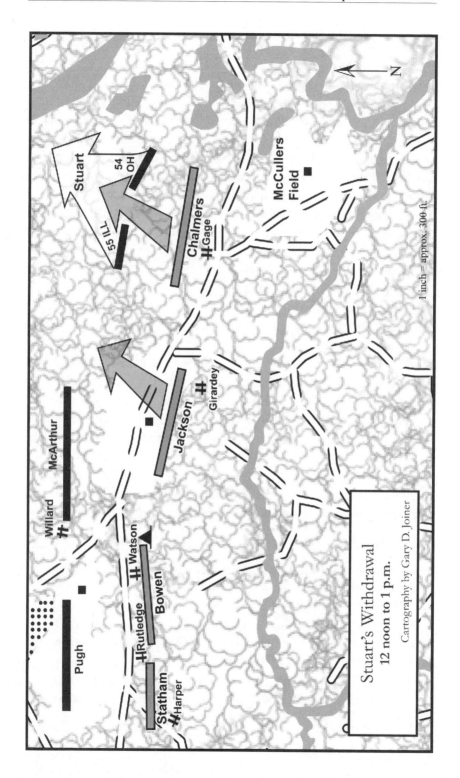

N

Stuart

54 OH

55 ILL

Chalmers
Gage

McCullers
Field

1 inch = approx. 300 ft.

McArthur

Jackson
Girardey

Willard

Watson

Bowen

Rutledge

Pugh

Statham
Harper

Stuart's Withdrawal
12 noon to 1 p.m.

Cartography by Gary D. Joiner

division, who acted as a guide, Wallace moved his First and Third Brigades forward to support McClernand and Sherman; his Second Brigade he split up, the regiments being detached to various parts of the battlefield. McArthur took the Ninth and Twelfth Illinois over to help Stuart, and a little later Wallace ordered the Fiftieth Illinois, Colonel T. W. Sweeny's Third Brigade, to follow McArthur and link up with him on the extreme Union left.[64] In route to the left, the Ninth Illinois picked up a number of recruits. Sword in hand, a young officer of the regiment insulted, shamed, and threatened a number of stragglers from other units into joining McArthur. The brave, young lieutenant took each name down in a little notebook, which he placed in his coat pocket. Unfortunately he was killed as his brigade went into action. With their colorful Scots bonnets perched on their heads, McArthur's "Highlanders" confidently moved into position on Hurlbut's left.[65]

Advancing against Jackson's Confederate brigade, General McArthur deployed his three regiments, the Fiftieth Illinois having caught up, from left to right: the Fiftieth Illinois, Colonel Moses M. Bane, Twelfth Illinois, Lieutenant Colonel Augustus L. Chetlain, and the Ninth Illinois, Colonel August Mersy, in addition to Lieutenant Peter P. Wood's Battery A, First Illinois Light Artillery. Jackson's Alabamans moved forward toward the Illinoisans, while Captain Isodore Girardy's Battery opened up with four of his guns, blasting the Illinoisans with canister.[66]

The Twelfth Illinois took heavy casualties, and Lieutenant Colonel Chetlain was obliged to withdraw about seventy-five yards to get relief from the gunfire, leaving behind a number of wounded personnel

---

64 Wills de Hass, "The Battle of Shiloh," *The Annals of the War Written by Leading Participants North and South* (Philadelphia: Times Publishing Company, 1879), 686; Reed, *Shiloh*, 48, 50.

65 Wills de Hass, "The Battle of Shiloh," *The Annals of the War Written by Leading Participants North and South* (Philadelphia: Times Publishing Company, 1879), 686; Reed, *Shiloh*, 48, 50.

66 Wills de Hass, "The Battle of Shiloh," *The Annals of the War Written by Leading Participants North and South* (Philadelphia: Times Publishing Company, 1879), 686; Reed, *Shiloh*, 48, 50.

including Captain Frank B. Ferris and Lieutenant Richard K. Randolph.[67] Chetlain, suffering for several days from dysentery, had been advised the previous day by the regimental surgeon to go to the hospital at Paducah. Still in camp on Sunday morning, Chetlain watched the regiment pull out without him. The minutes ticked by and finally, arising from his bed, the young officer put on his uniform, mounted a horse, and headed for the front. Just after taking cover from Girardy's fire, Chetlain had his horse shot from under him by a Confederate sniper, the fall badly bruising the already ailing officer, but he gamely continued in command.[68]

In the face of heavy fire from the three Illinois regiments and their supporting battery, the Alabamans' advance slowed down. Jackson's left regiment, Lieutenant Colonel Robert C. Farris, Seventeenth Alabama, pushed in so close to McArthur's men that they could see Yankees not only on their front but on both sides as well. Six Bluecoats, probably stragglers from earlier actions, suddenly wandered into Farris' position. These Yanks naively asked whose side the Alabamans were on. The confused Federals were told to surrender or be shot down. All six wisely chose to raise their hands. Then two Northern officers wandered by, one of them leading a horse. Farris' men yelled for them to surrender. One of them jumped on the horse and tried to ride away, but a company officer brought him down with a pistol bullet. The other Northerner hid behind a tree and began yelling for his men to come up. The officer must have been bluffing, for no more Federals appeared. The Confederates gave the Union officer a chance to surrender, but he gamely peppered them with his revolver. A dozen musket balls spattered his tree before the Northerner dropped his sword and pistol and yelled, "Don't kill me—I surrender!"[69] Unfortunately someone shot him anyway.

McArthur's men opened with their rifles, and the Seventeenth and Eighteenth Alabama regiments replied in kind. Part of Bane's Fiftieth Illinois moved upon the Seventeenth Alabama's right flank, advancing

---

67 Cockerill, "A Boy at Shiloh," 18, 19. The three Illinois regiments occupied a position to the right and several hundred yards behind Stuart's right. Jackson's Brigade attacked in a sort of slanted, staggered formation.

68 *OR* 10, pt. 1, 565; Charles B. Kimbell, *History of Battery "A" First Illinois Light Artillery Volunteers* (Chicago: Cushing Printing Co., 1899), 40, 41.

69 *OR* 10, pt. 1, 156.

within pistol range. The lieutenant colonel of the Fiftieth fired three pistol balls at Sergeant Bob Mosley and Lieutenant Edward Crenshaw. The two Alabamans returned his fire, their bullets simultaneously breaking one of his legs. Mosley ran out, disarming and capturing the fallen officer. The following day the Seventeenth Alabama returned the lieutenant colonel to his own lines under a flag of truce, a yellow handkerchief tied to a sapling pole.[70]

An enthusiastic fire fight developed between Jackson's left wing and McArthur's Illinoisans, with probably part of the Forty-first Illinois, Hurlbut's left wing regiment, joining in. Slugs flew fast and thick, and soon the Seventeenth Alabama ran short of ammunition. Colonel Farris told his men to fire slowly and deliberately. The non-commissioned officers started stripping cartridges from the dead and wounded. Luckily the Yanks began to give ground.[71]

At one stage in the fighting some of the Seventeenth Alabamans began to waver. Temporarily forgetting his ecclesiastical duties, the Reverend Isaac Tickenor, the regimental chaplain, moved out and began rallying the men, finally even leading a charge. Grabbing a rifle, he battled like a Trojan, much to the delight and admiration of his flock. According to the soldiers, the Baptist chaplain killed one Federal field grade officer, one captain, and four privates, besides capturing a dozen other fellows.[72]

Casualties on both sides were heavy. Girardy's Battery took a particularly bad beating from McArthur's riflemen. Lieutenant J. J. Jacobus was mortally wounded, shot through the forehead. Private August Roesel was picked off by an Illinois rifleman, who put a ball through his head while the gunner was in the act of aiming his 6-pounder. Lieutenant Charles Speath caught a ball through his right arm, while Private John Halbert was shot through both arms. Three other enlisted men were badly wounded before McArthur's riflemen were pushed back.

70 Chetlain, *Recollections*, 77, 78.

71 Kirkpatrick Scrapbook, Alabama Department of Archives and History.

72 "Diary of Edward Crenshaw," 269; Cincinnati *Commercial*, April 11, 1862.

(These were the last casualties the battery sustained that day, although it was repeatedly engaged all afternoon.)[73]

There was no massive all-out assault on the extreme Union left. The rugged terrain forbade that. The Confederates attacked in short spurts and rushes, gradually pushing the Yankees backward, gobbling up seventy-five or a hundred yards of terrain at a bite. With little bites, Withers' Division continued to push closer to the Tennessee River and Pittsburg Landing. By 12:30 or 12:40 p.m., the Mississippians and Alabamans were threatening to roll over the Union left, and there were no other Federal troops between them and the river.

73 Kirkpatrick Scrapbook, Alabama Department of Archives and History.

Chapter 10

The Crossroads

EXECUTING A WITHDRAWAL UNDER fire is always a hazardous proposition, but by a few minutes past 10:00 a.m., William Sherman's Fifth Division, or what was left of it, was established in a new position linking up with John McClernand's First Division.[1] Colonel Jesse Hildebrand stayed with his remaining regiment, the Seventy-seventh Ohio, until it started retiring from the Shiloh Church position. The regiment fell into disorder, the men disappearing in all directions. Hildebrand became separated, lost heart, and washing his hands of the affair galloped over to McClernand's headquarters, where he attached himself to the First Division as a volunteer aide.[2]

1 Grant's comrade in arms, biographer and friend, Adam Badeau, maintained that Sherman at this time took command of McClernand's division as well as his own. This is a dubious claim. It is true that Sherman was a West Pointer, while McClernand's only military experience prior to 1861 was as a private in the Black Hawk War, but the idea that the ambitious and grasping McClernand would allow any fellow officer, let alone Sherman, who was still suffering from the stigma of his earlier so-called mental breakdown, and with whom he had been quarreling some days earlier, assume command, is highly questionable. McClernand served with distinction at Belmont and Fort Donelson under Grant, and he was as qualified as any man in the Union army to run a division at this stage in the war. McClernand certainly had more combat experience than Sherman. See Adam Badeau, *Military History of Ulysses S. Grant, From April, 1861, to April, 1865* (New York: D. Appleton and Company, 1881), 7, 79; Comte de Paris, *History of the Civil War in America,* 1: 542.

2 *OR* 10, pt. 1, 249, 250, 263; Duke *Fifty-third Ohio*, 49.

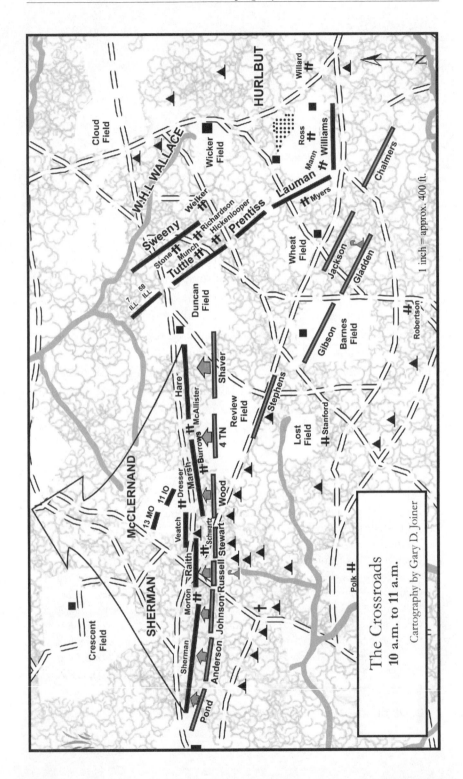

The Crossroads
10 a.m. to 11 a.m.

Cartography by Gary D. Joiner

1 inch = approx. 400 ft.

Buckland's three regiments also reached the Purdy Road line in a state of confusion. Cockerill and part of the Seventieth Ohio wandered off, but eventually wound up with McClernand. Colonels Sullivan and Buckland made repeated efforts to rally the brigade, but the more faint-hearted soldiers went scattering in all directions.[3] Cursing and yelling, officers managed to collect fragments from the various regiments and formed them up about two hundred yards west of the crossroads.

General Grant located Sherman and briefly chatted with him as to how things were going. Sherman was riding a wounded horse, and he had a minor wound in one hand. He was covered with dust and mud. Sherman informed Grant that ammunition was running a little short. Dispatching an aide to the rear to order additional cartridges, Grant rode off toward McClernand's division.[4]

Sherman's ammunition situation was particularly tricky, since the division employed six different types of shoulder arms. Hildebrand's brigade alone used three different kinds of muskets. Many of Sherman's soldiers insisted on carrying wounded comrades to the rear, and although many of these fellows later returned to the firing lines, the practice further weakened the already depleted division.[5]

Sherman missed McDowell's brigade. He had ordered the still unengaged unit to fall back on the Purdy Road line, but there was no sign of it.[6] Generals Anderson's and Cleburne's skirmishers cut the Purdy Road about one-third of a mile west of the crossroads just after McDowell's lone battery galloped down the road toward the crossroads, save one 12-pound howitzer detached to guard the Owl Creek bridge. McDowell ordered the remaining gun brought up and it was soon in

3 *Ibid.*; *OR* 10, pt. 1, 267.

4 Badeau, *Military History of Ulysses S. Grant*, 78, 79; Fuller, *The Generalship of Ulysses S. Grant*, 112; Richard Miller Devens, *The Pictorial Book of Anecdotes and Incidents of the Rebellion* (Hartford: Hartford Publishing Company, 1867), 253; Richardson, *Personal History of U. S. Grant*, 241, 242. Years later Grant wrote he "never deemed it important to stay long with Sherman." *Battles and Leaders*, 1: 473.

5 Duke, *Fifty-third-Ohio,* 48.

6 *OR* 10, pt. 1, 250.

action, showering the Southerners with canister. Musket balls sprinkled all three of McDowell's regiments, and the colonel decided against trying to force the road. Turning his regiments in a northeasterly direction, McDowell moved across Crescent Field and into Sowell Field before swinging about and linking up with McClernand's division about 11:30.[7] Even with McDowell out of position to help, Sherman still prepared to resist with the regiments of his other two brigades and Raith's brigade, which also arrived a little earlier at the new line.

The new Purdy Road position lacked the natural strength of the Shiloh Church ridge, but at least the Union army presented a fairly continuous front for the first time in the battle. Colonel Stuart's command held the extreme Union left, supported by McArthur's regiments. Next in line was Hurlbut's command holding the Peach Orchard, and the remnants of Prentiss' division, reinforced by Colonel Jacob Tindall's Twenty-third Missouri Infantry, which occupied part of a sunken road to the right of Hurlbut. W. H. L. Wallace's division held the rest of the road, commanding a clear field of fire across the northern end of Duncan's Field. General McClernand's First Brigade under Colonel Abraham Hare (including two veteran regiments) occupied a position eighty to one hundred yards in front of the Purdy Road and just north of the Review Field. The left portion of the brigade was about 300 yards to the south of Wallace's right flank, and so in a position to receive supporting fire from that unit.

From left to right Hare's brigade consisted of Captain James H. Ashmore's Eighth Illinois, Major Samuel Eaton's Eighteenth Illinois, and Colonel Marcellus Crocker's Thirteenth Iowa. Captain Edward McAllister's Battery D, First Illinois Light Artillery, was positioned on the right flank of the Thirteenth Iowa, perhaps seventy-five yards north of the Purdy Road. To the right of the battery McClernand's veteran Second Brigade, Colonel C. Carroll Marsh commanding, braced itself. From left to right Marsh deployed the Forty-fifth Illinois, Colonel John

---

7 *Ibid.*, 255; Reed, *Shiloh*, 256. McDowell said he was ordered to join McClernand by Major W.D. Sanger, one of Sherman's chief aides. Sherman said he ordered Buckland and McDowell to link with McClernand about 10:30. Buckland's unit did not execute the order because it was disorganized. *OR* 10, pt. 1, 250, 255.

E. Smith, Forty-eighth Illinois, Colonel Isham Haynie, Twentieth Illinois, Lieutenant Colonel Evan Richards, and the Eleventh Illinois, Lieutenant Colonel Thomas Ransom. Captain Jerome Burrows' Fourteenth Ohio Battery unlimbered on a little patch of high ground just to the rear of the Twentieth Illinois. After its successful withdrawal from the Shiloh Church line, Raith's brigade deployed just behind and to the right of Marsh on the north side of the crossroads, the Forty-ninth Illinois lying across the Shiloh Church Road. Sherman directed Nispel's Battery to unlimber on Marsh's right, while Captain James Timony's Battery D, Second Illinois, formed up on the left of the Forty-ninth Illinois. The Eleventh Iowa, of Hare's brigade, deployed just behind the batteries at the crossroads as infantry support. General Sherman's men were on the north side of the Purdy Road, on Raith's right.

McClernand's soldiers moved into position with enough time to organize and get ready for a fight, but Raith's and Sherman's men reached the new line with Confederate skirmishers hot on their heels and the main body of Southerners only six or eight minutes away.[8] Johnson's skirmishers advanced on Sherman's position as Behr's Sixth Indiana Battery galloped up the Purdy Road, reaching the crossroads. Sherman rode up and directed Behr to unlimber just to the right of the crossroads.[9]

Chanting, "Bull run, Bull run," and "Get up there, you Damn Yankee Sons of Bitches, and fight like men," the Rebel skirmishers raked Behr's Battery with musket balls. The captain's lifeless body fell off his horse, and several of his enlisted gunners were wounded. Drivers and gunners alike panicked and headed for the rear without firing a shot, abandoning the four 6-pound smoothbores and the 12-pound howitzer.[10]

---

8 *Ibid.*, 115, 116, 124, 126, 127, 128, 130, 133, 137, 146, 249, 273, 276, 278, 291; Douglas Hapeman, Diary, April 6, 1862, Douglas Hapeman Papers, Illinois State Historical Library; Reed, *Shiloh*, 45-47; Atwell Thompson Map of Shiloh; Map of Shiloh battlefield, presumably drawn by T. Lyle Dickey, Wallace-Dickey Papers, Illinois State Historical Library; Duke. *Fifty-third Ohio*, 49; Shiloh National Military Park markers; *OR* 10, pt. 1, 250.

9 *Ibid.*

10 T. W. Connelly, *History of the Seventieth Ohio Regiment, from its Organizations to its Mustering Out* (Cincinnati: Peak Brothers, 1902), 148.

Major Schwartz took personal command of Nispel's remaining guns and opened fire on the advancing Confederates. The battery began catching heavy musket fire and the major asked Colonel Raith for infantry support. The brigade commander personally led the Seventeenth and Forty-third Illinois forward. Both Schwartz and Raith were immediately wounded, the former seriously, the latter mortally with a Minie ball through his right thigh.[11] Southern soldiers captured the wounded colonel and placed him in a tent, from which point he was later recovered by the Federals.[12]

The Confederate advance slacked off somewhat as hundreds of Southerners straggled toward the rear, either deliberately malingering to minimize the risk of death or maiming, or carrying wounded comrades to sanctuary. Beauregard worked frantically to get these men back to the firing lines. His personal escort under Captain J. G. Dreux, broke up a party of men plundering a captured encampment, while his staff officers collected stragglers.[13]

When all of his aides were employed, Beauregard rode about looking for additional assistance. Spotting a Southern officer, General Beauregard asked him to identiy his unit. Captain Samuel Latta replied that he was a member of the Thirteenth Tennessee. Failing to recognize the general, Latta asked, "And who are you, sir?" Beauregard told him,

11   *OR* 10, pt. 1, 144, 139, 146; Reed, *Shiloh*, 47; Adolph Engelman to wife, April 8, 1862, Adolph Engelmann Papers, Illinois State Historical Library.

12   *OR* 10, pt. 1, 144; Thomas J. McCormack, (ed.). *Memoirs of Gustave Koerner 1809-1896* (Cedar Rapids: Torch Press, 1909), 215; Adolph Engelmann to wife, April 8, 1862, Adolph Engelmann Papers, Illinois State Historical Library. Raith was treated at Pittsburg Landing, but his leg was so badly mangled that McClernand ordered the colonel taken to Savannah on board the steamer *Hannibal*. John McClernand to Captain A. S. Martin, Order of April 9, 1862, John A. McClernand Papers, Illinois State Historical Library. A second letter to Martin directed the captain to give Raith special attention. *Ibid.*; Adolph Engelmann to wife, April 11, 1862, Adolph Engelmann Papers, Illinois State Historical Library. Raith's leg was amputated Wednesday; but he died from loss of blood Friday morning at 11:00 a.m. *OR* 10, pt. 1, 144.

13   S. W. Ferguson to General Beauregard, Miscellaneous Collections, Shiloh National Military Park.

and within minutes Latta was headed for the front in charge of a hundred stragglers.[14]

The Confederates were nearly as disorganized and confused as Sherman's battered division. There was no single individual coordinating the various brigades, and the advance on the Purdy Road line was disorganized. From left to right, the Southern order of advance was Anderson's Brigade with bits and pieces from Cleburne's Brigade on the west side of the Corinth and Pittsburg Road. Bushrod Johnson's Brigade should have been on Anderson's right, but the wounding of General Johnson left the unit leaderless because it took a while to locate the senior colonel, Preston Smith. Only the One hundred fifty-fourth Tennessee, Smith's own regiment, advanced along or just to the left of the Corinth- Pittsburg Road, taking part in the assault against the Union Purdy Road position.

By order of General Hardee and General Ruggles, the Fifth and Twenty-third Tennessee and Thirteenth Arkansas of Stewart's Brigade moved up just behind Colonel Smith, supporting him in his advance on the Federals at the crossroads.

Part of Russell's Brigade, on the right of General Johnson's, was badly disorganized after the Shiloh Church assault but took part in the advance. By some rapid and rather confusing reshuffling, Wood's and part of Stewart's brigades changed positions, so Wood actually hit the right position at the crossroads, while Stewart and the Fourth Tennessee advanced on Wood's right. Shaver's Brigade completed the line-up, moving up on Stewart's right. As this second push commenced against the Union right only three of Anderson's regiments moved forward, the Seventeenth and Twentieth Louisiana and the Ninth Texas.[15]

---

14 Samuel Latta to wife, April 12, 1862, Confederate Collection, Tennessee State Library and Archives. With the permission of his commanding officer, Captain Latta was taking the body of a fallen friend and fellow officer to a place of safety when he encountered Beauregard. *Ibid.*

15 || Dr. Cunningham originally stated that Russell's Brigade took no part in the 11:00 a.m. assault on McClernand's line. Actually, two of his regiments did. After the 12th and 13th Tennessee were detached away from the brigade, Russell and the 11th Louisiana and 22nd Tennessee took part in the assault. See *OR* 10, pt. 1, 417; Shiloh Battlefield Commission Tablet #302.

At the beginning of the attack the Seventeenth Louisiana lost its lieutenant colonel to one of Sherman's riflemen, who put a Minie ball through Jones' left arm. With their leader gone, the regiment faltered.[16] Reichard's Twentieth Louisiana charged Sherman, but was stopped by heavy fire. As the German-Louisianan temporarily retired, Captain Herman Muller, Company C, was struck in his knee by a bullet. One of the men yelled to First Lieutenant Charles DePetz, "Captain Muller has fallen!" DePetz sent two men to pick up the captain and carry him to a hospital.[17] DePetz assumed command of the company, and Reichard quickly rallied the regiment. Within minutes the Twentieth went forward again. At the identical spot where Captain Muller was hit, Lieutenant DePetz was struck in the back by a shell fragment, sending him sprawling to the ground. DePetz's fingers nervously felt his back but found the fragment had only struck his rolled up raincoat. Pulling himself together, the greatly relieved lieutenant climbed to his feet and ran after his still advancing regiment. Heavy fire hit the Twentieth, but they pressed steadily on toward Sherman.[18]

On the right of Anderson's Brigade, Stanley's Ninth Texas resolutely advanced toward the Purdy Road, although hit heavily by Sherman's fire. The Washington Artillery raked Sherman's soldiers with 6 and 12-pound projectiles to cover the advance,[19] but Union

16 *OR* 10, pt. 1, 506.

17 Charles DePetz to wife, April 15, 1882, in Clark, "The New Orleans German Colony in the Civil War," 1003. In the confusion of battle, Muller wound up a prisoner. Enlisting in the army December 21, 1861, at Camp Lewis, Louisiana, Muller was elected second lieutenant of Company C. On January 8, 1862, he was elected captain. After the battle he was taken by steamer to the military hospital in Cincinnati, Ohio. On July 30, he was forwarded to the military prison at Camp Chase, Ohio. On September 11, 1862, he was exchanged from the steamer *John H. Done*, near Vicksburg; Mississippi. His leg was permanently crippled by the Shiloh wound, and he was never able to rejoin his command. He retired from the army November 2, 1864. Booth, *Louisiana Records*, 3, Book 1: 1086.

18 Charles DePetz to wife, April 15, 1862, in Clark, "The New Orleans German Colony in the Civil War," 1003.

19 *OR* 10, pt. 1, 509.

sharpshooters in the woods and some unidentified tents sprinkled the battery with rifle fire, causing many casualties. One man was struck as he moved the trail of one of the pieces. Private Richard Pugh, in the battery since March 6, was hit by two bullets that tore his pants legs without scratching him. The battery was forced to a new position in order to avoid some of the sniper fire.[20]

Still acting under Bragg's order to advance, Colonel Preston Smith quickly out-distanced the rest of the brigade, unaware of General Johnson's mishap. With his five hundred or so remaining Tennesseans behind him, Smith led the One hundred fifty-fourth across the wooded area heading straight for Raith's position at the crossroads. The Confederates lashed the Illinoisans with musketry and with fire from the single gun of Polk's battery under Sergeant J. J. Pirtle, which had somehow managed to keep up with Smith's advance.[21]

Smith was already sharply engaged with Raith's command when Stewart's regiments came up to support him. McNeeley's Thirteenth Arkansas moved up to support Pirtle's gun, some of his men assisting the gunners in shifting firing positions. The Thirteenth did some sharpshooting with the Illinoisans, but was not heavily engaged, losing only six men. Lieutenant R. A. Duncan, Company A, was wounded, and two sergeants and three privates were killed.[22]

---

20 Richard Pugh to wife, April 8, 1862, Richard L. Pugh Papers, Louisiana State University Archives; Washington Artillery Order Book, Louisiana Historical Association Collection, Howard-Tilton Memorial Library, Tulane University.

21 *OR* 10, pt. 1, 446, 447.

22 *Ibid.*, 430, 431. || Dr. Cunningham originally included the 11th Iowa in with Raith's brigade action, but there is little evidence to substantiate such a claim. The 11th Iowa was deployed in the rear of Veatch's brigade, which was in the rear of Marsh's command. Thus, the 11th Iowa was not with Raith's men. See *OR* 10, pt. 1, 130. The 11th Iowa did some fighting earlier than the 11:00 a.m. Confederate assault, which could have been some long-range support of Raith, and the *effect* of Raith's break could have resulted in the enemy flanking the 11th Iowa, as Lieutenant Colonel William Hall makes clear in his report. That relationship, however, is the closest we can place the Iowans with Raith's brigade. We have slightly clarified the original text. See Shiloh Battlefield Monument #102.

Venable's Fifth Tennessee advanced on Smith's right, but quickly retired in the face of extremely heavy fire.[23] This left it up to the Thirty-third and One hundred fifty-fourth to do the job. After raking the Northerners with musketry, Smith's and Campbell's regiments charged, driving the Federals back from the crossroads, the One hundred fifty-fourth taking two guns.[24]

General S. A. M. Wood's Brigade passed through Raith's brigade camp, trading shots with McClernand's skirmishers. Informed of the strength of the Purdy Road position, Wood halted his brigade, rearranged his regiments, and angled them for a charge to the left. His new dispositions from left to right were the Ninth Arkansas Battalion, Eighth Arkansas, Twenty-seventh Tennessee, Sixteenth Alabama, Forty-fourth Tennessee, Fifty-fifth Tennessee, and the Third Mississippi Battalion. General "Sam" notified Hindman of the situation and the divisional commander immediately ordered Shaver's Brigade to support Wood's Brigade in an advance.[25]

Wood's Southerners headed straight for Marsh's brigade. The batteries on both sides banged enthusiastically away, but the infantry held their fire, saving the all important first shot for maximum effect at close range. Some of Marsh's enlisted men grumbled about the decision, muttering, "Why don't our officers give the command to fire?" But the officers waited. As the strain mounted, a few nervous fingers tightened on triggers, and occasional puffs of smoke spurted from the line of waiting Blue infantry. One hysterical officer in the Forty-fifth Illinois screamed, "Cease fire, those are our troops." An irate private in Company A yelled back at him, "The hell they are! You will find out pretty damned soon they are not."[26]

The Gray regiments moved in closer until finally the Federal line erupted in a deadly volley of musketry. The Southerners quickly returned the fire. Large numbers of men on both sides fell to the ground or

23   *OR* 10, pt. 1, 433.

24   *Ibid.*, 435.

25   *OR* 10, pt. 1, 592.

26   Crammer, *With Grant at Fort Donelson*, 57, 58.

clutched torn parts of their bodies. For at least five minutes the soldiers of Marsh's and Wood's brigades simply stood in line and cut each other to pieces. Burrows' six rifles spewed death into the Gray lines, but the Confederates fought back savagely. Burrows and twenty-five of his men were wounded and four others killed by the musketry. Seventy battery horses were cut down by the deadly fire.[27]

If the fire from Marsh's men was not bad enough, the Confederates suddenly found themselves being mauled by musketry from Rebel troops in the rear, who mistook Wood's left regiments for Federals. Colonel Patterson ordered his Eighth Arkansas to take cover on the ground or behind trees. The shots from the rear soon ceased, and Patterson's men quickly scrambled to their feet and poured a blistering fire into the Eleventh and Twentieth Illinois.[28]

Losses in all of Wood's units except Hardcastle's Battalion, which was not engaged, were heavy. Colonel Christopher Williams of the Twenty-seventh Tennessee fell with a bullet through his heart. Lieutenant Colonel B. H. Brown of the same regiment dropped with a severely fractured leg. Many enlisted men and junior officers, including Captain Isham G. Hearn, Company E, were killed outright. The Confederates, however, resolutely continued firing into the men from Illinois. [29]

Union losses were even heavier, especially in field officers. Colonel Haynie and Lieutenant Colonel William Sanford, Forty-eighth Illinois, were both badly wounded, and the regiment began to gradually give ground.[30] The Twentieth Illinois was the next to crack, and then the Eleventh, having lost two commanding officers (Lieutenant Colonel T. E. G. Ransom and Major Garrett Nevins badly wounded in less than five minutes, plus a third or more of its other personnel), broke and headed for the rear. The Eleventh had sustained 329 casualties at Fort Donelson two

---

27 *OR* 10, pt. 1, 137; Bearss, "Project 17," 4; Kelly, "General John Herbert Kelly, The Boy General of the Confederacy," 41, 42.

28 *OR* 10, pt. 1, 598.

29 *Ibid.*, 605.

30 *Ibid.*, 138.

months earlier and was still pitifully under strength.[31] The Forty-fifth followed its sister regiments, and the Confederates followed the retreating Federals.[32]

Although Wood's men had routed an entire brigade, their fight was actually only half over. Immediately behind Marsh's abandoned position lay a second Federal brigade of fresh troops, many of them combat veterans: Veatch's brigade of Hurlbut's division.

When Hurlbut was first notified of the attack on Sherman that morning, he immediately dispatched Colonel James C. Veatch's brigade to reinforce Sherman's left.[33] Lieutenant J. C. Long of Hurlbut's staff brought Veatch the news of his assignment.[34] Bugles blew and drums beat, and soon Colonel Veatch's four regiments were on the road to the front. It was a long walk, and the brigade met "crowds of stragglers skulking to the rear, . . . a humiliating sight." The Fourth Division's men shouted curses and insults to the stragglers, who retorted with a wide variety of excuses for their conduct. Sometimes the brigade saw two and three able bodied men carrying or helping along one slightly scratched Federal soldier.[35]

Veatch's orders were to deploy his brigade behind the camp of the Seventeenth Illinois, to the right of the Review Field, but by the time the marching Federals reached the bordering area, Confederate infantry was already approaching the Illinois camp site. Veatch wisely decided that to attempt to take his assigned position would mean a disaster, and besides there were Federal troops (McClernand's) between him and the camp. The forty-two year old veteran of Fort Donelson deployed his men behind Hare's brigade. An officer, claiming to be acting under Sherman's orders, rode up and told Veatch to move to the right. The Federals slung

31 *Ibid.*, 116; Douglas Hapeman Diary, April 6, 1862, Douglas Hapeman Papers, Illinois State Historical Library; *OR* 7, 133, 137.

32 Crummer, *With Grant at Fort Donelson*, 59.

33 *OR* 10, pt. 1, 203.

34 *Ibid.*, 220.

35 Barber, *Army Memoirs*, 51, 52; Alvin Q. Bacon, *Thrilling Adventures of A Pioneer Boy While A Prisoner of War* (n.p., n.d.), 61, 62.

their rifles over their shoulders and moved to the right to some uneven ground directly behind Marsh, where the regiments were deployed again. From left to right Veatch's command consisted of the Twenty-fifth Indiana, Lieutenant Colonel William Morgan (Veatch's old regiment), Fourteenth Illinois Colonel Cyrus Hall, Forty-sixth Illinois, Colonel John Davis, and the Fifteenth Illinois, Lieutenant Colonel Edward Ellis.[36] The brigade took position on a slight rise in the ground, in front of which was a hill.[37] They were less than thirty yards behind Marsh.[38] Veatch apparently thought he was behind part of Sherman's division, for there is no record of him communicating with either Marsh or McClernand. When Marsh's men broke, the pursuing Rebels occupied his position and kept on after the retreating Yanks. Veatch's men had difficulty in opening fire for fear of shooting their own people fleeing ahead of the Confederates. To add to the problems, Burrows' surviving battery horses broke loose and stampeded through Veatch's lines, routing Company A, Fourteenth Illinois.[39]

Lying on the ground or sheltered behind the numerous trees, the Northerners fired at will into Wood's men.[40] But the Confederates, stimulated by their victory and probably not realizing they were facing a fresh Federal force, kept right on coming. Some of the Federals lit out for

---

36 *OR* 10, pt. 1, 226, 228, 230; Bacon, *Thrilling Adventures*, 4, 5; Foster, *War Stories*, 62.

37 Barber, *Army Memoirs*, 53; Foster, *War Stories*, 62.

38 *OR* 10, pt. 1, 228. || Dr. Cunningham originally stated that Veatch was 150 to 200 yards behind Marsh, and cited Colonel John A. Davis of the 46th Illinois as his source. Colonel Davis might have been referring to one of Raith's forward regiments, although it is difficult to be certain. In actuality, Veatch's line was less than thirty yards behind McClernand's. Veatch does not state his position in relation to McClernand, but the Shiloh Battlefield Commission, as well as the Illinois Shiloh Battlefield Commission, placed the brigade's monuments at the shorter distance. See *OR* 10, pt. 1, 220; Shiloh Battlefield Monuments #51, 52, 64, and 84.

39 *Ibid.*, 225.

40 Payson Shumway to wife, April 13, 1862, Payson Z. Shumway Papers, Illinois State Historical Library.

the rear, "not to return unless drove at the point of a bayonet."[41] The fleeing troops from Marsh's brigade swept over Veatch's position, disrupting his line completely and seriously disordering the Fifteenth and Forty-sixth Illinois.

About the same moment, Smith's One hundred fifty-fourth Tennessee crashed through the crossroads, driving back Colonel Raith and turning Veatch's right flank as well as the Eleventh Iowa's. Some of the Tennesseans started shooting into the Fifteenth Illinois' right companies, while General Wood's determined soldiers strongly peppered the Northern regiments from in front.[42] Lieutenant Colonel E. P. Ellis caught a ball in an arm, but he continued to lead the Fifteenth until another musket ball tore through his heart.[43] Moments before, Major William Goddard was killed while admonishing the Fifteenth to "stand firm; stand your ground. . . . Take good aim."[44] All but two of the company commanders and more than one hundred in the ranks fell in the deadly crossfire, but still the regiment held.[45]

The Sixteenth Alabama and the Twenty-seventh Tennessee swarmed over Burrow's Battery, abandoned now, save for the dead and wounded men and horses. A Confederate sergeant planted the "Stars and Bars" over the battery, but he was immediately shot down by Fifteenth Illinois riflemen.[46] Finally in the midst of such confusion, the Fifteenth could stand no more, and its members headed for the rear.[47] The Forty-sixth was next to crack. Colonel Davis' men were hit by heavy and accurate

---

41 Bacon, *Thrilling Adventures*, 4; *OR* 10, pt. 1, 220.

42 Foster, *War Stories*, 62; *OR* 10, pt. 1, 220.

43 *Ibid.*, 226; Barber, *Army Memoirs*, 54. Private Barber, Company D, said Ellis was first hit in the hand.

44 *OR* 10, pt. 1, 226.

45 *Ibid.* || Dr. Cunningham once again wrote that Raith was driven back with the 11th Iowa. We have slightly corrected the text to read that the 11th Iowa was outflanked as a result of Raith's break. See *OR* 10, pt. 1, 130; Shiloh Battlefield Monument #102.

46 Barber, *Army Memoirs*, 53.

47 *OR* 10, pt. 1, 220.

fire which killed or wounded eight company officers and many enlisted men. Among the casualties was former militiaman John Musser, captain of Company A. When the Confederates charged, the twenty-nine year old officer sheathed his sword, grabbed a musket, and began firing until a Southern bullet caught him in the leg. Musser was transported to Quincy, Illinois, by means of a hospital ship, and his leg was amputated. He died April 23, leaving a wife and two children. Major Benjamin Dornblaser was among those wounded at this time. A musket ball, which he carried the rest of his life, hit him in the left shoulder joint of the arm. Davis finally ordered the regiment to fall back to prevent its annihilation.[48]

Confederate infantry, probably from the Fourth Tennessee, turned Veatch's left flank so the Twenty-fifth Indiana was subjected to a deadly two-way fire. Lieutenant Colonel Morgan ordered his men to fall back, but as they started the execution of his command, he was shot through the leg. Major John Foster took over the command and managed to withdraw part of the regiment to comparative safety in the rear. It was a fighting retreat, many of the men pausing to load and fire every few yards.

Seeing everyone else pulling back, Colonel Hall decided to do likewise. His men headed for the rear in complete confusion, but the colonel managed to collect some of them and linked up with Foster. Some of the men did not hear the order to fall back and were left behind and were overrun.[49]

With a little assistance from other units, Wood's command had defeated two enemy brigades, rolling them pell-mell, but the price was dear and Wood was among the casualties. The noise of battle frightened his mount and the general was flung to the ground with such force as to disable the brigade commander for more than three hours. The temporary loss of their commanding officer, plus the confusion engendered by their successful attack, threw the Southerners of this brigade into a complete state of disorder, the remnants of the various battalions and regiments wandering off in all directions.

Major Samuel Love, the Twenty-seventh's last field officer, was not with the command. He was taking part in an operation on another part of

---

48 *Ibid.*, 228, 229; Jones, *46th Illinois*, 37, 25.

49 *Ibid.*; Bacon, *Thrilling Adventures*, 5.

the field, and the regiment was low on ammunition. The captains marched the surviving men to the rear,[50] where they met General Beauregard. By the general's orders Lieutenant Colonel Ferguson took command of the Twenty-seventh. Collecting ammunition from the supply wagons, the lieutenant colonel distributed cartridges to the Tennesseans and ordered them to "rest and refresh themselves with coffee, etc." He later turned the command over to the senior captain, but it was three hours until the regiment was ready to go back into action.[51]

If Wood had broken through, the rest of the Confederate push against McClernand's position had met with only a little success. General Alexander Stewart became involved in the assault in a rather peculiar fashion. In response to orders from a staff officer, Stewart moved his brigade over to the left, and then forward. But Colonel R. P. Neely failed to hear the order, and the Fourth Tennessee wandered to the right. Stewart led his three other regiments across a small stream and ordered them to lie on the ground to protect themselves against enemy fire until he could ride back and locate Colonel Neely. While he was gone, Hardee and then Ruggles came by and ordered the three regiments to join in on the attack at the crossroads. Finding the Fourth, Stewart led them to where he assumed the rest of his brigade was waiting. Finding the regiments gone, he had little time to ponder the matter, for one of General Bragg's staff officers rode up and ordered Stewart to storm a Federal battery located in the northwest corner of the Review Field. Stewart told his men what Bragg wanted done and asked if they could do it. The men replied, "Show us where it is; we will try."[52]

The battery in question was that of Captain Edward McAllister. It had been dropping 24-pound shells on the Fourth Tennessee for several minutes, causing the soldiers to take cover on the ground. The bursting shells killed Captain John Southerland, Company G, and several privates also. Major John F. Henry was mortally wounded. It was about eight hundred yards to McAllister's position, but the Tennesseans scrambled

---

50 *OR* 10, pt. 1, 592, 601, 606.

51 Lieutenant Colonel S. W. Ferguson to General Beauregard, April 9, 1862, Miscellaneous Collection, Shiloh National Military Park.

52 *OR* 10, pt. 1, 427.

to their feet and double-quicked forward slightly to the left, and then straight on for the battery. The big guns belched flame, smoke, and death as the exploding projectiles tore nasty gaps in the advancing lines. Wood's and Shaver's brigades were attacking at the same time, thus much of the infantry fire was diverted from the Fourth Tennessee to the other units; however, the Tennesseans were struck by rifle fire from the Forty-fifth Illinois and Thirteenth Iowa of Hare's brigade.[53]

The Fourth Tennessee averaged the loss of a man for every four yards of ground it advanced across, but the regiment did not turn back. Halting near McAllister's position, the Tennesseans poured in a volley and charged. McAllister and many of his men were struck. Despite his injury, the game captain ordered his guns hitched up. So many horses had been hit by the Fourth's musketry that there were only enough to hitch up three pieces. Battery D, First Illinois, less one gun and two men, made a hasty withdrawal as Neely's regiment swarmed into their position, capturing two gunners.[54]

As the Fourth Tennessee captured the shiny 24-pounder, Shaver and his brigade drove Hare's three regiments from their position. After helping crack Peabody's brigade, Shaver was ordered to halt and reform his command, and upon performing this function, Hindman ordered him to "make an oblique change of front to the left," the idea of attacking a Federal encampment there. Before completing this movement, however,

---

53 McClernand to U. S. Grant, March 3, 1862, John A. McClernand Papers, Illinois State Historical Library; *OR* 10, pt. 1, 432, 116.

54 *OR* 10, pt. 1, 432, 116; Bearss, "Project 17," 2. There is some question as to whom led the Confederate charge. General Stewart referred to "Neely's" regiment, and the general commended Neely for his gallantry at the end of his report. *Ibid.*, 427, 429. The report of the Fourth Tennessee at Shiloh was signed by Lieutenant Colonel Otho Strahl, who flatly stated that he made the charge. He did not even mention Neely's name in the report. *Ibid.*, 432, 433. A. J. Meadows, of the Fourth Tennessee, maintained that Strahl led the charge which captured Captain McAllister's "famous" battery. A. J. Meadows, "The Fourth Tennessee," *Confederate Veteran* 14 (July 1906): 312. Colonel Neely died of natural causes the following month, and Strahl was elected colonel. *Tennesseans in the Civil War*, 1: 183. Either Stewart was confused about Neely's presence or something happened to the colonel before the charge was made and Strahl did not refer to it, perhaps from a feeling of delicacy.

Shaver was ordered to make a flank movement, cross the Review Field, and storm McClernand's left.[55]

Shaver's regiments moved across Review Field, running into only light fire. By the time they reached within eighty or a hundred yards of Hare's position, the Fourth Tennessee had chased McAllister's gunners away and Wood's men were driving Marsh's brigade back. Realizing they were outflanked, Hare's brigade began to dissolve. Shaver's men raked the Eighth Illinois position with musketry, wounding the commanding officer, Captain James Ashmore. Captain William Harvey, Company K, assumed command but he was killed almost instantly, and the regiment headed for the rear. The Thirteenth Iowa fired one volley before Colonel Crocker gave the order to pull back.[56]

The collapse of Veatch's brigade spelled the end of the Purdy Road line, and by about 11:20 a.m. the Confederates were in complete possession of the position. McClernand ordered his regiments to regroup about two hundred yards north of the crossroads. Giving the order, however, was much easier than seeing it executed.[57] The Federals were badly scattered and brigade organization was completely disrupted. Most of the regimental commanders simply fell back to where they could find a decent spot to make a stand. Sherman and McClernand no longer had a fairly continuous formation. Instead, they found themselves with a score of confused regiments strung out along three-quarters of a mile of uneven terrain.

The only saving grace of the situation was that the Confederates were just as confused. Wood was by this time out of the fight, while Preston Smith was just beginning to round up his scattered units. Russell's command was also badly scattered, and many of his men were in need of cartridges. Only Anderson's battered brigade possessed any kind of cohesive aggressiveness. Despite the best efforts of many officers on both sides, along most of this area the fighting simply degenerated into a prolonged exchange of heavy musket and cannon fire.

55 *OR* 10, pt. 1, 574.

56 *Ibid.*, 124, 126, 128, 132, 574, 576, 578.

57 *Ibid.*, 116.

On McClernand's left, Colonel Crocker managed to collect most of his regiment and part of the Eighth and Eighteenth Illinois, and they engaged opposing Confederate infantry in a sharp fire fight.[58]

Captain James Timony's Battery D, Second Illinois, came up and McClernand ordered it into position along the road. Timony's men opened fire on Anderson's slowly advancing Texans and Louisianans. Lieutenant DePetz had another near encounter with death. The lieutenant later wrote his wife, telling her that "two shots sounded and one of them went through my trousers leg and fell in my boot, the other cut away my watch-chain, and went through my coat without hurting me in the slightest."[59]

Confederate musketry was very heavy, and Battery D's few infantry supports quickly melted away. Confederate artillery, probably some of Irving Hogdson's gunners, shelled the Illinois battery. An exploding projectile knocked Captain Timony senseless, while gunners and horses dropped all around. Lieutenant T. D. Tozer was killed while helping work his gun, and at least four enlisted men lost their lives, besides many that were wounded under the heavy Confederate fire. Lieutenant J. D. Whitall took command of Timony's Battery and managed to withdraw two of the battery's pieces and some other equipment, but the Ninth Texas seized four of the ponderous iron tubes.[60]

After the loss of Timony's guns, McClernand ordered another withdrawal, his various regiments establishing a jagged line along the southern end of the Jones Field. After this last withdrawal,[61] offensive activities on this portion of the front temporarily halted. Sherman and McClernand reorganized their commands and prepared for a counterattack.

*   *   *

58 *Ibid.*, 132.

59 Charles DePetz to wife, April 15, 1862, in Clark, "The New Orleans German Colony in the Civil War," 1003, 1004.

60 *OR* 52, 23; 10, pt. 1, 116, 509.

61 *OR* 10, pt. 1, 117.

Shortly after the battle began, General W. H. L. Wallace formed his Second Division up in preparation for a move to the front, wherever that might be. But before moving out Wallace ordered Colonel Crafts Wright to take his regiment, the Thirteenth Missouri Infantry of McArthur's brigade, and report to General Sherman over at or near the Purdy Road.[62] Wallace then sent B. S. Compton's Fourteenth Missouri and Colonel Thomas Morton's Eighty-first Ohio over to guard the Snake Creek Bridge, on the road leading to Crump's Landing.[63] Wallace directed General McArthur to take the two remaining regiments of his brigade, plus Battery A, First Illinois, and move south along the Hamburg Road to support Colonel Stuart.[64] With his two remaining brigades, Wallace started out on the fatal two mile march to the battle front, not knowing that his lovely wife, Ann, was on the steamer *Minnehaha*, already tied up at the Landing.[65]

Arriving at the Duncan Field, in a gap between Hurlbut's position in the Peach Orchard and McClernand's near the Purdy Road,[66] Wallace immediately moved his First Brigade, commanded by Colonel James Tuttle, into position along an old road behind the Duncan Field. From left to right Tuttle's line consisted of the Fourteenth Iowa, Colonel William T. Shaw, Twelfth Iowa, Colonel Joseph Woods, Seventh Iowa, Lieutenant Colonel James C. Parrott, and Second Iowa, Lieutenant Colonel James Baker. Wallace brought up his Third Brigade, led by Colonel T. W. Sweeny, with the Fifty-eighth and Seventh Illinois, Colonels William Lynch and Major Richard Rowett respectively

---

62 *Ibid.*, 159.

63 *Ibid.*, 161.

64 *Ibid.*, 155, 156; Reed, *Shiloh*, 50.

65 Mrs. W. H. L. Wallace to her Aunt Mag, April 29, 1862, Miscellaneous Collection, Shiloh National Military Park. According to Colonel Tuttle, writing many years after the event, Wallace was in his tent dressing to go meet his wife when the news of the attack came. Byers, *Iowa in War Times*, 129.

66 Bell, *Tramps and Triumphs*, 15; Reed, *Shiloh*, 48. Within a few minutes after Wallace reached his position, Hurlbut's right flank was reinforced by Prentiss and the reorganized regiments of his division. During the battle Prentiss actually covered Wallace's left.

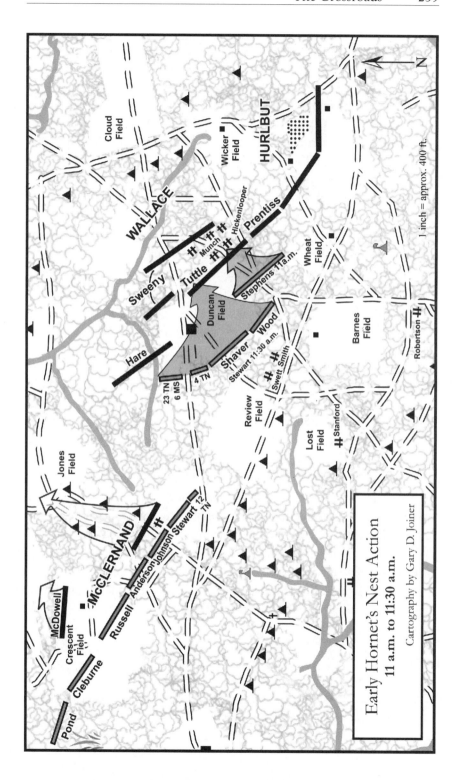

N

1 inch = approx. 400 ft.

Early Hornet's Nest Action
11 a.m. to 11:30 a.m.

Cartography by Gary D. Joiner

commanding, moving forward to take up the position on Tuttle's right and on McClernand's extreme left. The Fiftieth Illinois was soon ordered to move to McArthur's support, while the Eighth Iowa and Fifty-seventh Illinois were held in divisional reserve.[67]

Tuttle's First Brigade was one of the finest in Grant's army. The Second Iowa had served with honor in Missouri throughout most of 1861, but had failed to see action. Its first colonel, Samuel R. Curtis, had been promoted to major general, and on March 7 and 8 defeated General Earl Van Dorn's army in a difficult combat at Pea Ridge, Arkansas. Even as the Second took its position in line on the morning of April 6, Van Dorn's army was hurrying toward Corinth. The Second Iowa's second colonel, James Tuttle, had performed with distinction at Fort Donelson, leading the Second in a determined charge on the Confederate works. Tuttle was now brigade commander and in line for a brigadier generalship. All four regiments had fought at Fort Donelson, and the Seventh had been engaged at Belmont, Missouri, the previous November.[68]

Tuttle's brigade established its position along a landmark that has since become synonymous with Shiloh—the Sunken Road. The road was a simple wagon track running from the Corinth-Pittsburg Landing Road eastward to the Hamburg-Savannah Road. It ran across the three principal roads to Pittsburg Landing; thus it was an unforeseen barrier to the Confederate plan to drive a wedge between the Federal left and the Landing. Union and Confederate officers alike were strongly impressed by the inherent strength of General Wallace's and General Prentiss' positions, but to their eyes that strength lay in the thick underbrush on the left and the clear field of fire provided by Duncan's Field on the right. Only one "Official Report" cites the position, Cheatham's, referring to it merely as "an abandoned road."[69]

General Don Carlos Buell later said that "it was equally formidable against attack from both directions," adding that the position consisted of

---

67 Thomas, *Soldier Life*; *OR* 10, pt. 1, 149, 151, 153, 162, 164, 165.

68 *Ibid.*, 7, 168, 111, 275.

69 *Ibid.*, 10, pt. 1, 438. || For more information on the historiography of the Sunken Road, see Smith, *The Untold Story of Shiloh*, 29-34.

"a wood in the center with a thick undergrowth, flanked on either side by open fields, and with open but sheltering woods in front and rear."[70] The Southerners referred to the whole position, road and all, simply as the "Hornet's Nest." Confederate Private Thomas Chinn Robertson, Fourth Louisiana, who took part in several attacks on the Hornet's Nest, described it as "an old road, which by frequent travel had become worn about three feet deep." Robertson also said the road ran across a hill which "was covered with the thickest undergrowth of blackjack I ever saw."[71]

The ground in front of Prentiss' position was covered with many hickory and oak trees that had not yet leaved. The Federals could see to shoot through the trees, but the timber acted as a screen for their own

---

70 *Battles and Leaders*, 1: 50.

71 Thomas Chinn Robertson to mother, April 9, 1862, Thomas Chinn Robertson Papers, Louisiana State University Archives. Robertson's description is borne out by one Union source which mentioned "an old washed out road ... three feet deep," with a low ridge and a dense thicket to the left. Byers, *Iowa In War Times*, 129, 130. See also Mildred Throne, (ed.). "Erastus B. Times, History of Company D, the 12th Iowa Infantry, 1861-1866," *The Iowa Journal of History* 56 (April 1958): 178. ‖ Historians have long been puzzled by Robertson's statement about the Sunken Road, which is the only contemporary account describing the road as "about three feet deep." As Smith, *The Untold Story of Shiloh*, 34, makes plain, "Not one single report in the *Official Records* mentions the road as being sunken. Likewise, no soldiers' letters or diaries exist that refer to it as sunken. Many buffs quote a soldier, Thomas Chinn Robertson, of the 4th Louisiana in Gibson's Brigade as describing the road as three feet deep. In reality, that soldier was in no position to see the road. Gibson's Brigade never reached the Sunken Road and fell back in confusion. Robertson described a tangle of undergrowth, which precluded sight, and even remarked that corps commander Braxton Bragg stated that he would lead them to where they could see the enemy. The unit thereafter moved forward to the right, thus never allowing the quoted soldier to view how deep the road actually was. In all likelihood, the unclear Louisianan was describing the Eastern Corinth Road or possibly even the main Corinth Road, both of which were heavily traveled thoroughfares and thus would have been eroded. Federal regiments, at times during the battle, aligned on both roads." Smith concludes by writing, "Robertson[also claimed] . . . that twenty-seven Federal regiments defended the position he had attacked." *Ibid.*, 178.

position. To Private Charles Morton, Twenty-fifth Missouri, the Sunken Road was a position "about fifteen inches or more deep, affording excellent cover and good rest while firing."[72] Private Leander Stillwell, Sixty-first Illinois, spoke of the position as an "old, grass-grown country road that ran through thick woods. The wheels of wagons, running for many years right in the same ruts, had cut through the turf, so that the surface of the road was somewhat lower than the adjacent ground." Stillwell added that "this afforded a slight natural breastwork, which was substantial protection."[73] Captain Andrew Hickenlooper, Fifth Ohio Battery, remembered the Sunken Road as a "roadway . . . cut for some distance through a low hill." The road was washed out, forming "a protecting parapet only a few inches in height but enough partially to protect the infantry, with its front covered by an almost impenetrable growth."[74]

General Lew Wallace remembered the Sunken Road as "an abandoned road washed out by rains to a depth of twenty or thirty inches, and screened by a thicket."[75] Whether or not the Sunken Road, or the Hornet's Nest, was a massive trench or just a slightly washed out road bed, it still provided a good logical position for the Union army to rally.

By around 9:30, Tuttle's men began taking their position along the road. A Confederate battery opened fire on the Second Iowa, killing and mangling Union men with exploding shells. One member of Company C had his foot crushed so badly by a shell fragment the doctors were later forced to amputate it. The men were ordered to lie down in the roadbed to get some cover from the fire, but casualties still mounted. Captain Bob Littler was struck as he hugged the earth, a jagged slice of iron tearing his arm off from the shoulder, except for a tiny piece of muscle. Crazed with pain, Littler jumped to his feet screaming, "Here, boys! here!" before

---

72 Morton, "A Boy at Shiloh," 62.

73 Stillwell, *Common Soldier*, 64. Colonel Tuttle cited the "old sunken road" in a speech after the war. James M. Tuttle, "Brigade Report," *First Reunion of Iowa's Hornet's Nest Brigade Held at Des Moines, Iowa, Wednesday and Thursday, October 12 and 13, 1887* (Oskaloosa: n.p., 1887), 12.

74 Hickenlooper, "The Battle of Shiloh," 417, 418.

75 Wallace, *An Autobiography*, 481.

mercifully fainting. Terrified by the exploding shells, a trembling rabbit ran up and snuggled alongside a soldier.[76] Occasionally Tuttle's and Sweeny's men exchanged shots with distant Confederate skirmishers, but for the most part of an hour the position remained comparatively quiet, except for the artillery fire.

In the attack on Hare's brigade position, Shaver's right wing regiment, Colonel Marmaduke's Third Confederate, was exposed to heavy rifle fire from Wallace's men. Shaver immediately sent word to General Bragg that strong Federal forces were massing to the right and in front of his command. General Bragg ordered Captain Charles Swett's Battery to move over and support Shaver. Confederate sharpshooters also joined in the fight.[77] Swett and his men fought their way over the extremely rough terrain until they reached the Third Confederate's position. Colonel Marmaduke was standing there, waiting, and he told the battery commander, "Swett, these fellows are in that piece of woods on our front, let's go for them." Captain Swett replied, "Alright, I'm with you." Marmaduke's men advanced toward Wallace skirmishers, while Swett's 6-pounders and 12-pound howitzers covered the advance.[78]

General Hindman rode over to investigate and ran into the line of fire of a Federal battery. A cannon ball, probably from one of Hickenlooper's remaining smooth-bores, killed General Hindman's mount, and that officer was badly bruised by his fall to the ground.[79]

Shaver's men were exhausted and they were low on ammunition. After Hindman was disabled, Shaver withdrew to regroup. Stewart, with his Fourth Tennessee and fragments of the Sixteenth Alabama and Fifty-fifth Tennessee, also took part in this movement, although not closely engaged.[80]

76 Bell, *Tramps and Triumphs*, 16, 17.

77 *OR* 10, pt. 1, 574.

78 Charles Swett, "Shiloh," Miscellaneous Collection, Shiloh National Military Park.

79 D. C. Govan to the Honorable Shiloh Park Commission, April 14, 1900, Miscellaneous Collection, Shiloh National Military Park; *OR* 10, pt. 1, 574.

80 *Ibid.*, 574, 428; Reed, *Shiloh*, 70. || Although technically correct, Dr. Cunningham does not give ample credit to this operation. Around 11:30 a.m.

At this stage in the fighting, a new unit moved upon the scene, Cheatham's Second Brigade commanded by Colonel William H. Stephens. Cheatham's other brigade under Bushrod Johnson had previously been engaged on the Confederate left, but the general remained in reserve with the Second. As the brigade headed for the front, General A. S. Johnston detached the First Tennessee Battalion, Colonel George Maney, to unite with Colonel N. B. Forrest's cavalry and Colonel D. H. Cummings' Nineteenth Tennessee. These three units moved to the right to guard Greer Ford over Lick Creek.[81]

General Johnston halted the First Tennessee and personally addressed them as they moved toward their new station. Informing Maney's men that he had selected them for this post of honor, Johnston explained that if General Buell's army arrived and crossed the Tennessee River at Hamburg, the Confederates would be in serious trouble. He directed the Tennesseans to hold their position no matter what the price might be. To wind up his speech, he asked the soldiers if they had been issued the required forty rounds. It was a solemn moment, and then one very serious private, Dave Adams, soberly drawled, "No, General, I ain't got but thirty-eight." General Johnston smiled and replied, "Very well, my friend, see your orderly sergeant and get your full number."[82]

Stewart, who took over Shaver's Brigade, made the largest attack of the day (3,600 men) on the Hornet's Nest with that brigade, the 4th Tennessee, and the 16th Alabama and 55th Tennessee of Wood's Brigade, which Cunningham describes. Also joining this advance were portions of Cleburne's Brigade (the 6th Mississippi and 23rd Tennessee). This advance, which stretched from the Corinth Road to the Eastern Corinth Road, was perhaps the only significant assault to move directly through Duncan Field. Because of the geographical nature of the assault area, the advance petered out quickly, with Shaver reporting his brigade out of ammunition and headed for the rear. The remainder of the participants withdrew as well. The attack probably did not penetrate more than one-third of the way into Duncan Field. See Smith, *The Untold Story of Shiloh*, 47.

81 *Ibid.*, 454; William Preston, Diary, April 6, 1862, Miscellaneous Collection, Shiloh National Military Park.

82 A. S. Horsley, "Reminiscences of Shiloh," *Confederate Veteran* 2 (August 1894): 234.

The rest of the brigade executed a series of movements along the front, deploying to the left in support of General Bragg's line; and then, by General Beauregard's orders, deploying to the right, taking up a position in front but well away from the Hornet's Nest.

Shortly after 10:00 a.m., Captain Melancthon Smith opened fire on the Hornet's Nest with his four Napoleons and two 6-pound smoothbores. The Mississippians suffered heavily from Wallace's batteries, but they kept the contest up for an hour.[83] Wallace's Missouri gunners not only pounded Smith's Mississippi Battery, but they raked the entire brigade as well. Cheatham ordered his men to lie on the ground, and the Federal gunners quickly shifted to a more lucrative target, Colonel A. J. Lindsay's First Mississippi Cavalry, which was screening Cheatham's rear.

The Mississippians saw the first shots pass over their heads, but the Northern gunners lowered their sights. Projectiles dropped among the cavalry with increasing accuracy. One solid shot fell just short and richocheted toward Captain H. W. Foote. Sinking his spurs into his horse's flanks, Foote narrowly got out of the way. The projectile struck Lieutenant E. T. Deupree's stallion, killing him, and grazing the lieutenant's thigh, breaking his saber in two. Several more horses were struck by cannon shot, including Lieutenant J. G. Deupree's mount, Bremer. In the excitement of battle, the horse's tail was raised high, and the shot "cut away about half of it, bone and-all, and ever afterwards he was known as 'bob-tail Bremer." With iron balls bouncing in all directions, Colonel Lindsay decided to countermarch the First Mississippi, and they took shelter in a nearby ravine.[84]

About 11:20, General Breckinridge moved a force of infantry into position on Cheatham's right, and opened with rifle fire on the opposing Federals. Moments later, Beauregard's assistant adjutant general, Colonel Thomas Jordan, rode up and informed Cheatham that General Beauregard ordered him to attack Wallace's position. Cheatham then personally led forward his Second Brigade, Colonel Charles Wickliffe's

83   *OR* 10, pt. 1, 438.

84   J. G. Deupree, "The Noxubee Squadron of the First Mississippi Cavalry," 31, 32.

Seventh Kentucky on the left, Colonel Henry Douglass' Ninth Tennessee in the center, and Lieutenant Colonel Timothy P. Jones' Sixth Tennessee on the right. With Smith's Mississippi Battery providing covering fire, Cheatham, Stephens, and the three regiments double-quicked toward the Sunken Road.

The Iowans hit the attacking forces heavily with musketry and artillery fire.[85] Cheatham's soldiers slowed down. Then they stopped altogether, many of the men taking cover behind trees and bushes to return the Federal fire. Many officers lost their lives here, including Major W. J. Welhorn, Seventh Kentucky, and Captains Joe B. Freeman and G. G. Person. Not all of the officers were as brave as these. One Sixth Tennessee officer named Fussell headed for cover behind a log, and he cringed there all through the fight.[86]

The three Confederate regiments quickly fell back to the rear, minus many of their best men either killed or wounded. During this movement Colonel Stephens, who was already suffering from illness, was disabled by a bad fall from his horse. Within minutes he was forced to leave the field. Returning to his original position on the Hamburg Road, Cheatham moved to the right, where he was not seriously engaged again until that afternoon.[87]

85   *OR* 10, pt. 1, 438, 151. The Seventh Kentucky had already been under long range artillery fire. About 9:00 a.m., an exploding shell wounded Captain J. G. Pirtle, Company A. George, *History of the 3d, 7th, 8th, and 12th Kentucky, C. S. A.*, 29.

86   John Johnston, "Personal Reminiscences of the Civil War," John Johnston Papers, Tennessee Department of Archives and History.

87   *OR* 10, pt. 1, 453, 438.

Chapter 11

Hornet's Nest

BY NOON THE SITUATION on the Shiloh battlefield was
thoroughly confused. Except for a few regiments, both armies were fully
committed in the battle, yet neither side had scored a decisive blow. On
the Union right, McClernand and Sherman busily collected their men,
positioning them in a rough line in front of Hare's brigade camp. Their
job was made a little easier by the arrival of fresh troops, McDowell's
brigade and the Thirteenth Missouri, along with the Fifteenth and
Sixteenth Iowa. After his long complicated journey from the brigade
camp area, McDowell and his three regiments reached General
McClernand's right a little before noon, and the newly arrived regiments
were soon busy fighting Confederate skirmishers.[1]

Colonel Crafts J. Wright brought the Thirteenth Missouri of
McArthur's brigade to help Sherman, and he joined on that commander's
left.[2] The Fifteenth and Sixteenth Iowa went in to reinforce McClernand
by orders of General U. S. Grant.[3] The six regiments quickly deployed,
and by their presence helped stem further Confederate advancing for the
time being.

It was a trying ordeal for the Fifteenth Iowa, for the unit had only
completed its organization at Keokuk on February 22, and lacking
muskets and equipment, the regiment had been able to do very little

1 Hart, *Fortieth Illinois Infantry*, 88.

2 *OR* 10, pt. 1, 159.

3 *Ibid.*, 160.

training.[4] They were issued weapons, .58 caliber Springfield rifles, March 26, but had not had a chance to practice using them before embarking for Pittsburg Landing.[5] Their march to McClernand's line was something of a nightmare, as the inexperienced Colonel Hugh Reid galloped up and down the line on his horse yelling somewhat confused orders to his men. The lieutenant colonel, William Dewey of Sidney, Iowa, also rode up and down the line, unleashing a prodigious flow of swear words at the soldiers. Occasionally he paused and reined in his horse to "take some consolation through the neck of a pint bottle."[6] Passing the usual crowd of stretcher bearers and stragglers on the road, the regiment reached the battle line to the south and east of Hare's brigade camp.

The ten companies started deploying as Confederate skirmishers began hitting them with musketry. Some of the Iowans promptly shot back. Forty-year-old Colonel Reid rode up and sarcastically yelled, "Cease firing; there is not an enemy within two miles of you!"[7] As if in answer to his remark, a Confederate sniper sent a ball through the colonel's neck, plowing a deep furrow and causing him to fall from his horse.

Major Belknap rode over and asked his fallen superior officer how badly he was hurt. The half stunned colonel replied, "I am killed. Tell my wife I died fighting gloriously."[8] Within a few minutes, however, Colonel Reid was on his feet and resumed command of the regiment for the rest of the day.[9]

---

4 McElroy, *Undying Procession*, 38.

5 Throne, *Cyrus Boyd Diary*, 24, 29.

6 *Ibid.*, 29. The assistant regimental surgeon later remarked that Lieutenant Colonel Dewey was on the sick.

7 Day, "The Fifteenth Iowa at Shiloh," 182.

8 *Ibid.*

9 Belknap, *15th Regiment Iowa*, 15; Day, "The Fifteenth Iowa at Shiloh," 182, 183. Later in the war Reid supported the recruiting of Negro troops. When some of his soldiers protested, he explained, "Remember that every colored

The Fifteenth Iowa, along with its sister regiment the Sixteenth on its flank, soon was fully deployed for action, and enthusiastically fired at the distant Southern snipers.[10]

McClernand ordered a counterattack, and just about 12:00 noon, Federal troops began moving forward. Only part of the division responded to the attack order, Hare's brigade standing purely on the defensive, except for his detached Eleventh Iowa. The Eleventh, Twentieth, Forty-third, Forty-fifth, and the Forty-sixth Illinois, of Veatch's brigade, the Eleventh Iowa, Thirteenth Missouri, plus a detachment of forty men belonging to the Seventieth Ohio, under Henry Philips, regimental adjutant, in addition to McDowell's three regiments, advanced to the attack.[11]

The counterattacking Federals hit Bushrod Johnson's Brigade, now commanded by Preston Smith, and sharply pushed it back.[12] McDowell's brigade advanced on McClernand's right, but it suddenly halted as it ran into Confederate reinforcements, R. T. Trabue's Brigade of Breckinridge's Reserve Corps. The counterattack broke up into two separate engagements, that on the right between McDowell, with a few loose bodies of Federal soldiers aiding him, and Trabue's Brigade, which was supported by scattered Confederate units, and that on the left between McClernand and the remnants of his division, which attacked and drove back Preston Smith's Brigade plus a few assisting Confederate troops from other units.

Trabue's Brigade consisted of the Third Kentucky, Lieutenant Colonel Benjamin Anderson, Fourth Kentucky, Lieutenant Colonel Andrew Hynes, Fifth Kentucky, Colonel Thomas H. Hunt, Sixth

---

soldier who stops a rebel bullet saves a white man's life." Belknap, *15th Regiment Iowa*, 15.

10   Throne, *Cyrus Boyd Diary*, 30; *OR* 10, pt. 1, 288.

11   *Ibid.*, 117, 137, 133, 134; Douglas Hapeman, Diary, April 6, 1862, Douglas Hapeman Papers, Illinois State Historical Library; *OR* 10, pt. 1, 159, 271; Crummer, *With Grant at Fort Donelson*, 63. The two newly arrived Iowa regiments probably did not take part in this counterattack and probably more than Philip's detachment of Sherman's division participated.

12   *OR* 10, pt. 1, 447; Reed, *Shiloh*, 84.

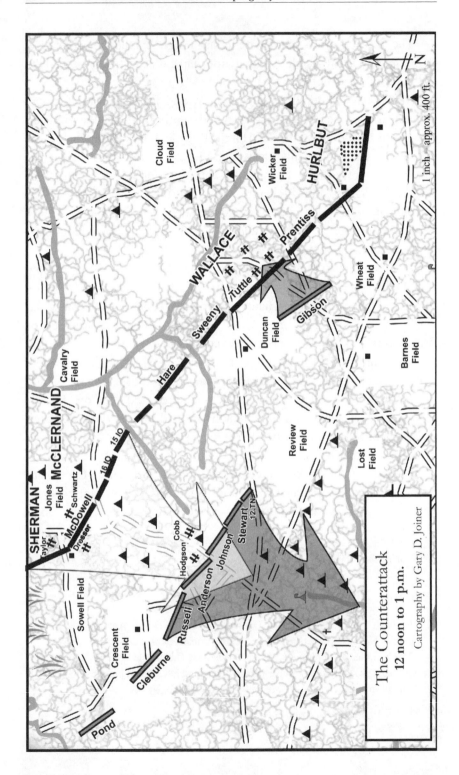

The Counterattack
12 noon to 1 p.m.

Cartography by Gary D. Joiner

1 inch = approx. 400 ft.

Kentucky, Colonel Joseph Lewis, Thirty-first Alabama, Lieutenant Colonel Montgomery Gilbreath, Fourth Alabama Battalion, Major James M. Clifton, Tennessee Battalion, Lieutenant Colonel James M. Crews, Kentucky Cavalry Squadron, Captain John H. Morgan, and the artillery batteries of Captain Edward Byrne and Captain Robert Cobb.[13]

As the battle began Breckinridge ordered Colonel Trabue to move forward in the rear of Polk's Corps. The colonel proceeded some distance when he received a note from Breckinridge ordering him to move up on Polk's left. Executing this order caused his brigade to run into long range fire from a Federal battery. Union gunners fired many rounds into the brigade but caused few casualties. Governor George W. Johnson of Kentucky and Colonel Robert McKee, both acting as military aides to Trabue, had their horses killed by this fire. The governor grabbed a musket and joined with the Fourth Kentucky as a simple volunteer private.

A courier from General Beauregard reached Trabue and the latter, in response to new orders, detached the Third Kentucky, Fourth Alabama, Crews' Battalion, and Byrne's Battery to the right to support Brigadier General Patton Anderson. The brigade was further weakened when an unidentified officer from another unit borrowed Cobb's Battery without Trabue's knowledge, leaving the brigade without artillery. Trabue resumed his forward movement without further incident, but about noon he observed Union troops in front of him. The Confederates frantically deployed in line of battle just as McDowell's brigade and the Thirteenth

13 *OR* 52, pt. 1, 29. Byrne's Battery was referred to as the Kentucky and Mississippi Battery. Byrne was a native Kentuckian, but resided in Washington County, Mississippi, in 1861. At Greenville, Mississippi, in the summer, he organized a battery which included both Mississippians and expatriate Kentuckians. Thompson, *History of the Orphan Brigade*, 857-859. In some accounts Byrne's name is spelled Burns. L. D. Young, *Reminiscences of A Soldier of the Orphan Brigade* (Paris: n.p., n.d.), 32. Crews' Tennessee Battalion was one of those strange hybrid units that frequently showed up in the Confederate army, especially in the early days of the Civil War. It was apparently organized at Savannah, Tennessee, in February 1862, and consisted of six companies. The unit lacked equipment, training, and weapons. *Tennesseans in the Civil War*, 1: 163; *ORN* 22, 573.

Missouri hit them.[14] Trabue's line of battle was from left to right the Fourth Kentucky, Sixth Kentucky, and the Fifth Kentucky, with the Thirty-first Alabama in reserve, while McDowell's arrangement from left to right was the Fortieth Illinois, Thirteenth Missouri, Sixth Iowa, and Forty-sixth Ohio.[15]

Worthington's Forty-sixth Ohio poured a deadly volley of rifle bullets into the Fourth Kentucky, wounding Lieutenant Colonel Hynes. Major Thomas Monroe, Jr. took command. Cautioning the inexperienced Kentuckians to aim low, Monroe gave the order to fire.[16]

For over an hour, the two brigades exchanged volleys of musketry while bits and pieces of other regiments joined with both commands. The Fortieth Illinois had forty-six men killed and many wounded. Colonel Hicks rode up and down in front of his men encouraging them. One of Trabue's men put a bullet through the colonel's horse, spilling the rider to the ground. The Yankee colonel stumbled to his feet and was immediately hit in the left shoulder by a musket ball. His orderly and several soldiers picked him up and carried him to the rear to obtain medical aid.[17]

All four Union regiments were badly hurt by the heavy firing. Lieutenant Colonel Joseph St. James of the Thirteenth Missouri was carried off the battlefield mortally wounded, while several company commanders were also wounded. The regimental major was struck in the chest by a bullet, but he escaped without a scratch, thanks to his iron body armor. Badly jarred by the blow, he withdrew from the field, leaving Colonel Wright alone to manage the regiment.[18] Colonel McDowell rode over to the Sixth Iowa, but his horse was killed and he was knocked senseless.[19]

---

14   *OR* 10, pt. 1, 614, 615.

15   *Ibid.,* 614, 615, 255, 159.

16   Young, *Soldier of the Orphan Brigade,* 27.

17   Hart, *Fortieth Illinois Infantry,* 88.

18   *OR* 10, pt. 1, 159.

19   Byers, *Iowa In War Times,* 139; Wright, *Sixth Iowa,* 84.

Union artillery opened on Trabue's men, but within a few minutes Captain Cobb returned from his unexplained excursion and took a position on Trabue's right. His four 6-pound smoothbores and two 12-pound iron howitzers quickly began dropping projectiles on the enemy battery. Federal gunners changed their sights and began raking the Kentucky Battery. A shell exploded in the battery, killing two of the Confederate gunners. The same round tore off another cannoneer's hands. The wounded gunner stood there with his bleeding stumps and calmly remarked, "My Lord that stops my fighting."[20]

The Federal battery's next shell exploded in the Fifth Kentucky's ranks, killing three men and ripping off the leg of a fourth. Several color bearers dropped from Union fire, including youthful John Green, who had a musket ball glance off his "hard head." Recovering consciousness on a stretcher while being carried to the rear, Private Green insisted on returning to the firing line declaring, "There is too much work here for a man to go to the rear as long as he can shoot a gun."[21]

Additional Confederates units, fragments of both Russell's and Cleburne's brigades, filtered toward Trabue. R. M. Russell brought part of the Eleventh Louisiana, the Twenty-second Tennessee, plus Venable's Fifth Tennessee of Stewart's Brigade. Colonel Ben Hill, of Cleburne's Brigade, brought up what was left of his Fifth Tennessee, and another of Cleburne's regiments, the Twenty-fourth Tennessee, also joined the fight.[22]

McClernand's counterattack on Preston Smith's and Pat Anderson's brigades overlapped on the Trabue-McDowell fight. The Eleventh and Twentieth Illinois approached close enough to Cobb's Battery to hit it with musketry, killing or wounding most of the men and horses. The Illinoisans silenced the guns, but they failed to occupy the battery position.[23] The momentum of McClernand's push carried the Union

---

20 Kirwan, *Johnny Green*, 26.

21 *Ibid.*, 27.

22 *OR* 10, pt. 1, 417, 585.

23 *Ibid.*, 117, 137, 134. The whole action cost Cobb's Battery twelve men killed and twenty-nine wounded. Sixty-eight animals were killed and ten others

soldiers back to and beyond the First Division's headquarters, but their losses mounted rapidly. Lieutenant Colonel Pease of the Forty-ninth Illinois and Lieutenant Colonel Richards of the Twentieth Illinois were both wounded, and casualties among all ranks ran high. Many Union soldiers ran out of ammunition and the Confederates in front of McClernand showed no sign of breaking.[24]

Around 1:00 p.m., troops from Anderson's Brigade moved up to support Trabue, and with these additional reinforcements, the colonel ordered an all out charge with fixed bayonets.[25] The regimental commanders received Trabue's order and passed it to the company commanders. Bayonet blades were quickly attached to the men's muskets and the Confederates moved forward on the double-quick. After gallant resistance, Worthington's Forty-sixth Ohio broke under the bayonet charge and it headed for the rear.[26] Sherman rode up and ordered the Sixth Iowa to fall back, and the rest of the brigade quickly followed. The Confederates moved out in pursuit, thus turning McClernand's right flank.[27] Retracing their steps, McClernand's men fell back to the Jones' Field position, from where they had started.[28]

McClernand's counterattack delayed the Confederate advance during the early afternoon, but afterwards there were no more fresh Union troops to commit on the right. Basically McClernand's and Sherman's divisions and Veatch's brigade were reduced to a confused mass of individual soldiers and pieces of regiments. Many soldiers dropped their guns and headed for the rear. In the search for safety, knapsacks, overcoats, and everything with weight was dropped to the ground as excess baggage. Some soldiers simply collapsed, too

---

wounded. *Ibid.*, 621; Bearss, "Project 17," 46, 47. According to T. J. Lindsey, Cobb lost seventy-nine of his eighty-four battery horses killed. Lindsey, *Ohio at Shiloh*, 48.

24   *OR* 10, pt. 1, 116.

25   *Ibid.*, 615.

26   Young, *Soldier of the Orphan Brigade*, 30.

27   Byers, *Iowa in War Times*, 139.

28   *OR* 10, pt. 1, 117.

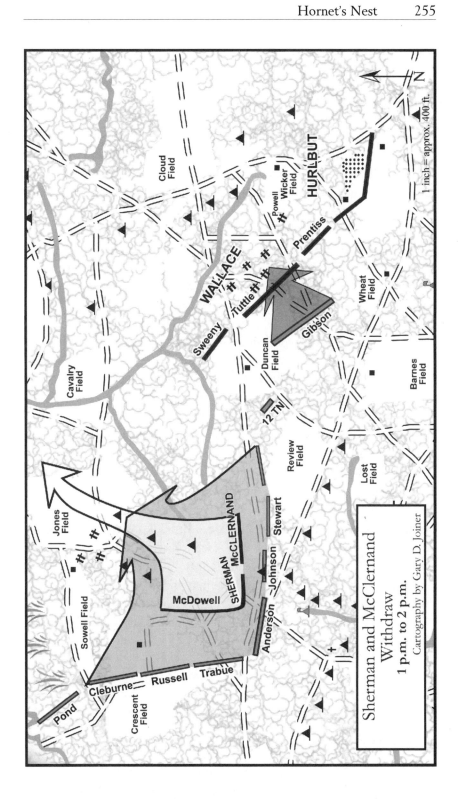

Sherman and McClernand
Withdraw
1 p.m. to 2 p.m.
Cartography by Gary D. Joiner

exhausted and panic-stricken to flee further. Cavalrymen rode in all directions, shouting at the top of their lungs and waving sabers at the fugitives, while officers coaxed and begged the men to stop fleeing. Stray cannon balls and shells tore through the trees, clipping limbs, which sometimes fell on the stragglers. The rear of the Union right presented a scene of disaster and defeat.[29]

Still McClernand, Sherman, and some thousands of Union soldiers fought on at their new position. The Federal right was mauled, but not routed. Just a few hundred yards to McClernand's left, the Union situation looked much better, for at the Hornet's Nest Prentiss' and Wallace's men repulsed charge after charge.

The Southerners opened the afternoon's activities at the Hornet's Nest with an assault by Gibson's Brigade, part of Ruggles' Division. After their unfortunate accidental encounter with Stewart's Brigade, Gibson's men moved to the right under orders from General Bragg. The brigade deployed in the wooded terrain where the Eastern Corinth Road crossed the Hamburg-Purdy Road. From left to right Gibson deployed the Fourth Louisiana, Colonel Henry Watkins Allen, Thirteenth Louisiana, Major Anathole P. Avegno, First Arkansas, Colonel James F. Fagan, and the Nineteenth Louisiana, Colonel Benjamin L. Hodge. After arranging his men, Gibson, in obedience to Bragg's orders, moved forward toward the section of the Hornet's Nest held by remnants of Prentiss' division.[30]

In good order the four regiments surged toward General Prentiss' position, although receiving heavy Federal musketry and artillery fire. In the dense undergrowth, the Confederates' formation was broken and the Southerners accidentally fired into each other. Fagan sent word to Captain H. M. F. Favrot of the Delta Rifles for him "For God's sake to cease firing, that we were killing his men and he was killing ours."[31] Prentiss' riflemen raked the men from Louisiana and Arkansas with Minie balls, while Hickenlooper's four guns belched shrapnel and

---

29 Throne, *Cyrus Boyd Diary*, 32, 33.

30 *OR* 10, pt. 1, 480.

31 Thomas Chinn Robertson to mother, April 9, 1862, Thomas C. Robertson Papers, Louisiana State University Archives.

canister.[32] Confused and disorganized, the brigade fell back several hundred yards, where the officers started reforming the men.

Losses for the Confederates were extremely heavy in the first charge. Twenty-eight year old Captain Edgar Martin Dubroca, Company C, Thirteenth Louisiana, presented the goriest spectacle in the brigade. An exploding shell had burst in the ranks of his company, killing six men and splattering their brains and blood all over the swarthy captain.[33]

Within minutes Gibson led his brigade forward again, across the wheat field and into the heavy brush in front of the Hornet's Nest. This time Prentiss' men reserved their fire until the Confederates were within twenty-five or thirty yards of the road. Suddenly an extra long row of flashes appeared from the roadbed area. Dozens of Southerners crumbled under the volley, and the brigade faltered. The Federals frantically poured powder and rammed slugs down the barrels of their rifles to rake Gibson's men with another volley and then another. The Fourth Louisiana started the charge in two lines, but the intense undergrowth broke the lines so badly that some of the men in the rear actually fired into those in front. The grimly determined Louisianans, unable to press forward, emptied their muskets into the thick clouds of blackish smoke that marked the Federal lines.[34]

Captain John Bunyon Taylor, Company I, Fourth Louisiana, was mortally wounded,[35] and Captain John T. Hilliard, Company G, was killed. Gray-eyed twenty-nine year old Captain William F. Pennington, Company C, a former bartender from Lake Providence, Louisiana, was also wounded. His Shiloh injuries were not nearly as embarrassing as

32 Hickenlooper, "The Battle of Shiloh," 420.

33 Thomas Chinn Robertson to mother, April 9, 1862, Thomas C. Robertson Papers, Louisiana State University Archives. Dubroca escaped injury on this occasion, but he was later captured in the war at Bardstown, Kentucky. He was exchanged at Vicksburg, Mississippi, November 29, 1862. He returned to his regiment, later becoming lieutenant colonel and he led his regiment in Tennessee and Georgia. Booth, *Louisiana Records*, 2: 690.

34 Thomas Chinn Robertson to mother, April 9, 1862, Thomas C. Robertson Papers, Louisiana State University Archives.

35 Booth, *Louisiana Records*, 3: 780.

those he sustained on January 28, 1863, when he was beaten up. Drunken Second Lieutenant Daniel McArthy, Company D, was one of the men who took part in this attack.[36]

The Thirteenth Louisiana advanced over fairly easy terrain, maintaining two lines, with about fifty yard intervals between them. But Union fire proved too much for the Thirteenth, and Major Avegno gave the command to fall back. In the confusion some of the men failed to get the word and continued firing into the Hornet's Nest. Eventually everyone was notified, and the troops retired to an old cowpen.[37]

Hodge's Nineteenth Louisiana became entangled in the heavy brush. Unable to make out the Union position, Hodge was forced to order his men to stop charging and return the Federals' fire. Observing that his gun fire was having little effect on the Federal position, Hodge reluctantly gave the order to withdraw, having lost about fifty men in the attack.[38]

Fagan's First Arkansas fared no better in the tangled undergrowth and in the face of Prentiss' stubborn defense. The colonel escaped unhurt, but his lieutenant colonel, John B. Thompson, fell mortally wounded with seven balls through his body.[39]

All four regiments withdrew beyond effective range of Union fire. They then regrouped for a third try. Although most of the Confederate

---

36   *OR* 10, pt. 1, 489; Booth, *Louisiana Records*, 3: 103; Taylor, *Reluctant Rebel*, 83, 84. As young Robert Patrick told the story, McArthy was drunk. He began beating Private Thomas Shipwith, Company A, and Pennington, then a major, tried to arrest the lieutenant, who refused to be arrested. Instead, he knocked Pennington down, and proceeded to pound the major's head in an open fireplace. Apparently no action was taken against the lieutenant, who later was mortally wounded near Atlanta, August 9, 1864. Taylor, *Reluctant Rebel*, 83, 84; Booth, *Louisiana Records*, 3: 1136. Pennington survived the beating and was elected lieutenant colonel, and he led the Fourth Louisiana in a number of actions in Georgia and Tennessee. He was captured at the Battle of Nashville, but survived the war. *Ibid.,* 103. This incident clearly illustrates the rather informal Confederate discipline.

37   Richardson, "War As I Saw It," 99; *OR* 10, pt. 1, 491.

38   *Ibid.*, 492, 493.

39   Howard, *Illustrated Comprehensive History of the Great Battle of Shiloh,* 79; *OR* 10, pt. 1, 488.

fire was aimed blindly, it was not totally without effect, for Prentiss' casualties slowly but steadily mounted. Among those who fell was the officer who had first discovered the Confederates and had brought on the action, Major James Powell. The former regular army officer was mortally wounded,[40] and died that night.[41]

Inside the Hornet's Nest, the normally straight-laced private Leander Stillwell, Sixty-first Illinois, was so overcome by the sight of his comrades dropping around him that he indulged in some "wicked profanity." Stillwell was so shaken by the enormity of his "sin" that he held his breath, expecting "summary punishment on the spot." Nothing happened, however, so Stillwell kept on shooting Rebels.[42]

Some of Gibson's men quickly prepared blanket stretchers to carry their wounded off the field, while Colonel Allen, Fourth Louisiana, went over and talked to General Bragg, who was watching the operation. Allen asked the general for artillery support, but Bragg was unable to provide it. As Colonel Allen started to ride back to his regiment, Bragg remarked, "Colonel Allen, I want no loitering now."[43] Allen quickly rejoined his men, and Gibson ordered another charge. Unfortunately in the excitement, the colonel failed to notify Hodge. The Nineteenth was slow in starting. Bragg noticed the Nineteenth was not moving, and he dispatched a staff officer to order Hodge forward. The Louisianan agreed to charge, but he told the staff officer that he "thought it impossible to force the enemy from this strong position by a charge from the front."[44]

For a third time the brigade advanced, and for a third time was quickly stalled by the terrain and enemy fire. Gibson's men took cover where they could find it, and fired at the enemy position for about sixty minutes.[45] Colonel Allen was hit in his face, and Colonel Fagan's horse

40   *OR* 10, pt. 1, 284.

41   Hoburt, *The Truth About Shiloh*, 12; Morton, "A Boy at Shiloh," 63.

42   Stillwell, *Common Soldier*, 59.

43   Richardson, "War As I Saw It," 100.

44   *OR* 10, pt. 1, 493.

45   *Ibid.*, 491, 493.

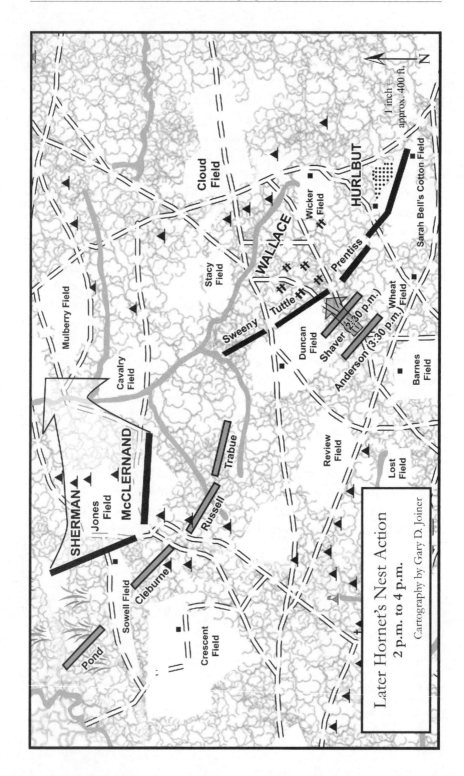

Later Hornet's Nest Action
2 p.m. to 4 p.m.

Cartography by Gary D. Joiner

was killed. Finally Gibson gave the order to withdraw to Barnes' Field. The brigade, as a unit, was not engaged any more that day.[46]

Not all of Gibson's men fell back on the main body, however. Having good spots from which to snipe at the Federals, some of the Louisianans continued firing into the Hornet's Nest. Private James G. Muggar, Company G, Thirteenth Louisiana, was one of these determined troopers. He fired at Prentiss' men until a ball struck him in the eye, blinding him, although temporarily. Another Louisiana soldier carried Muggar to safety.[47] Recovering from his injury, Muggar was later able to rejoin his regiment and he fought until he was captured in 1864.[48]

Even as Gibson's men attacked the left side of the Hornet's Nest, other Southern troops attacked the right opposite the Duncan Field. A little just before 1:00 p.m., Cleburne, with what was left of his Sixth Mississippi and Twenty-third Tennessee, supported by the Eighth Arkansas of Wood's Brigade, opened fire on Sweeny's brigade. The Southerners quickly became involved in a fire fight with Sweeny's skirmishers. Troops from the Seventh Illinois captured some of Cleburne's men and sent them to the rear under heavy guard. Federal skirmishers retired on their position, and Cleburne disengaged his battered little command.

The Sixth Mississippi, now commanded by Captain W. A. Harper, was so thoroughly disorganized by its earlier losses that Cleburne ordered it off the battlefield. He then ordered the Twenty-third Tennessee to fall back and regroup and, if possible, to link up with the rest of the brigade.

---

46 *Ibid.*, 484; Reed, *Shiloh*, 77; Richardson, "War As I Saw It," 101; Thomas Chinn Robertson to mother, April 9, 1862, Thomas C. Robertson Papers, Louisiana State University Archives. D. W. Reed said the brigade attacked four times. Apparently he was basing this on Gibson's report of the action. *OR* 10, pt. 1, 480. It seems however, from all sources this writer has perused, that only three attacks took place, the last occurred about 2:00 p.m. || Daniel, *Shiloh*, 213, argues that Gibson made four assaults; Sword, *Shiloh*, 288-289, and McDonough, *Shiloh*, 149, both argue that three attacks were made.

47 Booth, *Louisiana Records*, 3: 1081; Richardson, "War As I Saw It," 101.

48 Booth, *Louisiana Records*, 3: 1081.

Left without a command, Cleburne encountered Hardee, to whom he gave a report of his actions. The Third Corps Commander directed Cleburne to organize Confederate stragglers and to reassemble the fragments of Confederate units which were roaming aimlessly around behind the front.[49]

Gibson and Cleburne had tried and failed. Who would be the next to try and break the Hornet's Nest? Having replenished his ammunition supply, Colonel Shaver decided he would try. With his Sixth Arkansas detached by order of General Bragg, Shaver formed his three regiments for another charge on Tuttle's position. An ominous quiet settled over this portion of the battlefield as the Confederates started their attack. With perfect discipline, Tuttle's men held their fire until the Southerners were about fifty or sixty yards away. When the order was given, a battery of the Missouri Light Artillery opened with a salvo of shrapnel from its Parrott rifles while the Iowa infantry jerked and squeezed the triggers of their weapons. The dense undergrowth broke Shaver's line badly and his men's fire had little effect on the partially concealed enemy.[50]

Lieutenant Colonel Dean led his Seventh Arkansas toward the Fourteenth Iowa's position. When about fifty or fifty-five feet away, an Iowan put a Minie ball through Dean's neck, and he dropped to the ground. Major James T. Martin assumed command of the regiment, which took cover behind trees and brush and raked the Iowa men with heavy musketry.[51] Shaver ordered his men to withdraw, but some of the troops were unwilling or unable to disengage and a sharp fire fight ensued, lasting perhaps an hour.[52] Shaver managed to pull his men clear of the enemy zone of fire, and upon reporting to General Bragg, he was

49 *OR* 10, pt. 1, 162, 163; Reed, *Shiloh,* 71; *OR* 10, pt. 1, 582.

50 *Ibid.,* 574.

51 *Ibid.,* 578. Colonel William Shaw of the Fourteenth Iowa said he thought he saw Colonel Dean fall. After the attack was over, Captain Warren C. Jones, later a lieutenant colonel, went out and spoke to the dying officer. Jones turned the mortally wounded man on his back, placed a pocket handkerchief over his face, and crossed his hands. William Shaw to D. W. Reed, April 16, 1896, Miscellaneous Collection, Shiloh National Military Park.

52 *OR* 10, pt. 1, 574, 576, 578.

ordered to fall back and reform. The three regiments were not again engaged that day.

Some of Wallace's men were gradually cracking under the strain of repeated Confederate assaults. In one instance a Federal hid behind a tree. Other Northerners quickly moved up behind him. Eventually a grotesque daisy chain of thirty or forty men, each fellow clutching the waist of the man in front, swayed behind the tree while officers pleaded and begged the men to resume their places in the firing lines.[53]

Hosts of Wallace's men did not crack, however, but kept right on fighting. One Iowa private was told that his brother was dead. Directed by a friend, he soon found the corpse, and placing the butt of his musket beside his brother's head, he calmly reloaded and fired. Until his regiment was forced to fall back, he stood beside the body, exacting his own measure of vengeance.[54]

Private Samuel A. Moore of the Second Iowa dropped flat in the roadbed in an attempt to find some protection from a particularly heavy burst of Confederate gunfire. A big hulking private lay down by Moore's side. The rather diminutive Moore, in a very abstract fashion, remarked to the newcomer, "You are a great big, strong, muscular man and I am a little bit of a fellow, and lying down upon your right and the balls coming from that direction, they would pass directly over my body and take you about in the middle."[55] An increasing number of Federals were being struck by Southern buckshot, the pellets spreading out and striking at random.[56]

53 John Renick, *The 44th Indiana Volunteer Infantry* (LaGrange: Published by Author, 1880), 231.

54 *Ninth Reunion of Iowa's Hornet's Nest Brigade Held at Pittsburg Landing, April 6 and 1, 1912* (Des Moines: Bisland Brothers, Printers, 1912), 13.

55 Samuel A. Moore, "Ten Minutes With The Old Boys," *Third Reunion-Iowa Hornet's Nest Brigade, Held at Newton, Iowa, August 21 and 22, 1895* (Newton: Record Print, 1895), 28.

56 George Mills (ed.), "The Sharp Family Civil War Letters," *The Annals of Iowa* 24 (January 1959): 492; Adolph Engelmann to wife, April 17, 1862, Engelmann Papers, Illinois State Library and Archives; Henry Bellamy to

*   *   *

While Gibson, Cleburne, and Shaver tried to drive the Federals from the Sunken Road, other Confederate troops were moving to attack Hurlbut's command in the Peach Orchard. With the Second and Third Brigades, Brigadier General John Stevens Bowen and Colonel Winfield Statham, along with Brigadier General John C. Breckinridge, advanced along the Eastern Corinth Road. Guided by General Johnston, the Kentuckian deployed his two brigades in the wooded terrain. Under Johnston's personal supervision, Bowen arranged his brigade in a double line with the First Missouri (Bowen's old regiment) under Colonel Lucius Rich and the Second Confederate Regiment under Colonel John D. Martin in front, with the Ninth and Tenth Arkansas regiments, Colonels Isaac Dunlop and Thomas Merrick, in support. Bowen's men formed *en echelon* about one-half mile behind Jackson's Brigade line, his men having already shed their knapsacks in preparation for fast moving. Jackson's Brigade was to his right, with Statham's to his extreme left.

Confederate gunners brought two batteries forward to support the Reserve Corps, unlimbering their pieces on the south side of the Locust Grove Branch. Captain Alfred Hudson commanded the first battery, the Pettus Mississippi Flying Artillery, with two 3-inch rifles and two 12-pound howitzers. The second battery, the Watson Louisiana Flying Artillery, was commanded by Lieutenant Colonel Daniel Beltzhoover.[57]

As Breckinridge's batteries moved into position, sharp fighting continued on the left of the Peach Orchard, where Chalmers' and Jackson's brigades were steadily pressing back Stuart's and McArthur's commands. When Bowen's men attacked, Jackson's Brigade joined in with it, the two units complimenting each other's efforts. The brunt of the

parents, n.d., 1862, Henry Bellamy Papers, Michigan Historical Collection, University of Michigan.

57 Force, *From, Fort Henry to Corinth*, 151, 152; Reed, *Shiloh*, 85, 87, 88; *OR* 10, pt. 1, 621; Booth, *Louisiana Records*, 1: 17, 163. The Watson Battery fought in the Battle of Belmont, where it lost two guns, two men killed, and eight wounded or missing. *OR* 3: 359, 360. The battery is listed as part of Bowen's command as of November 23, 1861. *Ibid.*, 7: 728, and as belonging to Cleburne's Brigade on February 23, 1862. *Ibid*. See, R. R. Hutchinson, "Albert Sidney Johnston at Shiloh," *Confederate Veteran* 6 (July 1898): 311.

Confederate advance fell on McArthur's already battered Ninth, Twelfth, and Fiftieth Illinois posted east of the Hamburg and Savannah Road and Pugh's left flank regiments, the Forty-first and Twenty-eighth Illinois, supported by the four 6-pound smoothbores and two 12-pound howitzers of Battery A, First Illinois Light Artillery.[58]

When Bowen's Rebels stormed from the woods on the south side of the Peach Orchard, Pugh's riflemen blazed away, sending a shower of lead slugs into the oncoming Confederate battle line while Hurlbut's two batteries added to the din as they hammered the charging Confederates with exploding shells and solid shot. As the Southerners approached closer, Union gunners shifted to canister, spraying the Confederates with thousands of small metal balls.[59] The momentum of the attack was slowed by Union fire. Bowen's Arkansas regiments, green troops armed with old flintlock rifles, were unable to advance across a shallow ravine in front of McArthur's position. Union fire was so heavy and accurate that the Arkansans' regimental organization fell apart. Most of the men ceased trying to advance and began returning the Federal fire. Breckinridge and Bowen, with their respective staffs, rode up and down the south side of the ravine trying to persuade the men to advance. General Johnston rode up, a tin cup in his right hand that he had picked up as a souvenir in a Union camp earlier. He began speaking to the soldiers, saying, "Men of Arkansas, you who boast of using cold steel, don't waste your ammunition, . . . come and show us what you can do with the bayonet."[60] Encouraged by General Johnston's words and his calm, cool appearance, the troops responded to their officers' efforts to rally them and soon moved into the ravine. Quickly crossing it, they charged straight on for McArthur's men,[61] forcing the Illinoisans back.[62]

The Union batteries shelling Bowen were themselves on the receiving end of accurate fire from the Confederate batteries of Withers'

58 Kimbell, *Battery A*, 41; Reed, *Shiloh*, 49, 50.

59 *OR* 10, pt. 1, 245, 247; Force, *From Fort Henry to Corinth*, 152.

60 Hutchinson, "Albert Sidney Johnston at Shiloh," 311.

61 *Ibid.*, 312.

62 *OR* 10, pt. 1, 155, 157; Kimbell, *Battery A*, 41.

and Breckinridge's forces. A private in Lieutenant Peter Wood's Battery A, First Illinois, was torn open by a 6-pound shot through his body. Private Ed Russell lived just long enough to utter the usual last words of a dying Civil War soldier, "Tell them I died like a man at my post."[63]

Laing's Second Michigan Battery was repeatedly hit by Confederate fire, and two more of his gunners were wounded. Lieutenant A. F. Arndt's horse was shot from beneath him, while another officer's horse was also struck. Laing was forced to order his men to limber up and move the battery some distance to the rear.[64]

Meanwhile, Statham's Brigade advanced to support Bowen's left. Colonels William Preston and Thomas Jordan accompanied Breckinridge's advance and put Captain Arthur Rutledge's Tennessee Battery, four 6-pound smoothbores and two 12-pound howitzers, in position to act as support for the advance.[65] Statham's Brigade had suffered some casualties already, but not from enemy fire. One lieutenant in the Fifteenth Mississippi, nervously fiddling with his revolver, shot himself through the hand; another member of the Fifteenth was accidentally stabbed in the thigh by a bayonet.

---

63 *Ibid.*

64 *OR* 10, pt. 1, 313, 214, 245; W. B. Pippen, "Concerning the Battle of Shiloh," *Confederate Veteran* 16 (July 1908): 344. || In Dr. Cunningham's original text was an interesting paragraph that completely upset the timing of events in the Peach Orchard. In it, he declared that Pugh retired after McArthur's withdrawal uncovered his flank. Pugh, wrote Cunningham, fell back to the north side of the Peach Orchard. Cunningham also confused the cabins in the area, saying one Illinois regiment took position behind the Sarah Bell cabin. Bell's cabin sat on the south side of the field (south of the Peach Orchard). He probably meant the William Manse George cabin (George was Bell's son-in-law). At any rate, the larger picture was thrown off the established time line by this paragraph. Cunningham placed the attack that Johnston spurred forward and in which he was mortally wounded as moving toward the Federal line north of the Peach Orchard. The monuments in the line *south* of the orchard reflect that Pugh remained there until around 2:00 p.m. before falling back as a result of Johnston's attack. See Shiloh Battlefield Commission Monuments #56, 58, and 61.

65 William Preston Diary, April 6, 1862, Miscellaneous Collection, Shiloh National Military Park.

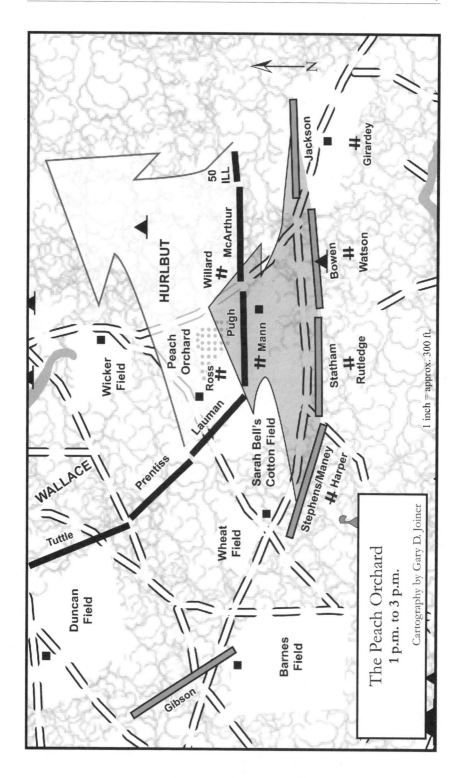

The Peach Orchard
1 p.m. to 3 p.m.

Cartography by Gary D. Joiner

1 inch = approx. 300 ft.

For hours Statham's men listened to the sounds of heavy firing, the men gradually growing more tense as they awaited their turn to move into action. Actually going into battle, much of this tension dissipated, but some of the soldiers watched with interest wounded Southerners and Union prisoners walking toward the Confederate rear. Here and there Statham's men stepped lightly to avoid treading on the mangled bodies, some still breathing, scattered along the line of advance. Union cannoneers began dropping rounds on the brigade, but it moved steadily onward.[66]

From left to right Statham's Brigade consisted of the following regiments: Colonel David H. Cummings' Nineteenth Tennessee, Major William F. Brantley's Fifteenth Mississippi, Colonel Frank Schaller's Twenty-second Mississippi, Colonel John Murray's Twenty-fifth Tennessee, Colonel Joel Battle's Twentieth Tennessee, and Lieutenant Colonel Ephraim Lytle's Forty-fifth Tennessee.[67]

To get to Pugh's brigade, Statham's men had to cross several small hills. As the Southerners moved steadily on, reaching the crest of the last of these hills, the Federals opened fire.[68] After some initial confusion, the Confederates again moved on, but Union fire inflicted grave casualties. In the excitement the Forty-fifth accidentally shot the left wing of the Twentieth Tennessee.[69] Troops of the Fifteenth Mississippi, harassed by

66 A. H. Mecklin Diary, April 6, 1862, Mississippi Department of Archives and History.

67 Doak "Memoirs," Confederate Collection, Tennessee Department of Archives and History; Bearss, "Project 17"; Edwin Bearss, "Painting Number 3, Shiloh National Military Park, #1, Background to Event Depicted-The Fight for the Peach Orchard," Miscellaneous Collection, Shiloh National Military Park; W. J. McMurray, *History of the Twentieth Tennessee* (Nashville: The Publication Committee, 1904), 126; Johnston, *Life of Gen. Albert Sidney Johnston*, 610.

68 Johnston, *Life of Gen. Albert Sidney Johnston*, 610.

69 A. H. Mecklin Diary, April 6, 1862, Mississippi Department of Archives and History; Doak, "Memoirs," Confederate Collection, Tennessee Department of Archives and History; McMurray, *Twentieth Tennessee*, 125, 126; W. J. Worsham, *The Old Nineteenth Tennessee, C. S. A.* (Knoxville: Press of Paragon Printing Company,1865), 39.

the Federals' deadly fire, took cover behind trees, brush, disabled wagons, or whatever they could find. Within seconds, six members of Company I were killed or wounded. Some of the men fired their muskets so fast that their weapons fouled, forcing the users to pick up weapons from the dead and wounded.[70] As Statham's men appeared along the edge of the Peach Orchard field, the divisional batteries hammered them with canister and shrapnel.[71] Statham's men continued on, climbed the fence on the south side of the field, and halted to dress their ranks. Laing's and Brotzmann's gunners tore great gaps in their ranks, but the Southerners quickly filled them. Officers shouted and waved their hats in the air as the brigade started across the field.

Union officers on the far side told their men to hold their fire. The only sounds heard were those of cannon going off and the tramping noise made by the advancing Confederate line. A few of Logan's Illinoisans could not restrain themselves any longer. Their fingers closed on the triggers of their rifles, and a Confederate officer crumbled to the ground. Seconds later, the Federal line erupted in a thunderous crash of rifle fire, the black powder smoke swirling about and obscuring their vision as they reloaded.[72]

The Confederate attack was stalled, but the Southerners poured such a heavy fire into the Forty-first Illinois that Hurlbut sent word to Logan to move over to their support. As Logan's men made the transfer, the Third Iowa and Twenty-eighth Illinois were slightly re-aligned to close the gap created in Pugh's line.[73]

The Forty-fifth Tennessee moved forward, straight for the Forty-first Illinois, but was promptly driven back. Lytle's men then tried another

---

70 A. H. Mecklin Diary, April 6, 1862, Mississippi Department of Archives and History.

71 *OR* 10, pt. 1, 245, 247.

72 Thompson, *Recollections With the Third Iowa Regiment*, 219. The blinding effect of the black powder smoke was a common phenomenon on the battlefield. Payson Shumway to wife, April 13, 1862, Payson Z. Shumway Papers, Illinois State Historical Library. See A. H. Mecklin Diary, April 6, 1862, Mississippi Department of Archives and History.

73 *OR* 10, pt. 1, 212, 213, 215.

advance, only to be again repulsed. Joel Battle's men no longer tried to advance, but simply held their position while firing at the enemy.[74]

Despite the appeals of their officers, the Forty-fifth Tennessee refused to charge again. Many of the soldiers continued shooting at Pugh's men from behind trees and rails, but they would not attack as a unit. General Breckinridge rode over to General Johnston complaining, "General, I have a Tennessee regiment that won't fight." The always sensitive and patriotic Governor Harris, who was with General Johnston, broke in, "General Breckinridge, show me that regiment." Riding over to Lytle's men, the Governor of Tennessee appealed to the soldiers' pride and patriotism, but with only partial success. Then General Johnston rode over. With a few well chosen words, he revived the enthusiasm of the men,[75] and led by General Johnston, Breckinridge, and the governor, the Tennesseans quickly moved forward, driving back Pugh's left regiments, the Forty-first and Thirty-second Illinois.[76] The right of Pugh's brigade held fast in the face of the assault mounted by Statham's left wing. The Iowans and Illinoisans sustained heavy casualties, but they continued firing through the thick clouds of smoke that covered their position until their officers made them stop. The smoke cleared, and the Federals cheered as they saw Statham's men retiring.[77]

To sit quietly waiting for an enemy army that does not show up was not an easy duty for a man of Colonel George Earl Maney's temperament. A native of Franklin, Tennessee, a veteran of the Mexican War, and a prominent Nashville attorney before Fort Sumter, Maney was originally captain of the First Tennessee, Company C, in May 1861.

---

74 Force, *From Fort Henry to Corinth*, 152; Johnston, *Life of Gen. Albert Sidney Johnston*, 610.

75 *Ibid.*, 610, 611.

76 Force, *From Fort Henry to Corinth*, 152, 153; *OR* 10, pt. 1, 212, 215, 217, 218; Johnston, *Life of Gen. Albert Sidney Johnston*, 611, 612; Walter Shotwell, *Civil War in America* 2 vols. (New York: Longmans, Green and Company, 1923), 1: 211.

77 Thompson, *Recollections With the Third Iowa Regiment*, 219, 220; A. H. Mecklin Diary, April 6, 1862, Mississippi Department of Archives and History.

Under his leadership, the regiment took part in various actions in western Virginia before being ordered to return to his native state in February 1862.[78] The regiment reached Chattanooga, where five companies were loaded on board a train belonging to the Memphis and Charleston Railroad. Unfortunately there was no room for the other five companies, and they were left behind in the town on provost duty.[79]

After faithfully watching for Buell's army several hours, Maney received a welcomed order from General Beauregard to rejoin the main army. The First Tennessee Regiment, or Battalion, was soon marching toward the battle area. Upon reaching the edge of the battlefield, the Tennesseans passed by fat and badly wounded Colonel Mathias Martin of the Twenty-third Tennessee, who was acting as an aide to General Cleburne. The colonel called to the First, "Give 'em Hail Columbia. That's right, my brave First Tennessee. Give 'em Hail Columbia."[80] With the wounded colonel's good wishes ringing in their ears, the First Tennessee continued until they reached General Breckinridge's Division, with which Cheatham had linked what was left of his brigade after the morning's repulse at the Hornet's Nest. Reporting to his immediate superior, Major General Franklin Cheatham, Maney was ordered to attack Hurlbut's position in the Peach Orchard.

General Cheatham instructed Maney to pick whatever other units from his brigade he wanted to go in with him, and the colonel selected the Ninth Tennessee; and he asked for the Nineteenth Tennessee from Statham's Brigade. It was quickly arranged that the Nineteenth would accompany the colonel in his attack, and about 2:30 p.m., while the rest of Statham's men still traded shots with the Northern men, the three Tennessee units started across the Peach Orchard toward Hurlbut's center.[81]

---

78 *Tennesseans in the Civil War*, 1: 172.

79 A. S. Horsley, "Reminiscences of Shiloh," *Confederate Veteran* 2 (August 1894): 454.

80 Watkins, *Co Aytch*, 41.

81 Thomas T. Harrison, "Shiloh," Thomas T. Harrison Papers, University of Tennessee Library.

Perhaps Private Tom Harrison of Colonel Maney's First Tennessee thought back to the day nine months earlier when his grandmother strapped his knapsack on his back and told him to "go and never surrender or turn traitor, and do not come back until the war is over, whether it be in victory or defeat."[82] In this charge, Harrison and his fellow Rebels would drive all the way if possible.

As Maney started forward, Gladden's former brigade, now commanded by Colonel Daniel Adams, began pressing the Federal right. Unfortunately one of Lauman's riflemen shot Colonel Adams in the side of his head, permanently blinding his right eye.[83] Colonel Z. C. Deas became the brigade's third commander that day, and he immediately moved forward to support Breckinridge and Cheatham. A vicious action, lasting many minutes, developed with Hurlbut's division, ending with the Federals being pushed back.[84]

With Maney pressing in the center, Deas on the left, and Statham and Bowen on the right, Hurlbut's division began to gradually give way. But it was Maney's charge that broke the back of the Federal position. With the Ninth Tennessee in the center, the First on the left, and the Nineteenth on the right, Maney stormed from the woods out onto the Peach Orchard Field, heading toward the sector of Pugh's line which was defended by the Third Iowa and Twenty-eighth Illinois. In the Peach Orchard, Maney's men encountered some of Statham's troops "retiring before a destructive fire."[85]

There was so much powder smoke over Pugh's position that his men had trouble spotting Maney's advance. Unable to ascertain Pugh's exact position, the aggressive Maney ordered his men to halt and lie on the ground. He gave the order to fire, and from this prone position, the Southerners blazed away in the general direction of the Federals. When the Northerners returned their fire, the canny colonel was able to ascertain their exact position and approximate strength. Before the

---

82 *OR* 10, pt. 1, 537; Warner, *Generals in Gray*, 1.

83 *OR* 10, pt. 1, 538, 542.

84 *OR* 10, pt. 1, 538, 542.

85 *Ibid.*, 455.

Federals could reload Maney ordered his men to their feet, and the Rebels quickly moved forward again.[86] As the momentum of their advance picked up in the Orchard, Minie balls ripped into their ranks, dropping men right and left, but the Confederates' battle blood was up; and, with wild Rebel yells, the Tennesseans tore into Pugh's line.[87]

In the face of the Confederate attack, Pugh's right wing withdrew, as did Brotzmann's Battery, which was forced to abandon a 6-pounder and two caissons.[88] The rest of Statham's Brigade quickly moved forward in hot pursuit.[89] Hurlbut was falling back, but Confederate losses were heavy, including General Albert Sidney Johnston.

As the troops of the Fourth Division fell back, many of them paused and reloaded their rifles and fired at the oncoming Confederates. One Union source said three fleeing Yankees turned around and, observing a mounted and obviously important Confederate officer in the distance, quickly loaded their muskets, and discharged them in his direction.[90] Battery A, First Illinois Light Artillery, claimed that a shot from one of their 12-pound howitzers killed General Johnston.[91] Whether the fatal bullet was fired by a soldier deliberately aiming to pick off a Confederate officer or whether it was simply fired at random by a running Federal, General Johnston was hit.

The mortal wound from a slug tore the popliteal artery in Johnston's right leg. It was a severe wound, but not necessarily a fatal one. The general could easily have stopped the bleeding himself with a simple

---

86 *Ibid.*, 439, 455; Hardy Murfree to James Murfree, May 12, 1862, James Murfree Papers, University of Tennessee Library.

87 Watkins, *Co Aytch*, 42.

88 *OR* 10, pt. 1, 213, 219, 249.

89 A. H. Mecklin Diary, April 6, 1862, Mississippi Department of Archives and History.

90 John Parish (ed.), "A Few Martial Memoirs," *The Palimpest* 1 (October 1920): 121.

91 Kimbell, *Battery A*, 45. The author wrote that the gun crew fired at some mounted officers, and that later the gunners learned that Johnston was hit by their fire. *Ibid.*

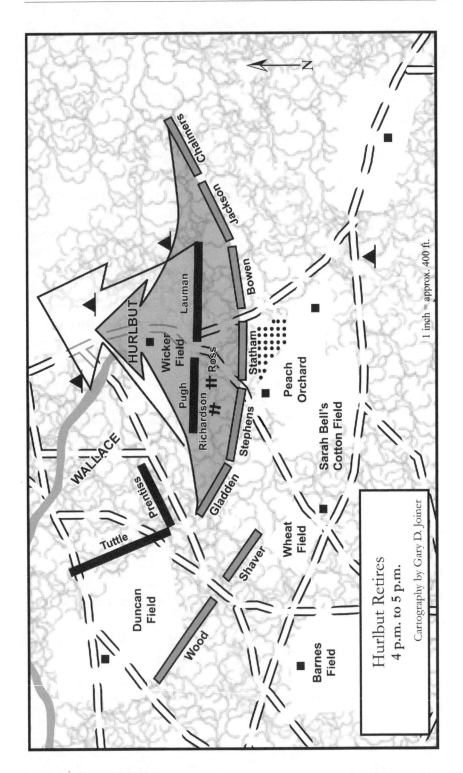

Chalmers

Jackson

Bowen

Lauman

HURLBUT

Wicker Field

Pugh

Ross

Statham

Peach Orchard

Richardson

Stephens

Sarah Bell's Cotton Field

WALLACE

Prentiss

Gladden

Tuttle

Shaver

Wheat Field

Duncan Field

Wood

Barnes Field

Hurlbut Retires
4 p.m. to 5 p.m.

Cartography by Gary D. Joiner

1 inch = approx. 400 ft.

tourniquet, if only he had been aware of the seriousness of the injury. In the excitement of the moment and in the flush of victory, the general failed to pay much attention to the deadly red trickle running down his leg.[92]

Throughout much of the day, Johnston's personal physician, Dr. D. W. Yandell, had accompanied the general across the battlefield, but when they rode upon a large cluster of wounded soldiers from both sides, the Kentuckian ordered Dr. Yandell to assist them. Before riding off to other duties, Johnston remarked to Dr. Yandell, "These men were our enemies a moment ago, they are our prisoners now; take care of them."[93]

Just before the fatal incident, the Confederate commander spoke to Governor Harris, and Johnston showed him where a musket ball had torn his shoe. A concerned Harris asked, "Are you wounded? Did the ball touch your foot?" The general simply replied in the negative and told Harris to carry an order to Colonel Statham. One of General Johnston's aides, Captain Leigh Wickham, remained with the general while Harris was on his errand. A few minutes later, Wickham heard the thud of a slug striking an object. Seconds later, he noticed blood dripping down General Johnston's leg, and remarked to the general about it. But the commander seemed unconcerned. Colonel Theodore O'Hara, the famed Southern poet and adventurer, rode up at this time and observed the blood. The author of *The Bivouac of the Dead* turned around and galloped for a surgeon.[94]

His mission fulfilled, the Tennessee governor was back at the side of his friend within a few minutes. Before Harris could report, General Johnston reeled in his saddle. The governor grabbed him with his left hand, helping to support him in the saddle. Harris asked the general if he

---

92 || For an in-depth examination of Johnston's wound and the circumstances surrounding it, see Sword, *Shiloh*, 461-471.

93 Johnston, *Life of Gen. Albert Sidney Johnston*, 615.

94 R. R. Hutchinson, "Albert Sidney Johnston at Shiloh," *Confederate Veteran* 6 (July 1898): 313; Johnston, *Life of Gen. Albert Sidney Johnston*, 613-615; George Withe Baylor, "With Gen. Albert Sidney Johnston at Shiloh," *Confederate Veteran* 5 (December 1897): 611; Roland, *Albert Sidney Johnston*, 336.

was hurt. Very softly Johnston replied, "Yes, and I fear seriously."[95] Governor Harris asked Wickham to go for a doctor. Supporting Johnston with one hand, the Tennessean led their horses to a sheltered spot a short distance away. Gently pulling the wounded general off his horse, Harris placed him on the ground and began searching his body for some other wound more serious than the seemingly minor one in his right leg.

William Preston and other staff officers collected around the bleeding general, who died perhaps twenty minutes after the wound was inflicted. There was little, if any, suffering. General Johnston simply lapsed into unconsciousness and died in this condition about 2:30 p.m.[96]

Couriers were immediately dispatched to notify General Beauregard that he was now the commanding general on the field. Governor Harris reached Beauregard with the news shortly after 3:00 p.m. From that point forward, the responsibility for the battle rested on the Creole's shoulders.[97]

95 Johnston, *Life of Gen. Albert Sidney Johnston*, 614.

96 *Ibid.*, 614, 615; George Withe Baylor, "With Gen. Johnston at Shiloh," *Confederate Veteran* 5 (December 1897): 611. For slightly different versions of General A. S. Johnston's death, see *Confederate Veteran* 17 (May 1909): 219, and 16 (December 1908): 629. William Preston Diary, April 6, 1862, Miscellaneous Collection, Shiloh National Military Park.

97 New Orleans *Daily Picayune*, April 11, 1862; J. S. Byers to William Preston Johnston, June 13, 1862, Mrs. Mason Barret Papers, Howard-Tilton Memorial Library, Tulane University; *Battles and Leaders*, 1: 590; William Preston Diary, April 6, 1862, Miscellaneous Collection, Shiloh National Military Park. Colonel Preston said he "wrote a note to Gen. Beauregard, informing him that he [Johnston] had fallen at the moment of victory, after routing the enemy at every point, and that the completion of the victory would devolve on him." *Ibid.* John Broome maintained that he carried word to Beauregard of the death of Johnston. John Broome, "How General Albert Sidney Johnston Died," *Confederate Veteran* 16 (December 1908): 629.

Chapter 12

Retreat

THE ARRIVAL OF THE news of Albert Sidney Johnston's death caused no panic in General Pierre Gustave Toutant Beauregard, the hero of Fort Sumter and Manassas. Johnston's death was tragic, but there would be time to mourn the Kentuckian later. Beauregard's only concern for the moment was winning the battle. Soldier-like, the new commander ordered the news of Johnston's death concealed from the army, lest it dishearten the men.[1]

Contrary to what many of Beauregard's critics said during the war and after, the new army commander possessed a fairly good picture of how the battle was developing. To coordinate the attack against the Hornet's Nest, he sent Massachusetts-born Daniel Ruggles to take charge. Any lull in the fighting following Beauregard's assumption of

---

[1] It was only after the army was safe at Corinth, three days after the battle, that Beauregard formally announced the news of Johnston's death, although by that time everyone on both sides knew it. Beauregard's message read as follows:

> Soldiers—Your late Commander-in-Chief, A. S. Johnston, is dead. A fearless soldier, a sagacious captain, a reproachless man has fallen. One who in his devotion to our cause shrunk from no sacrifice; one who, animated by a sense of duty and sustained by a sublime courage, challenged danger and perished gallantly for his country while leading forward his columns to victory. His signal example of heroism and patriotism, if generally imitated, will make this army invincible. A grateful country will mourn his loss, revere his name, and cherish his many virtues. *OR* 10, pt. 2, 408.

command was because of the disorganized condition of the Confederate army and not Beauregard's actions.[2]

It was becoming increasingly obvious to the new commanding general that the Confederate advance on the left had lost much of its momentum and that it was necessary to make the primary effort on the right and center of the Southern line to force the Federals from the Hornet's Nest position.[3]

On the Confederate left, Patton Anderson's Brigade moved over to join the attack at the Hornet's Nest, leaving only what was left of Cleburne's Brigade and Pond's still comparatively unscathed regiments to carry on the advance against Generals McClernand and Sherman. All other Confederate units were either reorganizing or shifting over to support the assault at the Hornet's Nest.

If the Confederate advance was waning, the Union defense was also weakened. When Grant visited Sherman about 3 p.m., the words exchanged by the two men could not have been very optimistic. Most of the remaining Federal regiments were mere skeletons of one hundred to two hundred men. Large numbers of Federal soldiers straggled to the rear or were serving with other units. One Union soldier wound up at the Hornet's Nest with Prentiss.[4] A number of the Federal regiments were so badly battered that it was necessary for McClernand and Sherman to order them out of the battle and back to the area around the Landing, where they could reform.[5]

In some of the Federal units ammunition began to run low. The men of the Forty-fifth Illinois stripped their dead and wounded for cartridges,

---

2 Roman, *Beauregard*, 1: 297, 298; *Battles and Leaders*, 1: 590; Williams, *P. G. T. Beauregard*, 140. Johnston's biographer, Charles Roland, suggested that the Confederate army suffered a serious loss of momentum, in part due to the disheartening news of Johnston's death as it spread across the field. Roland, *Albert Sidney Johnston*, 341, 342. || Dr. Cunningham was the first to question the Lost Cause idea that a lull occurred when Johnston died. Sword, *Shiloh*, 310, and Daniel, *Shiloh*, 235, both claim a lull developed. McDonough, *Shiloh*, 154-155, argues that there was no lull following Johnston's death.

3 *OR* 10, pt. 1, 496.

4 Barber, *Army Memoirs*, 54; Bacon, *Thrilling Adventures*, 6.

5 Bering and Montgomery, *Forty-eighth Ohio*, 21, 22.

but when this pitiful supply ran out Colonel Smith was forced to order his men to retire toward the rear to search for ammunition. The Illinoisans marched but a few hundred yards when they ran into a party of infantry heading for the front. Colonel Smith tried to borrow cartridges from these men, but unfortunately their ammunition would not fit the Forty-fifth's Enfields. The regiment resumed its march, but within minutes the captain of the rear company ran up to Smith, breathlessly exclaiming that Confederate cavalry was pressing in on the left rear. Colonel Smith told the excited captain, "Keep cool and don't say anything, the enemy don't know we are out of ammunition."[6] Fortunately the Confederates, if they were really Southerners and not some of Grant's own cavalry, did not attack, and Smith and his men soon located an ammunition wagon.

The Forty-fifth Illinois soldiers quickly scrambled on the supply wagon, tearing open the cases. Men crowded around the wagon, crying, "Give me some, give me more!" Pockets and cartridge pouches were quickly filled,[7] and soon the regiment moved to rejoin the brigade near the Landing, McClernand's last position of the day.[8]

The comparatively even battle lines of the Shiloh Church and Purdy Road positions were now only a fond memory to the two harassed Union commanders. The Federal line, if such it could be called, straggled over Jones' Field and the surrounding hills and ravines. Confederate and Union skirmishers were badly intermixed, and there was heavy musketry over all the area. One unidentified Ohio soldier, when wounded and ordered to the rear, wandered back within a few minutes and most aptly summed up the situation in a plea to his company commander, "Cap, give me a gun. This blamed fight aint got any rear."[9]

Staff officers rode furiously over the area trying to create order out of chaos. Captain Hammond even went so far as to try to encourage the men by telling them, "Sidney Johnston is killed! Beauregard is captured!

6 Crummer, *With Grant at Fort Donelson*, 64, 65.

7 *Ibid.*, 65.

8 *OR* 10, pt. 1, 134.

9 Duke, *Fifty-third Ohio*, 49. || Dr. Cunningham slightly misplaced this human interest story; according to the citation, it actually occurred a little earlier—on the Shiloh Church line.

Buell is coming."[10] Unwittingly, Hammond was right on two out of his three points. This officer experienced a dangerous afternoon. Twice his officer's cap was torn by Confederate bullets; twice his boots were torn by slugs; and twice he wound up sprawled on the ground, his horse shot from under him.[11]

Confusion or not, at least part of the Union army was still fighting, and a good thing for Grant for Cleburne was attacking again. After spending some time in the rear area collecting stragglers, Cleburne threw up his hands in disgust and began rounding up his own regiments. By around 4:00 p.m., he was attacking McClernand and Sherman with his Fifth, Twenty-third, and Twenty-fourth Tennessee, and the Fifteenth Arkansas. Taking cover behind trees, fences, posts, and brush, the Arkansans and Tennesseans poured a heavy fire into the Federals for perhaps an hour.[12]

Once again the Federals retreated, this time to a position along the Hamburg and Savannah Road. Sherman and his survivors held the right, with McClernand's battered fragments in the center. Veatch, with the remnants of the Fifteenth and Forty-sixth Illinois, was on the left while McAllister's Battery and an unidentified battery deployed behind McClernand's center. The battered Eighteenth Illinois, now commanded by Captain J. J. Anderson, was placed in reserve behind the batteries. The Seventh Illinois, of Sweeny's brigade, unexpectedly showed up, having retired from the Hornet's Nest line, and General McClernand ordered it to act as reserve for his command.[13]

Toward this new Federal position marched Pond's Louisianans. Occasionally under fire during the day, the brigade had not become seriously engaged. The Thirty-eighth Tennessee and the Crescent Regiment (Twenty-fourth Louisiana), supported by Lieutenant Phil

---

10   *Ibid.*, 52.

11   Orville J. Victor, *Incidents and Anecdotes of the War* (New York: James D. Torrey, 1862), 359.

12   *OR* 10, pt. 1, 582. || Dr. Cunningham's original text inadvertently left out the 23rd Tennessee, which Cleburne specifically noted joined in the attack. The 15th Arkansas advanced, but did not engage the enemy. *OR* 10, pt. 1, 582.

13   *OR* 10, pt. 1, 118.

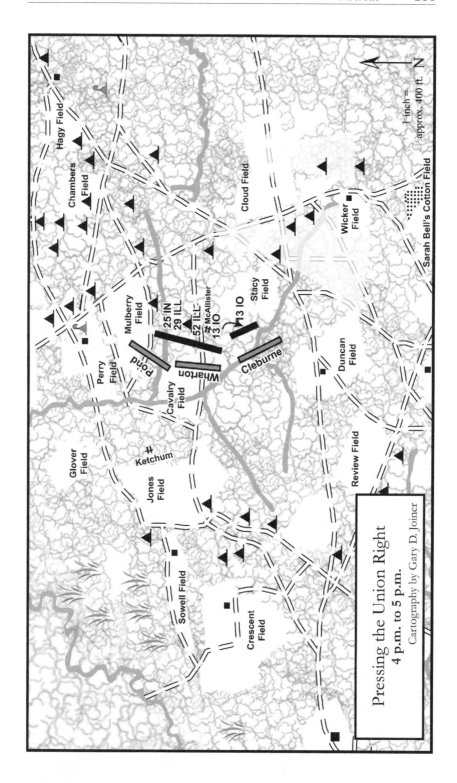

Pressing the Union Right
4 p.m. to 5 p.m.

Cartography by Gary D. Joiner

1 inch =
approx. 400 ft.

N

Hagy Field

Chambers
Field

Cloud Field

Wicker
Field

Sarah Bell's Cotton Field

Mulberry
Field

25 IN
29 ILL

52 ILL

McAllister

13 IO

13 IO

Stacy
Field

Point

Wharton

Cleburne

Duncan
Field

Perry
Field

Cavalry
Field

Glover
Field

Ketchum

Jones
Field

Review Field

Sowell Field

Crescent
Field

Bond's section of Ketchum's Battery, left the brigade early that morning to guard the Owl Creek-Purdy Road Bridge. After the remaining portion of the brigade was accidentally fired into by Confederate troops from another unit, Pond withdrew his unit a hundred yards to rest and reorganize.[14]

A little before 2:00 p.m., one of General Hardee's staff officers reported to Lieutenant Colonel S. W. Ferguson that Pond's Brigade was without a commander. Accompanied by the staff officer, Ferguson rode over and located General Hardee, who directed the lieutenant colonel to get the Louisiana units into the fight. The Sixteenth and Eighteenth Louisiana and the New Orleans Guard Battalion moved forward to within five or six hundred yards of McClernand's new position.[15]

14 Phil Bond to brother, April 23, 1862, in James G. Terry, "Record of the Alabama State Artillery from its Organization in May 1836 to the Surrender in April 1865," *The Alabama Historical Quarterly* 20 (Summer 1958): 316; *OR* 10, pt. 1, 516, 517.

15 S. W. Ferguson to General Beauregard, April 6, 1862, Miscellaneous Collection, Shiloh National Military Park. In the above report, Ferguson said he commanded the advance on McClernand. Lieutenant Colonel Alfred Roman stated flatly that he did not see the brigade commander on either day of the battle. Alfred Roman, "Memoirs of Shiloh," Confederate Collection, Tennessee Department of Archives and History. Pond gave an entirely different version of it in his official report. He said he was ordered to attack the position by Ferguson, who gave the order by virtue of the authority of General Hardee. *OR* 10, pt. 1, 517. Roman appended his name to an entirely different account of the action in his so-called biography of General Beauregard, which muddles the issue even more. Beauregard cooperated so closely in writing the book that it became, in effect, an "official" biography with overtones of an autobiography. The practical effect was that the account is Beauregard's own and not Roman's. This version stated that Beauregard was told by a staff officer that Pond's Brigade was leaderless. The Creole promptly ordered Ferguson to go over and take charge. The account stated that Pond's absence from the brigade was due to his undertaking a reconnaissance of the enemy's position, but it did not mention who actually led the charge. Roman, *Beauregard*, 1: 298. Sergeant L. M. Pipkin, the regimental quartermaster for the Sixth Louisiana, in a letter written half a century after the battle, confirmed Pond's report of the action in almost every detail, stating that Lieutenant Colonel Ferguson merely brought the order. L. M. Pipkin to D. W. Reed, March 17, 1909, Miscellaneous Collection, Shiloh National Military Park. Pond was elected colonel of the

Ferguson was a member of the class of 1857 at West Point and participated in the Mormon expedition of 1857-1858. Twenty-seven years old at Shiloh, he later served in the Vicksburg campaign and was appointed brigadier general on July 23, 1863. He fought against General Sherman in Georgia and the Carolinas, and in August 1864 was suggested for promotion to major general. Major General Joe Wheeler, his immediate superior and former classmate, vigorously objected, maintaining that Ferguson was a troublemaker and poor disciplinarian.[16]

As Ferguson checked the Federal position, Colonel Alfred Mouton sent two of his soldiers forward on a scout, Private Cesar Porta and Captain J. A. Druilhet. The two men soon returned and reported to Mouton the presence of two Federal batteries and a strong concentration of infantry.[17]

By order of General Hardee, the Washington Artillery moved into position on the right of the Sixteenth Louisiana to help cover the advance.[18] Ketchum, with his four remaining guns, was moving up to support the Louisianans when one of Hardee's aides arrived with orders to go to the left to help flush out a concentration of enemy infantry.[19]

When the order to attack was given, for some reason only Gober's Sixteenth and Mouton's Eighteenth Louisiana responded, starting the long quarter mile charge toward McClernand's position. Federal artillery and rifle fire were extremely accurate and heavy, and losses were high even before the two regiments reached anywhere near the enemy's position. Colonel Mouton's horse was killed, but quickly scrambling to his feet, the thirty-three year old colonel, who had exactly two years and

---

Sixteenth Louisiana on September 26, 1861. He resigned on May 2, 1862. Booth, *Louisiana Records*, 3, 2: 169.

16 Warner, *Generals in Gray*, 87; *OR* 47, pt. 2, 1004-1012, 1027, 1028, 1127.

17 Cesar Porta to J. B. Wilkinson, n.d., 1862, Louisiana Historical Association Collection, Howard-Tilton Memorial Library, Tulane University.

18 Order Book, Washington Artillery, Louisiana Historical Association Collection, Howard-Tilton Memorial Library, Tulane University. See *OR* 10, pt. 1, 527.

19 *OR* 10, pt. 1, 527.

two days of life left, continued leading the advance on foot. Major Gober's horse was also killed, but like Mouton, he came to his feet and continued to lead his men.[20]

The Eighteenth halted and delivered several volleys into the Northern position before resuming the charge. Mouton's men reached to within sixty or seventy yards of the Federal position before the deadly Union fire broke the charge. Both Louisiana regiments promptly retreated to avoid being annihilated. The Eighteenth alone lost 207 men in this one effort.[21] All during this attack Captain Walter O. Crain, former naval officer, fought in the ranks as a simple volunteer private, rifle in hand.[22]

---

20 *Ibid.*, 521; Cesar Porta to J. B. Wilkinson, n.d., 1862, Louisiana Historical Association Collection, Howard-Tilton Memorial Library, Tulane University; *Confederate Veteran* 9 (August 1901): 499.

21 *OR* 10, pt. 1, 118; Cesar Porta to J. B. Wilkinson, n.d., 1862, Louisiana Historical Association Collection, Howard-Tilton Memorial Library, Tulane University.

22 *OR* 10, pt. 1, 519. Captain Crain had one of the strangest careers of the Civil War. Shortly before the outbreak of war, he resigned from the U. S. Navy as a passed Midshipman. A native Louisianian, he enlisted in the First Infantry Battalion (First Battalion Louisiana). Enrolling as a private, he was soon promoted to a third lieutenant of Company D, July 20, 1861. Presumably he participated in the battalion's move to Virginia, perhaps even in its first action at the Curtis Farm on July 5, 1861. On August 24, 1861, he resigned from the battalion. Booth, *Louisiana Records*, 2: 472. On September 1, 1861, Crain was appointed captain of a battery of Tennessee light artillery, three guns. He was stationed at Memphis, Fort Henry, and Corinth, but for some reason the battery was disbanded in the latter part of March 1862. Serving as a rifleman in Pond's Brigade, Crain was severely wounded on Monday. On April 12, less than a week after the battle, he resigned his commission. *Tennesseans in the Civil War*, 1: 129, 130. On May 25, 1863, Crain was appointed a lieutenant in the Confederate navy and was assigned to the partially constructed ironclad *Missouri*. George I. Ness, Jr., "Louisiana Officers of the Confederate Navy," *Louisiana Historical Quarterly* 27 (April 1944): 483. On June 2, 1864, Crain was appointed a first lieutenant in the navy to rank from January 6, 1864. He served at Shreveport, Louisiana. His whereabouts during the last few months of the war are unknown, but he was paroled on June 3, 1865, at Alexandria,

After Mouton and Gober were repulsed the Orleans Guard Battalion charged. McClernand's riflemen and gunners promptly cut up the New Orleans soldiers, sending them reeling back after the two Louisiana regiments with a loss of about eighty men.[23] The Louisianians retired a few hundred yards to regroup and were not engaged again that day.[24]

The hard pressed Federals received one small and much needed reinforcement in the form of the Eighty-first Ohio Infantry. In company with the Thirteenth Missouri, Colonel Thomas Morton led his Eighty-first out to guard the Snake Creek Bridge, over which Lew Wallace's men would presumably arrive. From around 8:00 a.m. until 11:00 a.m., the Ohioans remained at the bridge until being ordered to move over and link up with the right wing of McDowell's brigade. The Eighty-first was not seriously involved in McDowell's engagement with Trabue, although the Ohioans did occasionally shoot at Confederate skirmishers who were endeavoring to turn McDowell's right.[25] About 3:00 p.m., General Grant rode up and ordered the Eighty-first to move farther to the left in support of McClernand and Sherman.[26]

Colonel B. S. Compton's Fourteenth Missouri, also assigned to guard the Snake Creek Bridge, was moved over to McArthur's brigade headquarters, presumably to avoid being separated from the rest of the army by the parties of Confederate cavalry beginning to threaten the road near the bridge. The Fourteenth and Eighty-first were next to each other

---

Louisiana. Booth, *Louisiana Records*, 2: 472; Ness, "Louisiana Officers of the Confederate Navy," 483.

23 Roman, "Memoirs of Shiloh," Confederate Collection, Tennessee State Library and Archives; Roman, *Beauregard*, 1: 298. Roman said the time was about 5 P. M. McClernand gave the time as 4:30 p.m. *OR* 10, pt. 1, 118.

24 *Ibid.*. 522.

25 Phil Jordan and Charles Thomas (eds.), "Reminiscences of an Ohio Volunteer," *Ohio Archaelogical and Historical Quarterly* 48 (October 1939): 311; *OR* 10, pt. 1, 118.

26 Chamberlain, *Eighty-first Regiment Ohio*, 16; *OR* 10, pt. 1, 118; Roman, "Memoirs of Shiloh," Confederate Collection, Tennessee State Library and Archives.

in position along the road, the Fourteenth presumably on the right, making it the extreme right of the whole Union army.

Around 4:00 p.m., Lieutenant Colonel R. H. Brewer's Mississippi Cavalry Battalion attempted to turn Grant's right flank, on orders from General Hardee. The Missourians opened fire with their muskets, killing one of Brewer's men and wounding three others. The Confederates returned the fire with their shotguns, killing two Missourians and wounding three others. A courier from Hardee arrived and ordered Brewer to abandon the effort, and he fell back. Compton quickly moved his regiments several hundred yards to the left so as to be in closer contact with Sherman's outfit.[27]

Even with their extreme right protected by two virtually fresh regiments, McClernand and Sherman were still having their problems. Pond's Louisianans were repulsed and out of the fight, but reorganized and supplied with fresh ammunition, Russell's and Trabue's brigades were now attacking again. Colonel Hare was badly wounded and Colonel Crocker assumed command of what was left of the First Brigade. Union casualties were heavy, and about 5:00 p.m., the Union position was abandoned, the Federals falling back several hundred yards toward the Landing to make another stand.[28]

* * *

While the Southerners pushed Grant's right back, heavy fighting continued at the Hornet's Nest. The big Confederate charges were about over. Most of the Confederate commanders on that part of the field realized that uncoordinated infantry attacks would avail but little against the strength and determination of Prentiss' and Wallace's divisions.

Unfortunately General Patton Anderson's Brigade was now swinging over from the left to help in the assault on Wallace's position. Lacking the exact knowledge of the strength of the Second Division, Anderson decided to attack across the Duncan Field. While moving into position to charge Wallace, Anderson met Colonel Marshall Smith of the Crescent Regiment. Separated from his own brigade, Smith suggested

27 *OR* 10, pt. 1, 161, 461.

28 *Ibid.*, 615, 616, 417, 118, 119, 124.

that the two commanders should link up, and Anderson quickly agreed. Smith's men formed up in line on the left and Anderson's on the right. Under heavy Union fire, the Rebels moved forward.[29] The brush and foliage in front of Wallace's position was so heavy that it was very difficult to see anything, and some of the bushes and grass were on fire, adding more smoke to hover over the Union position. Many of Anderson's men drove ahead blindly, unable to even see the enemy, grimly forced to hold their fire until they could see something to shoot. One enlisted man of the Twentieth Louisiana caught his rifle on some bushes, and the weapon accidentally went off. In an instant the Federal line erupted in a tremendous blast of musket and canister slugs. Blinded by the smoke and foliage and confused by the shower of balls, the Southerners faltered. Colonel Reichard of the Twentieth Louisiana suddenly slipped off his horse. He was immediately asked by one of his officers, "Are you wounded?" The husky former Prussian officer replied that it was only his horse that was hit.[30]

Harassed badly by Wallace's heavy fire, Anderson withdrew his unit, the Twentieth Louisiana taking cover on the safe side of a little rise in the ground, where they found a little protection from the Federal gunfire. Anderson detached an aide to ask General Ruggles for some artillery support, and then he rode up and down the edge of Duncan Field trying to locate a weak point in Wallace's position.[31] The Crescent Regiment did somewhat better, attacking and driving back on the main body some of Wallace's men posted in the Duncan Field as sharpshooters.[32]

Lieutenant Phil Bond's section of Ketchum's Battery had become separated from the regiment sometime earlier. Unable to follow the

---

29 *Ibid.*, 498.

30 Charles DePetz to wife, April 15, 1862, Clark, "The New Orleans German Colony in the Civil War," 1003, 1004.

31 *OR* 10, pt. 1, 498.

32 *Ibid.*, 523; Phil Bond to brother, April 23, 1862, in Terry, "Record of the Alabama State Artillery," 316, 317; Richardson, "War As I Saw It," 495,496; W. A. Howard to wife, April 9, 1862, Miscellaneous Collection, Shiloh National Military Park.

fleeter infantry across the rugged terrain, Bond tried to stick to solid, open, level, ground. Unfortunately he was given some wrong directions and his section, cannon, caissons, and all wound up entangled in a boggy thicket. It was nearly half an hour before the Alabamans dug and cut their way out, and Smith and the other men were long gone from sight. By sheer luck, Bond and his men arrived on the southwest edge of Duncan Field just as the Crescent Regiment was flushing Wallace's sharpshooters.

As the Alabamans unlimbered their pieces, one of the Missouri batteries opened fire on them. The Missourians had the range perfectly and they dropped round after round onto Bond's position. No one was killed or injured by the cannon fire, but the exploding shells frightened the horses and the inexperienced drivers were unable to control them. One driver was injured in this little panic before Bond wisely gave the order to move the two guns off the road and behind some cover. Once out of the enemy's line of fire, Bond left his weapons and went to locate Smith. Finding the Crescent's commander, Bond was directed to put his guns in position on that regiment's right and bombard the Hornet's Nest.[33]

While Bond's two guns peppered Wallace's position, Ruggles and his staff officers were moving back and forth across the battlefield, rounding up Confederate batteries in preparation for a massive barrage on the Union position. Bond's two pieces were on the extreme left of the line of guns set up at this time. To their right, Ruggles placed part or all of the Washington Artillery. One by one Confederate batteries showed up on the southern side of Duncan Field to be deployed. Swett's Mississippi Battery was ordered by Hardee to join the Duncan Field line, and their four 6-pound smoothbores and two 12-pound howitzers were in position and pounding Prentiss' position.[34] Byrne's Kentucky-Mississippi Battery went into position with its five 6-pound smoothbores and two 12-pound howitzers, and Robertson's Florida Battery shifted over from

---

33 Phil Bond to brother, April 23, 1862, in Terry, "Record of the Alabama State Artillery," 316, 317.

34 *OR* 10, pt. 1, 472; Charles Swett, "Memoirs," Miscellaneous Collection, Shiloh National Military Park. General Daniel Ruggles seems to have acted on his own initiative in deciding on this massive barrage on the Union position.

pounding Hurlbut's men to help shell Wallace, moving his four Napoleons into position on the edge of Duncan Field.[35] First Lieutenant James Thrall brought up two guns from Hubbard's Arkansas Battery on their right, and Roberts' Arkansas, Trigg's Arkansas, and Swett's Mississippi batteries on their left.[36] Trigg's Battery was equipped with two 6-pound smoothbores and two 12-pound howitzers. Roberts' Arkansas Battery had two 6-pound smoothbore guns and two bronze 12-pounders. Captain Arthur Rutledge brought up four 6-pound smoothbores and two 12-pound howitzers to the new position. Captain Thomas Stanford's Mississippi Battery took up its position with two 12-pound howitzers, one 3-inch rifle, and three brass 6-pound smoothbores. Captain Smith T. Bankhead's Tennessee Battery brought into position four 6-pound smoothbores and two 12-pound howitzers.[37]

35 *OR* 10, pt. 1, 472; Frank Peak, "A Southern Soldier's View of the Civil War, "'Frank Peak Papers, Louisiana State University Archives; S. H. Dent to wife, April 9, 1862, Shiloh-Corinth Collection, Alabama Department of Archives and History; Charles Swett, "Memoirs," Miscellaneous Collection, Shiloh National Military Park. Major F. A. Shoup, on orders from General Hardee, massed twenty guns along the Duncan Field to shell the Hornet's Nest. Proclaiming it was his idea, by implication, he intimated that General Ruggles took credit for his idea. Hardee's batteries did take part in this operation, and Major Shoup probably helped position them not realizing that Hardee's orders were in response to General Ruggles' request. F. A. Shoup, "The Art of War in '62—Shiloh," 8, 9.

36 *OR* 10, pt. 1, 479; Frank Peak, "A Southern Soldier's View of the Civil War," Frank Peak Papers, Louisiana State University Archives; *OR* 10, pt. 1, 475.

37 *OR* 10, pt. 1, 472. In his report General Ruggles listed a Captain Trabue's Kentucky Battery as being in the line-up. There was no such unit at the Battle of Shiloh, but it is possible that Ruggles was referring to Cobb's Kentucky Battery, of Trabue's Brigade. This unit had taken a very bad beating a little earlier in the day from McClernand's division, but it is possible that some of the battery's guns might have been able to have taken part in this Duncan Field operation. The marker at Shiloh National Military Park states that there were sixty-two guns under General Ruggles' direction firing into the Hornet's Nest. The late Kenneth P. Williams accepted this figure. Williams, *Lincoln Finds A General* 3: 372, 373. T. Harry Williams mentioned that Ruggles "collected more than sixty pieces of artillery." Williams, *P. G. T. Beauregard*, 140. See

By around 4:00 p.m., General Ruggles' artillery line was in action, heavily pounding Wallace's and Prentiss' soldiers. Considering the light caliber of the Southern weapons and the general quality of Civil War ammunition, especially Confederate army issued artillery rounds, it is questionable just how much damage Ruggles' guns caused, but the fusillade caused some casualties and it could not have helped Federal morale. The Confederate guns were emplaced a little less than a quarter of a mile from the Union position. This meant that the Southerners were beyond the range of accurate Northern rifle fire. But Civil War rifles could kill at more than a quarter of a mile range, even though inaccurate; so the Confederate cannoneers were exposed to fire not only from Federal cannon, but from enemy rifles as well.[38]

Several of the Southern batteries were badly mangled by this return fire. Captain Robertson's Florida Battery took a particularly heavy pounding. Unlimbering along the edge of the Duncan Field, the Floridians were the target of Federal riflemen. Minie balls spattered the position, kicking up the dirt and killing or mangling the artillery horses. Either Battery D or H, First Missouri Light Artillery, zeroed in on

---

also, Eisenschiml, *The Story of Shiloh*, 38; Howard; *Illustrated Comprehensive History of the Great Battle of Shiloh*, 74. The commander of the Washington Artillery, W. Irving Hodgson, in his report stated that his battery served on the left near Pond's Brigade, but mentioned nothing about taking part in the mass bombardment of the Hornet's Nest. *OR* 10, pt. 1, 54. The Order Book, Fifth Company, Washington Artillery, confirmed this, as does the letter of Richard Pugh to his wife written just after the battle. Order Book, Washington Artillery, Louisiana Historical Association Collection, Howard-Tilton Memorial Library, Tulane University; Richard Pugh to wife, April 8, 1862, Richard Pugh Papers, Louisiana State University Archives. Two guns were detached to help support Colonel Trabue, and it is possible they may have ended up with General Ruggles' line. Counting a section of pieces from Cobb's Battery and the two possible ones from Hodgson's Battery, makes a maximum total of fifty-one pieces in the Duncan Field position, according to General Ruggles' listing of the units. || Dr. Cunningham was the first to question the 62 pieces of artillery determined by Shiloh Battlefield Commission historian D. W. Reed. Sword, *Shiloh*, 326, sticks with the original 62 pieces, while Daniel, *Shiloh*, 229, argues there were 53.

38 || Dr. Cunningham was also the first to question the bombardment's importance. Daniel, *Shiloh*, 230, follows Cunningham's lead.

Robertson's position, hitting it with 20-pound Parrott shells. One gunner, standing in front of Lieutenant S. H. Dent, was torn to pieces by a Parrott round. More horses were hit, and more gunners. Finally Robertson, his Napoleons unable to match the superior accuracy of the enemy Parrotts, ordered his men to hitch up the guns and fall back. So many of their horses were dead or wounded by this time that the Florida unit was only able to withdraw two of their 1200 pound weapons, temporarily abandoning the others until later in the day.[39]

Strong concentrations of Confederate infantry moved in to support Ruggles' guns and quickly engaged Prentiss' embattled soldiers. Stewart's men traded rifle fire with the Federals in the Hornet's Nest while Captain Bankhead's gunners poured in 6- and 12-pound rounds.[40] Looney's Tennesseans of the Thirty-eighth regiment also arrived along the Duncan Field, as well as Colonel Preston Smith and his One hundred fifty-fourth Tennessee, which took up a position to support Swett's Battery.[41]

Fragments of other Confederate units and hundreds of disorganized troops also took up positions to support Ruggles. On orders from the Massachusetts-born Confederate general, Captain Samuel Latta, Thirteenth Tennessee, deployed a force of stragglers from various units and members of his own company to support the Confederate batteries. Latta's men worked their way forward, under heavy rifle fire, to take cover behind trees and fence posts, from where they were able to snipe at Wallace's men. Despite the presence of Confederate snipers, the Union fire slacked off little, if any, but at least many of the Federals diverted their rifle sights from the Southern gunners to Latta's men. Captain Latta picked up a rifle and fought like an enlisted man. Standing behind a tree, Latta lined up his rifle sight on a far off enemy rifleman and squeezed the trigger. The Bluecoat dropped to the ground and did not get up. To

39 S. H. Dent to wife, April 9, 1862, Shiloh-Corinth Collection, Alabama Department of Archives and History.

40 Joseph E. Riley, "The Military Service of Joseph E. Riley," Joseph E. Riley Papers, Chickamauga-Chattanooga National Military Park Archives.

41 *OR* 10, pt. 1, 428, 526, 448.

Captain Latta, this was partial or complete payment for wounds sustained by him at Belmont.[42]

The entire area along the Duncan Field and on down in front of General Prentiss' division presented a weird scene. The air was thick with the smell of blood and powder smoke, while the entire area trembled with sounds of artillery fire. Mangled men and animals added their cries of terror and pain to the confusion. Most of the men on both sides were badly frightened by the terrible and ghastly smells and sounds of the din. Still, somehow, most of them kept on fighting. One Confederate soldier in the Twenty-third Tennessee described it as follows:

> It was an awful thing to hear no intermission in firing and hear the clatter of small arms and the whizing minny balls and rifle shot and the sing of grape shot the hum of cannon balls and the roaring of the bomb shell and explosion of same seaming to be a thousand every minute.[43]

To Private William Swan of the Third Iowa Infantry, the "whole earth seemed in a blaze—the sharp, ringing crash of our musketry—our batteries belching forth their shot and shell, and roaring like the deep toned thunder." Cannon shot ripped into the Hornet's Nest, tearing bloody holes in the Yankee ranks. Exploding shells tore up the earth, shattering big oak trees as if struck by lightning, spattering the Federal soldiers with dirt and wood slivers. Still the determined Yanks held their ground.[44]

Battery F, Second Illinois, had earlier in the day galloped up behind Wallace's position and quickly unlimbered its six 6-pound guns in Duncan Field, but, losing one of them, soon took a less exposed position farther to the east, near Wicker Field. The Illinois soldiers did yeoman's work, but they were soon struck by heavy Confederate counter-battery fire. The battery commander, Captain John W. Powell, had his right arm

---

42 Samuel Latta to wife, April 12, 1862, Confederate Collection, Tennessee State Library and Archives.

43 W. A. Howard to wife, April 12, 1862, Miscellaneous Collection, Shiloh National Military Park.

44 Throne, "Letters from Shiloh," 244, 245.

shot off.[45] Undaunted by the loss of his limb, Powell later served with Grant at Vicksburg, and he wound up a major. After the war, the one-armed ex-soldier made the first trip down the turbulent Colorado River as well as many other exploring expeditions. Later he assisted in founding the U.S. Bureau of Ethnology, becoming its director in 1879. From 1881-1894, he was Director of the U. S. Geographical Survey. Powell died in 1902, at the age of sixty-eight, one of America's most respected and esteemed scientists and explorers.[46]

Despite all the noise and firing, the Hornet's Nest held. But what about Wallace's and Prentiss' flanks? McClernand's and Sherman's men were retiring on the right, and on the left things were no better. At the price of hundreds of casualties, including General Albert Sidney Johnston, Hurlbut had been driven out of his Peach Orchard position. But after reshuffling his units around to strengthen his left, Hurlbut established a new line that cut across the Hamburg-Savannah Road and touched the edge of the Wicker Field.[47] Now Hurlbut's own left was steadily crumbling. After a series of determined stands, Stuart's brigade, its ammunition exhausted, broke off its action with Chalmers and withdrew toward the Landing.[48]

McArthur's little command put up a game fight with Jackson's Confederate brigade and the right of Bowen's Brigade, but it too was

45 De Hass, *Annals of the War*, 49. || Dr. Cunningham originally confused Powell's movements, stating that he deployed behind Wallace's line only around 3:30 to 4:00 p.m. Powell's action in Duncan Field was as early as 9:30 a.m., where he lost one gun. He then moved to western Wicker Field, where he remained for about six hours. It was at Wicker Field that he lost his right arm. See Reed, *Shiloh*, 61; Shiloh Battlefield Commission Monument #43.

46 Unsigned sketch, "John W. Powell," Miscellaneous Collection, Shiloh National Military Park.

47 *OR* 10, pt. 1, 204. | | Interestingly, Dr. Cunningham does not go into any detail regarding large scale troop movements that occurred at this time. With McArthur's line giving way, Hurlbut pulled Lauman's entire brigade out of line west of the Hamburg-Savannah Road and placed it in line east of the road. See Reed, *Shiloh*, 55.

48 *Ibid.,* 259; Frank Peak, " A Southern Soldier's View of the Civil War," Prank Peak Papers, Louisiana State University Archives.

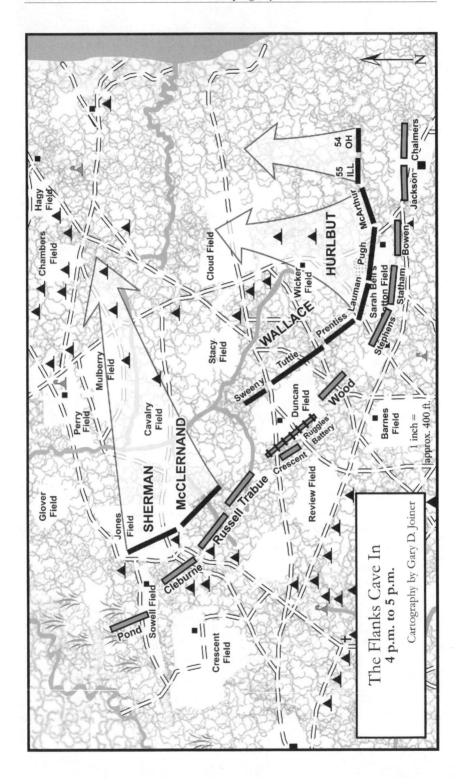

The Flanks Cave In
4 p.m. to 5 p.m.

Cartography by Gary D. Joiner

forced steadily back toward the river. Some Federal infantry concealed themselves in a small log building, but the Nineteenth Alabama charged and flushed them out while the Second Texas and the Seventeenth and Eighteenth Alabama cleared a line of Federal skirmishers from behind a fence. The Alabama and Texas soldiers climbed over the fence, pausing only to fire their muskets at McArthur's retreating men. McArthur finally managed to get his battered Illinoisans formed in a line with Hurlbut's new position.

At this point in the battle, McArthur received some much needed reinforcements, the Fifty-seventh Illinois. A little after 4:00, Colonel Silas Baldwin moved up the Fifty-seventh to support McArthur. Except for supporting one of Wallace's batteries for a few minutes at the Hornet's Nest, the Fifty-seventh was still fresh. Colonel Baldwin and his men were barely in position before Jackson's skirmishers passed over a hill several hundred yards in front of McArthur's position and opened fire. Baldwin's riflemen sprayed bullets at the Confederates, forcing one of Jackson's color bearers to take cover behind a stump.[49] The Seventeenth's color bearer was somewhat more determined, however. As McArthur's men riddled his banner with Minie balls, one of his comrades called to him to lower his burden. The plucky color bearer yelled back, "Never! I'll die before this flag shall be lowered."[50] At least for the moment the young Confederate kept his banner waving, but McArthur's fire was extremely accurate. Baldwin's skirmishers were gradually working their way toward the Confederates, some of them taking shelter behind a tree blown down by artillery fire. Colonel Wheeler recklessly galloped up and down his front encouraging his Alabamans, but a Federal marksman shot his horse and the pugnacious little colonel wound up sprawled upon the ground.

Ammunition was running out and some confusion developed in the brigade, although order was quickly restored. Hurlbut's position rapidly deteriorated. Chalmers' Brigade was speedily outflanking McArthur's

49 Kirkpatrick Scrapbook, Alabama Department of Archives and History; William Harvey Diary, April 6, 1862, Miscellaneous Collection, Shiloh National Military Park.

50 Kirkpatrick Scrapbook, Alabama Department of Archives and History.

little force, whose men were rapidly becoming exhausted. The Ninth Illinois alone had lost fifty-eight per cent of its effectives killed, wounded, or missing.

Hurlbut decided the only thing to do was to retreat to the Landing. He immediately issued orders to his regimental commanders to fall back, and within minutes most of his men were retiring in comparatively good order.[51] McArthur's brigade also withdrew when it became evident that Hurlbut was pulling back.

A sixty year old private in the Ninth Illinois refused to retreat when his regiment went to the rear. Instead, he joined up with another unit and fought with it until it also withdrew, whereupon he attached himself to still a third regiment. That night, rejoining his comrades in the Ninth, the elderly warrior displayed notes from officers of the units to which he had attached himself, stating that he had honorably fought with them.[52]

The Fifty-seventh Illinois started retreating when it saw the units on its right pulling back, but the Third Iowa, which connected Hurlbut's right with Prentiss, either failed to get the retreat order or was simply unable to execute it, for it remained near the Hornet's Nest, still determinedly fighting.[53]

General Bragg, nursing a badly bruised leg from a fall when his horse was shot out from under him, rode over his section of the battlefield frantically issuing orders for all units to advance. Spurred in part by Bragg's aggressiveness, Confederate units began moving forward into the vacuum created by Hurlbut's withdrawal.[54]

Hardee's troops, particularly Russell's brigades, were already moving behind Wallace's exposed right flank, and General Polk was

---

51 William Harvey Diary, April 6, 1862, Miscellaneous Collection, Shiloh National Military Park; Reed, *Shiloh*, 18, 19, 50; *OR* 10, pt. 1, 204, 550.

52 Morrison, *History of the Ninth Illinois*, 30-32.

53 William Harvey Diary, April 6, 1862, Miscellaneous Collection, Shiloh National Military Park; *OR* 10, pt. 1, 219.

54 Grady McWhiney, "Braxton Bragg at Shiloh," *The Tennessee Historical Quarterly* 21 (March 1962): 26. || Grady McWhiney, *Braxton Bragg and Confederate Defeat: Volume 1, Field Command* (New York: Columbia University Press, 1969), 235.

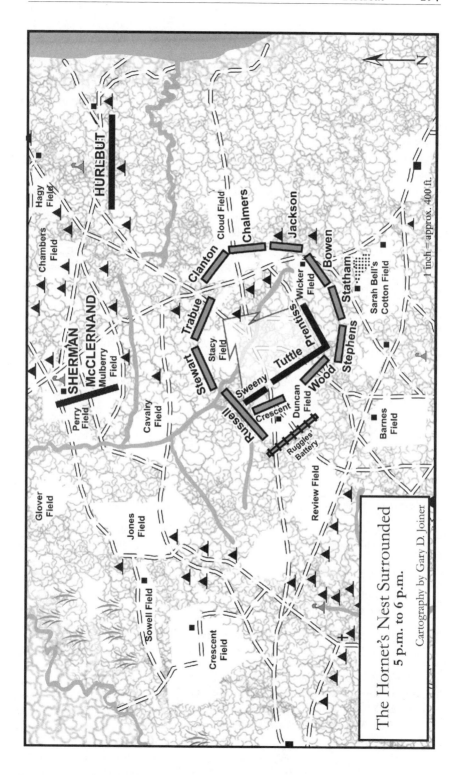

The Hornet's Nest Surrounded
5 p.m. to 6 p.m.

Cartography by Gary D. Joiner

moving in with the Crescent Louisiana Regiment. With Hurlbut's withdrawal, the Union center was left hanging in the air.[55] Gladden's and Chalmers' brigades quickly pressed in upon Prentiss' now exposed left.[56] General Prentiss moved part of his division back at right angles to protect himself from the Confederate advance. The Second and Sixth divisions were now in the strange position of fighting back to back.[57]

An aide brought General Wallace the news that his right was hanging in the air due to McClernand's withdrawal. Realizing that within minutes his division would be surrounded, Wallace gave the order to retreat along the Pittsburg Road.[58] With the Second and Seventh Iowa, Colonel Tuttle and General Wallace started down the road in their attempt to escape.

Confederate troops raked the retreating Federal column with heavy musketry, and near the forks of the Eastern Corinth Road, riding at the head of his troops, Wallace was shot down.[59] The general's brother-in-law, Cyrus Dickey, was riding by his side when the fatal bullet hit home. Dickey supposed Wallace to be dead, but wanted to save the body, and with the help of three orderlies tried to carry the general off the field. The firing was so heavy that the other three men let go and ran off, and Dickey was reluctantly forced to abandon what he supposed to be the general's corpse near some ammunition boxes.[60]

Tuttle and the Second and Seventh Iowa continued on down the road, but the rest of the brigade was unable to disengage in time. Confederate

---

55 OR 10, pt. 1, 417; Theodore Mandeville to Josephine Rozet, April 9, 1862, Theodore Mandeville Papers, Louisiana State University Archives.

56 Hugh Henry to mother, April 10, 1862, Shiloh-Corinth Collection, Alabama Department of Archives and History; OR 10, pt. 1, 550.

57 OR 10, pt. 1, 166.

58 Ibid., 149; T. Lyle Dickey to his Aunt Ann, May 19, 1862, Miscellaneous Collection, Shiloh National Military Park.

59 OR 10, pt. 1, 149; John Mahon (ed.), "The Civil War Letters of Samuel Mahon, Seventh Iowa Infantry," Iowa Journal of History 51 (July 1953): 238.

60 Cyrus Dickey to John J. Dickey, April 10, 1862, W. H. L. Wallace Papers, Illinois State Library and Archives. The musket ball entered above and behind the general's left ear, and taking a slanting course, passed up and out his left eye. Ibid.; Wallace, Life and Letters of General W. H. L. Wallace, 196.

infantry were already in the rear of the Fourteenth Iowa when Shaw gave the order to fall back. Some of the Iowa infantry straggled behind the main body, determined to get a few more shots off. Even these die-hards soon realized, however, that it was hopeless and fell back, trying to catch up with Shaw and the others.[61] The Iowans found themselves being fired into from all sides, and Shaw quickly realized he was surrounded and that further resistance was futile. Ordering his men to cease fire, the explorer-soldier personally surrendered to Major F. E. Whitfield of the Ninth Mississippi, Chalmers' Brigade.[62]

The Fourteenth Iowa's stragglers caught up with their regiment at this point. Seeing their comrades surrender, they began smashing their rifles rather than turn them over. Although the Iowans were now at least theoretically prisoners, there was still heavy firing going on across the area. Parties of Confederate troops, having swarmed into the Hornet's Nest, were still shooting at anybody wearing a blue uniform. One of Chalmers' officers told Shaw and his men to take cover in the army tents scattered around the area. Some of the Federals decided to follow the advice of the Mississippian and hid in the tents, where their uniforms were concealed.

Unfortunately stray bullets continued raking the area, dropping Mississippians and Iowans alike. One of Shaw's privates was killed by a slug through his head, and a Mississippi captain was dropped as if pole-axed, struck in the chin by a spent slug. The Fifty-fifth Tennessee wandered into the area and Lieutenant Colonel Wiley M. Reed assigned part of the outfit the task of rounding up the badly scattered Iowans.[63]

From a vantage point in the rear, Captain Charles Swett could see the Confederates swarming over Wallace's and Prentiss' regiments, and he noted that the Blue and Gray were badly intermingled.[64] The Twelfth Iowa retreated along Shaw's left, but it too failed to get beyond General

---

61   Thomas, *Soldier Life.*

62   *OR* 10, pt. 1, 550.

63   Thomas, *Soldier Life.*

64   Charles Swett, "The Battle of Shiloh," Miscellaneous Collection, Shiloh National Military Park. A Confederate officer confirmed that some of his men kept on firing for a little while after the white flags were raised. Captain Robert

Hurlbut's First Brigade camp. The Thirty-eighth Tennessee of Pond's Brigade charged Wallace's line as the division started to fall back. Looney's Tennesseans rounded up most of the regiment while a few of the men were picked up by Chalmers' Mississippians. Some mounted Confederates grabbed up the Twelfth's flags and began dragging them through the mud.[65] Colonel J. G. Woods was still with the regiment, but he was so badly wounded that as the retreat started, he turned the command over to his senior company commander, Captain Samuel R. Edgington. General Polk arrived in the Third Iowa camp just as Edgington ordered his men to drop their weapons, and the captain surrendered his sword to the "Fighting Bishop." Always courteous, General Polk saluted Captain Edgington and returned the blade, although the captain and future colonel of the regiment had the sword taken away from him by his guards later.[66]

A few yards to the west from where Edgington gave up, the charging Confederates caught up with Sweeny's command. Running for their lives, a good part of the Fifty-eighth Illinois managed to break through the Southerners and escaped to the Landing, but over three hundred men did not make it, and these were collected by Confederate infantry.[67] The Seventh Illinois, however, slipped through and escaped with only one or two stragglers lost. Despite all the excitement and turmoil, the one-armed Sweeny, suffering from a nasty wound in his remaining good left arm and another in one foot, managed to escape to the Landing.[68]

H. Wood to his father, June 1, 1862, Robert H. Wood Papers, University of Tennessee Library.

65 Luther Jackson, "A Prisoner of War," *The Annals of Iowa* 19 (July 1933): 24; *OR* 10, pt. 1, 154; Reed, *Shiloh*, 49; Thomas, *Soldier Life*; William Harvey Diary, April 6, 1862, Miscellaneous Collection, Shiloh National Military Park.

66 Throne, "Erastus Sarpers' History of Company D, 12th Iowa Infantry, 1861-1866," 181.

67 *OR* 10, pt. 1, 164.

68 *Ibid.*, 101; Albert D. Richardson, *The Secret Service, The Field, The Dungeon, and The Escape* (Hartford: American Publishing Company, 1867), 239.

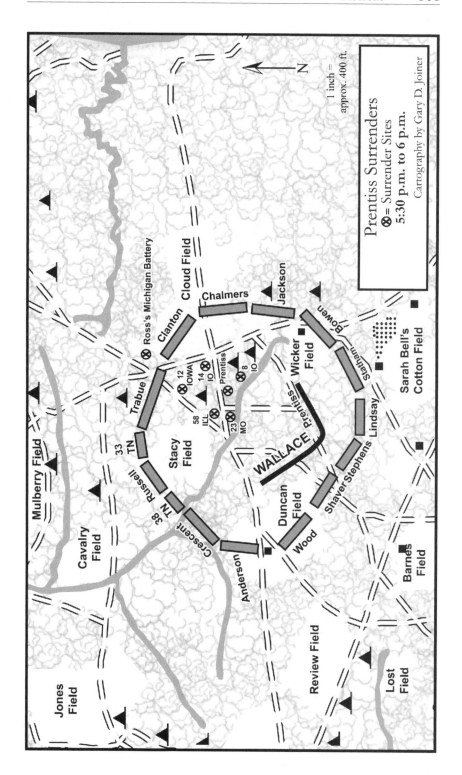

Prentiss Surrenders
⊗ = Surrender Sites
5:30 p.m. to 6 p.m.

Cartography by Gary D. Joiner

1 inch =
approx. 400 ft.

N

Chalmers

Jackson

Bowen

Clanton   Cloud Field

Ross's Michigan Battery

Statham

Wicker
Field

Sarah Bell's
Cotton Field

Prentiss

12
IOWA

14
IO

8
IO

Prentiss

Trabue

58
ILL

23
MO

Prentiss

WALLACE

Lindsay

TN
33

Stacy
Field

Russell

Stephens

Shaver

Duncan
Field

TN
38

Crescent

Wood

Barnes
Field

Mulberry Field

Anderson

Cavalry
Field

Review Field

Jones
Field

Lost
Field

Fortunately all of Wallace's batteries pulled out before the collapse, and they escaped to the Landing area. Prentiss' division fared little better than Wallace's in its attempt to fall back from the Hornet's Nest. Troops from Withers' Division were all over the rear area, while the Thirty-third Tennessee charged directly behind the retreating Federals.[69] Prentiss' and Withers' men became so thoroughly mixed up that some of the Federals simply surrendered while others found or blasted gaps through the badly scattered Mississippians and Alabamans. The men of Chalmers' Mississippi brigade managed to round up Lieutenant Colonel Isaac V. Pratt and more than a hundred members of his Eighteenth Missouri Regiment, plus some stragglers from Hurlbut's Twenty-eighth Illinois, who failed to fall back with their division.[70]

The Eighth Iowa met an even more stringent fate. A few of the men managed to slip through to the Landing, but the wounded Colonel Geddes and 335 of his men were cut off and taken prisoners.[71] Some of the Iowans were reluctant to quit, and they kept firing at anyone wearing the wrong color uniform, even after Geddes surrendered and white flags were up. A Confederate officer rode over to try and stop the senseless killing. He yelled to the Iowans, "My God! lay down your arms; you will all be killed." The Federals shot him down. Finally the firing eased, and the last die-hard surrendered.[72]

The Sixty-first Illinois got out before the Confederates were able to surround it, and it lost only a few captured stragglers. But Prentiss' other regiments took a pretty bad beating in terms of prisoners. The Rebels grabbed up some four hundred members of the Twenty-third Missouri, including its commanding officer, Lieutenant Colonel Quin Morton. His

---

69   *OR* 10, pt. 1, 533, 550.

70   *Ibid.*, 550, 104.

71   *Ibid.*, 164; McElroy, *Undying Procession*, 25. The Eighth Iowa was part of Sweeny's brigade, but he had ordered it over to assist General Prentiss a little before noon, and the regiment fought in the Hornet's Nest until the order for the withdrawal came. *OR* 10, pt. 1, 165, 166.

72   Bacon, *Thrilling Adventures*, 6; Theodore Mandeville to Josephine Rozet, April 9, 1862, Theodore Mandeville Papers, Louisiana State University Archives.

First Brigade, so badly mauled in the early morning's fight, lost two hundred or more men captured and temporarily ceased to exist as a unit.[73]

And what of the Sixth Division's commander? He wound up a prisoner. A number of different Confederate units claimed to have captured the general.[74]

As Prentiss rode around the field with a white flag, trying to prevent any more of his men from being shot, the Thirty-third Tennessee came up screaming and yelling in triumph at the sight of hundreds of Union soldiers standing or walking around, their hands in the air. Still defiant, Prentiss reined in his horse, raised himself in his stirrups, and said, "Yell, boys, you have a right to shout for you have captured the bravest brigade [division] in the U. S. Army."[75]

73 *OR* 10, pt. 1, 104, 105.

74 Private Theodore Mandeville, Crescent Regiment, said his regiment captured Prentiss. He said Colonel Smith personally received Prentiss' sword. Theodore Mandeville to Josephine Rozet, April 9, 1862, Theodore Mandeville Papers, Louisiana State University Archives. This was confirmed by another Crescent enlisted man, Yves LeMonier, "Shiloh," Louisiana Historical Association Collection, Howard-Tilton Memorial Library, Tulane University. Another account said Prentiss surrendered to the Nineteenth Tennessee. Worsham, *The Old Nineteenth Tennessee Regiment, C. S. A.*, 41.

75 Jackson, "A Prisoner of War," 24; Joseph E. Riley, "The Military Service of Joseph E. Riley," Joseph E. Riley Papers, Chickamauga-Chattanooga National Military Park Archives. A slightly different version by a member of the Crescent Regiment said Prentiss turned about to the screaming Confederates and said directly to the commanding officer, "Let them cheer, let them cheer, for they have, this day, captured the finest Brigade in the United States Army." Yves LeMonier, "Shiloh," Louisiana Historical Association Collection, Howard-Tilton Memorial Library, Tulane University. Later on, by implication, Grant censored Prentiss for not retreating in time. Grant, *Memoirs*, 177. Grant's admirer and biographer, Adam Badeau, went further and accused Prentiss of poor generalship. Badeau, *Military History of Ulysses Grant*, 83. These criticisms take little account of the problem of executing a withdrawal in the face of an enemy not only in your front, but behind you as well. There may have been a personal pique between Grant and Prentiss, for in September of the previous year, the two men were engaged in slight controversy over the question of rank. Prentiss lost the argument, and he left Cairo, Illinois, and went to St. Louis. Prentiss remarked to a war correspondent, "Yes, I have left, I will

Most of the Confederate officers tried to reorganize their men and pursue the fleeing Federals. Many Confederates, however, considered the battle over and began drifting to the rear to find something to eat or drink. Several minutes of fighting followed as the Southerners haphazardly fanned out after retreating Union soldiers. One Rebel gun crew managed to get ahead of Tuttle's men. Some hundreds of yards from the Landing, this Confederate unit dashed through the ranks of the rapidly moving Federals. In the excitement no one seemed to notice that their uniforms were the wrong color. Unlimbering their pieces, the Rebels poured round after round into the Second Iowa, speeding it on its way toward the Landing.[76]

With the Peach Orchard-Hornet's Nest position at last overwhelmed, it seemed as though Beauregard was about to achieve the decisive victory so many of his soldiers had died for since early that morning. Just one more push would be necessary to sweep over and overwhelm the final remaining Federal line of resistance at the Landing and complete the annihilation of General Grant's army.

---

not serve under a drunkard." Richardson, *Personal History of Ulysses S. Grant*, 184. Prentiss was soon assigned to another command, but the relationship probably remained strained.

76 Bell, *Tramps and Triumphs*, 17, 18.

Chapter 13

Last Stand

DURING THE LONG DAY Union artillery helped delay or stop altogether attack after attack by the Confederate forces. After twelve hours of almost constant fighting, the Federal guns were privileged to repeat their role, this time at the Landing, their final stand of the day. The man in charge of the organization of this last stand effort was Colonel Joseph Dana Webster.

A graduate of Dartmouth College and a civil engineer by profession, Webster entered the U. S. Army as an officer in the topographical engineers in 1838. Serving in the Mexican War, Webster resigned from the army in 1854 with the rank of captain. When the Civil War broke out, he reenlisted in the army, eventually acquiring the duties if not the commensurate rank of chief of staff to General U. S. Grant. On February 1, 1862, he was appointed colonel of the First Illinois Light Artillery, but continued acting as chief of staff.

Sometime late in the afternoon that Sunday, Grant directed Webster to help form this new defensive position, and he set to work building a line. Using stragglers and assorted noncombatant personnel that he had rounded up, Webster soon prepared a fairly formidable defensive position.[1]

1 || Dr. Cunningham originally included a most unusual statement in this paragraph, claiming Webster built a line "of log and dirt breastworks in a semicircle around and across the Corinth Road, some two hundred yards out from the boat landing." No evidence of a line of breastworks is available. In fact, only minor use of any type of fortification has ever been located. For

Next came the guns. Swedish-born Captain Axel Silfversparre commanded a battery consisting of men, four 20-pound Parrotts, and almost nothing else. Mustered into service in Chicago on February 20 and arriving at Shiloh only the day before, Silfversparre's Battery H, First Illinois Light Artillery, lacked horses, harnesses, and most of the other innumerable items an artillery unit needs to function efficiently in battle. Undaunted by these shortages, Webster had the Illinoisans manhandling their ponderous iron tubes into line. There they were, with a little difficulty, pointed in the approximate direction from which a Confederate advance might come.

If at last the guns were in position, the men were still totally untrained, but under Webster's supervision, Battery H began practicing with its tubes. Unlike a normal firing range, however, the battery did not open fire at a distant artificial target, but instead, began dropping rounds in the general direction of the Confederate army.

Battered and torn by the battle's fury, Federal field batteries began falling back to the Landing to rest, regroup, and locate fresh ammunition. Probably some batteries simply had their fill of fighting. Whatever the reason, Webster quickly took over tactical command and ordered them to assist in holding the Landing.[2]

---

example, Schwartz's Battery piled up a small earthen rampart, and another battery apparently piled up sacks of corn. Out on the battlefield, Anderson's Confederate brigade made a hasty breastwork of logs on the second day. Other than these specific examples, there is no evidence of battle-related earthworks. Some post-battle entrenchments, however, still exist. We have slightly altered the text to reflect this. See Shiloh Battlefield Commission Tablets #57 and 361; Reed, *Shiloh*, 21.

2 "Editorial," *Journal of the Illinois State Historical Society* 9 (July 1916): 221, 222; *Annals the War*, 678; Willard Webb (ed.), *Crucial Moments of the Civil War* (New York: Bonanza Books, 1961), 59; Bouton, *Events of the Civil War*, 27, 28; *OR* 52, 24. Silfversparre was a former lieutenant in the Swedish Army. Arriving in America in 1861, he briefly served with Fremont in Missouri before organizing his battery. More than half of his personnel were Swedish Americans. An unpopular officer, because of strict disciplinary practices, Silfversparre resigned a few months after the battle. Nels Hokanson, *Sweedish Immigrants in Lincoln's Time* 2nd. Ed. (New York: Harper, 1942), 72,113, 114;

The First Minnesota arrived with its four remaining guns after escaping from the Hornet's Nest before the surrender, and it was immediately placed in position, as was Battery E, Second Illinois Light Artillery, along with Captain Stone's Battery K, First Missouri Light Artillery.[3] Major John Cavender, Wallace's chief of artillery, added the six 20-pound Parrotts of Batteries H and D, First Missouri Light Artillery to Webster's rapidly growing command.[4] More cannon were added to the line, and then Captain Edward Bouton's Battery arrived to an enthusiastic greeting, the report having circulated at the Landing that the battery had been captured. Actually the Illinoisans had been badly shot up by a Confederate battery on the other side of Dill Branch, but with the help of some Ohio infantry all the guns were saved and dragged back to the Landing, where they were quickly placed in the line.[5]

While Webster positioned the incoming guns, Federal infantry units trudged wearily in and Webster cooperated with their commanding

---

Ella Lonn, *Foreigners in the Union Army and Navy* (Baton Rouge: Louisiana State University Press, 1951), 135, 136, 285.

3 Edwin Hannaford, *The Story of A Regiment: A History of the Campaigns and Associations in the Field, of the Sixth Regiment Ohio Volunteer Infantry* (Cincinnati: Published by Author, 1868), 257; Reed, *Shiloh*, 59; *OR* 10, pt. 1, 337.

4 *OR* 10, pt. 1, 204.

5 Bouton, *Events of the Civil War*, 23, 24. Accounts vary as to just how many guns Webster positioned along the bluff. Grant merely said twenty or more. Grant, *Memoirs*, 179. One of General Grant's earliest and most able biographers said there were "sixty field-pieces and siege guns at the position. Richardson, *Personal History of Ulysses S. Grant*, 244, 247. See Eisenschiml, *The Story of Shiloh*, 41. Private Cyrus Boyd, who was an eye witness, said there were about "40 pieces." Throne, *Cyrus Boyd Diary*, 34. The largest estimate of the number of guns was one hundred pieces. Conger, *The Rise of U. S. Grant*, 258. Colonel Thomas Jordan of the Confederate army believed there were at least fifty guns in the Federal position. Jordan, "The Campaign and Battle of Shiloh," 395. || Daniel, *Shiloh*, 246, says 41 guns, while Sword, *Shiloh*, 356, vaguely relates there were "at least ten batteries." McDonough, *Shiloh*, 162, says 62 guns. Oddly, Dr. Cunningham failed to mention the five siege guns of Battery B, 2nd Illinois Light Artillery, on which Webster studded the line. See Shiloh Battlefield Commission Monument #40.

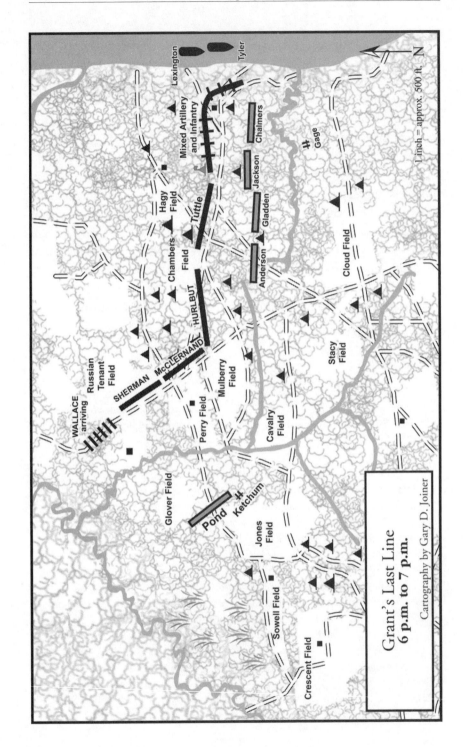

**Grant's Last Line
6 p.m. to 7 p.m.**

Cartography by Gary D. Joiner

officers in deploying them along the Landing front. The Sixth Iowa, now commanded by Captain M. W. Walden, arrived after a frantic withdrawal from McClernand's last line, and Webster arranged for the regiment to move in as support for the big guns. Mounted on his horse in front of the Iowans, Webster addressed the soldiers saying, "I pledge you my men at the guns will do their duty, and if the Rebels come on, I want you to meet them with the cold steel."[6]

General Grant ran across Major William Belknap, who was rallying part of the Fifteenth Iowa, and the general asked him his name and unit. The major replied, and Grant promptly asked him, "Any relation of Colonel Belknap of the Old Army?" The young major answered, "He was my father!" Holding his hand out, Grant said, "I knew your father well, and was with him in Mexico."[7]

Sherman's, McClernand's and Hurlbut's commands all gradually straggled to the Landing, adding their riflemen and cannon to the force already there, but some units were slow in falling back. Lieutenant Cuthbert Laing's Second Light Michigan Battery paused in a ravine to trade shots with Captain Melancthon Smith's Mississippi Battery. The delay proved fatal. Prentiss' surrender had freed the First Mississippi Cavalry to move forward. Its commander, Colonel A. J. Lindsay, was directed to take charge of all cavalry on that side of the field and sweep to the river. Lieutenant Colonel John Miller assumed command of the regiment, and they galloped forward about a quarter of a mile, yelling like mad men. Then Laing's Battery was observed about three hundred yards ahead, in the act of limbering up. The Mississippians charged wildly forward towards the guns and the Federals, realizing escape was impossible, decided to try and fight it out. Unlimbering their pieces, the Yanks frantically tried to swing their weapons around to bear on the charging enemy. Before a single cannon could be loaded, aimed, and fired, the Mississippians reached the battery, riding down the hapless gunners. Resistance was hopeless and the Federals quickly raised their hands, fifty-six gunners surrendering, along with the five cannon. (Laing was on another part of the battlefield recovering his sixth gun, which was

6 Byers, *Iowa in War Times*, 139.

7 Belknap, *15th Regiment Iowa*, 190.

damaged earlier in the day.) The prisoners and guns were quickly ordered to the rear, and the Mississippians continued their advance toward the Tennessee River.[8]

Other Confederate cavalry units also tried to harass the retreating Union army. On the other side of the field, not far from Jones Field, Confederate Colonel John Hunt Morgan attempted to bring his unit into action with McClernand's rear most retreating units. After observing the repulse of Pond's Brigade, Morgan, acting under orders from Hardee to advance, followed McClernand's troops when they began to withdraw toward the Landing. Byrne's Battery appeared and began unlimbering to shell McClernand's men also. Bluecoated riflemen suddenly attacked out of a clump of woods. Morgan immediately gave the command to charge and the Kentuckians followed the Federals into the thick foliage, losing all trace of formation in the process. Morgan's men suddenly found themselves on the receiving end of a heavy fire from a strong force of McClernand's infantry. Men and horses went down, but the Kentuckians did not falter. It was an awkward, clumsy, stumbling affair, with some of Morgan's men trying vainly to hack and slash at the Union infantry in the underbrush. Some of the Kentuckians put their trust in their shotguns and pistols and were able to kill or wound twelve or fifteen of the enemy. Within moments the action abruptly ended and the Bluecoats continued retreating toward the Landing. The brief fight cost Morgan the lives of Lieutenant James West and Privates Samuel Buckner and James Ghiselin, and several wounded.[9]

Confederate infantry commanders were also trying to organize some kind of pursuit of the retreating Federals, but it was no easy matter. When Prentiss and the other Unionists who had escaped from the Hornet's Nest were captured, many of the Confederate infantry assumed the battle was over and casually left their units to find something to eat and drink or hunt for wounded buddies.[10] Despite the loss of these additional

---

8 E. D. Winston, *Story of Pontotoc* (Pontotoc: Pontotoc Progress Printing, 1931), 233; Deupree, "The Noxubee Squadron of the First Mississippi Cavalry," 33, 34; *OR* 10, pt. 1, 460, 461, 246.

9 Duke, *Morgan's Cavalry*, 148-150; Holland, *Morgan and His Raiders*, 92.

10 Kirkpatrick Scrapbook, Alabama Department of Archives and History.

defectors, Confederate officers soon managed to round up at least part of their commands and started off for the Landing. There was still almost continuous firing from scattered points across the field as the somewhat awkwardly advancing Southerners collided with parties of Union stragglers.

Chalmers' and Jackson's brigades of Withers' Division, which were probably the first two infantry units to undertake the last advance, were particularly troubled by Federal stragglers. Some of the Second Texas came upon a squad of Union infantry, consisting of about a dozen men, led by a sergeant. One of the group waved a white piece of cloth from a musket rammer, and the Texans naturally assumed the Yanks were an isolated party who wanted to give up. The Northerners walked within about fifty feet of the Confederates when the sergeant suddenly yelled in a single breath, "Halt—ready—aim—fire!" The Yankee volley killed two Texans and wounded several more, and the plucky Federals, their guns empty, tried to retreat to safety. Angered by what they considered Northern treachery, the Confederates wiped out the entire squad.[11]

A little further on toward the river, the Texans' commanding officer, Colonel John Moore, captured a solitary soldier. Several hundred yards from the river the regiment came upon an isolated log cabin, which the Rebels immediately proceeded to deploy around for a quick search. The precaution was not necessary, for from the door of the cabin a lone Union defender walked out, his bayoneted rifle high in the air. Moore's men quickly disarmed the Irish Yankee, and jokingly asked him what he was doing. The disarmed Federal replied casually, "And sure, I wanter surrinder meself." The fellow was quickly obliged, and he was sent to the rear with the other prisoners.[12]

As the tail end of the Fortieth Illinois headed for the new position near the Landing, an officer, Lieutenant John McLean, had a foot shot off. Five members of the regiment dropped behind to help the hapless officer. Private John Hunt took the rifles of the other four men while they picked up the crippled McLean. Confederate skirmishers moved in on the

11 Houston, "Shiloh Shadows," 331.

12 John C. Moore, "Shiloh Issues Again," *Confederate Veteran* 10 (July 1902): 317.

little party and one Southerner shot McLean's own musket out of his hands, ruining it, but the little group finally managed to make it to the Landing and at least temporary sanctuary.[13]

Skirmishers from the Fifteenth Mississippi of Statham's Brigade also ran into a hot fight with retreating Federals. Company E deployed behind a corn crib while Northern riflemen deployed along the rim of a ravine and peppered them with slugs. Private Dick Wood took cover behind a large Federal army medical chest filled with and lined on the top with jars and bottles. Union riflemen sniped at Wood, their heavy slugs ripping into the chest, sending wooden splinters and bits of glass and medicine flying in all directions. Wood was cut in the neck by a fragment, and he finally took the butt of his Enfield and smashed the remaining jars and bottles from off the top in order to get a little relief.[14] With the barrage of flying missiles now reduced to merely some Federal slugs, Wood quickly resumed his less personal fight with the distant Union riflemen, who were soon driven back.

But a disturbing new element was rapidly being added to the fight. Heavy shells, much larger than anything the Confederates had encountered before, were beginning to explode among and around the advancing Southerners. These shells were coming from an important new entry in the battle, the United States navy gunboats *Lexington* and *Tyler*.

When the battle began that Sunday morning, the *Tyler* commanded by Lieutenant William Gwin and the *Lexington* commanded by Lieutenant James W. Shirk were idly steaming by on the Tennessee River, not performing any particular function. After listening to the sounds of battle for a good while, Gwin, who was the senior naval officer present, decided to move his gunboat up above the Landing so as to be in a position to support the troops should they be driven back to the river's bank.[15]

13 John Hunt, "Reminiscences of Dr. John B. Hunt," Miscellaneous Collection, Shiloh National Military Park.

14 J. B. Foster, "Mississippi Histories," *Confederate Veteran* 10 (December 1902): 554.

15 || For a modern analysis of the navy's role at at Shiloh, see Smith, *The Untold Story of Shiloh*, 53-66.

About 10:15 a.m., the *Lexington*, which had been at Crump's Landing when the battle began, arrived to find out what was going on. Determining that a battle was raging, Shirk turned the *Lexington* around and returned to Crump's to support Wallace. With Shirk gone, Gwin stood off Pittsburg Landing, vainly awaiting some orders from Grant or someone in authority as to what action to take. Occasionally Confederate overshots splashed water around the little wooden gunboat, but caused no damage. Frustrated by the lack of orders, Gwin finally decided to take action. About 1:25, p.m., he dispatched an officer ashore to find someone in authority to get orders from. Locating General Hurlbut, arrangements were quickly made for the gunboat to open fire on the Confederate army.

About 2:50, p.m., the *Tyler* opened fire with her six 8-inch smoothbores and lone 32-pounder, firing in the direction of some Confederate gun positions. After an hour, Gwin ordered his gunners to cease fire, and he moved his ship down opposite the Landing, sending Gunner Herman Peters ashore to "communicate with General Grant for further instructions."[16] Grant immediately sent word back to Gwin for him to use his own judgment. Shirk arrived with the *Lexington* and the two wooden vessels assumed a new position about three-quarters of a mile above the Landing, shelling some Confederate batteries. It is questionable just how effective the gunboats' fire was, but the sounds of the big shells exploding did not help Confederate morale.[17]

Bragg's orders were to pursue the Federals to the Tennessee River, but Chalmers, Jackson, and the other Confederate leaders were encountering increased difficulties in executing this order.[18] Many of the Confederates were short of ammunition, and the gunboats' fire was hitting with increasing accuracy as the Southerners neared the river. The Tennessee was at high water, and by elevating their guns to the maximum and using reduced charges, Gwin and Shirk punished Withers men severely. Gwin opened fire on Chalmers' Brigade at 5:35 p.m., sending

16 *ORN* 22, 763.

17 *Ibid.*; A. H. Mecklin, Diary, April 6, 1862, Mississippi Department of Archives and History.

18 *OR* 10, pt. 1, 533, 534.

shell after shell crashing into the Southerners position.[19] One of the big naval shells landed right in the middle of the remaining part of the Fifty-second Tennessee of Chalmers' Brigade, cutting down several of the men. Private William F. Mosier's uncle was knocked on his back, lamed for life by a shell, his musket barrel bent. Several more shells immediately hit among the Fifty-second, and the soldiers quickly scattered to find whatever cover they could, leaving only three enlisted men with Captain Wilson.[20] The Fifth Tennessee was also hit by the fire from the Union gunboats. Private James Bouie, Company C, was torn to pieces by an exploding shell, as was at least one other man in another company.[21]

The Confederates unknowingly were racing against time, for the *Lexington* and *Tyler* were not the only Federal reinforcements available to General Grant. Other help was coming, and indeed was practically arrived, for the advance of Buell's army was already being ferried across the Tennessee.

About 7:00 a.m. Sunday morning the troops of the Fourth Division, Army of the Ohio, were astir, putting the finishing touches to their breakfasts and toilets in preparation for a dress parade. The scattered crackle of musket fire could be heard in the distance, but no one paid any particular attention to it. Then a little past 7:00, the sound of cannon fire began drifting in, steadily increasing in tempo until it was almost a solid roll. Awakened by the sounds, the gigantic General William Nelson sprang to his feet from his cot and called an aide, Lieutenant Richard Southgate, formerly of the Sixth Ohio, and ordered him to tell Colonels William Hazen, S. D. Bruce, and Jacob Ammen to have their brigades in

19 B. B. Carruth, "Vivid Recollections of Shiloh," *Confederate Veteran* 9 (April 1901): 166; *ORN* 22, 763.

20 William Mosier to D. W. Reed, December 11, 1912, Miscellaneous Collection, Shiloh National Military Park.

21 Rennolds, *The Henry County Commands*, 34. || For an interesting theory on the gunboats' shelling of the battlefield, see Gary D. Joiner's contribution to the History Channel television program *Battlefield Detectives: Shiloh* (2006). Dr. Joiner argues that the gunboats were able to shell the interior of the battlefield by ricocheting shells off the ridges surrounding Dill Branch ravine.

"readiness to move at any moment after the end of the hour."[22] He dispatched another aide to go down to the river to see if any transports were available. As the sounds of battle rapidly increased, Nelson paced up and down in front of his tent, scowling at and tongue lashing anyone within range. Finally he turned to one of his staff, Dr. Bradford, and vehemently exclaimed, "By God, Bradford, if I get no orders by twelve o'clock, I will move without them. I will do so, if I have to go back to the deck of my ship for it."[23]

Finally a little after 8:00 a.m., unwilling to endure the suspense, Nelson mounted his long-suffering horse and rode over to the Cherry House to find out what was going on and what his orders were. At the Cherry House, Nelson found the order that Grant had dictated to Rawlins an hour before, directing him to move his division to the river opposite Pittsburg Landing. The order seemed to indicate no particular urgency, and indeed the attitude around Savannah was one of calm, suggesting that the whole affair was a large-scale picket fight. Whatever the sense of urgency, the Kentuckian quickly rode back to his headquarters and immediately dictated orders to get ready to move.[24]

Considering Grant's previous remarks concerning the impractibility of the local roads, it is a little difficult to see how he meant for Nelson to get to the high ground opposite Pittsburg Landing. The citizens of Savannah were not very much help. Most of the potential guides were already enlisted with Grant and busy fighting Johnston's army. The few remaining sympathizers were under the impression that the route to the bluff opposite Pittsburg was impassable due to high water. Nelson quickly ordered his assistant adjutant general, Captain J. Mills Kendrick, to take a detachment of cavalry and reconnoiter in the direction of the river.

Even while Prentiss' and Sherman's divisions were crumbling under the fierce Southern onslaught, the troops of Nelson's Fourth Division

22 Jacob Ammen Diary, April 6, 1862, Illinois State Historical Library; Hannaford, *The Story of A Regiment*, 241; W. B. Hazen, *A Narrative of Military Service* (Boston: Ticknor and Company, 1885), 24.

23 Hannaford, *The Story of A Regiment*, 242.

24 *Ibid.*, 243-246; Hazen, *A Narrative of Military Service*, 24.

lolled about checking equipment, impatient and eager to move, but lacking orders. Nelson could only stump about growling at his aides while waiting for Kendrick's report or for some of Grant's empty transports to come up to Savannah.

Taking advantage of the delay, Nelson's subordinate officers checked and rechecked the state of readiness of their commands, making sure that every man had an adequate supply of rations and ammunition. Nelson finally rode over to see Colonel Ammen,[25] ordering him to be ready to move either through the swamps, if Kendrick's report was favorable, or by boat from the Landing. The general then rode on off toward the Landing to look for the transports.

Colonel Ammen stood around awhile, awaiting orders; but none came, and he finally mounted his horse and rode aver to the Cherry House, where he met an impatient Buell and Nelson. No boats had arrived, and the first reports from Kendrick's patrol were unfavorable. The sounds of battle from Shiloh continued to increase in intensity, and rumors of a Union disaster began to spread around Savannah. Someone remarked to Colonel Ammen that his old friend, General C. F. Smith, was upstairs, and the colonel went up the stairway. Upon finding his old comrade, they began chatting. In cheerful spirits, the crippled Smith laughed at the idea of a major battle, claiming that it was simply a large picket fight. The minutes passed as the two men chatted and the firing continued to increase. Finally Smith agreed that perhaps part of Grant's army might be seriously involved in battle. An orderly knocked on Smith's door requesting that Colonel Ammen go downstairs to meet with Buell and Nelson.[26] Ammen was told that Buell had decided to proceed upstream on a little steamer to talk to Grant, and that Kendrick's men had returned without finding a useable path. Nelson had managed to locate a Tennessee Unionist who knew the country and had agreed to guide the army to a point opposite Pittsburg Landing.[27] According to the guide, the

25 Hannaford, *The Story of A Regiment*, 246-248.

26 Jacob Ammen Diary, April 6, 1862, Illinois State Historical Library; William R. Hartpence, *History of the 5lst Indiana Veteran Volunteer Infantry* (Cincinnati: The Robert Clack Company, 1894), 36, 37.

27 Hartpence, *History of the 5lst Indiana Veteran Volunteer Infantry*, 36, 37.

river road was impassable, but there was another route that could be navigated by infantry and cavalry, although not by artillery or baggage.

Between 1:00 and 1:30 p.m., Nelson's brigades moved out, following the guide's directions. General Nelson dashed up to the head of the column, telling Colonel Ammen to follow.[28] Ammen's brigade led the way, Colonel William Grose's Thirty-sixth Indiana in front, followed by Lieutenant Colonel Frederick C. Jones's Twenty-fourth Ohio and Lieutenant Colonel Nicholas Anderson's Sixth Ohio in the rear. Colonel Sanders' men, Buell's Twenty-second Brigade, followed behind Ammen's force, while Colonel William Hazen's Nineteenth Brigade brought up the rear. The Fourth Division had approximately eight miles to march in order to reach the point where the transports would presumably be waiting, and the journey was necessarily a rigorous one, considering the poor state of the path.

General Nelson, mounted on his large and powerful bay, and accompanied by part of his staff, quickly left the column behind. Somewhere along the road Nelson ran into one of Grant's aides, who handed him a written message from the general which read as follows:

> You will hurry up your command as fast as possible. The boats will be in readiness to transport all troops of your command across the river. All looks well, but it is necessary for you to push forward as fast as possible.[29]

A short distance from the Tennessee River, Nelson received a second courier from General Grant. The newcomer was riding Grant's own mount and had a verbal message that the Fourth Division should press forward with all speed or the fight would be lost.[30] On orders from Nelson, his men started moving forward on the double-quick, but soon had to abandon the swift pace due to the extreme muddiness of the roadway. At last Ammen's Bluecoats debouched into a clearing opposite Pittsburg Landing.

---

28 *Ibid.*; Hazen, *A Narrative of Military Service*, 24; *OR* 10, pt. 1, 323.

29 Badeau, *Military History of Ulysses S. Grant*, 77.

30 Jacob Ammen Diary, April 6, 1862, Illinois State Historical Library.

After leaving Savannah aboard the little steamer, accompanied by his chief of staff, Buell proceeded up the river only to be halted by a descending steamer, which came alongside and delivered Grant's early morning order, which had been dictated to Rawlins and sent wandering all over the area until finally it came into Buell's hands at this time. Nearing the Landing, Buell could make out large numbers of fugitives fleeing from the battlefield. Indeed the mouth of Snake Creek was full of them swimming across.

About 1:00 p.m., the little steamer tied up at Pittsburg Landing and Buell went hunting for Grant. Informed that the general was on his headquarters boat, tied up only a few yards away from his own steamer, Buell quickly went on board and found his superior in conversation with several members of his staff. After exchanging salutations, Grant remarked that he had just come in from the front, and he held up his scabbard to show Buell a dent made in it by a Rebel projectile.[31] Buell inquired as to the progress of the battle, and he requested his senior to send some steamers to Savannah to pick up Crittenden's division, which would be coming into Savannah shortly. The conference then ended, and the two men parted, Grant and several staff officers riding off in one direction while Buell walked up hill in another.[32] After separating from

31 *Battles and Leaders*, 1: 492, 493. See Richardson, *Personal History of Ulysses S. Grant*, 243, for details of how Grant's scabbard was dented.

32 Grant, *Memoirs*, 178, 179; *Battles and Leaders*, 1: 492, 493. A rather fanciful story, primarily promulgated by Adam Badeau, appeared to the effect that Buell asked Grant, "What preparations have you made for retreating?" to which Grant replied, "I have not yet despaired of whipping them, general." Badeau, *Military History, of Ulysses S. Grant*, 82; *OR* 10, pt. 1, 186. A slightly different version said Grant did utter the aforementioned, to which Buell replied, "Of course; but in case of defeat?" Grant replied, "Well, we could make a bridge across the river with the boats and protect it with artillery. But if we do have to retreat, there won't be many men left to cross." Richardson, *Personal History of Ulysses S. Grant*, 244. In his *Memoirs*, General Grant alluded to Buell's mentioning something about a line of retreat. Grant, *Memoirs*, 179. Buell flatly denied exchanging any such remarks with General Grant, saying the whole thing was "ridiculous and absurd." *Battles and Leaders*, 1: 493.

Grant, Buell busied himself trying to create a little order at the Landing, but with only limited success.[33]

When Nelson's men reached the point opposite Pittsburg Landing, the last big dramatic moment in the combat at Shiloh was rapidly approaching. It was around 5:00 in the afternoon, or a little earlier, when the first of Ammen's men reached the point. The Hornet's Nest was just yielding, and Prentiss' and Wallace's men were already trying to retreat to the Landing. Having reached the point some minutes earlier, Nelson was already busy trying to round up some transports. Several stern-wheel steamers were lying along the eastern bank, laden with fugitives from Grant's army, and the captains had no enthusiasm about risking their boats on the dangerous western side of the river. Moments passed while Nelson cursed and harangued the reluctant river sailors; but by threats and appeals, the saltwater sailor finally persuaded several of the steamboat captains to agree to take his men across. Nelson, Colonel Grose, and part of the Thirty-sixth Indiana boarded the first steamer, while Ammen was ordered to quickly follow with the rest of his brigade about 5:40 p.m.[34]

Nelson climbed ashore at the Landing and began pushing his way through the horde of stragglers crowded at the Landing. He quickly found Buell and Grant, who were anxiously awaiting him. To Grant, Nelson saluted, and in his own inimitable style proclaimed, "Here we are, General, we don't know many fine points or nice evolution, but if you want stupidity and hard fighting, I reckon we are the men for you."[35]

33 Grant, *Memoirs*, 179; *Battles and Leaders*, 1: 493.

34 Hannaford, *The Story of A Regiment*, 256; Jacob Ammen Diary, April 6, 1862, Illinois State Historical Library. There is some question as to the exact time Nelson and his men began landing. Nelson's volunteer aide-de-camp, Horace N. Fisher, said that he was on the first steamer, and he had landed at 5:20 p.m. Horace N. Fisher to D. W. Reed, March 27, 1905, Miscellaneous Collection, Shiloh National Military Park. || Sword, *Shiloh*, 362, says 5:20 p.m. Daniel, *Shiloh*, 246, 249, does not state, only saying between 5:00 and 6:00 p.m. McDonough, *Shiloh*, 178, says "about 5 p.m."

35 Richardson, *Personal History of Ulysses S. Grant*, 247; Richardson, *The Secret Service The Field, The Dungeon and the Escape*, 241.

Buell immediately ordered the late arrival to deploy his men along the position, remarking, "You have had the advance throughout the march and here, General, is your opportunity. There is still one hour left in which to decide this fight."[36]

Pushing their way through the numerous stragglers, Grose and his men quickly moved out to help support the beleaguered last position of Grant's army. By this hour, with less than one hour's light remaining, the scene at the Landing, and indeed the entire battlefield, was one of utter and complete confusion. Many thousands of Union soldiers were standing around the Landing in utterly abject panic, some of them attempting to hide from the occasional stray Southern projectiles that came flying over, while others attempted to beg their way on board what they supposed to be the safety of the various steamers. Many of Grant's steamers had been gradually filled with wounded soldiers, rendering them unavailable for any other duty for the moment; but this made no difference to the panic-stricken Bluecoats. Several steamers were compelled to slip their lines and swing out into mid channel in order to avoid being swamped by the horde of crazed men. One hysterical Union officer threatened the pilot of the *Minnehaha* with his revolver in an attempt to make him take on board the officer's soldiers, but the boat's pilot resolutely refused to yield, thus saving his ship from being overrun.[37]

Not all of the wretches gathered at the Landing had completely lost their sense of duty. Here and there one of Grant's officers went about trying to rally the men, sometimes asking the fellows why they did not rejoin their units. The usual reply to his question was, "I can't find it [the regiment]." One officer wandered about delivering a frenzied Fourth of July tirade, reminding the men of the honor of their various states, their mothers, their homes, and a list of other inducements; however, the only

---

36 Hannaford, *The Story of A Regiment,* 256; Jacob Ammen Diary, April 6,1862, Illinois State Historical Library; Horace N. Fisher to D. W. Reed, April 12, 1905, Miscellaneous Collection, Shiloh National Military Park.

37 Ambrose Bierce, *The Collected Works of Ambrose Bierce* (New York: 1909), 1: 245; Mrs. W. H. L. Wallace to her Aunt Mag, April 29, 1862, Miscellaneous Collection, Shiloh National Military Park.

reaction to his speech was an occasional remark to the effect that it was a very good speech.[38]

When the Sixth Ohio started to disembark, a crowd of the rabble tried to climb on board their boat, blocking the men's debarkation. Nelson went dashing down into the middle of the crowd, shouting, "Get out of the way, you damned cowards! Get out of the way! If you wont fight yourselves, let these men off that will. Sixth Ohio, follow me!"[39]

Even as the first of Nelson's men climbed up the Landing to hold the line, sharp fighting had broken out along the last Union position. Chalmers' and part of Jackson's brigades moved up in front of Grant's position and opened up with a fairly strong burst of fire in preparation for

---

38 Devens, *The Pictorial Book of Anecdotes*, 240.

39 Hannaford, *The Story of A Regiment*, 257. To Buell and his men, it seemed as though a large part of Grant's army crowded around the Landing in a pusillanimous display of abject cowardice. The commander of the Army of the Ohio estimated the number as 15,000. *Battles and Leaders,* 1: 494. Colonel Hazen, who arrived just before dark, estimated the number of stragglers as "twenty or thirty acres worth." Hazen, *A Narrative of Military Service*, 25. With some embarrassment, Grant said that "there probably were as many as four or five thousand stragglers lying under cover of the bluff, panic stricken." Grant, *Memoirs*, 178, 179. Actually Hazen and Buell were probably nearer right in their estimates, for the crowd at the bluff included not only panic-stricken stragglers from the combat units, but a large number of noncombat and miscellaneous personnel such as sutlers, musicians, clerks, teamsters, etc. According to General Halleck, Grant's army, including Lew Wallace's division, numbered 53,669, as of the end of March. *OR* 10, pt. 2, 84. Since his combat troops on early Sunday morning numbered less than 40,000, this figure would indicate the presence of about 7,000 or so auxiliary troops. Add to this the undoubted thousands who did break and run for the bluff, plus what must have amounted to several thousand more men who were disorganized in the withdrawal to Webster's position and did not have sufficient time to reorganize before the arrival of Buell's army, and the figure 15,000 would seem to have a fair degree of accuracy. The eminent British historian J. F. C. Fuller stated that were about 11,000 noncombatant troops at Shiloh, and between 4,000 and 5,000 unwounded stragglers. Fuller, *The Generalship of Ulysses S. Grant*, 105. || Daniel, *Shiloh*, 246, says "between 10,000 and 15,000"; Sword, *Shiloh*, 361, and McDonough, *Shiloh*, 178, mostly quote participants' numbers.

assault. Webster rode up and down behind the Union line shouting encouragingly, "Stand firm, boys; they can never carry this line in the world."[40] General Grant rode along the lines, urging the men to keep up a steady fire on the Confederates.[41]

One of General Grant's scouts, Captain Irving Carson, rode up to the general, reported, and then started riding away. His horse had taken no more than two or three steps when a cannon shot tore off that officer's head, except for the chin, spattering Grant with bits of brains and blood, leaving him rather messy but unhurt,[42] although the shot went on to rip the saddle of W. Preston Graves, a volunteer aide to Nelson. General Sherman, who was directing things on the Union extreme right, also had a very narrow escape. Captain J. H. Hammond was holding the reins of Sherman's horse while the general mounted. A bullet ripped the reins two inches from Hammonds' fingers and only inches from the general's head.[43]

Even with Nelson's arrival Grant's situation was still serious. Much of his army was disorganized, and many of his soldiers were roaming around, trying to find their units. One incompetent officer roamed around, adding to the confusion, claiming General Grant had surrendered and the battle was ended. When asked how he knew the fighting had ended, the officer replied that he had seen the troops lined up and laying down their arms. Fortunately most of the battle hardened veterans took the report with a grain of salt.[44]

Around 6:00 p.m., Chalmers and Jackson actually attacked over the rugged terrain. Grant's weary infantry fired into the oncoming

---

40 Richardson, *Personal History of Ulysses S. Grant*, 247.

41 Byers, *Iowa In War Times*, 139; Kimbell, *Battery A*, 43-45.

42 Victor, *Incidents and Anecdotes of the War*, 359; Richardson, *Personal History of Ulysses Grant*, 247; Kimbell, *Battery A*, 44.

43 Victor, *Incidents and Anecdotes of the War*, 359. || Dr. Cunningham originally stated that the scout Carson was the famous Kit Carson. It was actually Irving Carson. See "The Dead of Companies A and B, Chicago Light Artillery," *Chicago Tribune*, April 17, 1862. The name has been altered accordingly.

44 Duke, *Fifty-third Ohio*, 53, 54.

Confederate infantry, while Webster's guns joined in with shrapnel and canister. Chalmers' advance was covered by the 3-inch rifles and 12-pound howitzers of Gage's Alabama Battery, but in the face of the massed Union artillery, the Southerners found the going difficult. Observing the Confederate advance, Lieutenant Shirk of the *Lexington* ordered his gunners to open fire on the advancing Southerners. In ten minutes the navy cannoneers sent thirty-two rounds into the Confederates with excellent effect.[45]

Right in the middle of the attack the Thirty-sixth Indiana went stumbling into position along Webster's line, with orders to support Stone's First Missouri Battery K, (the rest of the regiment having been ferried over on a second steamer). Before the Indianans could be deployed, a Confederate projectile killed an enlisted man, the first casualty suffered by Buell's command in the Battle of Shiloh. Grose quickly arranged his men in the proper position and then immediately opened up with heavy musket fire on Chalmers' Mississippians. The four hundred odd Indianans got off some fourteen or fifteen rounds per man at the oncoming Mississippians, having one man killed and one wounded from the return fire.

Gage's Alabama Battery was knocked out by Federal artillery fire, thus depriving the Southerners of artillery support at the very height of the attack. In the face of the fire from Webster's guns, the *Tyler* and *Lexington*, Grant's infantry, and Buell's Thirty-sixth Indiana, along with the incredibly poor terrain, Chalmers and Jackson were forced to withdraw.[46]

It was now after 6:00 and the sun was slipping perilously low along the horizon. From his headquarters in the rear, General Beauregard sent his staff officers to the various corps commanders with instructions to break off operations and withdraw to the captured enemy camps for the

---

45 *OR* 10, pt. 1, 550; *ORN* 22, 786.

46 *OR* 10, pt. 1, 337; Hannaford, *The Story of A Regiment*, 258, 259; James R. Chalmers to R. H. Looney, April 3, 1895, Miscellaneous Collection, Shiloh National Military Park; Jacob Ammen Diary, April 6, 1862, Illinois State Historical Library; Roman, *Beauregard*, 1: 301; Micajah Wilkinson to brother, April 6, 1862, Micajah Wilkinson Papers, Louisiana State University Archives.

night.[47] He did not know that reinforcements were already reaching Grant's army, and assumed the Confederate army would be able to resume the action on Monday morning, still facing the same men beaten on Sunday. Since a night action was dangerous, and assuming that the enemy was completely beaten, Beauregard issued this order, thereby laying the ground work for one of the bitterest controversies of the Battle of Shiloh, and indeed of the Civil War.

For a century, critics have maintained that the Creole forfeited a magnificent opportunity to completely destroy Grant's army—one more assault and the Federals would have been driven into the river and captured. Such an opinion completely ignores the existing situation on the Shiloh battlefield on late Sunday evening, April 6, 1862. It was nearly 5:30 p.m. before General Prentiss and his troops, as well as General Wallace and his men, were finally rounded up after falling back from the Hornet's Nest.[48]

The Confederate army was badly disorganized and only Withers' troops were able to cross the rough terrain toward Grant's last position

---

47 *OR* 10, pt. 1, 386, 387; N. Augustine to General. Beauregard, April 10, 1862, Miscellaneous Collection, Shiloh National Military Park; N. Augustine to General Beauregard, (Report) April 10, 1862, Louisiana Historical Association Collection, Howard-Tilton Memorial Library, Tulane University; Theodore Mandeville to Josephine Rozet, April 9, 1862, Theodore Mandeville Papers, Louisiana State University Archives. Mandeville said his regiment was being heavily shelled by the gunboats when ordered to withdraw "about sundown." *Ibid*. William Preston Johnston, son and biographer of the dead Confederate hero, commented that "complete victory was in his [Beauregard's] grasp, and he threw it away." *Battles and Leaders*, 1: 568. See Kirwan, *Johnny Green*, 28; Richardson, "War As I Saw It," 102.

48 General Prentiss gave the time of his surrender as 5:30 p.m. *OR* 10, pt. 1, 279. Colonel Thomas Jordan, of Beauregard's staff, gave the time of the Union general's surrender as between 5:30 p.m. and 6:00 p.m. Jordan, "The Campaign and Battle of Shiloh," 395. ‖ Most historians have concluded Beauregard had no chance to break the last line. Sword, *Shiloh*, 449-452, seems to exonerate Beauregard; McDonough, *Shiloh*, 181, argues that Beauregard was justified in his actions; Daniel, *Shiloh*, 256, 249, believes the Confederates had no chance to break Grant's last line, although he tempers this a bit by describing the line "far from impregnable." See also Smith, *The Untold Story of Shiloh*, 31-32.

and make anything like an organized attack. Other Rebel units were only able to peck away slightly at the Union's last position. With sunset falling at 6:25 p.m., there simply was not time to organize the sort of attack needed to blast Grant's soldiers out of what amounted to a very strong defensive position. It is true that Grant's men were somewhat dispirited by their frequent reverses, but the arrival of Colonel Ammen's brigade strongly boosted the morale of Grant's soldiers, giving them the feeling that they were no longer isolated.

One of the biggest obstacles to Beauregard's ordering a strong attack on the Webster position was the very confused state of his various commands, most of which were badly separated.[49] It would have taken Beauregard at least an hour or probably longer to have collected enough infantry and artillery to have risked an attack on the Landing. Time simply ran out.

At the time of the battle, many participating Confederates believed Beauregard gave the withdrawal order due to the presence of the *Lexington* and *Tyler*, whose fire had begun to take considerable effect on the Southerners as they approached closer to the river.[50] Although he did not cite the gunboats' fire as a reason for the withdrawal, Beauregard did mention it in some detail, indicating that it may have subconsciously influenced his decision.[51]

The Creole's order to break off the action did not actually end the fighting, for isolated skirmishing went on for the next fifteen or twenty minutes of light, when the curtain of darkness ended the day's carnage. In

---

49 Shoup, "The Art of War," 10; Crenshaw, "Diary of Captain Edward Crenshaw," 269; Liddell Hart, *Sherman*, 129; Conger, *The Rise of U. S. Grant*, 259. At least some of the Southerners heard a rumor passing around the battlefield that Johnston was dead. It is possible that the news added to the general state of Confederate disorganization. Richardson, "War As I Saw It," 102.

50 Mobile *Evening News*, April 14, 1862; The Charleston *Daily Courier*, April 20, 1862; Shoup, "The Art of War," 10; Richard Pugh to wife, April 8, 1862, Richard Pugh Papers, Louisiana State University Archives.

51 Mobile *Evening News*, April 14, 1862; *OR* 10, pt. 1, 387; Frank Peak, "A Southern Soldiers View of the War," Frank Peak Papers, Louisiana State University Archives.

these remaining minutes, part of the Tenth Mississippi, of Chalmers' Brigade, swung way around to the right, crossed the big pond just off the river, and began sniping at the Federal gunboats. Shirk's and Gwin's gunners fired a few blasts from their big guns at the Mississippians, who hastily beat a retreat in the direction of the Indian mounds.[52]

One other interesting controversy arose out of the last few minutes of the day's battle. Did Nelson's arrival save General Grant's army? The answer to this must remain problematical. Grant's admirers and friendly biographers, and even some serious scholars such as the late Kenneth P. Williams, maintained that Grant could have held out that evening without the arrival of Ammen's brigade.[53] The Comte de Paris, an eminent French historian, was of the opinion that the arrival of Buell's troops saved the last Union position from being carried by Chalmers' and Jackson's attack.[54] Among Grant's soldiers, a majority seem to have believed the position could have been held without the arrival of Ammen's brigade,[55] but there were some who gave these troops credit for saving the day. One of Grant's soldiers, Andrew Hickenlooper, remarked that the arrival of Buell's troops "changed the fate of the battle."[56] Whatever Grant's men thought of the situation, Buell's troops remained convinced that their arrival saved the Union army.[57]

---

52 R. F. Learned to D. W. Reed, March 22, 1904, Miscellaneous Collection, Shiloh National Military Park.

53 Williams, *Lincoln Finds A General*, 3: 378, 379; Richardson, *Personal History of Ulysses S. Grant*, 247, 248; Badeau, *Military History of Ulysses S. Grant*, 84, 85; Grant, *Memoirs*, 180.

54 Comte de Paris, *History of the Civil War*, 1: 548.

55 George R. Lee, "Shiloh," George Read Lee Papers, Illinois State Historical Library.

56 Hickenlooper, "The Battle of Shiloh," 436; Payson Shumway, Diary, April 13, 1862; Payson Z. Shumway Papers, Illinois State Historical Library; Unidentified Union soldier to Emily Rice, April 11, 1862, Miscellaneous Collection, Shiloh National Military Park.

57 "John A. Joyce, *A Checkered Life* (Chicago: S. P. Pounds, 1883), 60-62; John Hunt, "Reminisces," Miscellaneous Collection, Shiloh National Military Park; Alexis Cope, *The Fifteenth Ohio Volunteers and Its Campaigns: War of*

But it would be some time before the Shiloh controversies began in earnest. As darkness settled over the battlefield Sunday night, April 6, 1862, the soldiers were more concerned with finding something to eat and drink than in bothering about discussing the fine points of who saved whom. Thousands of Rebel soldiers believed the main battle was over. As soon as dawn came, they would simply make one more brief push and destroy what was left of Grant's army. It was a relaxing and pleasant thought to lie down and sleep with.

1861-65 (Columbus: Published by Author, 1916), 125; R. W. Johnson, *A Soldier's Reminiscences in Peace and War* (Philadelphia: J. P. Lippincott, 1886), 189. || Sword, *Shiloh*, 370-371, 449-452, stresses that Buell's arrival was a factor in maintaining the final position, emphasizing "the situation was grave" upon his arrival; McDonough, *Shiloh*, 179, argues that Buell made little difference in the fighting; Daniel, *Shiloh*, 249, seems to argue that Grant had the situation under control, but admitted his final line was "far from impregnable." See also Smith, *The Untold Story of Shiloh*, 27-28.

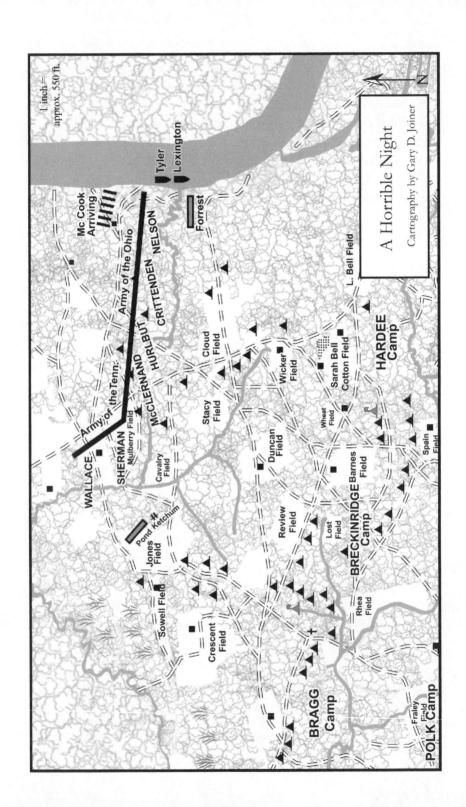

A Horrible Night

Cartography by Gary D. Joiner

1 inch = approx. 550 ft.

Chapter 14

Buell, Grant, and Beauregard

IT HAD BEEN A long and bitter thirteen hours, but at least most of the Southern army could take some feeling of joy in the knowledge that they had won. But at Confederate headquarters there was one group who felt only sorrow. Albert Sidney Johnston was dead.

The hero of Monterrey, the Mormon expedition, the Texas troubles, and the man who had led them to Shiloh lay wrapped in a muddy army blanket. General Beauregard had relieved Johnston's staff officers of any duties so as to allow them to take charge of their fallen leader's body. However, they remained with the Creole until about 9:00 p.m. that evening, when it was obvious the fighting for the day was completely over. Some of the men attempted to get a little sleep, while others sat around talking. But at dawn the next day, Colonel William Preston and the other members of the staff started for Corinth, the beginning of a long, sad journey.

In Corinth, the staff took their beloved leader's body to the William Inge house, the structure that had served as Johnston's headquarters during his stay in the little Mississippi town. The door to Johnston's quarters was jammed, but a staff officer quickly forced it open, and soon the general's body was placed on the bed in the room.

Mrs. Inge and a neighbor lady ushered the distraught officers out and began cleaning the face and uniform of the fallen commander. As Johnston had ridden from Corinth only three days earlier, Mrs. Inge had given him two sandwiches and a piece of cake to eat during his journey to the front. While washing the mud and blood away, she found one of the sandwiches and part of the cake in his coat pocket. One of the Inge neighbor's daughters, Miss Eugenia Polk, entered the room and took two locks of hair from Johnston's head, one of which she sent to his widow, Eliza.[1]

Johnston's staff then accompanied the body to New Orleans, arriving on April 9, to be met at the railroad station by Governor Moore and General Lovell. The corpse was borne to the New Orleans city hall, where it lay in state for two days before being laid to rest in the Monroe family tomb, at the suggestion of Mayor John T. Monroe. After some years, the body was removed and taken to Austin, Texas.[2]

General Johnston and his staff were not the only ones traveling south on the road, toward Corinth. As soon as the Hornet's Nest fell and Prentiss' and Wallace's men were all rounded up, the Southerners immediately began sending the unfortunate captives en route to Corinth, where they could be handled more easily. The first batch of prisoners headed down the road to Mississippi even before darkness ended the day's fighting.

The captives and their captors traveled but a few yards when a shell from one of the gunboats came whistling over. Everyone, Blue and Gray alike, scrambled for cover as the big shell burst about sixty feet from the road. No one was hurt, and the men were soon on their feet, sloshing through the mud again. After marching a short distance, the troops settled down to camp for the night.

On Monday morning the prisoners and guards rose about dawn and started off without bothering with the formality of a breakfast, for the simple reason they had no food. At about 5:00 p.m., the column reached Corinth and the prisoners were assembled in front of the Inge house, where Johnston's body had been cared for earlier in the day. One Confederate housewife remarked to the prisoners, "Well, Yanks, this is pretty good work our boys have done for a breakfast spell." One Union prisoner answered her, "Mother, I hope before dinner you will have cause to change your mind."[3]

---

1 Eisenschiml, *The Story of Shiloh,* 75, 76; William Preston Diary, April 6, 1862, Miscellaneous Collection, Shiloh National Military Park.

2 Roland, *Albert Sidney Johnston*, 352, 353.

3 Thomas, *Soldier Life.*

A Confederate officer recognized one of the prisoners as a Southern deserter named Roland (or Rowland). The deserter was taken away from the others and convicted by a court-martial several days later. A detail of Rebels dug a grave and erected a thick post beside it. Guards brought the prisoner to the place of execution, but the rain had filled the grave, and things were delayed while the water was dipped out. Defiant to the bitter end, Rowland asked, "Please hand me a drink of that water, as I want to drink out of my own grave so the boys will talk about it when I am dead, and remember Rowland."[4] A soldier gave the condemned man some of the water, which he quickly drank and then asked for more, on the grounds that he had heard that water was very scarce in Hell. He was granted his wish and escorted to the post. As the firing squad made ready, Rowland cursed President Jefferson Davis, Bragg, and the whole Confederacy, winding up his tirade by saying that he would show the Southerners how a Union man could die. He was not bound to the pole, but simply knelt there of his own accord. The officer in charge of the detail gave the order, "Ready, aim, fire!" A few seconds later the deserter, or patriot, lay in his wet grave, covered with Mississippi mud.[5]

After standing around out in the open for some time, most of the prisoners were loaded on board box and passenger cars for a short train ride to Memphis, where they were unloaded late in the afternoon of April 8 and were confined in a three story warehouse on the wharf. The soldiers were all fed pork and crackers, but there was a shortage of containers to hold water.[6] After a short stay in the Mississippi River town, the Federal soldiers were again loaded on board trains and taken to Jackson, Mississippi, and finally shipped to Mobile, Alabama, where they were confined until exchanged.

General Prentiss was not sent along with the other prisoners, but was taken to meet with General Beauregard. The fighting was still in progress

---

4 *Ibid.*; Watkins, *Co. Aytch*, 50.

5 *Ibid.*

6 Eisenschiml, *The Story of Shiloh*, 57; Bacon *Thrilling Adventures*, 7; Jackson, "A Prisoner of War," 24. For further details of the subsequent fate of the prisoners, see Mildred Throne, "Iowans in Southern Prisons, 1862," *Iowa Journal of History* 54 (January 1956): 67-70.

when the two men confronted one another. They quickly shook hands and exchanged pleasantries. "General Beauregard," Prentiss remarked, "we have felt your power today and been compelled to yield to it." Beauregard, somewhat forgetting his manners, launched into a dissertation on the merits of the South and the Confederacy, proclaiming that the North would never be able to conquer it. Prentiss politely declined to argue the point, but stood by his contention that the Union was indissoluble. Beauregard finally casually asked the Union general how big the Federal army was, and Prentiss hesitated for a second, and then deciding it would do no harm, remarked that it consisted of six divisions of about seven thousand men each.[7] The conversation continued for some time. Prentiss became somewhat more unguarded in his remarks and finally let it slip that General Buell was coming. He may have said it deliberately to try and frighten the Creole, but Beauregard was seized by the thought that the Federal officer was lying.

After a lengthy conversation, the Creole turned his prisoner over to Colonels Thomas Jordan and Jacob Thompson, the latter an old pre-war friend of Prentiss. The three men made up a makeshift bed of tents and captured blankets and chatted quite amiably of their day's experiences. Just before going off to sleep, Prentiss laughingly remarked to his Southern hosts: "You gentlemen have had your way today, but it will be very different to-morrow. You'll see! Buell will effect a junction with Grant to-night, and we'll turn the tables on you in the morning."[8] The Southerners paid little attention to their prisoner's remarks, thinking he was only trying to frighten them.

General Beauregard did not believe the captured Union general because of the receipt of a dispatch from Brigadier General Ben Hardin Helm in Northern Alabama, which stated that Buell was marching toward Decatur and not toward Pittsburg Landing. Helm's message caused a dangerous feeling of over confidence to develop in the Southern leaders,[9]

---

7 New Orleans *Daily Picayune*, April 11, 1862; Mobile *Evening News,* April 14, 1862.

8 *Battles and Leaders* 1: 602.

9 Williams, *P. G. T. Beauregard*, 143. It has not been ascertained exactly when Beauregard received the Helm message. Jordan maintained that the

who felt they could leisurely take their time in destroying Grant's army Monday morning. A sense of lassitude settled over Beauregard's headquarters in Sherman's tent alongside Shiloh Church.

Generals Hardee and Breckinridge went in to see Beauregard to find out the plans for the next morning. Bragg also came in. Beauregard instructed the officers to assemble their commands for action at the earliest possible moment the next morning. There would be no effort to round up the scattered Confederate commands that night. The other officers soon drifted off, leaving Beauregard and Bragg, who climbed into Sherman's bed for some much needed sleep.[10]

At least one Confederate officer was not so sanguine about Buell's exact position. Colonel Nathan Bedford Forrest sometime before midnight sent his men to infiltrate Grant's position; they worked their way down to the Landing, where they could see fresh Federal troops disembarking from steamboats. Forrest's scouts then worked their way back to Confederate lines, carrying this vital information. The first senior officer Forrest came across was General Cleburne, whom he awakened about midnight. Forrest asked Cleburne where headquarters were, but unfortunately the general did not know.

Offering a candid appraisal of the situation, Colonel Forrest remarked to Cleburne, "If the enemy comes on us in the morning, we'll be whipped like hell."[11] Forrest left to continue his search for General Beauregard, Bragg, or someone in authority.

---

dispatch arrived late in the afternoon and was only handed to Beauregard after 6:30 p.m. *Battles and Leaders*, 1: 602, 603. Beauregard reported that the message said Buell had been delayed and could not possibly reach Grant before Tuesday at the earliest. *OR* 10, pt. 1, 385. It is possible that there were two dispatches from Helm. See Williams, *P. G. T. Beauregard*, 143. If a dispatch reached the Creole late in the afternoon, it might have helped reinforce his decision to break off the action.

10 *Battles and Leaders*, 1: 602.

11 Henry, *First With The Most Forrest*, 79; Wyeth, *That Devil Forrest*, 63; James R. Chalmers, "Forrest and His Campaigns," *Southern Historical Society Papers* 7 (October 1879): 458. || Dr. Cunningham originally stated that Forrest infiltrated enemy lines himself, but this was not the case. See Sword, *Shiloh*, 381, and Daniel, *Shiloh*, 263. We have slightly altered the text to reflect this.

Sometime around 1:00 a.m., the cavalryman located Generals Hardee and Breckinridge. He suggested to them that the army should either launch an immediate night attack or withdraw before the reinforced Federals could assault. The Third Corps commander told Forrest to go ahead and give his information to Beauregard, but somehow in the darkness Forrest missed the Shiloh Church headquarters. He dispatched scouts to go to the river to keep an eye on the Federals, and about 2:00 a.m. they reported that Federal troops were landing. Forrest located Hardee again and was directed to keep an eye on the Yanks and to maintain a strong picket line in case of a sudden Federal surprise attack.

The condition of the Confederate rank and file was grim. Probably one-fifth of the men who had marched from Corinth were dead or wounded, and thousands more were scattered all over several thousand acres of shell and bullet scarred terrain. Even many officers were lost.[12]

Major Francis A. Shoup wandered over the battlefield about 10:00 p.m., looking for someone in authority. After vainly searching through several bodies of sleeping men, Shoup came upon his good friend Cleburne, who was sitting on a tree stump drinking coffee from a bucket. The major tried to get some picture of what was going on and where everybody was. The Irishman candidly told him he did not know where Hardee or anyone else was, and that he wasn't too sure where the tree stump was. The general said he had only a few of his own men left, but that he had managed to gather a large number of stragglers from a variety of other commands.

The cold and privations of the march to Shiloh dangerously weakened many of the soldiers, but thousands of them were still able to wander around the battlefield searching for food or other forms of booty. Stragglers from the First Tennessee ate a late supper of crackers and coffee, while members of Byrnes' Kentucky Battery feasted on champagne and cheese.[13] Most of the soldiers who bothered to hunt food

12 Thomas Jordan and Roger Pryor, *The Campaigns of Lieut.-Gen. N. B. Forrest, and of Forrest's Cavalry*, 136, 137; Samuel Latta to wife, April 12, 1862, Confederate Collection, Tennessee State Library and Archives.

13 Shoup, "The Art of War," 11; Hardy Murfree to James Murfree, May 12, 1862, James B. Murfree Papers, University of Tennessee Library; Frank Peak,

managed to find something even if it were not champagne. Some of the Confederates found things to delight more than their taste buds. Various types of loot were picked up, including large quantities of shoes, clothing, and blankets.[14]

Private Jessie W. Wyatt, Company B, Twelfth Tennessee, picked up a small pocket Bible belonging to Private Samuel Lytle, Company F, Eleventh Iowa. The Iowan greatly regretted the loss, for it was a keepsake from his father; but fortunately, many years after the war, it was returned to him by C. W. Keeley, lately a private in the Seventy-third Illinois. Keeley picked off a Confederate sharpshooter near Adairsville, Georgia, on May 17, 1864. The dead man was Wyatt, and he had the Bible in his haversack. Lytle's address was still in the Bible; thus Keeley was able to return it after the war.[15]

Many of the Southerners were less interested in looting and eating than in getting a little sleep. Besides the physical exertions of the march to Shiloh and the day's horrific combat, the soldiers suffered from a lassitude, or lethargy, induced by the day's extreme tension. Thousands of the Southern soldiers eagerly headed for captured Union tents for some rest.

About midnight, it began to rain heavily, while great thunderclaps pealed through the air. Private Sam Houston, Jr., Second Texas, pulled a complete blank for the night. Wrapping himself in his blanket, he dropped down on the muddy ground. The ice cold rain drenched him through and through, although he did not notice it until he awakened the next morning.[16] Like Private Houston, Lieutenant Dent, Robertson's Battery, was unable to find a captured Union tent so he simply wrapped

---

"A Southern Soldier's View of the Civil War," 2, Frank Peak Papers, Louisiana State University Archives.

14 Phil Bond to brother, April 23, 1862, in Terry, "Record of the Alabama State Artillery," 318.

15 "A Bible Twice Captured in Battle," *Iowa Historical Record* 1 (July 1885): 132-134.

16 Sam Houston, Jr., "Shiloh Shadow," 332; Theodore Mandeville to Josephine Rozet, April 9, 1862, Theodore Mandeville Papers, Louisiana State University Archives; Richardson, "War As I Saw It," 103.

up in his blanket, stretched out in the mud beside his guns, and dozed off, cold rain or not. Fifteen year old Private Thomas Duncan, Forrest's Cavalry, spent the night sitting up with his back against a tree to keep from drowning. Private Anderson Jetton, First Tennessee, wandered around in the rain until he finally found part of his regiment sleeping in some captured Union tents. Jetton very quietly and quickly slipped into an unoccupied section of the tent, but was forced to spend the night awkwardly sprawled on his stomach, a Minie ball having passed through the back of his trousers at their tightest point. Troops from the Twenty-second Alabama slept in Union tents, but the canvas was so bullet-riddled it kept very little rain out; however, the men slept soundly in spite of it.[17]

The *Lexington* and *Tyler* fired shells in the general direction of the Confederates at the rate of one every fifteen minutes, but most of the Southern soldiers slept through the fitful bombardment.[18]

There was very little activity on the battlefield except for an occasional nervous picket's shot. Colonel Forrest's fifteen-year old son Willie and two other daring young Confederates slipped quietly across no-man's-land into Union lines, where they surprised a group of tired Federals. The three boys fired their shotguns at the Yanks and charged. A worried Colonel Forrest found out later that night that the three boys had brought in fifteen prisoners.[19]

Some enlisted men from the Eighteenth Louisiana were on picket duty so close to the Federals that they could hear the enemy talking. Tired of standing guard in the cold rain, two of the Louisianans slipped over past the Union picket post and rounded up a large quantity of pork,

17 S. H. Dent to wife, April 9, 1862, Shiloh-Corinth Collection, Alabama Department of Archives and History; Duncan, *Recollections,* 61; Hardy Murfree to J. B. Murfree, May 12, 1862, James B. Murfree Papers, University of Tennessee Library; Hugh Henry to parents, April 10, 1862, Shiloh-Corinth Collection, Alabama Department of Archives and History.

18 Abernethy *Elisha Stockwell,* 15; Frank Peak, "A Southern Soldier's View of the Civil War," Frank Peak Papers, Louisiana State University Archives; *ORN* 22: 764, 786.

19 Jordan and Pryor, *The Campaigns of Lieut.-Gen. N. B. Forrest, and of Forrest Cavalry,* 135.

potatoes, and blankets, which helped make picket duty slightly less irksome.[20]

If the rain and cold and fear were not depressing enough, the night added its own little touches of macabre horror. Two Texans filled their canteens in the darkness from what they supposed was a little spring. The water tasted a little peculiar, but they drank it anyway.

The next morning one of them started drinking from the canteen again, only to find the water reddish in color. In disgust and repugnance, he poured the bloody water on the ground.[21] Private Johnny Green went to Shiloh Branch to fill a bucket with water to make coffee early in the night. Green stepped over a log half way in the water, only upon taking a second look, he discovered it was a body of a soldier, his blood staining the water. After a few seconds of thought, Green filled his bucket anyway, and he walked on back to his regiment.[22]

As thousands of Southern soldiers went to sleep Sunday night, they had different weapons from the ones they had cradled in their arms Saturday night. All day long, as the Confederates drove the Federals back toward the Landing, these soldiers exchanged their shotguns and antiquated muskets for the Enfield, Springfield, Austrian, and Belgian rifles dropped by the dead, wounded, or fleeing Yanks.[23]

To one group of men in particular, the night offered no opportunity for rest. Confederate chaplains, Catholic and Protestant alike, went about their dreary duties of administering sacraments and offering comfort to the dying and wounded, who were scattered over the Shiloh battlefield.[24]

Across in the Union lines, conditions were probably even worse, since the Southerners had most of the Federal tents. Grant spent the first

---

20 Cesar Porta to J. B. Wilkinson, n.d., 1862, Louisiana Historical Association Collection, Howard-Tilton Memorial Library, Tulane University.

21 Sam Houston, Jr., "Shiloh Shadows," 332.

22 Kirwan, *Johnny Green*, 28, 29.

23 Henry M. Doak, "Memoirs," Confederate Collection, Tennessee State Library and Archives; *Confederate Veteran* 8 (May 1900): 211.

24 Sidney J. Romero: "Louisiana Clergy and the Confederate Army," *Louisiana History* 2 (Summer 1961): 287-291.

part of the night under a tree a few hundred yards from the river bank. His injured ankle was still aching badly, and the cold rain drenched his face and body. The general decided to limp back to the log cabin near the Landing. He reached the building in a few minutes, but found it was being used as an emergency hospital. Several doctors busily dressed wounds or sawed off arms and legs as the case called for. Wounded and delirious soldiers screamed and shrieked in their agony, while orderlies carried outside the amputated limbs. After a few minutes of this, Grant decided he preferred the rain, and he returned to the comparative sanity of his tree.[25]

Grant's soldiers were in little better shape than their commanding general. Many of his soldiers could not resist wandering off, trying to find food or hunting for word of missing relatives or friends. Orders were for the men to stay on the alert, however, and to be prepared in case of a Rebel night attack. The rainfall only added to the miseries of the hungry, unhappy Union soldiers, while gunfire from the *Lexington* and *Tyler* interrupted the sleep of many of the fellows who tried to nap in the mud.[26]

Much of the ammunition supplies that lay around at the Landing became completely watersoaked, while the many individual soldiers were hard pressed to keep their muskets and cartridges dry. The only light was from bolts of lightning, and the men who tried to move around in the darkness tripped and stumbled over broken down wagons, holes, or bodies. Wounded horses and wounded men added cries of terror and pain to the loud thunderclaps and the sharp explosions of the naval guns.[27]

The only cheering note for the Union army at Pittsburg was the arrival of massed reinforcements. Just after dark Lew Wallace's tardy division arrived along the Federal right. After the initial confusion caused by Grant's order to Wallace Sunday morning, the Third Division finally left Crump's Landing along the Shunpike Road. Wallace believed he was supposed to follow this route and move in to the battlefield at about this point, where he assumed Sherman was engaged near Shiloh Church.

25 Grant, *Memoirs*, 181.

26 Jordan and Thomas, "Reminiscences of an Ohio Volunteer," 312; Barber, *Army Memoirs* 56; Cockerill, "A Boy at Shiloh," 28, 29.

27 Throne, *Cyrus Boyd Diary*, 35.

With all of his division, except a small detachment to guard Crump's Landing, Wallace made a fairly quick march toward the battlefield. Grant apparently assumed the Third Division would come by the road nearest the river, the Hamburg and Savannah Road, instead of by the longer and more circuitous route they actually took.

When Wallace failed to arrive at the battlefield in what Grant assumed to be adequate time, he sent messengers to hurry Wallace. These aides, notably his aide de camp, thirty-eight year old Captain William Rowley, finally found Wallace on what they assumed was the wrong road. When Rowley demanded to know what the Indianan was doing, Wallace became slightly rattled and agreed to countermarch his division, using some short country roads, and link up with Grant across the Snake Creek Bridge on the Hamburg and Savannah Road. Ironically by following the Grant-Rowley urgings, Wallace did the Union army a major disservice. If Wallace had ignored Grant's urgings and continued along his original line of march, he would have struck the Confederate army on its exposed left flank. At the very least, Johnston would have been forced to divert Breckinridge's troops toward the Shiloh Church position to contain the Union Third Division. It is even possible that Wallace might have routed the Southern army.[28]

About 6:30 p.m., the advance elements of Wallace's men crossed over Snake Creek Bridge and within a few minutes joined up with the main Union army.[29] Nelson's division was already being ferried across the Tennessee, the last units crossing the river around 8:30 or 9:00 p.m. This gave Grant two fresh divisions already in position, and still more troops arriving every few minutes.

During the long Sunday, Grant apparently forgot he had troops in Savannah other than Nelson's. Around 9:00 p.m., one of Grant's staff

28 Jordan and Thomas, "Reminiscences of an Ohio Volunteer," 312. || Although Wallace made this claim in his autobiography, most historians do not agree. For more on Wallace's march, see Allen, "If He Had Less Rank," 63-89; Smith, *The Untold Story of Shiloh*, 25-27.

29 Reed, *Shiloh*, 51; *OR* 10, pt. 1, 169, 170, 175-190; W. T. Sherman to W. R. Rowley, July 15, 1881, W. R. Rowley Papers, Illinois State Historical Library; Lew Wallace to Henry Halleck, March 4, 1863, W. R. Rowley Papers, Illinois State Historical Library; Wallace, *An Autobiography,* 2: 503-603.

officers reached Savannah and ordered David Wood's Fourteenth Wisconsin Infantry to disembark at once and proceed to Pittsburg Landing. The regiment, which had been under arms all day, waiting for orders to move, was immediately drawn up in line. Colonel Wood announced to his men that he had permission to move. He then asked them if they were ready. The men shouted, "Yes," although Private Elisha Stockwell, Jr. kept his mouth shut, thinking that he would rather remain where he was. The regiment quickly boarded a steamer, reaching Pittsburg around 11:00 p.m., where the men were quickly disembarked.[30]

Where was the rest of Buell's army? The Second, Fifth, and Sixth divisions were badly strung out along the road to Savannah early Sunday morning. About eight or nine o'clock in the morning, the soldiers, privates and generals alike, were alarmed by the sounds of artillery fire in the distance. The troops were ordered to drop everything except their muskets and to increase their pace. The Fifth Division began straggling into Savannah around 8:30 p.m. or 9:00 p.m. Sunday night. By midnight or a little after, all of Brigadier General T. L. Crittenden's Fifth Division was in Savannah, either already on steamers heading for Pittsburg or waiting at the landing for an empty steamer.[31]

About midnight, Brigadier General Alexander McCook's unit started arriving in Savannah, the last troops reaching the town about 3:00 or 4:00 a.m. A sizeable traffic jam developed in downtown Savannah, as the soldiers arrived too fast for the steamers to transport them to Pittsburg. Even Grant's headquarters vessel, the *Tigress*, was pressed into the service of hauling troops and equipment; but the snarl-up in the town continued.

Some of the steamboats' captains had little enthusiasm for their jobs, probably fearing their boats would be damaged if caught under fire at the Landing. Many of the vessels brought loads of cowardly stragglers to

---

30   Edgar Houghton, "History of Company I, Fourteenth Wisconsin Infantry, from October 15, 1861 to October 9, 1865," *The Wisconsin Magazine of History* 11 (September 1927): 27; *OR* 10, pt. 1, 371; Abernethy, *Elisha Stockwell*, 14; Unidentified Union soldier of the Thirty-fourth Illinois Infantry, "Shiloh," Miscellaneous Papers, Illinois State Historical Library.

31   Charles Briant, *History of the Sixth Regiment Indiana Volunteer Infantry* (Indianapolis: W. B. Burford, 1891),101, 102; Cope, *Fifteenth Ohio* 108.

Savannah, while others arrived filled with wounded. Between the stragglers and the wounded, it proved a slow and difficult process to empty them and then reload transports at the comparatively small Savannah landing.[32]

Around midnight it started raining, then hailing. Most of the town's houses were filled with wounded, so many of the army had to lie down to sleep in the backyards, gardens, and streets. Sleeping in the mud would ordinarily have been counted as a hardship, but most of Buell's men were so tired from the hot march that day they quickly dozed off. A few of the more finicky tried to find an unoccupied porch or shed to sleep under.[33]

About 4:00 a.m., a steamer carried part of the Sixteenth U. S. Infantry Regiment to Pittsburg, and the men scrambled ashore, pushing back a crowd of stragglers who tried to force their way on the boat. Many of Buell's regiments had trouble with stragglers at the Landing, but one by one the units of the Army of the Ohio disembarked and were gradually moved into position.[34]

Buell's men had a bad time trying to find their assigned positions in the dark, for the ground seemed to be literally covered with Grant's sleeping soldiers. The new arrivals kept stepping on the sleeping beauties, causing a certain amount of bad language to be exchanged. One Indianan tripped and landed on top of a group of sleeping men. Awakened from his slumber so suddenly, one bruised and startled Federal yelled, "There is a horse lose in camp; he has just passed right over us, and I believe has broke some of my ribs."[35] Another sleeping

32 Abernethy, *Elisha, Stockwell*, 14, 15; Unidentified Union soldier of the Thirty-fourth Illinois infantry, "Shiloh," Miscellaneous Papers, Illinois State Historical Library.

33 Harry Carman, "Diary of Amos Glover," *The Ohio Archaeological and Historical Quarterly* 44 (April 1935): 265; Edwin W. Payne, *History of the Thirty-fourth Regiment of Illinois Volunteer Infantry* (Clinton: Allen Printing Company, 1903,) 16; Cope, *Fifteenth Ohio*, 108.

34 *Harper's Weekly*, April 5, 1913. || Dr. Cunningham originally listed only the "Sixteenth Regiment," which obviously is the 1st Battalion, 16th U.S. Infantry. See *OR* 10, 1: 307.

35 Briant, *Sixth Regiment Indiana*, 104.

soldier, possibly a member of the Forty-third Illinois, woke up with a man standing on his leg.[36]

Besides stumbling over Grant's sleeping men, some of the new arrivals ran into trees, banging their heads and bloodying their noses thoroughly. In the confusion and darkness, some of Grant's soldiers accidentally captured General Buell while he was trying to guide some of his troops into position.[37]

The landing of troops and artillery lasted all night and on into the morning, with the combat strength of the Union forces at Pittsburg steadily increasing. Grant and Buell do not seem to have discussed any coordinated counterattack plan, but by common consent both the Army of the Ohio and the Army of the Tennessee prepared to advance at first light of day.

None of Buell's regiments had been in a major battle before, although many participated in minor actions in Tennessee, Kentucky, and western Virginia. Troops from the Thirty-fourth Illinois had clashed with John Hunt Morgan's Confederate Raiders near Nashville in March, while the Fifteenth Ohio had fought in actions at Philippi, Laurel Hill, and Carrick's Ford, Virginia, and at Woodsonville, Kentucky.[38]

All of Buell's regiments were well trained, well equipped, and itching for a fight with the wicked "rebs." As the sun rose, those of Buell's soldiers who were already at Pittsburg munched hard tack and drank bad coffee in preparation for what was obviously going to be an exciting morning.

Only a few hundred yards away, Confederate soldiers began waking up at the order of their officers. Most of the Southerners were about to get the shock of their lives.

---

36 Briant, *Sixth Regiment Indiana*, 104; Fritz Haskell (ed.), "Diary of Colonel William Camm, 1864 to 1865," *Journal of Illinois State Historical Society* 18 (January 1926): 853.

37 Unidentified Union soldier of the Thirty-fourth Illinois Infantry, "Shiloh," Miscellaneous Papers, Illinois State Historical Library.

38 S. H. Dent to wife, April 9, 1862, Shiloh-Corinth Collection, Alabama Department of Archives and History; Thomas C. Robertson to mother, April 8, 1862, Thomas C. Robertson Papers, Louisiana State University Archives.

On Sunday afternoon, after receiving Beauregard's order to withdraw, the Confederate army pulled back an average of one-half mile. Just about every brigade in the Southern army had lost its organizational integrity during the day-long fight, and during the hours of darkness little was or could be done to patch up the various scattered units. At dawn, Monday morning, the Southern army was stretched out in a confused line running from Jones Field to the edge of the Cantrell Field. There was no particular order of battle. Rebel units would fight on Monday in about the order they camped the night before. From right to left, Beauregard's line of battle was very roughly Chalmers' Mississippians, some scattered units from the rest of Withers' Division, the Crescent Regiment, Maney's First Tennessee, the remnants of Stewart's Brigade, reinforced by Bate's Second Tennessee and Tappan's Thirteenth Arkansas, Cleburne, with fragments of three of his regiments and a large number of stragglers from other commands, Statham's Brigade, Trabue's command, Anderson's command, Gibson's Brigade (which was in comparatively good shape), Wood's and fragments of Russell's Brigade, and Pond's Louisianans on the extreme Confederate left.

Partly by accident and partly by design, Grant's army took over the right third of the battlefield, with Buell's army assuming the responsibility of the center and left. Lew Wallace's fresh division occupied Grant's extreme right. Sherman, with fragments of his division, was to Wallace's left. McClernand had perhaps forty percent of his April 5 effectives in position on Sherman's left, while Hurlbut's division held the left of the Army of the Tennessee. The Fourth Division was probably in the best shape of those participating in Sunday's fighting. Prentiss' and W. H. L. Wallace's units simply no longer existed, except as scattered fragments attached to units of other divisions, including some in Buell's army. Many of Grant's other regiments were so badly battered that they could not be deployed in the battle line and were held in what was euphemistically called the reserve.[39] Nelson's division, which was the first to land at Pittsburg, held the extreme Union left, while the rest of

---

39 Throne, *Cyrus Boyd Diary*, 36; Ruff, "Civil War Experiences of A German Emigrant," 298; Jordan, "Campaign and Battle of Shiloh," 405; Houston, "Shiloh Shadows," 332, 333.

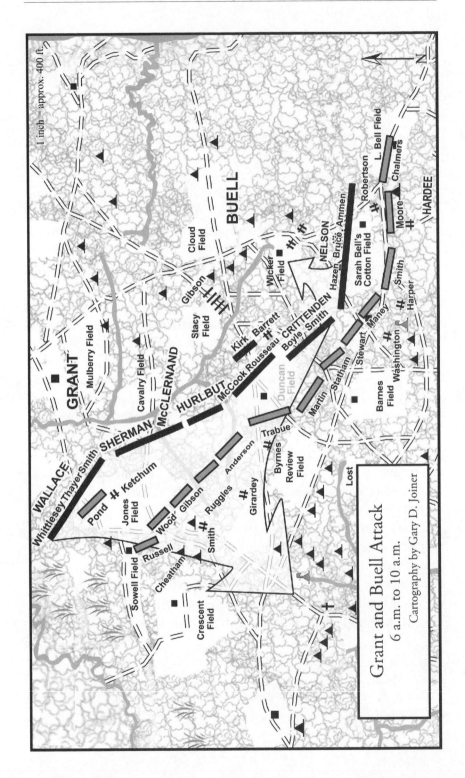

1 inch = approx. 400 ft.

N

BUELL

L. Bell Field

Robertson

Chalmers

Moore

HARDEE

Hazen Bruce Ammen

NELSON

Smith

Sarah Bell's Cotton Field

Harper

Cloud Field

Wicker Field

Washington

Maney

Stewart

Gibson

Stacy Field

Kirk   Barrett

McCook Rousseau

CRITTENDEN

Boyle Smith

Statham

Barnes Field

GRANT

Mulberry Field

Cavalry Field

McCLERNAND

HURLBUT

Duncan Field

Martin

Lost

SHERMAN

Trabue

Byrnes

Review Field

WALLACE

Whittlesey Thayer Smith

Ketchum

Pond

Jones Field

Wood Gibson

Ruggles

Anderson

Girardey

Smith

Russell

Sowell Field

Cheatham

Crescent Field

Grant and Buell Attack

6 a.m. to 10 a.m.

Cartography by Gary D. Joiner

Buell's troops were deployed in roughly the same order of disembarkation. Crittenden's division was on Nelson's right, while McCook's division was gradually deployed on Crittenden's right, as it reached the front.

The giant Nelson, a black plume in his hat, aroused his three brigades well before daylight Monday morning. About 3:00 a.m, he waded through the mud and drizzle to reach Colonel Ammen's command post at the foot of a large tree. "Colonel Ammens," Nelson thundered, "you will put the Tenth in motion, as soon as you can see to move at dawn; find the enemy and whip him." Wheeling his magnificent, if somewhat bedraggled, black horse about, Nelson headed for his Nineteenth Brigade to give the same message to Colonel William Hazen.[40]

Ammen's soldiers washed down their breakfast crackers with long gulps of Tennessee River water before falling into line. Two companies from each of the brigade's three regiments were ordered forward as skirmishers, to develop the enemy's position.[41] Meanwhile Hazen and Bruce, Nelson's two remaining brigade commanders, received word of the coming advance and were busy forming their regiments into line.

Nelson dispatched an aide to go tell General Buell that the Fourth Division was ready to go. Just as the sun came up, Buell directed Nelson to start his advance. With Ammen's Tenth Brigade on the left, Hazen's Nineteenth Brigade on the right, and Bruce's Twenty-second Brigade in the middle, the division moved forward into Dill Branch.

Slipping and sliding on the wet grass and gingerly stepping around an occasional bloated corpse, Nelson's Bluecoats crossed Dill Branch and cautiously ascended the opposite ridge. Most of the men were thoroughly soaked from the night's deluge, while their breakfast was scarcely filling; but their minds hardly noticed their bodies' discomforts. The only thing on the soldiers' minds was: where were the Rebels? At least their percussion rifles would work, despite the dampness.

Mounted on "Old Bob," Colonel Ammen rode ahead of the brigade, disregarding the spray of water when he bumped stray bushes and limbs. From a few hundred yards in front, the soldiers could hear occasional

40   Jacob Ammen Diary, April 7, 1862, Illinois State Historical Library.

41   Hannaford, *The Story of A Regiment*, 571, 572.

bursts of firing as the skirmishers encountered Breckinridge's pickets. The sun was out and started almost immediately drying out the soldiers' clothing, but it did little good as the troopers stumbled into the still wet bushes.[42]

To the right and slightly behind the Fourth Division, the Second Division advanced along and parallel to the Corinth-Pittsburg Road.[43] Pressing onward, the Fourth Division crossed a number of deep ravines, passing several of their skirmishers lying dead or wounded from Confederate picket fire. Their feet soaking wet from wading through ankle deep mud, the division passed through Brigadier General J. G. Lauman's looted brigade camp and then crossed Cloud Field.

As Hazen's brigade marched a few hundred yards farther in its approach toward Wicker Field, Confederate artillery opened fire upon it, the 10-pound and 12-pound projectiles sprinkling the Federals and spreading some discomfort in the ranks. Buell sent an aide to order Nelson to halt and reconnoiter the position. At the same time Buell directed Crittenden to move up and support Nelson's right flank.[44]

Colonel Ammen rode up and down the line to reassure his men, casually telling them, "Now, boys, keep cool; give'em the best you've got!"[45] Nelson's and Crittenden's divisions soon resumed the advance, pushing back the Southern skirmishers toward their artillery support. Within a few minutes, the two divisions reached the area which Prentiss, Wallace, and Hurlbut had defended so gallantly the day before. The Peach Orchard was directly in front of Nelson's division, while Crittenden's right flank overlapped in front of the Hornet's Nest. In this badly torn up region, the Federals found the Confederates in strength.[46]

Just beyond the Peach Orchard Field, the Rebels were deployed. Captain Felix Robertson's Florida Battery, with its four Napoleon guns, was deployed at the southeast edge of the Peach Orchard. At the east end

42 *OR* 10, pt. 1, 293, 340, 348; Hannaford, *The Story of A Regiment*, 571.

43 *Battles and Leaders*, 1: 525; *OR* 10, pt. 1, 293, 355.

44 *OR* 10, pt. 1, 324, 340, 341; Hannaford, *The Story of A Regiment*, 263, 572.

45 Hannaford, *The Story of A Regiment*, 572.

46 *OR* 10, pt. 1, 293, 355.

of the Wheat Field, about a quarter mile west of what came to be known as the "Bloody Pond," was Captain Irving Hodgson's Fifth Company of the Washington Artillery, with its two 6-pound smoothbores and two 12-pound howitzers. From this vantage point, the Louisianans could sweep Crittenden's left, as well as Nelson's right regiments.[47]

Both Confederate batteries discharged an accurate, steady fire into Nelson's right regiments, sending them reeling back in disorder. The Fourth Division left its batteries at Savannah for lack of transport, so Nelson had no effective means of countering the deadly fire. In desperation, he sent word to Buell for help. In response, the major general sent Batteries H and M of the Fourth United States Artillery, consisting of two 12-pound howitzers and two 3-inch Rodman rifles under Captain John Mendenhall. The guns and caissons careened wildly as the cannoneers raced up the Hamburg-Savannah Road to assist Nelson.

Mendenhall's gunners quickly unlimbered their pieces along the southern edge of the Wicker Field, firing round after round of shrapnel and shell at the Confederate pieces. Suddenly another Rebel battery, possibly McClung's, opened fire on Mendenhall from a distant clump of woods. The Union gunners quickly shifted their guns around to meet their new foe, and a half hour fire fight ensued.[48]

Taking advantage of the Confederate gunners' distraction, skirmishers from Colonel Gideon Moody's Ninth Indiana and Colonel Walter Whitaker's Sixth Kentucky, both of Hazen's brigade, worked their way up close enough to pepper the Rebel gunners with rifle fire. The Confederates abandoned several of their tubes, but before Hazen's men could spike or carry them off, Southern infantry attacked and sent the

47 *Ibid.*, 293, 294; Atwell Thompson Map of Shiloh; S. H. Dent to wife, April 9, 1862, Shiloh-Corinth Collection, Alabama Department of Archives and History; Washington Artillery Order Book, Louisiana Historical Association Collection, Howard-Tilton Memorial Library, Tulane University. S. H. Dent to wife, April 9, 1862, Shiloh-Corinth Collection, Alabama Department of Archives and History; *OR* 10, pt. 1, 293, 324, 373; Hazen, *A Narrative of Military Service*, 25-27.

48 S. H. Dent to wife, April 9, 1862, Shiloh-Corinth Collection, Alabama Department of Archives and History; *OR* 10, pt. 1, 293, 324, 373; Hazen, *A Narrative of Military Service*, 25-27.

Federals running back to the main force. Hazen ordered Moody to take his remaining companies and support the retreating skirmishers. The Indianans moved forward a short distance until they came to a rail fence near a cabin. Taking cover behind posts, the Indiana soldiers engaged in a fierce exchange of musketry with troops from Cleburne's and Stewart's commands.

Bate's Second Tennessee and Tappan's Thirteenth Arkansas moved up and began a heavy fire into the Hoosiers and the rest of Hazen's brigade. Some of the Second Tennessee took cover behind a large fallen tree, while much of the regiment drew some protection from a slight rise in the ground. The Tennesseans possessed a beautiful flag, presented to them by Miss Matilda Cheney of Galatin County, a relative of Captain Joe Tyree. Corporal Andrew Island rested the flag against a tree while he did some shooting, and Hazen's sharpshooting country boys promptly riddled it. Indeed, standing or crawling near the flag proved an excellent way to get shot. One Federal Minie ball shattered the stock of Private W. E. Yeatman's prized Springfield rifle, although he escaped unhurt. After thirty or forty minutes of steady firing, the Hoosiers ran short of cartridges and Moody ordered them to fall back a few yards and take shelter while more ammunition was brought up.[49]

While the Indianans had their show going, Colonel Walter C. Whitaker and his Sixth Kentucky engaged the Confederate infantry and artillery in the woods north of the Peach Orchard. The Southerners were apparently trying to penetrate a gap between Crittenden's division and Nelson's right flank, but their plan was thwarted by Hazen's quick perception of the situation and his transfer of infantry over to the gap.[50]

Mendenhall was having his problems with the Southerners. His regular army gunners silenced a force of Confederate artillery, firing on them from the front; but other Southern guns opened up on the Federal battery's right flank. The Rebels had the range, and the Yankee captain was forced to suddenly disperse his tubes to avoid having them

49 *OR* 10, pt. 1, 294, 324, 325, 341, 342, 348, 349; Hazen, *A Narrative of Military Service*, 26; W. E. Yeatman, "Memoirs,' Confederate Collection, Tennessee State Library and Archives.

50 *OR* 10, pt. 1, 341, 344; Hazen, *A Narrative of Military Service*, 26.

overwhelmed. For perhaps an hour, the regulars and the Confederates traded rounds with indecisive effect. Then soon a new trouble broke out, and Mendenhall was forced to abandon his duel in order to proceed pounding a Rebel infantry assault.

Just to the west of Wicker Field Confederate infantry assaulted Hazen's brigade. Three companies of the Sixth Kentucky were posted to support the guns while the rest of the Sixth Kentucky, the Ninth Indiana, and the Forty-first Ohio were posted to its right. The regular army gunners poured in round after round of case shot at the Southerners, finally shifting to canister as the Confederates closed in. Hazen's riflemen discharged a heavy shower of Minie balls at the Rebels, who promptly halted and began firing.

Fearing the Southerners might overwhelm the battery, Hazen ordered his drummers to sound the charge. As the drums beat out the harsh staccato of the charge, his soldiers fixed bayonets and surged forward. The Rebels were forced back, losing several pieces of artillery. After advancing six or seven hundred yards, the attack was finally stalled, as the Southerners made a stand and Hazen was reluctantly forced to order his brigade to fall back to its original position.[51]

While Hazen was busy with his part of the battle, sharp fighting flared to the left of the Hamburg-Savannah Road. Cautiously advancing to avoid walking into an ambush, Ammen's soggy soldiers traded shots with retreating Confederate pickets. The men were wet but cheerful, and eager to engage the Rebels. As they moved forward, the men cast cautious glances at the right, in the direction of the heavy fire from Hazen's engaged brigade. When Mendenhall's tubes let go their first round, the Tenth Brigade enthusiastically cheered. The line of advance was fairly uneven, as the soldiers carefully stepped around the hundreds of dead and wounded soldiers sprawled all around on the ground. Dying men screamed, "Oh God, have mercy! Oh God! Oh God!"[52]

Finally, as the brigade neared the so-called "Bloody Pond," the men were brought under heavy fire from two Confederate batteries, one to their right, west of the famous Peach Orchard, and the other, Robertson's

51 *OR* 10, pt. 1, 314, 342-348, 373.

52 *OR* 10, pt. 1, 335; Hannaford, *The Story of A Regiment*, 265, 573.

Florida Battery, directly in front of the brigade. As the Rebel projectiles began slicing the Federal ranks, the Northern infantry was ordered to lie down on the ground while skirmishers were deployed forward to scout the ground for Confederates.[53]

Trying to dislodge two enemy batteries without artillery support was apt to be a nasty business, so Colonel Ammen called a halt to proceedings until some Federal artillery could come up. Fortunately it was not long before Captain William R. Terrill reported to General Nelson with his Battery H, 5th United States Light Artillery, with two 10-pound rifles and four 12-pound Napoleons. Nelson decided to break up the battery in order to afford at least some protection to his entire division. Lieutenant Francis Grunther's two gun section was dispatched to the right to support Hazen, while the other two sections, West Point trained Lieutenant Jacob Smyser's and Lieutenant Israel Ludlow's, were sent to the aid of Ammen.[54]

Terrill went riding up the Hamburg-Savannah Road, and with a quick sweep of his eyes took in the situation. His gun crews galloped up with their four Napoleons, and were soon in position and enthusiastically firing away.[55] After firing a few rounds from his first position, Terrill advanced his four tubes to the edge of the Peach Orchard, where he warmly engaged Robertson's Battery. The Southerners were temporarily silenced, but they immediately bounced back, for Robertson's orders were to hold his position "at all cost."[56]

Terrill was soon too busy to bother with the Florida Rebels, for Southern infantry was attacking. Screaming like berserkers, Confederate infantry swarmed in, dead ahead at Terrill's Battery. In the face of the onslaught the Federal battery was withdrawn several hundred yards to a new position, from which it reopened fire at the advancing Rebels. Three times the Southerners charged the battery in its new position, only to be

---

53 Hannaford, *The Story of A Regiment*, 573; *OR* 10, pt. 1, 335-340.

54 *OR* 10, pt. 1, 321, 325.

55 Hannaford, *The Story of A Regiment*, 574.

56 *OR* 10, pt. 1, 322; S. H. Dent to wife, April 9, 1562, Shiloh-Corinth Collection, Alabama Department of Archives and History.

stopped with heavy bursts of canister and rifle fire from the supporting Union infantry. Terrill's gunners began dropping right and left. Wounded battery horses screamed in pain as Rebel bullets tore their bodies. Several members of the Twenty-fourth Ohio ran over to assist the beleaguered Napoleon gun crews. Finally the Southerners charged a fourth time, but Colonel Ammen's right wing stood firm.

The Confederates had suffered enough. Terrill's gunners continued hammering as the Southerners suddenly retired. Ammen rode over to talk to Terrill, and to also borrow some binoculars. The Union gunners let go a round from one of the tubes, and the brigade commander's horse, "Old Bob," took fright and stampeded away from the battery in the direction of the Confederate infantry. Ammen was finally able to get his mount under control, or the Union army might well have lost the services of a tolerably good brigade commander.[57]

Confederate infantry also hit Ammen's left wing, but his sturdy Midwesterners held their ground. Generals Nelson and Buell rode by to investigate the situation and expressed their admiration at the cool way the Federal infantry drove back the Rebels. Finally, Nelson's division shifted over to the offensive and successfully stormed the Peach Orchard. The Confederate extreme right was badly mauled and dangerously weakened by the Monday morning action.[58]

The Southerners were still in good spirits and exhibited determined aggressiveness, but they were rapidly being overwhelmed and outfought by the ever increasing numbers of Federal reinforcements.

57 *OR* 10, pt. 1, 301, 321, 322; Hannaford, *The Story of A Regiment*, 572.

58 *OR* 10, pt. 1, 335-340, 342, 353.

Chapter 15

Victory?

BY 8:30 A.M., THERE was sharp skirmishing all across Shiloh field, although the heaviest fighting was on the Union left where Nelson was engaged. Gradually General Crittenden's Fifth Division developed Breckinridge's battle line, and by 9 or 9:30 a.m., heavy fighting raged along the area defended by Prentiss and W. H. L. Wallace the day before.[1]

The guns of the Washington Artillery, which had plagued Nelson's right wing, shifted around to bear on Crittenden's advance elements. The Kentucky Unionist chose to attack with his Fourteenth Brigade, commanded by Colonel William Sooy Smith, a thirty-one year old West Point-trained Ohioan. Smith had the Thirteenth Ohio, Lieutenant Colonel Joseph Hawkins, on the left, the Twenty-sixth Kentucky on the right, Lieutenant Colonel Cicero Maxwell, and the Eleventh Kentucky, Colonel Pierce Hawkins, in reserve. The Fourteenth Wisconsin, Colonel

---

1 || Lew Wallace supporters will find fault with Dr. Cunningham's original statement that only the Army of the Ohio was engaged heavily by 8:30 a.m. Wallace began his move by 6:00 a.m., but had to cross Tilghman Branch before he began to fight in earnest. Reports from Wallace's division state the men began moving out around 6:00-6:30 a.m. See *OR* 10, pt. 1, 170, 190-191, 193, 197; Shiloh Battlefield Commission Tablets #292, 126, 293, and 294. Buell's forces were operating within a similar time frame on the other side of the battlefield, where they had to contend with Dill Branch. They were not heavily engaged until 7:30-8:00 a.m. See *OR* 10, pt. 1, 324; Shiloh Battlefield Commission Tablet # 275, Shiloh Battlefield Commission Monuments # 78, 89, and 126. Smith, *This Great Battlefield of Shiloh*, 86.

David Wood, was attached to the brigade, and it fought to the right of the Twenty-sixth.

The brigade boldly pushed back some small parties of Southern skirmishers, but was gradually brought to a halt by accurate fire from the Washington Artillery and by a sharp attack from Breckinridge's somewhat jaded infantry. Smith's infantrymen, however, stood firm, raking the Confederates with a heavy and accurate artillery fire. Captain Joseph Bartlett supported the embattled brigade with his Battery G, First Ohio Light Artillery, which consisted of four 6-pound guns and two 12-pound Wiard rifles.

Union gunners fired the first of the six hundred rounds they would expend that day. Raked and torn by the heavy Federal fire, Statham ordered his Mississippians and Tennesseans to fall back. A second charge was ordered, and again Statham's Brigade broke on the rock-like Fourteenth Brigade. The Confederates were finally persuaded of the futility of driving the Yanks from their position, and began to fall back to establish a new line.[2]

Now it was the Federals' turn to go over to the offensive. In concert with Hazen, Smith led his regiments forward, the men walking slowly but steadily across the battlefield. The Louisiana gunners poured some fifty rounds into the advancing enemy line, the iron fragments tearing large gaps in it. Captain L. D. McClung brought up two of his four pieces to back up the Louisianans, and the crews of these weapons joined in the barrage.

The Kentuckians, Wisconsians, and Ohioans halted several times to deliver crushing volleys of rifle fire into the Confederate gun position. Part of the Crescent Louisiana Regiment was deployed around and in support of the Southern field pieces. The Louisianians emptied their muskets at Sooy Smith's men, but with little effect. Disregarding heavy casualties, the Federals simply kept on coming. The gunners began dropping like flies, while more than a dozen of the precious horses also went down. A few of the gunners abandoned their pieces and fled, but

---

2 *OR* 10, pt. 1, 355, 366; Washington Artillery Order Book, 48; Louisiana Historical Association Collection, Howard-Tilton Memorial Library, Tulane University; Henry Melville, "Memoirs," Confederate Collection, Tennessee State Library and Archives.

most of them stayed and fought, discharging loads of canister at twenty yards' range.[3]

The supporting infantry, badly torn up by the rifle fire, started falling back. Lieutenant John Dimitry and Captain William Graham, Company C, did not hear the order to retreat and kept on discharging their pistols at Smith's men. A Union soldier shot Graham in the chest with a rifle slug, but Dimitry grabbed him and tried to carry him away. Another slug hit the captain, and Dimitry was forced to abandon the body. As the young lieutenant turned to follow his men, he was shot through his right leg, but managed to escape in the confusion.[4]

The Federals swarmed into the artillery position, seizing McClung's guns and at least one Louisianan. Before the Northerners could overrun the other five, Colonel Marshall J. Smith counterattacked with the rest of the Crescent Regiment. Bartlett's Ohio gunners chopped the Louisianans up as they rushed Sooy Smith's men, but resolutely the Southerners continued, not faltering. They smashed pell-mell into the enemy brigade. The Federals abandoned their pieces and fell back about a hundred yards. Union officers quickly rallied their men and tried to charge the battery again. Just then the First Missouri Confederate Regiment came up in support of Marshall Smith's hard pressed men. After a vicious exchange of musket fire, lasting for several minutes, the Unionists fell back, and the Washington Artillery, along with McClung's guns, were saved.

The Mississippians pressed the retreating Federal soldiers, routing out stragglers from behind trees, bushes, and from small gullies. Gage's and Girardy's batteries moved up in support and opened fire on the retreating Yanks. Unfortunately, their first rounds were short and landed in the ranks of the First Missouri, killing and wounding many. The Missourians were upset by the unexpected hazard, but Corporal John O'Neil, Company D, relieved the tension and raised a great big laugh by yelling to the soldiers, "Yesterday mornin' you were afeared you would

3 *Ibid.*; Washington Artillery Order Book, Louisiana Historical Association Collection, Howard-Tilton Memorial Library, Tulane University; John Dimitry to William Bullitt, n.d., John Dimitry Papers, Louisiana State University Archives; *OR* 10, pt. 1, 513-515.

4 "John Dimitry," *Confederate Veteran* 11 (February 1903): 72.

niver git into this battle, and I'm dammed if I ain't afeared we will niver git out of it! Faith, there's no dress parade about this situation."[5]

The Southern attack was soon contained, and General Crittenden unleashed his reserve Eleventh Brigade. The Confederates felt the pressure of Crittenden's division keenly, for about 10:00 a.m., Statham's and Bowen's regiments were pulled from the right and sent over to bolster the Confederate left around Shiloh Church.[6]

The badly mixed Rebel forces aggressively fought the Federals, but were gradually forced to yield ground, won at such a price the day before. At one point, a Confederate captain commanded personnel from the Fourth, Twenty-second, and Thirteenth Tennessee. Stumbling over the muddy ground and tripping through briar patches, the Tennessee command manfully helped oppose Crittenden's advance.

One young Tennessean, wandering to the rear to get a wounded left hand dressed, ended up in a Union aid station. A doctor cleaned and dressed the Rebel's wound and gave him a shot of brandy. Private Henry Doak, who had studied violin for years, naively asked the doctor if he would be able to play again. The doctor, who had no desire to see such an amiable young man rot in a prison, replied, "Young man, you will never play the fiddle again. If you don't leave and get to Corinth, the chances are you will never play your part in life; you will be very ill— your state of health low—and you're going to suffer very much. Now, go."[7]

5   *OR* 10, pt. 1, 524; Theodore Mandeville to Josephine Rozet April 9, 1862, Theodore Mandeville Papers, Louisiana State University Archives; John Dimitry to William Bullitt, John Dimitry Papers, Louisiana State University Archives; A. Gordan Blakewell, "Fifth Washington Artillery," Louisiana Historical Association Collection, Howard-Tilton Memorial Library, Tulane University; Joseph Boyce, "Second Day's Battle," Louisiana Historical Association Collection, Howard-Tilton Memorial Library, Tulane University.

6   Samuel Latta to wife, April 12, 1862, Confederate Collection, Tennessee State Library and Archives; Theodore Mandeville to Josephine Rozet, April 12, 1862, Theodore Mandeville Papers, Louisiana State University Archives; Worsham, *The Old Nineteenth Tennessee, C. S. A.*, 43.

7   Theodore Mandeville to Josephine Rozet, April 9, 1862, Theodore Mandeville Papers, Louisiana State University Archives; Henry M. Doak, "Memoirs," Confederate Collection, Tennessee State Library and Archives.

Confederate organization continued to break down on the right, and the Southerners were forced to gradually give ground. At one point, Colonel Marshall Smith picked up the Crescent Regiment's flag and led a reckless bayonet charge, halting for a little while the Federal advance. The Washington Artillery was so badly battered that it had to be withdrawn from the field, leaving behind six men and thirty horses dead. All twenty of the battery's wounded were carried off successfully.[8]

By noon, Crittenden's men had taken the Hornet's Nest and Duncan Field, and were preparing to move toward Barnes' Field. Without fresh reserves, the Confederates were simply unable to withstand their numerically superior enemy.

McCook's Second Division went into action much later than Nelson's and Crittenden's units, due to its late arrival from Savannah. It was about 12:00 p.m., when General Alexander McCook led his three brigades under fire. McCook immediately launched his Fourth Brigade under General Lovell Rousseau at Colonel Trabue's Confederate brigade. For more than an hour, these two units slashed and pounded at each other, while the rest of the Second Division moved up into position. Rousseau was supported by Captain George Stone's Battery K, First Missouri, while Trabue was backed up by Byrne's Kentucky Battery. There was little in the way of wild charging, the men on both sides preferring a less spectacular and less strenuous long-range fire fight.[9]

Solid shot and shells passed freely over the heads of the contending infantry as Stone's and Byrne's batteries fought it out. Finally after more than an hour, the Union guns were silenced, probably from a shortage of ammunition. The Southern gunners then depressed their sights and began harassing McCook's infantry. Some of the fire was quite accurate, while Confederate sharpshooters also took a goodly number of casualties in

---

8 Samuel Latta to wife, April 12, 1862, Confederate Collection, Tennessee State Library and Archives; Theodore Mandeville to Josephine Rozet, April 9, 1862, Theodore Mandeville Papers, Louisiana State University Archives; Order Book, Washington Artillery, Louisiana Historical Association Collection, Howard-Tilton Memorial Library, Tulane University.

9 Carman, "Diary of Amos Glover," 266; Reed, *Shiloh*, 65; *OR* 10, pt. 1, 303; Kirwan, *Johnny Green*, 30; Robert Barry, "A Soldier's Letter from Shiloh," in *Harper's Weekly* 57 (April 5, 1913): 9.

Rousseau's inexperienced brigade. Suddenly one company of regulars, belonging to the First Battalion, Sixteenth U. S. Infantry, Captain Edwin Townsend, broke and headed for the rear, seized by one of those curious panics that sometimes hit experienced troops. Federal officers quickly rallied the men, one officer striking at them with his sword blade and pistol barrel. With cries of "get back to your places, back or die," and "back, back! Meet your fate like men, not cowards!" the regulars were finally driven back to their places in line.[10]

Several times the Southerners did advance, once trying to seize Stone's Battery, but Rousseau's brigade held. The Fourth Brigade ran short of ammunition, but did manage to advance to the Wolfe Field when part of Trabue's Brigade was shunted off to another part of the battlefield. The Federals captured a couple of pieces of artillery, taken by the Southerners the day before, but they failed to score any kind of decisive kill, and the Confederates, including Byrne's Battery, were easily able to regroup.[11]

His supply of cartridges finally exhausted, Rousseau pulled back, and McCook sent in his newly arrived Fifth Brigade under Colonel Edward N. Kirk. Its order of battle from left to right was Colonel Frederick Stumbaugh, Seventy-seventh Pennsylvania, the only Eastern regiment serving with either Grant or Buell, the Thirty-fourth Illinois, Major Charles Levanway, Thirtieth Indiana, Colonel Sion Bass, and the Twenty-ninth Indiana, Lieutenant Colonel David Dunn.

From its second position of the day, Byrne's Battery gave Kirk's brigade its baptism of fire, sprinkling it with 6- and 12-pound rounds. Some of the shots were a little high and passed through the trees overhead of the brigade, but many struck home. As the Confederates zeroed in on the Thirty-fourth Illinois' flag, an officer finally told the color bearer to "lower the flag. They can see it and have our range." It was a little late, for just then a shell burst in the midst of the Illinois men. Corporal Charles

---

10 Frank Peak, "A Southern Soldier's View of the War," 23, Frank Peak Papers, Louisiana State University Archives; Barry, "A Soldier's Letter from Shiloh," April 5, 1913, in *Harper's Weekly* 57 (April 5, 1913): 9.

11 Briant, *Sixth Regiment Indiana*, 108, 109; *OR* 10, pt. 1, 309; Kirwan, *Johnny Green* 305; Frank Peak, "A Southern Soldier's View of the War," 23, Frank Peak Papers, Louisiana State University Archives.

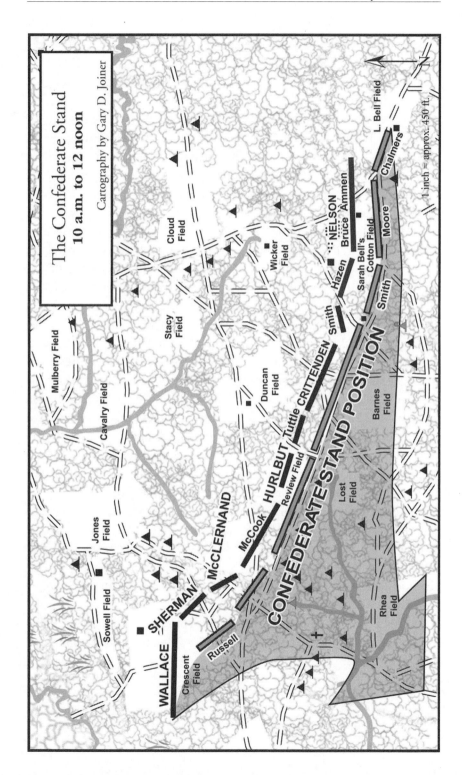

The Confederate Stand
10 a.m. to 12 noon

Cartography by Gary D. Joiner

1 inch = approx. 450 ft.

L. Bell Field

Chalmers

NELSON
Bruce Ammen

Moore

Hazen

Sarah Bell's
Cotton Field

Smith

Cloud
Field

Smith

Wicker
Field

CONFEDERATE STAND POSITION

Tuttle
CRITTENDEN

Stacy
Field

Barnes
Field

Duncan
Field

HURLBUT

Mulberry Field

Review Field

Lost
Field

Cavalry Field

McCook

McCLERNAND

Rhea
Field

Jones
Field

SHERMAN

Russell

Sowell Field

WALLACE

Crescent
Field

Haines was tossed twenty or thirty feet and was considerably cut up, but the officer who had just spoken lay on the ground, both legs shattered. Several other members of the Thirty-fourth were also struck down by the same projectile.[12]

The Seventy-seventh Pennsylvania successfully tangled with the Twentieth Tennessee, capturing its colonel, Joel Battle. Amidst heavy firing, Kirk's men kept up a somewhat jerky advance, driving in the direction of the Water Oaks Pond. Rousseau managed to obtain more cartridges for his men and soon rejoined the advance, helping push back the miscellaneous collection of Rebel units.[13]

About 1:30 or 2:00 p.m., McCook sent in his last brigade, Gibson's Sixth. Confederate sharpshooters peppered the brigade as it moved up, killing or wounding many soldiers. Gibson deployed three of his regiments, the Forty-ninth Ohio, Lieutenant Colonel Albert Blackman, Fifteenth Ohio, Major William Wallace, and the Thirty-ninth Indiana, Colonel Thomas Harrison, on the left flank of McCook. Confederate artillery suddenly opened up on the Fifteenth Ohio as it deployed, bursting a shell in the regimental line and badly mauling Companies H and E. A Corporal Deniston, Company K, had a foot smashed by the explosion. He jumped around the battlefield on his undamaged foot, screaming in extreme agony, before stretcher bearers finally managed to carry him to the rear. A Corporal Campbell, Company E, was terribly mangled by the explosion. Knowing he could not live, he begged his friends to shoot him and end his agony, but no one was willing. The Fifteenth Ohio was soon forced to take cover on the ground.

The terrain was uneven and covered with trees and undergrowth. As the Ohioans fired their heavy .69 caliber muskets, the haze from the smoke added to the other unfavorable conditions and made visibility impossible. Most of the Union soldiers simply fired blindly in the direction of the enemy or at muzzle flashes as the wind sometimes wafted the smoke away.

Gibson had one other regiment, the Thirty-second Indiana, under Colonel August Willich, an ardent communist and revolutionary and one

---

12 Payne, *History of the Thirty-fourth Illinois*, 342, 343.

13 Reed, *Shiloh*, 65, 66.

of the most experienced soldiers in the entire United States Army. As the Thirty-second moved up, McCook detached Willich and his German-Americans to strengthen Rousseau's left wing. The regiment advanced at the double-quick and executed a well disciplined bayonet charge against a party of Confederates threatening Rousseau. The German-Americans were hit by withering blasts of musketry and canister from their enemy's guns, but they forced the Southerners to fall back.[14]

In this attack, thirty-one year old John Leonhard Huber, Company D, lost his life. He had been in America only eight months, having arrived from Germany in August 1861. Unable to find work in Lawrenceburg, Indiana, he decided to join some old friends from Germany who had already enlisted in the army with Willich. He "went cheerfully into battle, but unfortunately had to sacrifice his life."[15]

In the face of repeated Confederate counterattacks, McCook still managed to gain ground, but neither he nor any other unit of Buell's army was able to achieve a break through. The Federals were making the same mistake their enemy had committed the day before in not concentrating their forces on one sector of the battlefield and overwhelming the Southern line. Instead, Federal strength was spread along the three-mile front, and hence lost a good deal of its potency.

While Buell's army hammered at the Rebel right and center, Grant attacked on the Confederate left. Elements of Lew Wallace's, Sherman's, McClernand's, and Hurlbut's divisions, plus a few bits and pieces of W. H. L. Wallace's and Prentiss' defunct organizations, assaulted the Confederate left, the commands of Generals Ruggles and Cheatham.[16]

14 Cope, *Fifteenth Ohio*, 124, 125; *OR* 10, pt. 1, 303, 317.

15 John Leonhard Huber to his sister, February 8, 1862, Miscellaneous Collection, Shiloh National Military Park; Gottlib Probst to Mr. and Mrs. Schneider, August 20, 1862, Miscellaneous Collection, Shiloh National Military Park.

16 *OR* 10, pt. 1, 120, 125, 127, 135, 159, 205, 206, 251, 252; Jordan and Thomas, "Reminiscences of an Ohio Volunteer," 312; Franklin H. Bailey to parents, April 8, 1862, Franklin H. Bailey Papers, Michigan Historical Collection, University of Michigan.

It was 9:00 or 9:30 in the morning before Grant's weary troops were able to seriously engage the even more weary enemy. If the Southerners were tired, they were still filled with fighting spirit, for Grant's soldiers soon found themselves under heavy attack. The fighting rocked back and forth for perhaps an hour, with neither side able to score decisively.

About 10 a.m., General Ruggles ordered Randall Gibson's Brigade to attack. Lacking the Nineteenth Louisiana, which had become separated the night before, Gibson nevertheless struck with a great deal of force. The attack was somewhat bogged down because of the muddy ground over which the brigade had to pass, but Beauregard seized a battle flag and galloped out in front of the men and urged them to advance again. The Louisianans' and Arkansans' martial spirits were raised by Beauregard's example, and they swarmed into the Union position. A Federal battery was overrun and captured, and a number of prisoners ware taken. Some of the Northern infantry rallied in an oak grove and hit the Thirteenth Louisiana with rifle fire. Several Southerners went down, but the Louisianans quickly rushed the new Union position, causing the Federals to break. One Union soldier stepped out from behind a tree to surrender, but the Confederates' battle blood was up. The Southern soldiers raked the Yank with musket balls, although several Rebel officers ordered their men to hold their fire.

The fight rocked back and forth in seesaw fashion as first the Southerners and then the Federals would rally and counterattack. Major Avegno was badly wounded, but his men kept on firing. Finally the Thirteenth Louisiana and First Arkansas were forced to fall back to near Shiloh Church.[17] The Fourth Louisiana assaulted a second Union battery and was badly cut up and finally driven to take cover in a deep ravine about one-fourth of a mile from Shiloh Church.[18]

Even as Gibson's men were finally repulsed, heavy fighting raged on the extreme Confederate left, or Union right, as Lew Wallace's Third Division finally went into battle, a day late but certainly no less willing. Confederate forces in front of Wallace's unit were comparatively weak, consisting of parts of Pond's Brigade, fragments of a couple of Tennessee

17 *OR* 10, pt. 1, 480, 481; Richardson, "War As I Saw It," 104, 105.

18 Thomas Chinn Robertson to mother, April 9, 1862, Thomas C. Robertson Papers, Louisiana State University Archives.

regiments, and a section of artillery belonging to Ketchum's Battery. When Wallace's men first advanced that morning the two guns were ordered forward to support the Confederate infantry. Wallace's Ninth Indiana Battery, Captain Noah Thompson commanding, opened first fire on the Southern gunners. The two Confederate guns, brought into action despite the Union fire, were soon busy dropping rounds into the enemy's ranks. The Indiana gunners averaged almost two hundred rounds per gun on Monday, a good portion of them fired at Ketchum's guns; but most of them either overshot or fell short. A 6-pound ball did bowl over one of the Alabama gunners, but he was the only casualty for over an hour.[19]

The Eighteenth Louisiana advanced and engaged Wallace's skirmishers, but was brought under a particularly accurate artillery barrage, probably from Battery I, First Missouri Light Artillery. Exploding shells killed or wounded a number of enlisted men, while solid shot ripped through trees, spattering the Louisianans with jagged wooden splinters. Mouton finally ordered his men to fall back a few hundred yards and take cover on the ground.[20]

Gradually the whole of Pond's Brigade, including Colonel Robert F. Looney's long lost Thirty-eighth Tennessee, was committed to the fight with Wallace. General Bragg began moving up additional batteries and infantry to oppose Wallace, and after a sharp artillery duel, the Southerners launched a vicious attack on Lieutenant Thurber's Battery I, First Missouri. After a sharp exchange of fire, Wallace's First Brigade repulsed the Confederates.[21]

About 10:30, Wallace ordered his three brigades to advance, the Federals driving back Confederate skirmishers until they ran into a strong force of Rebels under General Bragg. Wallace sustained sharp losses from Ketchum's guns and from the fire of the Tennesseans and

---

19   Phil Bond to brother, April 23, 1862, in "Record of the Alabama State Artillery," 318. || Dr. Cunningham again seems to give Wallace a tough grade for not engaging earlier in the day of April 7, 1862. See footnote #1 in this chapter for an explanation of his time line of action.

20   Cesar Porta to J. B. Wilkinson, n.d., Louisiana Historical Association Collection, Howard-Tilton Memorial Library, Tulane University.

21   *OR* 10, pt. 1, 171.

Louisianans. Believing he was about to be assaulted, Wallace halted and began bringing up his reserves. After waiting some minutes, Wallace found he was not under attack, and he decided to again take the initiative. Before he could act, Confederate troops under Hardee counterattacked McCook and Crittenden, and Bragg suddenly threw part of Pond's Brigade and several other regiments against Wallace's left flank.[22]

For a few minutes it seemed as though the peppery Indianan might be isolated from the rest of the Union army and perhaps destroyed.[23] The attack, however, began to flag, and Beauregard decided to personally intervene. Grabbing up a battle flag, he led the Eighteenth Louisiana and a Tennessee regiment forward against Wallace. It was to no avail, however, for the exhausted Rebels were unable to rout their numerically superior foe. The Indianan had won. By refusing to panic and by carefully employing his reserves, Wallace stalled Bragg's counterthrust.[24]

About 1:00 or 1:30 p.m., Wallace again shifted to the offensive, steadily pushing back the Confederate extreme left. The Southern army was not physically capable of containing its larger foe. By 2:00 p.m., Beauregard probably had no more than twenty thousand effectives capable of opposing the Union attack. Grant's army counted at least ten or twelve thousand effectives from the troops that had started the battle Sunday, while Buell's arrival added more than twenty-five thousand fresh troops to the Union total. The situation grew increasingly critical.

---

22 || Dr. Cunningham's original text included a reference to an officer named "Buckner" counterattacking with General Hardee. The only Buckner we could locate on the field was Captain John A. Buckner of the 8th Kentucky, who was acting as a volunteer aide on Brigadier General Charles Clark's staff. With his general officer wounded on the first day, perhaps Buckner led a conglomeration of reformed units on the second day, but we will never know for sure who exactly Cunningham was referencing. See *OR* 10, pt. 1, 415.

23 Phil Bond to brother, April 23, 1862, in Terry, "Record of the Alabama State Artillery," 318, 319; *OR* 10, pt. 1, 171.

24 || Dr. Cunningham does not place Beauregard's act at any certain position, but Beauregard's aide, Colonel Jacob Thompson, reported that the event took place "to the left and rear of the church." See *OR* 10, pt. 1, 402.

All during the morning the Creole hoped and prayed for the arrival of Van Dorn. If these twenty thousand fresh troops arrived, Beauregard planned a devastating flank and frontal assault on the Union right. When a courier arrived from Corinth with news that Van Dorn was still miles away, Beauregard knew the game was up. Without fresh troops, there was no possible hope of a Southern victory, and indeed the entire Confederate army might be destroyed.[25]

About 1:00 p.m., Beauregard started preparations for a withdrawal to Corinth, Mississippi. He issued orders to staff officers to notify the various unit commanders of his decision. Arrangements were also made to deploy troops and artillery to cover the retreat. In particular, batteries were arranged in front of Shiloh Church and on the Ridge Road. Confederate cavalry units were ordered to burn or wreck everything that could not be carried off. Hundreds of tents and great mounds of supplies, dried off by the warm midday sun, were soon ablaze, while soldiers smashed and cut at the material that was still too damp to burn.[26] Colonel Numa Augustin was dispatched to Corinth to prepare things there, arranging for food and shelter for the wounded.[27]

At least one Southerner did not want to retreat. One of Beauregard's staff officers stopped at the Shiloh Church hospital to arrange for the movement of the wounded to Corinth. He noted a young Confederate soldier, perhaps thirteen or fourteen years old, having a wounded hand dressed by a doctor. The boy calmly remarked, "Make haste, please,

25 Cesar Porta to J. B. Wilkinson, n.d., 1862, Louisiana Historical Association Collection, Howard-Tilton Memorial Library, Tulane University; N. Augustine to General Beauregard, April 10, 1862, Louisiana Historical Association Collection, Howard-Tilton Memorial Library, Tulane University; Roman, *Beauregard*, 1: 319, 320.

26 *Ibid.*, 320; Richard L. Pugh to wife, April 9, 1862, Richard Pugh Papers, Louisiana State University Archives; Theodore Mandeville to Josephine Rozet, April 9, 1862, Theodore Mandeville Papers, Louisiana State University Archives.

27 Colonel N. Augustine to General Beauregard, April 10, 1862, Louisiana Historical Association Collection, Howard-Tilton Memorial Library, Tulane University.

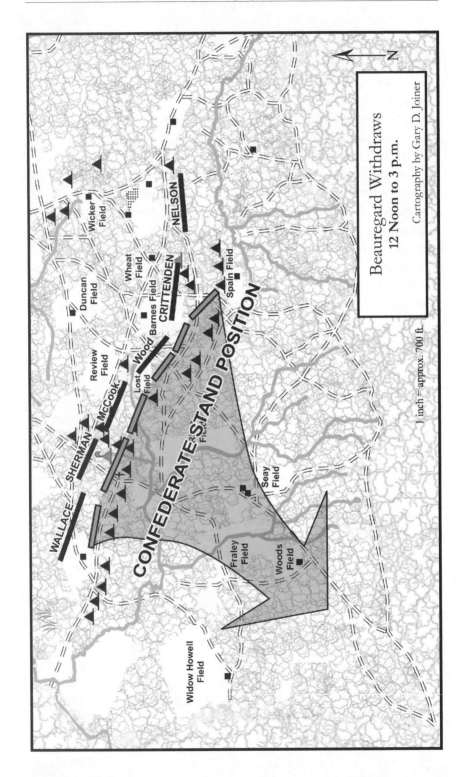

Beauregard Withdraws
12 Noon to 3 p.m.

Cartography by Gary D. Joiner

1 inch = approx. 700 ft.

doctor, I want to go back and take another shot at the Yankees."[28] It was rapidly becoming too late for even such fighting spirit to prevail.

About 2:00 p.m., the corps commanders started the withdrawal. Breckinridge moved first, forming a rear guard position near Shiloh Church. Beauregard told him that the army must be saved at all costs, adding that "this retreat must not be a rout."[29]

A little past 2:00 p.m., General Thomas J. Wood's division reached the field. His Twentieth Brigade under Brigadier General (and later President) James A. Garfield moved up in time to catch some scattered fire from retreating enemy troops. The men were excited and ready to fight. They could hear triumphant shouts and yells, which seemed to indicate a Union victory. Walking wounded from other brigades straggled past the fast moving new arrivals exuberantly exclaiming, "We've got 'em on the run, boy! Go for 'em! Give 'em the best you've got in the shop." None of Garfield's men were killed or wounded, although several were bruised by spent enemy slugs. Much to their dismay, they were unable to catch up with the retreating Southerners.[30]

Wood's Twenty-first Brigade, under Colonel George Wagner, marched swiftly across the battlefield but failed to make contact. Colonel Cyrus Hines, Fifty-seventh Indiana, was detached from the brigade and sent to support Hurlbut's Fourth Division. The regiment loaded its muskets, fixed bayonets, and charged the retiring Confederates. Small arms fire peppered the regiment, wounding four men, and several Confederate artillery rounds passed overhead, but the Indianans were able to round up some forty stragglers, including a chaplain.[31]

Confederate batteries unlimbered around Shiloh Church continued pouring a noisy fusillade in the general direction of the Union arms to

28 Roman, *Beauregard*, 1: 320.

29 E. A. Pollard, *The First Year of the War* (Richmond: West and Johnston, 1862), 1: 308.

30 Wilbur Hinman, *The Story of the Sherman Brigade* (Alliance: Published by Author, 1897), 145.

31 Asburry L. Kerwood, *Annals of the Fifty-Seventh Regiment Indiana Volunteers: Marches, Battles and Incidents of Army Life* (Dayton: W. J. Shuey, 1868), 56, 57; *OR* 10, pt. 1, 380, 381.

keep up the illusion that the main Confederate force was still present and in action. Gun crews poured rounds at the Federals in an extravagant and spectacular display of destructiveness. The Federals made no attempt to overwhelm the rear guard force, however, and around 3:30 p.m. the last of the guns were hitched up and hauled off down the long road toward Corinth. Except for a few scattered shots between Confederate stragglers and a few zealous Union skirmishers, the battle of Shiloh had ended.[32]

There was no pursuit. Why did Grant remain quietly on the battlefield instead of leading his men after the battered Confederates? His actions have never adequately been explained. In his *Memoirs*, Grant claimed that he did not have the "heart to order the men who had fought desperately for two days" to pursue, and that he did not order Buell to, since they were so nearly the same in seniority.[33]

Grant's argument remains a little shaky. As an old regular army officer, Grant knew full well that his few weeks army seniority did give him command on the field. This was standard army procedure, and Buell, as another army officer, knew it also. Buell maintained that Grant and his army did not want to pursue, and that he did not want to make such an effort on his own authority.[34]

Certainly the ultimate responsibility rested on Grant. Perhaps Sherman summed the matter up best in a conversation some years later after the war. When asked why Beauregard was not pursued, he replied, "I assure you, my dear fellow, we had had quite enough of their society for two whole days, and were only too glad to be rid of them on any terms."[35]

---

32 Shoup, "The Art of War," 12, 13; S. H. Dent to Wife, April 9, 1862, Shiloh-Corinth Collection, Alabama Department of Archives and History; Gordan Blakewell, "Fifth Washington Artillery," Louisiana Historical Association Collection, Howard-Tilton Memorial Library, Tulane University.

33 Grant, *Memoirs*, 184. || Daniel, *Shiloh*, 294, argues Grant should have sent Lew Wallace's fairly fresh division after the Confederates, while Sword, *Shiloh*, 425, states that Grant did mount a "limited pursuit." McDonough, *Shiloh*, 208, seems to agree with Sword: "it was not much of a pursuit."

34 *Battles and Leaders*, 1: 534.

35 John Fiske, *The Mississippi Valley in the Civil War* (Boston: Houghton Mifflin Company, 1900), 99.

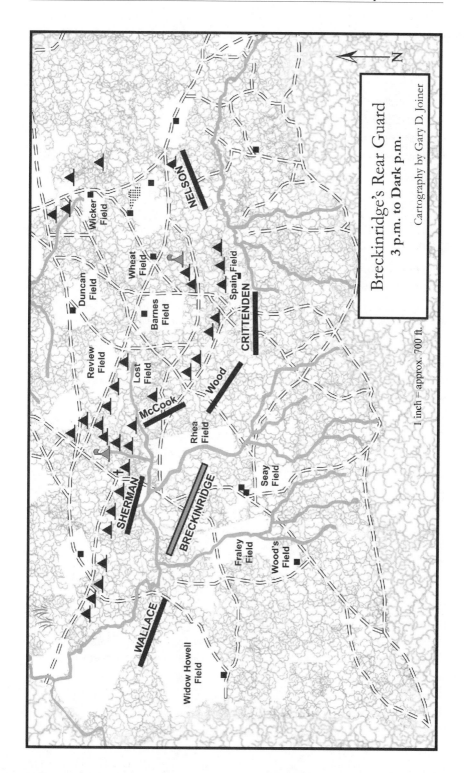

Breckinridge's Rear Guard
3 p.m. to Dark p.m.

Cartography by Gary D. Joiner

1 inch = approx. 700 ft.

NELSON

Wicker Field

Wheat Field

Duncan Field

Barnes Field

Spain Field

CRITTENDEN

Review Field

Lost Field

Wood

McCook

Rhea Field

Seay Field

BRECKINRIDGE

SHERMAN

Fraley Field

Wood's Field

WALLACE

Widow Howell Field

If Grant had pursued, the Confederates would have been in trouble for the march to Corinth quickly devolved into a nightmare. The roads were clogged as the retreating host wound out in a jerky line seven or eight miles long. The crude country roads were already in bad condition from the march to Shiloh, and the additional rain that fell Saturday and Sunday night made them nearly impassable. Soldiers often sank nearly to their knees in the mud; wagons and guns were engulfed up to their axles. Cursing and sweating, the hungry teamsters lashed their mules and horses, trying to move with their cargos of supplies and wounded.

Only the worst shot-up Southerners were accorded a crude bed in the ambulances, country wagons, and carts. When these were all filled, some of the more mangled men were loaded on stretchers and carried the twenty-two miles by hand. Men with smashed eyes, deafened ears, and mangled arms trudged through the mud along with the weary but unwounded soldiers. Everything was in a state of turmoil. Each time a wagon hit a rut, the delirious wounded groaned and screamed in agony.

About 6:30 p.m. it started to rain, and soon the temperature began dropping. The rain turned into hail, and marble-sized balls lacerated and bruised the pitifully tired, animals and soldiers alike. Most of the wounded did not even have a blanket to protect them from the barrage in their open vehicles. Many of the unwounded were in almost as bad shape. The exertions of the battle and the privations of the past five days had materially weakened them. Each step was harder than the last, for many of the men had badly blistered feet inside soggy and cracked shoes.[36]

Breckinridge halted his command at Mickey's to see what would turn up, while the rest of the Southern army tramped onward into Corinth, dumping out along the route three hundred wounded who had died.[37]

---

36 Henry Elson, *The Civil War Through the Camera* (New York: McKiney, Stone and Mackenzie, Publishers, 1912), 62-64; W. E. Yeatman "Shiloh," Confederate Collection, Tennessee State Library and Archives; Joseph Boyce, 'Second Day's Battle," Louisiana Historical Association Collection, Howard-Tilton Memorial Library, Tulane University; Theodore Mandeville to Josephine Rozet, April 9, 1862, Theodore Mandeville Papers, Louisiana State University Archives.

37 Horn, *Army of Tennessee*, 143; Elson, *The Civil War Through the Camera*, 64; Theodore Mandeville to Josephine Rozet, April 9, 1862, Theodore Mandeville Papers, Louisiana State University Archives.

As the first wounded reached the little Mississippi town, the whole place was converted into a gigantic hospital. Churches, homes, schools, and every other conceivable structure was taken over for the mangled men, while hundreds had to be placed out on porches, sidewalks, and platforms at the railroad depot. There were not enough doctors and nurses to go around, and available medical supplies were inadequate to meet the demand. Soon the doctors were busy sawing off mangled and torn arms and legs, limbs hopelessly smashed by Minie balls or shell fragments. With their crude nineteenth century medical skill, surgeons could do little but amputate. Weakened by their ordeal, many of the soldiers could not stand the shock of amputation, and many expired within a few hours. Tetanus stalked through Corinth, while the faint sickening smell of gangrene was vividly detected on many of the Rebel soldiers.[38]

Twenty-two miles away the Union army faced a similar medical crisis. Only regimental medical units were available to care for their wounded, and these were quickly overtaxed by the sheer volume of the task. Even before the fighting ceased, volunteer nurses, male and female, labored with the wounded, applying temporary bandages. Ambulances carried hundreds to emergency tent hospitals or to the few permanent structures available, but on Tuesday the majority still lay where they had fallen, pitifully crying for succor.

People passing by the medical centers were often sickened by the sounds and odors. Amputated limbs lay in large piles unburied, while there was the sweet smell of blood everywhere. Grant telegraphed for emergency medical aid, and a number of transports were soon busy evacuating thousands of soldiers to Northern cities.

One of Buell's surgeons, B. J. D. Irwin, worked medical miracles on the bloody battlefield. Working at least twenty hours a day, he constructed a modern field hospital composed of commandeered army tents capable of housing two thousand five hundred soldiers. The patients were segregated according to their ailments, while the medical staff was assigned specialized functions. Irwin organized a central administration

---

38 Wiley, *The Life of Johnny Reb*, 263; Horn, *Army of Tennessee* 148, 149; William G. Stevenson, *Thirteen Months in the Rebel Army* (New York: Barnes and Burr, 1862) Elson, *The Civil War Through the Camera*, 64, 65.

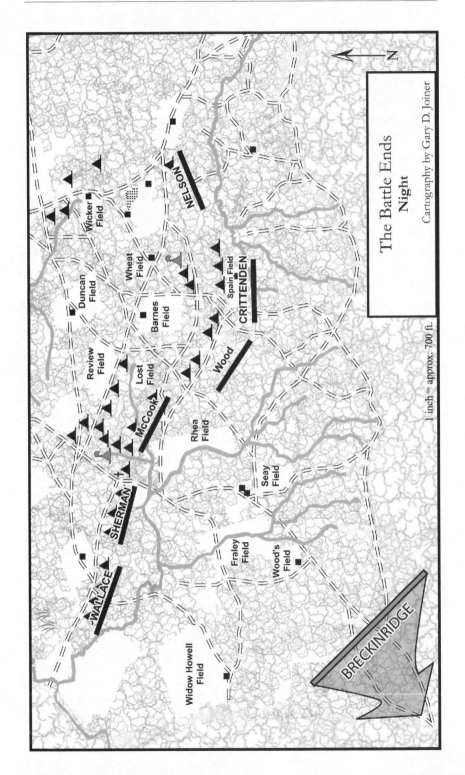

The Battle Ends
Night

Cartography by Gary D. Joiner

1 inch = approx. 700 ft.

NELSON

CRITTENDEN

WOOD

McCOOK

SHERMAN

WALLACE

BRECKINRIDGE

Wicker
Field

Duncan
Field

Wheat
Field

Spain Field

Barnes
Field

Review
Field

Lost
Field

Rhea
Field

Seay
Field

Fraley
Field

Wood's
Field

Widow Howell
Field

to handle food, drugs, laundry, and admittance—a streamlined method of hospital administration far in advance of existing practices.[39]

One of the wounded collected off the battlefield on Monday was General W. H. L. Wallace. He was found about 10:00 a.m. by Federal soldiers. He was cold and soaked through and through from the night's dampness. Stretcher bearers quickly carried him to the Landing, from where he was taken to Savannah. Cyrus Dickey, brother-in-law of Wallace, went on board the *Minnehaha* to tell his sister, Ann, that her husband was alive but mortally wounded.

Mrs. Wallace soon reached Savannah to find her husband on a cot in the Cherry House. Ann spoke to her unconscious spouse, who promptly awoke and clasped her hand. The chances for his survival were not good, but he seemed to rally and his pulse was strong and healthy. Such was his condition on Tuesday and Wednesday that Ann and the rest of the family thought he might live. But on Thursday, he became feverish and his pulse began to drop. Wallace was frequently conscious, and was able to carry on short conversations, but he seemed to realize that he could not survive. He touched his wife and said, "We meet in heaven." Soon his pulse dropped. He slipped into unconsciousness and passed away later in the day, apparently without any pain.[40]

Tuesday morning found General Breckinridge's jaded command covering the Confederate retreat with a force of about three hundred and fifty cavalry under Colonel Nathan Bedford Forrest out on patrol. The Confederate cavalry was reconnoitering behind the retiring Southerners when they observed Union cavalry and infantry moving toward them. It

39 George Adams, *The Medical History of the Union Army in the Civil War* (New York: Henry Schuman, 1952), 81, 82; Hannafard, *The Story of A Regiment*, 286; "Missourians," *Missouri Historical Review* 27 (April 1943): 323. || For a modern account of Irwin and his hospital, see John H. Fahey, "The Fighting Doctor: Bernard John Dowling Irwin in the Civil War," *North and South* 9, no. 1 (March 2006): 36-50.

40 Mrs. W. H. L. Wallace to her Aunt Nag, April 29, 1862, Miscellaneous Collection, Shiloh National Military Park; Cyrus Dickey to Robert Dickey, April 10, 1862, Wallace-Dickey Papers, Illinois State Historical Library; Daniel H. Brush to David Brush, April 10, 1862, Daniel Harmon Brush Papers, Illinois State Historical Library.

was General Sherman with a reconnaissance force of two of his infantry brigades and the Fourth Illinois Cavalry under T. Lyle Dickey, father-in-law of W. H. L. Wallace. Sherman deployed two companies of the Seventy-seventh Ohio out in front as skirmishers, while about two hundred yards behind rode the cavalry. Forrest took the situation in at a glance, and decided to charge.

Screaming like wild men, the Southerners spurred their horses forward. Sherman's skirmishers took one look at the oncoming Rebels and headed for the rear. The Confederate troopers smashed into the Fourth Illinois Cavalry, driving it back in confusion on the main body of infantry. The Southerners paused for a moment to reload and then attacked again. Bursts of buckshot spattered the Ohio infantry, killing and mangling many officers and men and throwing the soldiers into disorder. Their shotguns empty, Forrest and his men drew their revolvers and spurred their mounts into the Bluecoats, raking the hapless infantry with .44 caliber balls. When their guns were emptied, the Confederates pulled their sabers and began slashing. Troopers who lacked blades clubbed their guns. The Ohioans had had enough and pulled back on their Second Brigade, which was waiting with fixed bayonets and loaded rifles.[41]

As the Confederates spotted the Second Brigade, they began reining in their mounts. Unfortunately Forrest was either carried away with the excitement of the affair or by a spirited horse that galloped right on into the new enemy force. The Ohioans quickly rushed at him from all sides, screaming, "Shoot that man! Knock him off his horse!" The Federals were so numerous that they tripped over each other. This was probably the only thing that saved Forrest from being killed or dragged off his mount. The Confederate colonel blazed away with his revolver in one hand and hacked with his saber in the other. His horse was shot twice, and

---

41 *OR* 10, pt. 1, 639, 640; Wyeth, *That Devil Forrest*, 64, 65; J. B. Blackburn, "Reminiscences of the Terry Rangers," *The Southwestern Historical Quarterly* 22 (July 1918): 59-62; John Stouffer Diary, April 8, 1862, John M. Stouffer Papers, Illinois State Historical Library; Cyrus Dickey to Robert Dickey, April 10, 1862, Wallace-Dickey Papers, Illinois State Historical Library; Andrew W. McCormick, "Sixteen Months A Prisoner of War," *Sketches of War History, 1861-1865, Military Order of the Loyal Legion of the United States, Ohio Commandery* (Columbus: 1903), 5: 69.

bullets whined about the rider's head. Finally one Ohioan shoved his musket barrel against Forrest's left side and pulled the trigger. The bullet entered just above the hip, tearing through his back muscles before lodging against his spine. Shaken by the blow, the colonel almost slipped from his saddle; but he quickly steadied himself and with a supreme effort, fought his way out, evading the clutching hands and menacing gun barrels. Although bleeding badly, he rounded up his troopers and the plunder, as well as their prisoners, and executed a withdrawal toward Mickey's.[42] Sherman did not attempt any kind of pursuit.

Reported Confederate losses in the action at Fallen Timbers were at least two killed and nine or ten wounded. Since most of the companies involved did not turn in casualty reports, the actual figures for the Confederates were probably two or three times higher. Sherman did not officially report his losses, but in his report of the action, he mentioned seeing fifteen of his soldiers on the ground and twenty-five others lying around wounded. Terry's Texas Rangers, of Forrest's command, bagged forty-three prisoners, and the other Confederate units undoubtedly took a few. A check of the casualty returns for the Federal units involved in the action indicates Federal losses for the action were not far short of two hundred.[43] This encounter ended the Shiloh campaign.

*   *   *

The Confederate army had inflicted great losses in men and material on the enemy, but had failed to score a decisive victory. Sunday, April 6, was a clear-cut Confederate victory, while Monday was tactically a drawn action. But if the Southern army achieved a tactical success, they suffered a major strategic defeat. The Union army was now united at Pittsburg, and the Confederacy could ill spare its losses on Shiloh field. Beauregard listed the official Confederate losses at 10,699, comprising

---

42   Eric Sheppard, *Bedford Forrest: The Confederacy's Greatest Cavalryman* (New York: Dial Press, 1930), 61, 62; Duncan, *Recollections*, 62, 63; Blackburn, "Reminiscences of the Terry Rangers," 59-62. || It is interesting to note that Dr. Cunningham did not include the propounded popular myth about Forrest grabbing a Union soldier and using him as a shield.

43   *OR* 10, pt. 1, 924, 640.

1,728 dead, 8,012 wounded, and 959 missing or captured. Actually true Confederate losses were much higher, probably running close to twelve thousand. The discrepancy in casualties was caused by the usual poor Confederate bookkeeping system and by the mortality rate of Confederate officers. In many cases accurate accounts of losses in individual Southern units were not made until weeks after Beauregard turned in his report.[44]

Official Union casualty returns show that Grant's army lost 1,513 killed, 6,601 wounded and 2,330 missing or captured, the latter occurring mostly in W. H. L. Wallace's and Prentiss' divisions. Buell's losses were officially listed as 241 dead, 1,807 wounded and 55 missing or captured, for a total of 13,047 casualties for both Union armies. Again poor bookkeeping and murderous officer losses concealed the true picture. Later casualty figures of the individual Union batteries and regiments indicate that most units suffered ten to twenty per cent higher losses than originally reported. Buell's figures seem to be very nearly correct, the discrepancies occurring in Grant's battered commands. Actual Union losses probably ran around 14,500 casualties. It was the first great battle of the Civil War, and up to that time the mightiest struggle ever to take place in the Americas.

Shiloh is one of the most "iffy" battles of the entire Civil War. The possibilities of the battle have fascinated generations of writers.

What would have happened if the Confederates had launched their attack on April 4 or even the following day?

What if Peabody had not sent out his pre-dawn patrol on the 6th?

What if W. H. L. Wallace had not reinforced the Union left?

If the Confederates had concentrated their forces against the Union left, would they have shattered the Federal line and captured Pittsburg Landing?

---

44 || It is worth noting that most historians do not view the April 7, 1862, fighting as a tactical draw, as Dr. Cunningham has described it. Since this statement is a matter of interpretation and not established fact, we have not seen fit to alter the text. It is the opinion of the editors, however, that the Confederates were soundly driven back in a tactical defeat on the second day. Dr. Cunningham's work with casualties is impressive in terms of recent (but as yet still unpublished) research in Compiled Service Records that reveals Confederate casualties ran some 25-30% higher than reported.

It is impossible to predict the might-have-beens of the battle, but a change in any of these or a wide variety of other factors could have changed the entire direction of the battle.

More ink was shed over Shiloh than any previous battle fought in the Western hemisphere. Altogether, participants turned in 229 official reports, encompassing 529 pages, plus at least three thousand pages of published unofficial materials.

Ink and blood alike, it was truly a magnificent spectacle.

Chapter 16

<hr>

Corinth

ON TUESDAY MORNING THE area around Shiloh looked as though a series of massive cyclones had swept over it. There were wrecked wagons, caissons, and field pieces strewn everywhere, while the vile odor of decaying flesh of thousands of horses and men poisoned the atmosphere. Young trees lay sprawled awkwardly on the ground, shot down by cannon balls or sawed through by the repeated impact of slugs. Canteens, bayonets, broken rifles, harnesses, bits of clothing, and a thousand other articles of military material littered the landscape.

Here and there Union stretcher bearers picked up wounded Federals and Confederates, some weakened by two nights of exposure on the battlefield. It would be Friday or perhaps even Saturday before the last battered body, still retaining a tiny spark of life, would be removed and carried to a field hospital.

Burial details were quickly assembled to dispose of all the corrupted flesh as a sanitary measure. The dead horses were piled in huge mounds, doused with kerosene, and ignited. The burning smell of animal flesh spread over much of the Federal camp area, much to the soldiers' distaste. Working with picks and shovels, the Federals soon cleared out burial pits roughly forty feet long by six feet wide and three feet in depth. The dead were disposed of in these shallow cavities.

Most of the Confederates were buried in as many as nine even larger pits, 721 bodies being planted in the last and deepest of these. Soldiers hitched ropes to the feet or hands and arms of the Rebel bodies and dragged them down to the waiting holes, where they were quickly pushed in. When the burial pits were full, Union soldiers walked along the edges, kicking and stomping at the jutting arms and legs, making them fit inside properly. Then the shovels were used to cover the holes with thin layers of Tennessee soil. It was a brutal, sickening job even for the most callous of men. By Thursday after the battle, all but a few stray bodies lay beneath the sod.[1]

Most of the Union soldiers at Pittsburg were in rather sorry shape. Buell's men had left their regimental wagons, containing their tents and other vital equipment, on the road to Savannah. Many of the soldiers in his regiments had also dropped their packs at or near Savannah. Until the wagons and knapsacks could be retrieved, most of the men of the Army of the Ohio had nothing but their weapons and the uniforms on their backs.

Grant's soldiers were in just as bad a condition, most of them having lost all their belongings when the Southerners overran and looted their army camps. Even the colonels and generals wound up with their belongings in possession of patched-pants Confederates. Lieutenant Colonel Adolph Engelmann, Forty-third Illinois, lost his shaving gear, new coat, underwear, extra uniforms, and a fifty dollar saddle. Captain Andrew Hickenlooper found his tent completely looted by the Southerners, and he was forced to remain in his muddy, bloody clothes of Sunday and Monday until supplies arrived and he was able to purchase

---

1 Bierce, *Collected Works*, 1: 254, 255; Throne, *Cyrus Boyd Diary*, 41, 42; Throne "Letters From Shiloh," 241; Briant, *Sixth Regiment Indiana,* 125, 126; Otto Eisenschiml, "Shiloh—The Blunders and the Blame," *Civil War Times Illustrated* 11 (April 1963): 34; Alice F. and Bettina Jackson, "Autobiography of James Albert Jackson, Sr. M. D.," *The Wisconsin Magazine of History* 28 (December 1944): 205; Albert Dillahaunty, *Shiloh: National Military Park, Tennessee National Park; Service Historical Handbook*, Series 10, (Washington: Government Printing Office, N. d.), 28, 29; Alfred Lacey Hough to wife, April 30, 1862, in Robert Athearn, *Soldier in the West: The Civil War Letters, of Alfred Lacey Hough* (Philadelphia: University of Pennsylvania Press, 1957), 61; W. Henry Sheak to Blair Ross, October 28, 1942, Miscellaneous Collection, Shiloh National Military Park. || Dr. Cunningham was mistaken when he originally stated the Confederates were placed in only five trenches. In addition to individual or small group graves, the Shiloh Battlefield Commission counted as many as nine burial trenches; almost certainly there are more waiting to be found. We have slightly altered the text to reflect this. Smith, *This Great Battlefield of Shiloh*, 76-77.

new uniforms.[2] A private in the Twelfth Michigan lost his knapsack, haversack, canteen, overcoat, blanket, and even a letter he had just written to his sweetheart back home.[3]

If the loss of clothing and personal effects was serious, the army was faced with an even more drastic immediate problem—the shortage of foodstuffs. It was a week after the battle before the army could bring provisions by steamer to replace those carried away or ruined by the Rebels. In the meantime, troops lived on what could be salvaged from the ruined supplies or what they were able to purchase from the helpful army sutlers. Most of the soldiers were able to find a few soda crackers to chew on, but these were not particularly tasty or filling. Even crackers were somewhat scarce, and a dozen thin slices sold for a dime. Eggs were selling at twenty-five cents a piece, while butter varied from thirty to forty cents a pound. Apples cost the previously unheard of price of two for a nickel. Postage stamps ran from five to eight cents each, although one soldier was able to pick up a bargain lot at thirty for one dollar. Writing paper was even more dear; however, many soldiers were able to buy small quantities to drop a few lines to the folks back home.[4]

Despite the handicaps and discomforts of the post-battle camp, the soldiers were doing some thinking and drawing conclusions. The attitude of the army, or at least a substantial part of it, was that the whole mess was Grant's fault. The soldiers told each other that Grant should have sent out patrols to avoid being surprised, while others claimed the army camps should have been fortified. If the commanding general was catching criticism at Pittsburg, it was no wonder the folks back home began asking a lot of embarrassing questions.

2 Adolph Engelmann to wife, April 9, 1862, Adolph Engelmann Papers, Illinois State Historical Library; Hickenlooper, "The Battle of Shiloh," 436.

3 Franklin H. Bailey to parents, April 8, 1862, Franklin H. Bailey Papers, Michigan Historical Collection, University of Michigan.

4 Franklin H. Bailey to parents, April 8, 1862, Franklin H. Bailey Papers, Michigan Historical Collection, University of Michigan; Francis Bruce to mother, April 14, 1862, Francis H. Bruce Papers, Illinois State Historical Library; Hickenlooper, "The Battle of Shiloh," 436; Throne, *Cyrus Boyd Diary*, 41.

Although vague rumors of the battle at Pittsburg first reached Washington, D. C. on the night of April 8, the country as a whole got its first concrete news about Shiloh from the April 10 issue of the New York *Herald*. It was an account by a correspondent, W. C. Carroll, who had served as a volunteer aide on Grant's staff.[5]

Carroll completely whitewashed Grant, ignoring any hint that the general had been taken by surprise. The enterprising correspondent went on to say that Grant had personally turned the tide on the second day of the battle by leading a heroic charge, a statement which was untrue. The story made a sensation, and the whole United States went mad with joy.[6]

The first warm glow of Northern enthusiasm soon wore off as young Whitelaw Reid, correspondent for the Cincinnati *Gazette* under the pen name Agate, fired off his account of the battle at Pittsburg to Cincinnati. The *Gazette* ran his massive letter, which was picked up by other prominent newspapers. The *Gazette* account was a revelation to many Americans who had gone overboard on the *Herald* account. Reid was convinced the army was taken by surprise, that Grant and the other generals were incompetent, and that the army had narrowly averted disaster. He charged the army was surprised in its tents and beds, and that some of the men were bayoneted before they could even put on their clothes. Reid made a number of errors, including the especially erroneous one that Prentiss was captured at 10:00 a.m., but on the whole his account was a remarkably reasonable appraisal of the battle, considering his own inexperience and the hectic conditions under which he worked.

By his article, Reid unleashed a hurricane of criticism of the Union command at Shiloh. Cowards who had run away from the battle and reached safety in Northern cities regaled frightened civilians with stories

---

5   Throne, "Letters from Shiloh," 237, 238; Payson Shumway to wife, April 13, 1862, Payson Z. Shumway Papers, Illinois State Historical Library; Throne, *Cyrus Boyd Diary*, 42; Howard K. Beale (ed.). *Diary of Edward Bates, 1859-1866* (Washington: Government Printing Office, 1933), 247, 248; Catton, *Grant Moves South*, 251.

6   New York *Herald*, April 10, 1862; Emmet Crozier, *Yankee Reporters, 1861-1865* (New York: Oxford University Press, 1956), 217; Throne, "Letters from Shiloh," 237-239; Payson Shumway to wife, April 13, 1862, Payson Z. Shumway Papers, Illinois State Historical Library.

of terrible command stupidity and incompetence, screaming the whole thing was the fault of Union superior officers.[7]

Governor David Tod of Ohio howled that the routed Fifty-third and Fifty-seventh Ohio Regiments were innocent, that the disaster that had befallen them was due to "criminal negligence" of Grant, Sherman, and other generals. Ohio editors and politicians castigated Grant as the villain in the picture, and in Congress, Representative James Harlan of Iowa declared that Grant had blundered at Belmont, Donelson, and Shiloh, and had only been saved at the latter by the arrival of Buell. Lieutenant Governor Benjamin Stanton of Ohio criticized Grant in a newspaper article on April 12, saying he ought to "be court martialed or shot."[8] Ugly rumors began to circulate that Grant was drunk at Shiloh, although the charge was untrue. For years stories of his drinking would recur again and again as his friends and enemies rushed to attack or to defend him.[9] The soldiers of Buell's army were convinced that Grant was not only incompetent, but also besotted on that fateful Sunday morning.[10]

7 Crozier, *Yankee Reporters*, 210-217; Cortissoz, *Life of Whitelaw Reid*, 87-89; Hickenlooper, "The Battle of Shiloh," 407-409.

8 Lloyd Lewis, *Sherman: Fighting Prophet* (New York: Harcourt, Brace and Company, 1958), 234. Colonel Thomas Worthington claimed the mess at Shiloh was due to treason on the part of Halleck, Grant, Sherman, and the Congressional Committee on the Conduct of the War. He demanded to be court-martialed and his wish was granted. Worthington lost the case, but later he put his sensational charges in writing. Thomas Worthington, *Brief History of the 46th Ohio Volunteers* (Washington: Published by Author, 1872). See also, Worthington, *Shiloh: Or The Tennessee Campaign of 1862* (Washington: McGill and Witherow, 1872); Worthington, *Colonel Worthington Vindicated: Sherman's Discreditable Record at Shiloh on His Own and Better Evidence* (Washington: F. McGill and Company, 1878). For an interesting view of Worthington's charges, see Eisenschiml, *The Story of Shiloh*, 52-56.

9 Douglas Putnam, "The Battle of Shiloh," Washington *Post*, July 11, 1897; Eugene Roseboom, "The Civil War Era, 1850-1873," *The History of the State of Ohio* (Columbus: Ohio Archaelogical and Historical Society, 1944), 395.

10 *Ibid.;* F. W. Keil, *The Thirty-fifth Ohio Regiment* (Fort Wayne: Housh and Company, 1894), 64; Henry Bellamy to parents, n.d., 1862, Henry Bellamy Papers, Michigan Historical Collection, University of Michigan.

If the army and the nation were upset by the accusations and charges arising out of Shiloh, then there was equally widespread jubilation over the news from Island No. 10. After several weeks of confused and almost bloodless fighting, the Confederate bastion surrendered on April 7 to the hero of New Madrid, General John Pope. Actually it was the United States Navy which made possible the capture, but Pope received most of the credit and was soon on his way to becoming the hero of the radical wing of the Republican Party, and many other Americans as well. The capture not only raised Union morale and freed Pope's army for operations against Corinth, but it also cost the Confederate army seven thousand irreplaceable men captured, besides a large amount of precious war material.[11]

The rest of Buell's army, including George Thomas' division, soon arrived at Shiloh to be followed a few days later by Pope's command, fresh from its Mississippi River victory. Additional fresh regiments came in from all quarters and the army swelled in fighting strength. The equipment and supplies left behind by the Army of the Ohio finally arrived at Pittsburg a week after the battle, while other supply shortages were quickly rectified. One handicap to Union efficiency was the persistent bad weather. It rained almost every day, and ten days after the battle, a sharp cold spell engulfed the Union army.[12]

The most significant event at Pittsburg Landing was not the rain, weather, or supplies, but the arrival of a new army commander: Major General Henry Wager Halleck. On April 11, Halleck arrived by steamer and promptly took charge, much to the curiosity and interest of the Union soldiers. Whatever the merits of Halleck as a soldier, his arrival certainly seemed to have been useful from the standpoint of army morale and discipline. Ever since the battle, the army had been at least partially in a state of chaos. Deserters kept wandering off by hitching rides on

---

11 Gosnell, *Guns on the Western Waters*, 82; Horn, *Army of Tennessee*, 145; Williams, *Lincoln and His Generals*, 120. || For Island No. 10, see Daniel and Bock, *Island No. 10*.

12 Ambrose, *History of the Seventh Illinois*, 64-66; Garman, *Amos Glover Diary*, 266; Douglas Hapeman, Diary, April 11, 1862, Douglas Hapeman Papers, Illinois State Historical Library.

steamers, while on occasion waves of panic swept through the troops. In one instance, someone yelled or shouted something about a Rebel attack, and hundreds of men started running for the river in wild panic. On Wednesday morning after the battle, the troops from the Twelfth Illinois abruptly lost their heads and raked Sherman's regimental camp with gunfire, wounding four men in the process. Just two days after this unfortunate experience, another bad panic swept through the army camp as some fool spread a false alarm about attacking Confederates. Fortunately, officers kept their heads and managed to restore order before anyone was hurt.[13]

Halleck quickly set to work restoring discipline and improving the conditions of the individual soldier. Each corps commander was made responsible for his own organization, discipline, and supply, while an all-out drive was launched to improve the health of the soldiers. These considered actions produced much good and reduced the number of occupied hospital beds.[14]

Southward at Corinth, General Beauregard similarly worked to prepare his army for action. Work parties were soon busy adding to the existing fortifications, while a steady stream of reinforcements arrived. Van Dorn's troops, as well as a few scattered regiments, reached camp in mid-April, but the Creole soon worked out a new table of organization allowing for the new units. Confederate morale was-fairly high, and the soldiers much better armed than when they had started the campaign, thanks to their capture of Union weapons. Unfortunately the Southern army suffered terribly from disease. Large numbers of soldiers contracted pneumonia during the marches to and from Shiloh, while the inadequate rations of the campaign worked havoc with the digestive tracts and bowels of the men. The pitifully overworked Confederate medical staff found themselves burdened with a staggering sick list on

---

13 *Ibid.*; Thompson, *Recollections With the Third Iowa Regiment*, 241; U. S. Grant to W. T. Sherman, April 9, 1862; Ambrose, *Halleck,* 47, 48. || For a recent biography of Halleck, see Marszalek, *Commander of All Lincoln's Armies.*

14 *Ibid.*; Douglas Hapeman, Diary, April 11, 1862, Douglas Hapeman Papers, Illinois State Historical Library.

top of the thousands of wounded to be cared for.[15] Typhoid fever soon made its deadly appearance, dropping privates and colonels with equal efficiency. The water supply at Corinth, already in bad shape before the battle, was soon almost completely polluted. During the last week in April and in the month of May, tens of thousands of Confederates became ill from drinking the germ-filled water. Southern reinforcements scarcely kept even with the daily decrease in effectives caused by disease.[16]

On top of all their other woes, the Southerners suffered greatly from hunger. Rations were scanty both as to quantity and quality. General Beauregard remonstrated with Richmond authorities, pleading for better commissary arrangements, but met with scant success.[17]

Confederate morale plummeted badly as the news of the fall of New Orleans reached the camp. To the men it seemed as though they were being surrounded by enemy armies on all sides.[18] Most of the soldiers would have welcomed a battle as a pleasant relief from the sickness and

15 "General Order No. 72, Chalmers' Brigade," April 7, 1862, T. Otis Baker Papers, Mississippi Department of Archives and History; John Cato to wife, April 10, 1862, John Cato Papers, Mississippi Department of Archives and History; Jimmy Knighton to sister, April 14, 1862, Jimmy Knighton Papers, Louisiana State University Archives; Samuel Latta to wife, April 13, 1862, Confederate Collection, Tennessee State Library and Archives; Charles J. Johnson to wife, April 15, 1862, Charles James Johnson Papers, Louisiana State University Archives.

16 Henry McNeill, Diary, April 28, 1862, Confederate Collection, Tennessee State Library and Archives; Jimmy Knighton to sister, April 20, 1862, Jimmy Knighton Papers, Louisiana State University Archives; Roman, *Beauregard*, 1: 383; Edwin H. Fay to wife April 21, 1862, in Bell I. Wiley, *"This Infernal War" The Confederate Letters of SGT. Edwin H. Fay* (Austin: University of Texas Press, 1957), 28; Taylor, *Reluctant Rebel*, 39; Wiley, *Life of Johnny Reb*, 247; Williams, *P. G. T, Beauregard*, 152; Theodore Mandeville to Josephine Rozet, April 19, 1862, Theodore Mandeville Papers, Louisiana State University Archives.

17 Roman, *Beauregard*, 1: 383; Taylor, *Reluctant Rebel*, 39; Edwin H. Fay to wife, April 21, 1862, in Wiley, *"This Infernal War,"* 51; George Blackemore, Diary, April 29, 1862, Confederate Collection, Tennessee State Library and Archives.

18 *Ibid.*

tedium of life at Corinth, but unfortunately the Union army was not too obliging about giving any kind of fight.

Halleck would not budge from Pittsburg Landing until his army was at maximum strength, fully equipped, well supplied, and at least comparatively competently trained; besides it was useless to take the offensive until the weather cleared and the roads dried up. Northern patrols from Pittsburg occasionally dueled with Confederate picket posts, but there would be no big push until the end of April.

With an eighth of a million men available, Halleck finally gave the order to advance on April 29. The Union army was completely different from the force that fought at Shiloh. The Second, Fourth, Fifth, and Sixth divisions of Grant's old army and the division of Major General George H. Thomas now formed the Union right wing, commanded by the Virginian Thomas. Buell's Army of the Ohio, reduced to the divisions of Wood, Nelson, and McCook, formed the center, while Pope's Army of the Mississippi became the Union left wing. McClernand commanded a reserve corps, consisting of his own division and those of Crittenden and Lew Wallace.[19]

Grant was appointed second in command of this new army, but the title only signified that he was shelved, for Halleck apparently felt that there was substance to the accusations made against Grant after Shiloh. The unhappy former army commander grieved about his new assignment and even considered handing in his resignation; however, fortunately for the Union cause, he was dissuaded by Sherman's good offices.[20]

Even with the massive numbers of men available, the Federal advance on Corinth was painfully slow. Halleck was determined to give Beauregard no opening for a vigorous counterattack. The Federals advanced cautiously behind screens of pickets and patrols, frequently halting to fortify the newly occupied ground. It would take four weeks for the army to reach the environs of Corinth, but it would make the short passage without fighting a major battle, and indeed with few battle

19 *OR* 10, pt. 1, 144. || For a modern account of the Siege of Corinth, see Smith, *The Untold Story of Shiloh*, 67-84.

20 Grant, *Memoirs*, 196; Sherman, *Memoirs*, 250; Lewis, *Sherman: Fighting Prophet*, 235, 236.

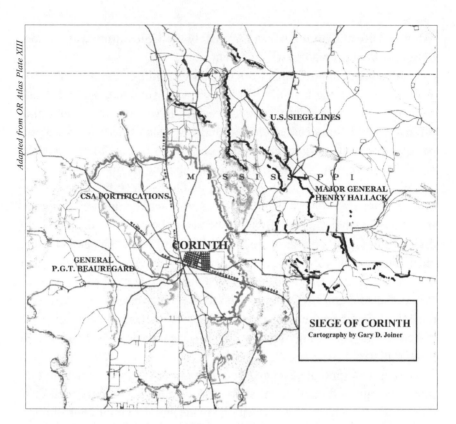

Adapted from OR Atlas Plate XIII

U.S. SIEGE LINES

M I S S I S S I P P I

CSA FORTIFICATIONS

MAJOR GENERAL
HENRY HALLACK

CORINTH

GENERAL
P.G.T. BEAUREGARD

SIEGE OF CORINTH
Cartography by Gary D. Joiner

casualties. The advance literally turned into a gigantic siege. But there was little lack of excitement despite the absence of big heroic clashes. Union and Confederate patrols frequently traded shots, and there was occasionally a brigade or even divisional strength engagement.

While thousands of soldiers labored at building roads, corduroying through the swamps for the heavy artillery and wagons to pass over, General Halleck's left wing drew first blood on May 3. Confederate skirmishers interfered with Union work parties along the road to Farmington, and Brigadier General James D. Morgan, of the First Division, deployed more than one thousand of his infantry and a battery of artillery to clear them out.

A casual meandering sort of battle developed, with the Southerners making a fighting retreat down the road in the face of vigorous enemy pressure. General Pope's soldiers finally entered Farmington, Mississippi, where they fought a second engagement with Confederate skirmishers south of the town. The entire affair lasted about three hours, until about 6:00 p.m., when the fighting died down. Probably no more than one hundred and fifty soldiers were killed or wounded on both sides, but it was still a noisy and bloody affair, and it was the biggest since Shiloh.

The Confederates were commanded by Colonel John S. Marmaduke and numbered about two thousand men, cavalry and infantry, and at least three pieces of artillery.[21] Sharp picket fighting broke out again on the following day, with Confederate soldiers trading Minie balls at long range. One Rebel scout crept up to a Federal work party and picked off a Union officer. Jumping to his feet, the Southerner made a wild but successful dash back to a Confederate picket post.[22]

The skies opened up again, raining on the Blue and Gray alike, but work on building fortifications and roads continued. Union and Confederate guns traded a few cautious long range shots to try and determine each other's positions and strength. Patrol activity flared on the Union right wing, and several Confederate prisoners were brought in to Thomas' headquarters.[23]

General Beauregard was eager to strike a blow against Halleck, and Pope's capture of Farmington seemed to provide the needed opportunity. Farmington was only about four miles from Corinth, and the swamp area around the little town meant that the hero of Island No. 10 was virtually isolated from the rest of the army. Beauregard's plan was for Bragg to distract Pope's attention with a frontal assault while Van Dorn attacked the Union left.[24]

---

21 *OR* 10, pt. 1, 714, 715; Edwin H. Fay to wife, May 5, 1867, in Wiley, *This Infernal War*, 46-48; Charleston *Daily Courier*, May 14, 1862; Robert Kimberly and Ephrain Holloway, *The 41st Ohio Volunteer Infantry in the War of the Rebellion* (Cleveland: W. R. Smellie, 1897), 28.

22 Charleston *Daily Courier*, May 13, 1862.

23 Adolph Engelmann to wife, May 4, 1862, Adolph Engelmann Papers, Illinois State Historical Library; Charleston *Daily Courier*, May 13, 1862; Phil Bond to brother, May 10, 1862, in Terry, "Record of the Alabama State Artillery," 323.

24 Williams, *P. G. T. Beauregard*, 151; Phil Bond to brother, May 10, 1862, in Terry, "Record of the Alabama State Artillery," 323.

On the morning of May 9, Bragg struck. Brigadier General Daniel Ruggles' Division actually made the assault, driving in Federal skirmishers and driving off the Second Iowa Cavalry. The Southerners swarmed into Farmington, captured a number of prisoners, grabbed up a newly established telegraph station, and secured a considerable quantity of Federal supplies. Just beyond the town, Ruggles encountered a strong force of Pope's infantry, which he engaged. Union skirmishers were chased off and several Federal infantry regiments badly mauled and forced to withdraw. The Southerners were finally ordered to halt lest they run into an ambush, but Private Charles Lamb, Thirteenth Louisiana, became so excited that he rushed after Pope's men until shot through the left leg. Lamb and the other Confederate wounded were picked up, and General Ruggles reluctantly gave the order to withdraw for Van Dorn had failed to make his flanking move. Ruggles' losses were ninety-nine men killed and wounded as against one hundred and seventy-eight Union casualties. Twelve Confederate regiments, one battalion, and four batteries were involved as compared to eleven Union regiments.[25] Pope pulled his troops back several miles so as to cooperate better with the rest of the army and to allay Halleck's fears about him becoming trapped in the exposed Farmington position. For more than a week operations languished in the Corinth area as both armies cautiously kept their horns in and continued digging.

Beauregard's situation steadily deteriorated as the Federals grew ever closer. His total effectives were only about fifty thousand men, thanks to the deadly effects of disease. If Halleck continued his siege-like approach, the Confederates would be forced to either fight under almost hopeless conditions or else evacuate Corinth and the surrounding fortifications.

To try and divert some of Halleck's army away, Beauregard launched raiding parties into Tennessee and Kentucky. The Creole hoped to pull troops away from the Corinth area to oppose these parties, but the

---

25 *OR* 10, pt. 1, 804-831; Richardson, "War As I Saw It," 226; Phil Bond to brother, May 10, 1862, in Terry, "Record of the Alabama State Artillery," 323; Edwin H. Fay to wife, May 14, 1862, in Wiley, *This Infernal War*, 50; Force, *From Fort Henry to Corinth*, 186,187; Augustine Vieira to an unnamed friend, May 14, 1862, Augustine Vieira Letters, Illinois State Historical Library.

plan failed as the raiders were too few in number to make any spectacular inroads on Federal communications.[26]

While the raiding parties were doing their part, Beauregard's soldiers skirmished and dug around Corinth. Miles of trenches and breastworks were thrown up, protecting the various approaches to the little Mississippi community. Grumbling soldiers dotted the countryside with a seemingly infinite number of rifle pits.

While thousands dug, hundreds traded shots with the Federals. Here and there a Southerner went down, his flesh torn by an enemy sharpshooter's round. One Southern private suddenly felt a tremendous blow on his leg, and looking down, he could see a small red mark which rapidly grew into a large whelp. A spent musket ball had hit him. Shaking with relief, the private sat down on the ground, emptying his stomach of his last scanty meal. The Sixth Tennessee was pestered by a Northern sniper who was peppering their picket post. The men finally spotted the Yank about five hundred yards away behind a large oak tree. But the fellow was too agile for their return fire. Finally Captain Ephrain Harbert, Company K, arrived at the post. A noted Tennessee squirrel hunter, Harbert watched the proceedings with a certain amount of disdain. Finally he took an Enfield rifle from one of the soldiers. He waited for the Yank to fire again and then gently squeezed the trigger. The Federal jerked backward behind the tree and did no more shooting that day.

Occasionally some of the Southerners got a little time off to visit the town. Most of the men vainly hunted for some liquor or decent food. One Confederate noticed some Federal soldiers being marched through the town and recorded in his diary that the "blue rascals looked like sheep killing dogs."[27]

The daily monotony was finally broken by a sharp fight caused when Sherman assaulted the Russell House on the extreme Confederate left.

26 Roman, *Beauregard*, 1: 381, 571, 572; Duke, *Morgan's Cavalry*, 155-166; Holland, *Morgan and His Raiders,* 95.

27 John Johnston, "Personal Reminiscences," Confederate Collection, Tennessee Department of Archives and History; George T. Blakemore, Diary, May 16, 1862, Confederate Collection, Tennessee Department of Archives and History.

Morgan L. Smith's brigade, supported by Bouton's Illinois Battery, assaulted the house and surrounding works, driving the Confederates out after an hour's fight. The Southerners were finally forced to give ground, although a Rebel officer made a gallant effort to rally his men. Private R. M. Snyder, Company G, Eighth Missouri, put a rifle ball through the Southern officer's head, ending his efforts. Federal losses were ten killed and thirty-one wounded, while Sherman reported that his men took one prisoner and found twelve bodies in and around the house.

The excitement died down but on May 21, Colonel Thomas T. Sedgewick led four regiments in a reconnaissance of the Corinth position on the Widow Serratt's house, where they were assaulted by a small force of Confederate infantry. A lively fight followed, lasting until darkness fell, when the troops retired on Buell's command. Confederate losses were unknown, but the Federals lost at least one killed and twenty-six wounded.[28]

The following morning the Southerners countered with a reconnaissance in force, consisting of a battalion-sized cavalry party under N. B. Forrest. The Southerners split into two groups, one party advancing directly on an enemy picket post while the other, led by Colonel Forrest in person, made a flanking movement. The Federals were taken by surprise and routed with several casualties, including a Reverend Dr. Ware and his sorrel stud, captured.[29] As Forrest succinctly put it, "I Suceded in gaining thir rear. . . . they wair not looking for me I taken them by surprise they run like Suns of Biches."[30]

The tempo of fighting gradually picked up with increased skirmishing and offensive patrolling on both sides. On May 27, Sherman launched a new attack on a log cabin, serving as a Confederate command post and strong point, in front of his position. Attacking with his own outfit, supported by James Veatch's and John Logan's, he moved up straight at and around on both flanks of the strong point. Federal artillery moved up within a few hundred yards of the Confederate position before

---

28 Bouton, *Events of the Civil War*, 38, 39; *OR* 10, pt. 1, 839-847.

29 Edwin Fay to wife, May 25, 1862, in Wiley, *This Infernal War*, 59.

30 R. S. Henry, *As They Saw Forrest* (Jackson: McCowat-Mercer Press, 1956), 287, 288.

unleashing a savage fire that literally demolished the building. Sherman's infantry then stormed the position. Union losses were light, and the Federals soon advanced on other Southern works in the rear of the shattered house. Southern artillery peppered the advancing Northerners, inflicting considerable casualties on Veatch's brigade. Confederate skirmishers also harried the advance, but the Bluecoats kept up the pressure until they were within three-fourths of a mile of the main Southern works outside Corinth.[31]

On May 28, almost the entire Federal army began a series of probing attacks on the Corinth works. The Northerners were within approximately four miles of Corinth all along the line of their siege works, and in most places they were less than a mile and a half from the main Confederate fortifications. If they could gain a few more yards of ground, they could bring up the heavy guns for the final bombardment, to be followed by an all-out assault that would capture the rail center, destroy Beauregard's army, and probably end the war in the Mississippi Valley. It was a nice dream, but it was not to be, for the Confederates were already quietly pulling out southward.

On May 19, Beauregard first began the delicate task of preparing Richmond for the idea of abandoning Corinth. In a clever opening gambit, he informed General Samuel Cooper that since he had received no orders as to what to do at Corinth, he was holding the town and risking a major defeat instead of evacuating and letting the enemy have the town. Having paved the way, the Creole then explained that if by some chance he had to leave the town, that his best line of retreat was along the Mobile and Ohio Railroad. He would defend Corinth to the last, unless the government wished him to do otherwise, or if the enemy's numbers proved overwhelming. Robert E. Lee, acting as President Jefferson Davis' advisor, answered Beauregard, approving of the suggested line of retreat. Even before Lee's missive arrived, the Rebels were already milling out of the town.[32]

On May 25, the Confederate high command met in council. Beauregard proposed an immediate retreat before the enemy isolated the

---

31 *OR* 10, pt. 1, 741, 742; Force, *From Fort Henry to Corinth*, 188.

32 *OR* 10, pt. 2, 529, 530; Roman, *Beauregard*, 1: 580, 581.

town. General Hardee was especially in favor of an immediate evacuation, and he drew up a lengthy memorandum advocating it.[33] Once the evacuation was agreed, it only remained to execute it. Secrecy was vital, and in order to help deceive the enemy, the corps and divisional commanders were to spread the rumor that an attack was being planned. Detailed instructions were issued for everyone, including specific orders on the routes to be used to reach Baldwin, Mississippi. On May 28, Beauregard telegraphed Richmond that he was retreating to Baldwin, where he hoped to be able to turn and smash any pursuers.[34]

The Creole's biggest worry was that the Federals would learn of the proposed retreat and attack while his army was half in and half out of the town and fortification. Partly to keep the Federals off balance and partly to keep Halleck's attention away from the town itself, the Confederates began a series of aggressive attacks on the advancing Federal army on May 28 and 29. On one occasion, Colonel Wesley Winans led the Nineteenth Louisiana in a vigorous charge on a party of attacking Yanks. The Eleventh and Thirteenth Louisiana joined in the fight, finally driving Halleck's soldiers back.[35]

The Southern soldiers not engaged were ordered to have their baggage packed and rations cooked and to be ready to move out at a moment's notice. The sick and wounded were shipped first, and about midday on May 28, the line troops began to move out. On the night of May 29, the last of the Southerners prepared to leave. Parties of men were detailed to keep the campfires burning, while drummers were ordered to stay behind and beat reveille at the usual hour. There were dummy guns posted all along the Confederate works, while an empty train of cars ran back and forth through the town. Occasionally the engineer would let go a loud whistle from his engine, while Rebel demolition parties cheered each time the train stopped to give the Federals the impression that

---

33 *Ibid.*, 388, 389; Williams, *P. G. T. Beauregard*, 153; Nathaniel Hughes, Jr., *General William J. Hardee: Old Reliable* (Baton Rouge: Louisiana State University Press, 1965), 118.

34 Roman, *Beauregard*, 1: 395, 578-586; *OR* 10, pt. 1, 770, 771.

35 *Ibid.*, 848-856; Richardson, "War As I Saw It," 227.

reinforcements were arriving. As the last parties of Southerners left the town, they burned all the nearby bridges and took down the road signs.[36]

About 5:00 a.m. on the morning of May 30, the Union army heard a series of explosions from Corinth, as the demolition parties blew up some supplies that could not be carried off. Generals Pope and Sherman decided the Rebels were evacuating and ordered patrols to probe the town's defenses. The patrols found no resistance, and indeed no sign of life except a few Southern soldiers who were too ill to be moved and some rather battered looking civilians.

Gradually the news spread around to the army that the Confederates had gone. One Union regiment informally received the news from an elderly Negro, who wandered into their picket line. He told them, "Dey's all gone, boss, shuah! . . . You-uns can jess walk right into de town ef yer wants to!"[37]

Halleck quickly ordered a pursuit, and Pope and Buell followed Beauregard for about thirty miles before breaking off the chase. Except for some light skirmishing, the Corinth campaign was over. The railroad center was under the Union flag, but little else was achieved, a singularly barren victory. Most of the Union soldiers were not overwhelmed with their prize. Ambrose Bierce described Corinth as "the capitol of a swamp."[38] Neither Corinth nor its female inhabitants caught the fancy of a young disgruntled Yankee. He described the little town as follows:

> I don't now remember that any of the Sixth boys got particularly struck on the place. Nor did I ever hear of any of them deserting the regiment to remain there on account of being captivated by any of Corinth's tobacco-chewing, snuff-rubbing, flax-haired, sharp-nosed, hatchet-faced, yellow-eyed, sallow-skinned, cotton-dressed, flat-breasted, big-footed, bare-headed, long-waisted, hump-shouldered, stoop-necked, bare-footed, straddle-toed, sharp-

36 George T. Blakemore, Diary, May 28-30, 1862, Confederate Collection, Tennessee State Library and Archives; Roman. *Beauregard*, 1: 390, 582-587; E. John Ellis to E. P. Ellis, June 2, 1862, Ellis Family Papers, Louisiana State University Archives; Duncan, *Recollections*, 77.

37 Hinman, *The Sherman Brigade*, 205.

38 Bierce, *Collected Works*, 1: 239.

shinned, thin-lipped, pale-faced, lantern-jawed, hollow-eyed, silly-looking female damsels.[39]

The Northerners had taken Corinth, but the escape of Beauregard's army meant the war was a long way from being over. Halleck thought he had gained a great victory, but Grant and many others believed he had botched the whole affair by permitting the Confederate army to escape.

From Fishing Creek to Corinth, Southerners had suffered a succession of staggering disasters that would be difficult and perhaps impossible to make good. Despite this, the Confederacy in the West was still very much alive and dangerous. The mob that fought at Shiloh was now a dangerous, experienced fighting army capable of quickly shifting over to the offensive once Halleck scattered his grand host across the upper South. After Fort Donelson, Grant and millions of others believed that one more battle would end the Civil War; instead the conflict was only just beginning.

Perryville, Stone's River, Chickamauga, and a vast array of bloody battles waited in the future for Grant, Sherman, Buell, Hardee, Polk, and all the others to fight.

39 Briant, *Sixth Regiment Indiana*, 135.

Organization of the Confederate Army

Army of the Mississippi
Gen. Albert Sidney Johnston (killed)
Gen. P.G.T. Beauregard

First Army Corps
Maj. Gen. Leonidas Polk

First Division
Brig. Gen. Charles Clark (wounded)
Brig. Gen. Alexander P. Stewart

First Brigade
Col. Robert M. Russell, 12th Tennessee
11th Louisiana:
Col. Samuel F. Marks (wounded)
Lieut. Col. Robert H. Barrow
12th Tennessee:
Lieut. Col. Tyree H. Bell
Maj. Robert P. Caldwell
13th Tennessee:
Col. Alfred J. Vaughan, Jr.
22d Tennessee:
Col. Thomas J. Freeman (wounded)
Bankhead's Tennessee Battery:
Capt. Smith P. Bankhead

Second Brigade
Brig. Gen. Alexander P. Stewart
13th Arkansas:
Lieut. Col. A. D. Grayson (killed)
Maj. James A. McNeely (wounded)
Col. James C. Tappan
4th Tennessee:
Col. Rufus P. Neely
Lieut. Col. Otho F. Strahl
5th Tennessee:
Lieut. Col. Calvin D. Venable
33d Tennessee:
Col. Alexander W. Campbell (wounded)
Stanford's Mississippi Battery:
Capt. Thomas J. Stanford

Second Division
Maj. Gen. Benjamin F. Cheatham (wounded)

First Brigade
Brig. Gen. Bushrod R. Johnson (wounded)
Col. Preston Smith, 154th Tennessee (wounded)
Blythe's Mississippi:
Col. A. K. Blythe (killed)
Lieut. Col. David L. Herron (killed)
Maj. James Moore
2d Tennessee:
Col. J. Knox Walker
15th Tennessee:
Lieut. Col. Robert C. Tyler (wounded)
Maj. John F. Hearn
154th Tennessee (senior):
Col. Preston Smith
Lieut. Col. Marcus J. Wright (wounded)
Polk's Tennessee Battery:
Capt. Marshall T. Polk (wounded)

Second Brigade
Col. William H. Stephens, 6th Tennessee
Col. George Maney, 1st Tennessee

7th Kentucky:
Col. Charles Wickliffe (mortally wounded)
Lieut. Col. William D. Lannom
1st Tennessee (Battalion):
Col. George Maney
Maj. Hume R. Field

6th Tennessee:
Lieut. Col. Timothy P. Jones
9th Tennessee:
Col. Henry L. Douglass
Smith's Mississippi Battery:
Capt. Melancthon Smith

<u>Cavalry</u>
1st Mississippi:
Col. Andrew J. Lindsay
Mississippi and Alabama Battalion:
Lieut. Col. Richard H. Brewer

<u>Unattached</u>
47th Tennessee:
Col. Munson R. Hill
(arrived on field April 7)

<u>Second Army Corps</u>

Maj. Gen. Braxton Bragg

<u>Escort</u>
Company Alabama Cavalry, Capt. Robert W. Smith

<u>First Division</u>
Brig. Gen. Daniel Ruggles

<u>First Brigade</u>
Col. Randall L. Gibson, 13th Louisiana
1st Arkansas:
Col. James F. Fagan
4th Louisiana:
Col. Henry W. Allen (wounded)
Lieut. Col. Samuel E. Hunter

13th Louisiana:
Maj. Anatole P. Avegno (mortally wounded)
Capt. Stephen O'Leary (wounded)
Capt. Edgar M. Dubroca
19th Louisiana:
Col. Benjamin L. Hodge
Lieut. Col. James M. Hollingsworth
Vaiden or Bain's Mississippi Battery:
Capt. S. C. Bain

Second Brigade
Brig. Gen. Patton Anderson
1st Florida Battalion:
Maj. Thaddeus A. McDonell (wounded)
Capt. W. G. Poole
Capt. W. Capers Bird
17th Louisiana:
Lieut. Col. Charles Jones (wounded)
20th Louisiana:
Col. August Reichard
Confederate Guards Response Battalion:
Maj. Franklin H. Clack
9th Texas:
Col. Wright A. Stanley
Washington (Louisiana) Artillery, Fifth Company:
Capt. W. Irving Hodgson

Third Brigade
Col. Preston Pond, Jr., 16th Louisiana
16th Louisiana:
Maj. Daniel Gober
18th Louisiana:
Col. Alfred Mouton (wounded)
Lieut. Col. Alfred Roman
Crescent (Louisiana) Regiment:
Col. Marshall J. Smith
Orleans Guard (Louisiana) Battalion:
Maj. Leon Querouze (wounded)
38th Tennessee:
Col. Robert F. Looney

Ketchum's Alabama Battery:
Capt. William H. Ketchum
Cavalry
Alabama Battalion
(5 companies-Jenkins, Cox, Robins, Tomlinson, and Smith)
Capt. Thomas F. Jenkins

Second Division
Brig. Gen. Jones M. Withers

First Brigade
Brig. Gen. Adley H. Gladden (mortally wounded)
Col. Daniel W. Adams (wounded), 22d Alabama
Col. Zach C. Deas
21st Alabama:
Lieut. Col. Stewart W. Cayce
Maj. Frederick Stewart
22d Alabama:
Col. Zach C. Deas
Lieut. Col. John C. Marrast
25th Alabama:
Col. John Q. Loomis (wounded)
Maj. George D. Johnston
26th Alabama:
Lieut. Col. John G. Coltart (wounded)
Lieut. Col. William D. Chadick
1st Louisiana:
Col. Daniel W. Adams
Maj. Fred H. Farrar, Jr.
Robertson's Alabama Battery:
Capt. Felix H. Robertson

Second Brigade
Brig. Gen. James R. Chalmers
5th Mississippi:
Col. Albert E. Fant
7th Mississippi:
Lieut. Col. Hamilton Mayson
9th Mississippi:
Lieut. Col. William A. Rankin (mortally wounded)

10th Mississippi:
Col. Robert A. Smith
52d Tennessee:
Col. Benjamin J. Lea
Gage's Alabama Battery:
Capt. Charles P. Gage

Third Brigade
Brig. Gen. John K. Jackson
17th Alabama:
Lieut. Col. Robert C. Fariss
18th Alabama:
Col. Eli S. Shorter
19th Alabama:
Col. Joseph Wheeler
2d Texas:
Col. John C. Moore
Lieut. Col. William P. Rogers
Maj. Hal G. Runnels
Girardey's Georgia Battery:
Capt. Isadore P. Girardey

Cavalry
Clanton's Alabama Regiment:
Col. James H. Clanton (wounded)

Third Army Corps
Maj. Gen. William J. Hardee (wounded)

First Brigade
Brig. Gen. Thomas C. Hindman (disabled),
commanding his own and Third Brigade
Col. R. G. Shaver, 7th Arkansas (disabled)
2d Arkansas:
Col. Daniel C. Govan
Maj. Reuben F. Harvey
6th Arkansas:
Col. Alexander T. Hawthorn
7th Arkansas:
Lieut. Col. John M. Dean (killed)
Maj. James T. Martin

3d Confederate:
Col. John S. Marmaduke
Warren Light Artillery or Swett's Mississippi Battery:
Capt. Charles Swett
Pillow's Flying Artillery or Miller's Tennessee Battery:
Capt. William Miller

Second Brigade
Brig. Gen. Patrick R. Cleburne
15th Arkansas:
Lieut. Col. Archibald K. Patton (killed)
6th Mississippi:
Col. John J. Thornton (wounded)
Lieut. Col. W. A. Harper
2d Tennessee:
Col. William B. Bate (wounded)
Lieut. Col. David L. Goodall
5th (35th) Tennessee:
Col. Benjamin J. Hill
23d Tennessee:
Lieut. Col. James F. Neill (wounded)
Maj. Robert Cantrell
24th Tennessee:
Lieut. Col. Thomas H. Peebles

Shoup's Battalion
Trigg's (Austin) Arkansas Battery:
Capt. John T. Trigg
Calvert's (Helena) Arkansas Battery:
Capt. J. H. Calvert
Hubbard's Arkansas Battery:
Capt. George T. Hubbard

Third Brigade
Brig. Gen. Sterling A.M. Wood (disabled)
Col. William K. Patterson, 8th Arkansas, temporarily
16th Alabama:
Lieut. Col. John W. Harris
8th Arkansas:
Col. William K. Patterson
9th (14th) Arkansas (battalion):
Maj. John H. Kelly

3d Mississippi Battalion:
Maj. Aaron B. Hardcastle
27th Tennessee :
Col. Christopher H. Williams (killed)
Maj. Samuel T. Love (killed)
44th Tennessee:
Col. Coleman A. McDaniel
55th Tennessee:
Col. James L. McKoin
Harper's (Jefferson Mississippi) Battery:
Capt. William L. Harper (wounded)
Lieut. Putnam Darden
Georgia Dragoons:
Capt. Isaac W. Avery

Reserve Corps
Brig. Gen. John C. Breckinridge

First Brigade
Col. Robert P. Trabue, 4th Kentucky
(Clifton's) 4th Alabama Battalion:
Maj. James M. Clifton
31st Alabama:
Lieut. Col. Montgomery Gilbreath
3d Kentucky:
Lieut. Col. Benjamin Anderson (wounded)
4th Kentucky:
Lieut. Col. Andrew R. Hynes (wounded)
5th Kentucky:
Lieut. Col. Thomas H. Hunt
6th Kentucky:
Col. Joseph H. Lewis
Crew's Tennessee Battalion:
Lieut. Col. James M. Crews
Lyon's (Cobb's) Kentucky Battery:
Capt. Robert Cobb
Byrne's Mississippi Battery:
Capt. Edward P. Byrne
Morgan's Squadron Kentucky Cavalry:
Colonel John H. Morgan

Second Brigade

Brig. Gen. John S. Bowen (wounded)

Col. John D. Martin

9th Arkansas:

Col. Isaac L. Dunlop

10th Arkansas:

Col. Thomas H. Merrick

2d Confederate:

Col. John D. Martin

Maj. Thomas H. Mangum

1st Missouri:

Col. Lucius L. Rich

Pettus Flying Artillery or

Hudson's Mississippi Battery:

Capt. Alfred Hudson

Watson's Louisiana Battery

Capt. Allen A. Burlsey

Thompson's Company, Kentucky Cavalry:

Capt. Phil. B. Thompson

Third Brigade

Col. Winfield S. Statham, 15th Mississippi

15th Mississippi:

Maj. William F. Brantley (wounded)

Capt. Lamkin S. Terry

22d Mississippi:

Col. Frank Schaller (wounded)

Lieut. Col. Charles S. Nelms (mortally wounded)

Maj. James S. Prestidge

19th Tennessee:

Col. David H. Cummings (wounded)

Lieut. Col. Francis M. Walker

20th Tennessee:

Col. Joel A. Battle (wounded and captured)

Maj. Patrick Duffy

28th Tennessee:

Col. John P. Murray

45th Tennessee:

Lieut. Col. Ephraim F. Lytle

Rutledge's Tennessee Battery:

Capt. Arthur M. Rutledge

Forrest's Regiment Tennessee Cavalry:
Col. Nathan B. Forrest (wounded)

Unattached
Wharton's Texas Regiment Cavalry:
Col. John A. Wharton (wounded)
Wirt Adams's Mississippi Regiment Cavalry:
Col. Wirt Adams
McClung's Tennessee, Battery:
Capt. Hugh L. W. McClung
Roberts Arkansas Battery:
Captain Franklin Roberts

Organization of the Union Army

Army of the Tennessee
Maj. Gen. U. S. Grant

First Division
Maj. Gen. John A. McClernand

First Brigade
Col. Abraham M. Hare (wounded), 11th Iowa
Col. Marcellus M. Crocker, 13th Iowa
8th Illinois:
Capt. James M. Ashmore (wounded)
Capt. William H. Harvey (killed)
Capt. Robert H. Sturgess
18th Illinois:
Maj. Samuel Eaton (wounded)
Capt. Daniel H. Brush (wounded)
Capt. William J. Dillion (killed)
Capt. Jabez J. Anderson
11th Iowa:
Lieut. Col. William Hall (wounded)
13th Iowa:
Col. Marcellus M. Crocker

Second Brigade
Col. C. Carroll Marsh, 20th Illinois
11th Illinois:
Lieut. Col. Thomas E. G. Ransom (wounded)
Maj. Garrett Nevins (wounded)

Capt. Lloyd D. Waddell
Maj. Garrett Nevins
20th Illinois:
Lieut. Col. Evan Richards (wounded)
Capt. Orton Frisbie
45th Illinois:
Col. John E. Smith
48th Illinois:
Col. Isham N. Hayniea
Maj. Manning Mayfield

Third Brigade
Col. Julius Raith (mortally wounded), 43d Illinois.
Lieut. Col. Enos P. Wood, 17th Illinois
17th Illinois:
Lieut. Col. Enos P. Wood
Maj. Francis M. Smith
29th Illinois:
Lieut. Col. Charles M. Ferrell
43d Illinois:
Lieut. Col. Adolph Endelmann
49th Illinois:
Lieut. Col. Phineas Pease (wounded)

Unattached
Dresser's Battery (D), 2d Illinois Light Artillery:
Capt. James P. Timony
McAllister's Battery (D), 1st Illinois Light Artillery:
Capt. Edward McAllister (wounded)
Schwartz's Battery (E), 2d Illinois Light Artillery:
Lieut. George L. Nispel
Burrows' Battery, 14th Ohio Light Artillery:
Capt. Jerome B. Burrows (wounded)
1st Battalion, 4th Illinois Light Cavalry:
Lieut. Col. William McCullough
Carmichael's Company Illinois Cavalry:
Capt. Eagleton Carmichael
Stewart's Company Illinois Cavalry:
Lieut. Ezra King

Second Division
Brig. Gen. W.H.L. Wallace (mortally wounded)
Col. James M. Tuttle, 2d Iowa

First Brigade
Col. James M. Tuttle
2d Iowa:
Lt. Col. James Baker
7th Iowa:
Lt. Col. James C. Parrott
12th Iowa:
Col. Joseph J. Woods (wounded and captured)
Capt. Samuel R. Edgington (captured)
14th Iowa:
Col. Wm. T. Shaw (captured)

Second Brigade
Brig. Gen. John McArthur (wounded)
Col. Thomas Morton, 81st Ohio
9th Illinois:
Col. August Mersy
12th Illinois:
Lieut. Col. Augustus L. Chetlain
Capt. James R. Hugunin
13th Missouri:
Col. Crafts J. Wright
14th Missouri:
Col. B. S. Compton
81st Ohio:
Col. Thomas Morton

Third Brigade
Col. Thomas W. Sweeny (wounded), 52d Illinois
Col. Silas D. Baldwin, 57th Illinois
8th Iowa:
Col. James L. Geddes (wounded and captured)
7th Illinois:
Maj. Richard Rowett
50th Illinois:
Col. Moses M. Bane (wounded)

52d Illinois:
Maj. Henry Stark
Capt. Edwin A. Bowen
57th Illinois:
Col. Silas D. Baldwin
Capt. Gustav A. Busse
58th Illinois:
Col. Wm. F. Lynch (captured)

Artillery
Willard's Battery (A), 1st Illinois Light Artillery:
Lieut. Peter P. Wood

Maj. J. S. Cavender's Battalion Missouri Artillery:
Richardson's Battery (D), 1st Missouri Light Artillery:
Capt. Henry Richardson
Welker's Battery (H), 1st Missouri Light Artillery:
Capt. Frederick Welker
Stone's Battery (K), 1st Missouri Light Artillery:
Capt. George H. Stone

Cavalry
Company A, 2d Illinois Cavalry:
Capt. John R. Hotaling
Company B, 2d Illinois Cavalry:
Capt. Thomas J. Larison
Company C, 2d United States Cavalry:
Lieut. James Powell
Company I, 4th United States Cavalry:
Lieut. James Powell

Third Division
Maj. Gen. Lew Wallace

First Brigade
Col. Morgan L. Smith, 8th Missouri
11th Indiana:
Col. George F. McGinnis
24th Indiana:
Col. Alvin P. Hovey

8th Missouri:
Lieut. Col. James Peckham

Second Brigade
Col. John M. Thayer, 1st Nebraska
23d Indiana:
Col. William L. Sanderson
1st Nebraska:
Lieut. Col. William D. McCord
58th Ohio:
Col. Valentine Bausenwein
68th Ohio:
(not engaged at Shiloh; remained at Crump's Landing)
Col. Samuel H. Steadman

Third Brigade
Col. Charles Whittlesey, 20th Ohio
20th Ohio:
Lieut. Col. Manning F. Force
56th Ohio:
(not engaged at Shiloh; remained at Crump's Landing)
Col. Peter Kinney
76th Ohio:
Col. Charles R. Woods
78th Ohio:
Col. Mortimer D. Leggett

Artillery
Thompson's Battery, 9th Indiana Light Artillery:
Lieut. George R. Brown
Buel's Battery (I), 1st Missouri Light Artillery:
Lieut. Charles H. Thurber

Cavalry
3d Battalion, 11th Illinois Cavalry:
(not engaged at Shiloh; remained at Crump's Landing)
Maj. James F. Johnson
3d Battalion, 5th Ohio Cavalry:
(not engaged at Shiloh; remained at Crump's Landing)
Maj. Charles S. Hayes

Fourth Division
Brig. Gen. Stephen A. Hurlbut

First Brigade
Col. Nelson G. Williams (wounded), 3d Iowa
Col. Isaac C. Pugh, 41st Illinois
28th Illinois:
Col. Amory K. Johnson
32d Illinois:
Col. John Logan (wounded)
41st Illinois:
Col. Isaac C. Pugh
Lieut. Col. Ansel Tupper (killed)
Maj. John Warner
Capt. John H. Nale
3d Iowa:
Maj. William M. Stone (captured)
Lieut. George W. Crosley

Second Brigade
Col. James C. Veatch, 25th Indiana
14th Illinois:
Col. Cyrus Hall
15th Illinois:
Lieut. Col. Edward F. W. Ellis (killed)
Capt. Louis D. Kelley
Lieut. Col. William Cam, 14th Illinois
46th Illinois:
Col. John A. Davis (wounded)
Lieut. Col. John J. Jones
25th Indiana:
Lieut. Col. William H. Morgan (wounded)
Maj. John W. Foster

Third Brigade
Brig. Gen. Jacob G. Lauman
31st Indiana:
Col. Charles Cruft (wounded)
Lieut. Col. John Osborn
44th Indiana:
Col. Hugh B. Reed

17th Kentucky:
Col. John H. McHenry, Jr.
25th Kentucky:
Lieut. Col. Benjamin H. Bristow
Maj. William B. Wall (wounded)
Capt. B. T. Underwood
Col. John H. McHenry, Jr., 17th Kentucky

Artillery
Ross's Battery, 2d Michigan Light Artillery:
Lieut. Cuthbert W. Laing
Mann's Battery (C), 1st Missouri Light Artillery:
Lieut. Edward Brotzmann
Myers's Battery, 13th Ohio Light Artillery:
Capt. John B. Myers

Cavalry
1st and 2d Battalions 5th Ohio Cavalry:
Col. William H. H. Taylor

Fifth Division
Brig. Gen. William T. Sherman (wounded)

First Brigade
Col. John A. McDowell (disabled), 6th Iowa
40th Illinois:
Col. Stephan G. Hicks (wounded)
Lieut. Col. James W. Boothe
6th Iowa:
Capt. John Williams (wounded)
Capt. Madison M. Walden
46th Ohio:
Col. Thomas Worthington

Second Brigade
Col. David Stuart (wounded), 55th Illinois
Lieut. Col. Oscar Malmborg, 55th Illinois
Col. T. Kilby Smith, 54th Ohio
55th Illinois:
Lieut. Col. Oscar Malmborg

54th Ohio:
Col. T. Kilby Smith
Lieut. Col. James A. Farden
71st Ohio:
Col. Rodney Mason

Third Brigade
Col. Jesse Hildebrand, 77th Ohio
53d Ohio:
Col. Jesse J. Appler
Lieut. Col. Robert A. Fulton
57th Ohio:
Lieut. Col. Americus V. Rice
77th Ohio:
Lieut. Col. Willis De Hass
Maj. Benjamin D. Fearing

Fourth Brigade
Col. Ralph P. Buckland, 72d Ohio
48th Ohio:
Col. Peter J. Sullivan (wounded)
Lieut. Col. Job R. Parker
70th Ohio:
Col. Joseph R. Cockerill
72d Ohio:
Lieut. Col. Herman Canfield (killed)
Col. Ralph P. Buckland

Artillery
Maj. Ezra Taylor, Chief of Artillery
Taylor's Battery (B), 1st Illinois Light Artillery:
Capt. Samuel E. Barrett
Waterhouse's Battery (E), 1st Illinois Light Artillery:
Capt. Allen C. Waterhouse (wounded)
Lieut. Abial R Abbott (wounded)
Lieut. John A. Fitch
Morton's Battery, 6th Indiana Light Artillery:
Capt. Frederick Behr (killed)

Cavalry
2d and 3d Battalions 4th Illinois Cavalry:

Col. T. Lyle Dickey
Thielemann's two companies Illinois Cavalry:
Capt. Christian Thielemann

Sixth Division
Brig. Gen. Benjamin M. Prentiss (captured)

First Brigade
Col. Everett Peabody (killed), 25th Missouri
12th Michigan:
Col. Francis Quinn
21st Missouri:
Col. David Moore (wounded)
Lieut. Col. H. M. Woodyard
25th Missouri:
Lieut. Col. Robert T. Van Horn
16th Wisconsin:
Col. Benjamin Allen (wounded)

Second Brigade
Col. Madison Miller (captured), 18th Missouri
61st Illinois:
Col. Jacob Fry
18th Missouri:
Lieut. Col. Isaac V. Pratt (captured)
18th Wisconsin:
Col. James S. Alban (killed)

Not Brigaded

16th Iowa:
(15th and 16th Iowa were on right in an independent command)
Col. Alexander Chambers (wounded)
Lieut. Col. Addison H. Sanders
15th Iowa:
(15th and 16th Iowa were on right in an independent command)
Col. Hugh T. Reid (wounded)
23d Missouri:
(arrived on field about 9:00 a.m. on April 6, 1862)
Col. Jacob T. Tindall (killed)
Lieut. Col. Quin Morton (captured)

Artillery
Hickenlooper's Battery, 5th Ohio Light Artillery:
Capt. Andrew Hickenlooper
Munch's Battery, 1st Minnesota Light Artillery:
Capt. Emil Munch (wounded)
Lieut. William Pfaender

Cavalry
1st and 2d Battalions, 11th Illinois Cavalry:
Col. Robert G. Ingersoll

Unassigned Troops
15th Michigan:
(temporarily attached Monday to Fourth Brigade, Army of the Ohio)
Col. John M. Oliver
14th Wisconsin:
(temporarily attached Monday to Fourteenth Brigade, Army of the Ohio)
Col. David E. Wood
Battery H, 1st Illinois Light Artillery:
Capt. Axel Silfversparre
Battery I, 1st Illinois Light Artillery:
Capt. Edward Bouton
Battery B, 2d Illinois Artillery, siege guns:
Capt. Reilly Madison
Battery F, 2d Illinois Light Artillery:
Capt. John W. Powell (wounded)
8th Battery, Ohio Light Artillery:
Capt. Louis Markgraf

Army of the Ohio
Maj. Gen. Don Carlos Buell, Commanding

Second Division
Brig. Gen. Alexander McD. McCook

Fourth Brigade
Brig. Gen. Lovell H. Rousseau
6th Indiana:
Col. Thomas T. Crittenden

5th Kentucky:
Col. Harvey M. Buckley
1st Ohio:
Col. Benjamin F. Smith
1st Battalion, 15th United States:
Capt. Peter T. Swain, Maj. John H. King
1st Battalion, 16th United States:
Capt. Edwin F. Townsend, Maj. John H. King
1st Battalion, 19th United States:
Maj. Stephen D. Carpenter, Maj. John H. King

Fifth Brigade
Col. Edward N. Kirk (wounded), 34th Illinois
34th Illinois:
Maj. Charles N. Levanway (killed)
Capt. Hiram W. Bristol
29th Indiana:
Lieut. Col. David M. Dunn
30th Indiana:
Col. Sion S. Bass (mortally wounded)
Lieut. Col. Joseph B. Dodge
77th Pennsylvania:
Col. Frederick S. Stumbaugh

Sixth Brigade
Col. William H. Gibson, 40th Ohio
32d Indiana:
Col. August Willich
39th Indiana:
Col. Thomas J. Harrison
15th Ohio:
Maj. William Wallace
49th Ohio:
Lieut. Col. Albert M. Blackman

Artillery
Terrill's Battery (H), 5th United States Artillery:
Capt. William R. Terrill

Fourth Division
Brig. Gen. William Nelson

Tenth Brigade
Col. Jacob Ammen, 24th Ohio
36th Indiana:
Col. William Grose
6th Ohio:
Lieut. Col. Nicholas L. Anderson
24th Ohio:
Lieut. Col. Frederick C. Jones

Nineteenth Brigade
Col. William B. Hazen, 41st Ohio
9th Indiana:
Col. Gideon C. Moody
6th Kentucky:
Col. Walter C. Whitaker
41st Ohio:
Lieut. Col. George S. Mygatt

Twenty-second Brigade
Col. Sanders D. Bruce, 20th Kentucky
1st Kentucky:
Col. David A. Enyart
2d Kentucky:
Col. Thomas D. Sedgewick
20th Kentucky:
Lieut. Col. Charles S. Hanson

Fifth Division
Brig. Gen. Thomas L. Crittenden

Eleventh Brigade
Brig. Gen. Jeremiah T. Boyle
9th Kentucky:
Col. Benjamin C. Grider
13th Kentucky:
Col. Edward H. Hobson
19th Ohio:
Col. Samuel Beatty
59th Ohio:
Col. James P. Fyffe

Fourteenth Brigade
Col. William Sooy Smith, 13th Ohio
11th Kentucky:
Col. Pierce B. Hawkins
26th Kentucky:
Lieut. Col. Cicero Maxwell
13th Ohio:
Lieut. Col. Joseph G. Hawkins

Artillery
Bartlett's Battery (G), 1st Ohio Light Artillery:
Capt. Joseph Bartlett
Mendenhall's batteries (H and M), 4th United States Artillery:
Capt. John Mendenhall

Sixth Division
Brig. Gen. Thomas J. Wood
(This division arrived upon the field about 2 o'clock on Monday. Wagner's brigade reached the front and became engaged, the 57th Indiana losing 4 men wounded.)

Fifteenth Brigade
Col. Milo S. Hascall, 17th Indiana
17th Indiana:
Col. John T. Wilder
58th Indiana:
Col. Henry M. Carr
3d Kentucky:
Col. Thomas Bramlette
26th Ohio:
Col. Edward P. Fyffe

Twentieth Brigade
Brig. Gen. James A. Garfield
13th Michigan:
Col. Michael Shoemaker
64th Ohio:
Col. John Ferguson
65th Ohio:
Col. Charles G. Harker

Twenty-first Brigade
Col. George D. Wagner, 15th Indiana
15th Indiana:
Lieut. Col. Gustavus A. Wood
40th Indiana:
Col. John W. Blake
57th Indiana:
Col. Cyrus C. Hines
24th Kentucky:
Col. Lewis B. Grigsby

Casualties at the Battle of Shiloh, April 6-7, 1862

Army of the Mississippi (Johnston)

	Killed	Wounded	Missing	Total
First Army Corps (Polk)	385	1,953	19	2,357
First Division (Clark)	190	933	3	1,126
First Brigade (Russell)	97	512	0	609
Second Brigade (Stewart)	93	421	3	517
Second Division (Cheatham)	195	1,020	16	1,231
First Brigade (Johnson)	120	607	13	740
Second Brigade (Stephens)	75	413	3	491
Second Army Corps (Bragg)	553	2,441	634	3,628
First Division (Ruggles)	255	1,137	318	1,710
First Brigade (Gibson)	97	488	97	682
Second Brigade (Anderson)	69	313	52	434
Third Brigade (Pond)	89	336	169	594
Second Division (Withers)	298	1,304	316	1,918
First Brigade (Gladden)	129	597	103	829
Second Brigade (Chalmers)	83	343	19	445
Third Brigade (Jackson)	86	364	194	644
Third Army Corps (Hardee)	404	1936	141	2,481
First Brigade (Hindman)	109	546	38	693
Second Brigade (Cleburne)	188	790	65	1,043
Third Brigade (Wood)	107	600	38	745

Reserve Corps (Breckinridge)	386	1,682	165	2,233
First Brigade (Trabue)	151	557	92	800
Second Brigade (Bowen)	98	498	28	624
Third Brigade (Statham)	137	627	45	809
Total	1,728	8,012	959	10,699

Army of the Tennessee (Grant)

	Killed	Wounded	Missing	Total
First Division (McClernand)	285	1,372	85	1,742
First Brigade (Hare)	100	458	9	567
Second Brigade (Marsh)	80	475	30	585
Third Brigade (Raith)	96	392	46	534
Artillery	9	42	0	51
Cavalry	0	3	0	3
Second Division (Wallace)	270	1,173	1,306	2,749
First Brigade (Tuttle)	39	143	676	858
Second Brigade (McArthur)	99	470	11	580
Third Brigade (Sweeny)	127	501	619	1,247
Artillery	4	53	0	57
Cavalry	1	5	0	6
Third Division (Wallace)	41	251	4	296
First Brigade (Smith)	18	114	0	132
Second Brigade (Thayer)	20	99	3	122
Third Brigade (Whittlesey)	2	32	1	35
Artillery	1	6	0	7
Cavalry	0	0	0	0
Fourth Division (Hurlbut)	317	1,441	111	1,869
First Brigade (Williams)	112	532	43	687
Second Brigade (Veatch)	130	492	8	630
Third Brigade (Lauman)	70	384	4	458
Artillery	4	27	56	87
Cavalry	1	6	0	7

Fifth Division (Sherman)	325	1,277	299	1,901
First Brigade (McDowell)	136	439	70	645
Second Brigade (Stuart)	80	380	90	550
Third Brigade (Hildebrand)	70	221	65	356
Fourth Brigade (Buckland)	36	203	74	313
Artillery	3	27	0	30
Cavalry	0	6	0	6
Sixth Division (Prentiss)	226	928	1,008	2,172
First Brigade (Peabody)	113	372	236	721
Second Brigade (Miller)	67	311	352	730
Not Brigaded	48	215	418	681
Artillery	4	27	0	31
Cavalry	3	3	0	6
Unassigned Troops	39	159	17	215
Total	1,513	6,601	2,830	10,944

Army of the Ohio (Buell)

	Killed	Wounded	Missing	Total
Second Division (McCook)	88	823	7	918
Fourth Brigade (Rousseau)	28	280	3	311
Fifth Brigade (Kirk)	34	310	2	346
Sixth Brigade (Gibson)	25	220	2	247
Artillery	1	13	0	14
Fourth Division (Nelson)	93	603	20	716
Tenth Brigade (Ammen)	16	106	8	130
Nineteenth Brigade (Hazen)	48	357	1	406
Twenty-second Brigade (Bruce)	29	138	11	178
Fifth Division (Crittenden)	60	377	28	465
Eleventh Brigade (Boyle)	33	212	18	263
Fourteenth Brigade (Smith)	25	157	10	192
Artillery	2	8	0	10

Sixth Division (Wood)	0	4	0	4
Fifteenth Brigade (Hascall)	0	0	0	0
Twentieth Brigade (Garfield)	0	0	0	0
Twenty-first Brigade (Wagner)	0	4	0	4
Total	241	1,807	55	2,103
Shiloh Grand Total	3,482	16,420	3,844	23,746

Appendix 4

Modern Photographic Tour of Shiloh

All photos courtesy of the authors

This appendix offers readers a photo gallery of many significant and interesting portions of the battlefield at Shiloh. We included this gallery for several reasons.

First, we believe it helps readers better understand the terrain of the battlefield and thus more fully appreciate the ebb and flow of the tactical action described in the main text. This is accomplished by numbering each photograph and keying each image to the map that appears on the following page (426). Simply find the number of the photograph on the map to determine where on the field the image was captured. The map also depicts the direction of the camera when the photograph was taken.

Second, this photo gallery can be used as a quick and useful guide for walking or driving the Shiloh battlefield.

Lastly, many people who study and enjoy Civil War history do not visit—for a wide variety of reasons—the battlefields they read about. Hopefully, these modern photographs will serve as a helpful (though admittedly poor) substitute for a tour in the flesh.

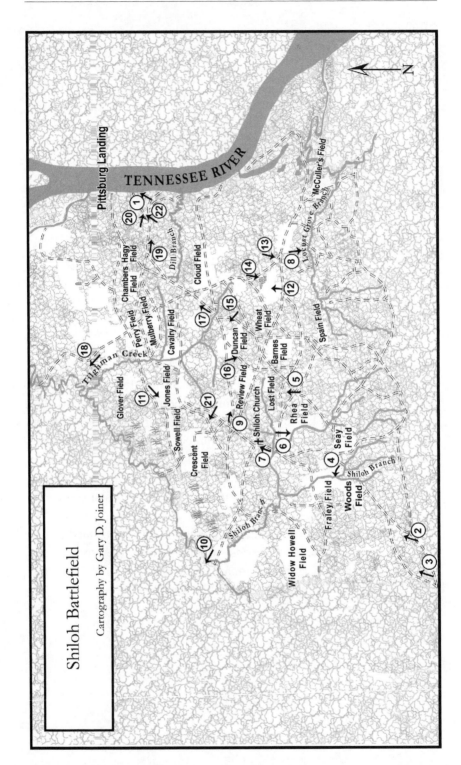

Shiloh Battlefield

Cartography by Gary D. Joiner

1. *Pittsburg Landing*. Named for Pittser Tucker, who owned a liquor store at the site, the landing on the Tennessee River was the chief staging area for the Federal armies. The Federal Army of the Tennessee landed here in mid-March 1862; U.S. Grant debarked here to take control of the disintegrating tactical situation on the morning of April 6, 1862; thousands of frightened Federal soldiers huddled along these bluffs; Don Carlos Buell's Army of the Ohio arrived here late in the day on April 6.

2. *Beauregard's Headquarters*. An impromptu Confederate council of war took place here on the afternoon of April 5, 1862, at the intersection of the Corinth and Bark roads. Beauregard argued that the Federals would be "entrenched to the eyes" and urged a withdrawal to Corinth. Albert Sidney Johnston ordered the attack to proceed, remarking, "I would fight them if they were a million."

3. *Confederate Headquarters*. This was the site of Albert Sidney Johnston's headquarters on the night of April 5, 1862. When he heard firing from the front at dawn the next morning, Johnston made his famous observation, "Tonight we will water our horses in the Tennessee River."

4. *Fraley Field*. The first shots of the battle erupted here when a small Federal patrol entered the area about dawn on April 6, 1862. The tablet in the foreground marks the position. Waiting in skirmish formation were Mississippians from Sam Wood's Brigade, denoted by the tablet at the far end of the field. Behind them was the entire Confederate Army of the Mississippi.

5. *Peabody's Headquarters.* From this spot, Everett Peabody sent out his patrol that uncovered the Confederate advance. The 25th Missouri camp is on the left, with Peabody's headquarters on the right. It was here Benjamin Prentiss scolded Peabody for bringing on the battle. In reality, Peabody's actions may well have saved the Federal army. The unfortunate colonel has only recently gained the credit he deserves; Peabody's headquarters monument doubles as his mortuary memorial.

6. *Rhea Field.* Larger at the time of the battle, this open area saw heavy fighting early in the battle as William T. Sherman's troops mounted a desperate defense. The 53rd Ohio (whose monument is visible on the right) fought well until its colonel fled the scene. Sherman was wounded in the hand near the edge of the far woods.

7. *Shiloh Branch*. This view looks north along the Corinth Road. The Confederates launched numerous assaults across it (from left to right) against William T. Sherman's camp line. The tablets on the left denote the positions of Patrick Cleburne's and Patton Anderson's brigades. Shiloh Church is visible in the distance.

8. *Locust Grove Branch*. This view looks south depicting the valley of Locust Grove Branch. It was on this high ground that David Stuart's brigade first defended the vital Federal left flank. Artillery fire from the high ground across the creek and infantry assaults from James R. Chalmers' and John K. Jackson's Confederate brigades eventually forced Stuart's withdrawal.

9. *McClernand's Crossroads Line.* This view looks along John A. McClernand's line of battle at the crossroads, where a series of regimental monuments now mark the site. A massed Southern attack struck McClernand and Sherman here around 11:00 a.m. on April 6, triggering some of the heaviest fighting of the battle. The Federals retreated, reorganized, and eventually counterattacked the Confederate left flank.

10. Owl Creek. The Tennessee River and Owl, Snake, and Lick creeks formed the basic parameters of the battlefield of Shiloh. This view of the Hamburg-Purdy Road crossing of Owl Creek looks west from the battlefield. John McDowell's brigade of Sherman's division defended this area early on April 6. This was also the route Lew Wallace would have taken to reach the battlefield had he continued on his march instead of countermarching to approach from a different direction.

11. Jones Field. One of the most important areas of the battlefield, Jones Field witnessed a badly needed reorganization of Sherman's and McClernand's shattered commands, followed by an audacious counterattack on the first day. It also witnessed heavy action on the second day when Lew Wallace's Federal division took possession of the area.

12. *The Peach Orchard.* This view of perhaps the battlefield's most famous landmark looks generally north. The monument-studded Federal line is visible in the distance across Sarah Bell's cotton field. In the foreground is the position tablet for Winfield Statham's Confederate brigade. On the left in the distance is the William Manse George cabin, the only wartime structure still standing on the battlefield.

13. The Site of Albert Sidney Johnston's Death. This view looks down the ravine in which Johnston died. After being wounded on the high ground to the north, staff officers moved the general into the ravine for cover. The tablet marks the spot where Johnston bled to death. He was the highest ranking American military officer ever killed in action.

14. *Bloody Pond.* The blood from scores of wounded soldiers on both sides turned this small body of water red. This photo, looking southwest, depicts the modern pond and the position of Willard's Battery late on the first day.

15. *The Hornet's Nest*. This view of the Sunken Road, looking northwest, shows the prominent knoll known today as the Hornet's Nest. The Confederate charges against this position were launched from the left. In the left center of this view is Munch's Minnesota Battery, with the position marker for the 21st Missouri on the right.

16. *Ruggles Battery*. After failing to break the Federal line with bayonet assaults, Confederate officers gathered artillery to blast the enemy out of the Sunken Road position. Some 50 to 60 pieces were wheeled into line, where they discharged as many as three shots a second into the Federals. The barrage was magnificent, but the Federal withdrawal came about because of pressure on the flanks and not the noisy but largely ineffective gunfire.

17. *Hell's Hollow.* This view, looking east up and out of Hell's Hollow, shows the area where the Hornet's Nest Federal defenders surrendered. The area was named "Hell's Hollow" because of the deadly Confederate crossfire that slammed shut the only avenue of escape. The tablet in center marks the site where the 12th Iowa Infantry surrendered.

18. *River Road.* It was along this obscure path that General Grant looked in vain all day for Lew Wallace's missing division. Although the label "lost" is undeserved, Wallace did not arrive at Shiloh until after dark on the first day's combat. When he finally reached the field, he did so along this route.

19. *Grant's Last Line*. This view of the Federal line, looking east, was taken on the ridge that begins at Pittsburg Landing and extends to the Snake Creek Bridge. It was on this ridge that Grant formed his last line of defense late in the day on April 6. Federal gunboats in the Tennessee River, massed infantry, and dozens of pieces of artillery defended the position.

20. *U. S. Grant's Headquarters*. General Grant made his headquarters under a large oak tree on the night of April 6, 1862. The tree no longer stands, but this monument marks the spot inside what later became the Shiloh National Cemetery. It was here Grant uttered his famous words to a pessimistic Sherman: "Lick 'em tomorrow, though."

21. *Confederate Burial Trench.* The killed from both sides were originally buried where they fell, but the Federal dead were disinterred in 1866 and taken to the Shiloh National Cemetery. Deep animosity still lingered in 1866, and the fallen Confederates were left on the battlefield. This photo depicts one of five marked Confederate burial sites at Shiloh. There are as many as four more documented burial trenches, and almost certainly many more awaiting discovery.

22. *Shiloh National Cemetery.* Established in 1866, this cemetery contains nearly 4,000 remains, mostly United States soldiers disinterred immediately after the war from common battlefield graves. Only four Confederates are interred in this cemetery; the vast majority of the Southern dead still lie in burial trenches scattered across the original battlefield.

Bibliography

Manuscripts

Ammen, Jacob. Diary. Illinois State Historical Library.

Andrews, Austin S. Papers. Illinois State Historical Library.

Bailey, Franklin H. Papers. Michigan Historical Collection, University of Michigan.

Baker, T. Otis Papers. Mississippi Department of Archives and History.

Barret, Mrs. Mason. Papers. Albert Sidney Johnston Collection, Howard-Tilton Memorial Library, Tulane University.

Bellamy, Henry. Papers. Michigan Historical Collection, University of Michigan.

Bragg, Braxton. Papers. William Palmer Collection, Western Reserve Historical Collection, Western Reserve Library.

Bruce, Francis H. Papers. Illinois State Historical Library.

Brush, Daniel Harmon. Papers. Illinois State Historical Library.

Cato, John. Papers. Mississippi Department of Archives and History.

Confederate Collection (Civil War Papers). Tennessee Department of Archives and History.

Dimitry, John. Papers. Louisiana State University Archives.

Ellis Family. Papers. Louisiana State University Archives.

Engelmann, Adolph. Papers. Illinois State Historical Library.

Engelmann-Kirchner. Papers. Illinois State Historical Library.

Gillett Family. Papers. Illinois State Historical Library.

Grant, U. S. Papers. Illinois State Historical Library.

Hapeman, Douglas. Papers. Illinois State Historical Library.

Harrison, Thomas. Papers. University of Tennessee Library.

Jackson, T. F. Papers. Mississippi Department of Archives and History.

Johnson, Charles James. Papers. Louisiana State University Archives.

Knighton, Jimmy. Papers. Louisiana State University Archives.

Lee, George Read. Papers. Illinois State Historical Library.

Louisiana Historical Association Collection, Howard-Tilton Memorial Library, Tulane University.

McLean, William. Papers. Illinois State Historical Library.

McClernand, John A. Papers. Illinois State Historical Library.

Mandeville, Theodore. Papers. Louisiana State University Archives.

Macklin, A. H. Diary. Mississippi Department of Archives and History.

Miscellaneous Collection on the Battle of Shiloh, Shiloh National Miliary Park.

Murfree, James B. Papers. University of Tennessee Library.

Peak, Frank. Papers. Louisiana State University Archives.

Pugh, Richard. Papers. Louisiana State University Archives.

Richardson, Thomas P. Papers. Louisiana State University Archives.

Ridgeway, S. P. Papers. University of Tennessee Library.

Riley, Joseph E. Papers. Chickamauga National Military Park.

Robertson, Thomas C. Papers. Louisiana State University Archives.

Rowley, W. R. Papers. Illinois State Historical Library.

Shiloh-Corinth Collection. Alabama Department of Archives and History.

Shumway, Payson Z. Papers. Illinois State Historical Library.

Sligh, James. Papers. Michigan Historical Collection, University of Michigan.

Smith, George. Papers. Iliinsis State Historical Library.

Stouffer, John. Papers. Illinois State Historical Library.

Tennessee Records. Papers. University of Tennessee Library.

Vieira, Augustine. Papers. Illinois State Historical Library.

Wallace, W. H. L. Papers. Illinois State Historical Library.

Wallace-Dickey. Papers. Illinois State Historical Library.

Wilkinson, Micajah. Papers. Louisiana State University Archives.

Newspapers

Charleston *Daily Courier*, May 13, 14, 1862.

Cincinnati *Commercial*, April 11, 1862.

Cincinnati *Daily Gazette*, October 25, 1861.

Miss Cottrill's *Scrapbook*, Alabama Department of Archives and History.

Harper's Weekly, March 1, 22, 1862.

Mrs. M. L. Kirkpatrick's *Scrapbook*, Alabama Department of Archives and History.

The Knoxville *Whig*, August 10, 1861.

Los Angeles *Times*, April 6, 1912.

Mobile Evening *News*, April 14, 1862.

Memphis *Appeal*, February 5, 1862.

Nashville *Gazette*, January 26, 1862.

New York *Herald*, April 10, May 3, 1862.

New York *Tribune*, May 10, 1862; February 15, 1864.

New Orleans *Daily Picayune*, April 11, 1862.

Washington *Post*, July 11, 1897.

Government Publications

Official Records of the Union and Confederate Navies in the War of the Rebellion. 30 vols. Washington: Government Printing Office, 1894-1922.

United States Bureau of the Census. *Eighth Census of the United States: 1860.* Washington: Government Printing Office,1894-1922.

The War of the Rebellion: A Compilation of the Official Records of the Union and Confederate Armies. 73 vols. in 128 parts. Washington: Government Printing Office, 1880-1901.

Memoirs, Letters, Diaries

Abernethy, Byron. (ed.). *Private Elisha Stockwell., Jr. Sees the Civil War.* Norman: The University of Oklahoma Press, 1958.

Anderson, John Q. (ed.). *Brokenburn: The Journal of Kate Stone, 1861-1868.* Baton Rouge: The Louisiana State University Press, 1955.

The Annals of War Written by Leading Participants North and South. Philadelphia: The Times Publishing Company, 1879.

Athearn, Robert G. (ed.). *Soldier in the West: The Civil War Letters of Alfred Lacey Hough.* Philadelphia: The University of Pennsylvania Press, 1957.

Bacon, Alvin Q. *Thrilling Adventures of A Pioneer Boy While A Prisoner of War.* N. p.: n.p., n.d.

Barber, Lucius. *Army Memoirs of Lucius W. Barber, Company D, 15th Illinois Infantry.* Chicago: J. M. W. Jones Stationery and Printing Company, 1894.

Basler, Roy. *The Collected Works of Abrahem Lincoln.* New Brunswick: Rutgers University Press, 1953.

Beale, Howard. (ed.). *The Diary of Edward Bates, 1859-1866.* Washington: Government Printing Office, 1933.

Bell, Jobn. *Tramps and Triumphs of the Second Iowa Infantry.* Des Moines: Valley Bank and Trust Company, 1961.

Bierce, Ambrose. *The Collected Works of Ambrose Bierce.* 12 vols. New York: The Neale Publishing Company, 1909.

Bouton, Edward. *Events of the Civil War.* Los Angeles: n.p., 1906.

Brinton, John. *Personal Memoirs of John H. Brinton.* New York: The Neale Publishing Company, 1914.

Brownlow, William. *Sketches of the Rise, Progress and Decline of Secession, With A Narrative of Personal Adventures Among the Rebels.* Philadelphia: G. W. Childs, Publishers, 1862.

Campaigns in Kentucky and Tennessee Including the Battle of Chickamauga, 1862-1864, Papers of the Military Historical Society of Massachusetts. Boston: 1908.

Chetlain, Augustus. *Recollections of Seventy Years.* Galena: The Gazette Publishing Company, 1899.

Coffin, Charles. *The Boys of '61.* Boston: Estes and Laurit, 1881.

Crummer, Wilbur. *With Grant At Fort Donelson, Shiloh, and Vicksburg.* Oak Park: E. C. Crummer Company, 1915.

Duncan, Thomas D. *Recollections of Thomas D. Duncan: A Confederate Soldier.* Nashville: McQuiddy Printing Company, 1922.

Foster, John. *Stories for My Grandchildren.* Cambridge: Riverside Press, 1918.

Geer, John. *Beyond the Lines or, A Yankee Prisoner Loose in Dixie.* Philadelphia: J. W. Dauyhaday, 1863.

Hazen, W. B. *A Narrative of Military Service.* Boston: Ticknor and Company, 1895.

Johnson, R. W. *A Soldier's Reminiscences in Peace and War.* Philadelphia: J. P. Lippincott, 1886.

Johnson, Robert and Clarence Buel (eds.) *Battles and Leaders of the Civil War.* 4 vols. New York: Century, 1887.

Jones, J. B. *A Rebel War Clerk's Diary at the Confederate States Capitol.* 2 vols. Philadelphia: J. B. Lippincott and Company, 1866.

Joyce, John. *A Checkered Life.* Chicago: S. P. Pounds, 1883.

Kirwan, A. D. *Johnny Green of the Orphan Brigade.* Lexington: University of Kentucky Press, 1956.

Long, E. B. (ed.). *Personal Memoirs of U. S. Grant.* Cleveland: The World Publishing Company, 1952.

McCormack, T. J. (ed.). *Memoirs of Gustave Koerner, 1809-1896.* Cedar Rapids: Torch Press, 1909.

Personal Recollections of the War of the Rebellion: Addresses Delivered Before the Commandery of the State of New York, Military Order of the Loyal Legion of the United States. New York: 1907.

Richardson, Albert. *The Secret Service, The Field, the Dungeon and the Escape.* Hartford: American Publishing Company, 1865.

Sherman, William T. *Memoirs of General William T. Sherman.* Bloomington: Indiana University Press, 1957.

Sketches of War History 1861-1865, Papers Prepared for the Commandery of the State of Ohio, Military Order of the Loyal Legion of the United States. Cincinnati: 1888-1908.

Stanley, Henry. *Autobiography of Henry Morton Stanley.* Boston: Houghton Mifflin, 1906.

Stevenson, William. *Thirteen Months in the Rebel Army.* New York: Barnes and Burr, 1862.

Stillwell, Leander. *The Story of A Common Soldier of Army Life in the Civil War, 1861-65.* Kansas City: Franklin Hudson Publishing Company, 1920.

Taylor, F. Jay (ed.). *The Secret Diary of Robert Patrick, 1861-1865: The Reluctant Rebel.* Baton Rouge: Louisiana State University Press, 1959.

Thomas, B. F. *Soldier Life: A Narrative of the Civil War.* Privately printed, 1907.

Thompson, Seymour. *Recollections With the Third Iowa Regiment.* Cincinnati: Published by the author, 1864.

Thorndike, Rachel Sherman. (ed.). *The Sherman Letters.* New York: Charles Scribner's Sons, 1894.

Throne, Mildred. (ed.). *The Civil War Diary of Cyrus F. Boyd, Fifteenth Iowa Infantry, 1861-1863.* Iowa City: State Historical Society of Iowa, 1953.

Wallace, Lew. *An Autobiography.* 2 vols. New York: Harper, 1906.

War Paper No. 3, Commandery of the State of California, Military Order of the Loyal Legion of the United States. Los Angeles: 1889.

War Paper No. 88, Commandery of the District of Columbia, Military Order of the Loyal Legion of the United States. Washington: 1912.

War Sketches and Incidents as Related Companions of the Iowa Commandery, Military Order of the Loyal Legion of the United States. Des Moines: P. C. Kenyon Press, 1893.

War Talks in Kansas: A Series of Papers Read Before the Kansas Commandery, Military Order of the Loyal Legion of the United States. Kansas City: Franklin Publishing Company, 1906.

Watkins, Sam. "Co. Aytch." *A Side Show of the Big Show.* New York: Collier Books, 1962.

Whittlessey, Charles. *War Memoranda: Cheat River to the Tennessee.* 1861-1862. Cleveland: William Walker, 1884.

Wiley, Bell I. (ed.). *"This Infernal War" The Confederate Letters of Sgt. Edwin H. Fay.* Austin: The University of Texas Press, 1958.

Wilkie, Fran *Pen and Powder.* Boston: Ticknor and Company, 1888.

Wilson, James. *The Life of John A. Rawlins.* New York: The Neale Publishing Company, 1916.

Young, L. D. *Reminscences of A Soldier of the Orphan Brigade.* Paris: N. p: N. d.

Younger, Edward. (ed.). *Inside the Confederate Government: The Diary of Robert Garlick Hill Kean.* New York: Oxford University Press, 1957.

Articles

"Amended Report of General Ruggles." *Southern Historical Society Papers* 7 (January 1879): 35-47.

Barry, Robert. "A Soldier's Letter from Shiloh." *Harper's Weekly* 57 (April 5, 1913).

"A Bible Twice Captured." *Iowa Historical Record* 1 (July 1885): 132-134.

Blackburn, J. "Reminiscences of the Terry Rangers." *Southwestern Historical Quarterly* 22 (July 1918): 38-77.

Buttgenbach, Walter. "Coast Defense in the Civil War." *Journal of the United States Artillery* 39 (March-April 1913): 210-216.

Campbell, Robert. "Brief History of the 17th Regiment Illinois Volunteer Infantry, 1861-1864." *Illinois Historical Society Transactions for 1914* (Springfield: 1914), 184-190.

Carman, Henry. (ed.). "Diary of Amos Glover." *The Ohio State Archaeological and Historical Quarterly* 44 (April 1935): 258-272.

Capron, Thaddeus H. "War Diary of Thaddeus H. Capron, 1861-1865." *Illinois State Historical Society* 12 (October 1919): 343-347.

Chalmers, James R. "Forrest and His Campaigns." *Southern Historical Society Papers* 7 (October 1879): 451-458.

Civil War History 8 (September 1962): 335, 336.

Clark, Robert, Jr. "The New Orleans German Colony in the Civil War." *Louisiana Historical Quarterly* 20 (October 1937): 990-1015.

Confederate Veteran, 1893-1932, Nashville: 40 vols.

Conger, A. L. "Fort Donelson." *The Military Historial and Economist* 1 (January 1916): 33-62.

Crenshaw, Edward. "Diary of Captain Edward Crenshaw." *The Alabama Historical Quarterly* 1 (Fall 1930): 261-270.

Crosley, George. "Some Reminiscences of an Iowa Soldier." *Annals of Iowa* 10 (July 1911): 119-136.

Deupree, J. G. "The Noxubee Squadron of the First Mississippi Cavalry." *Publications of the Mississippi Historical Society* 2 (Jackson: Mississippi Historical Society, 1918): 12-143.

"Editorial." *Illinois State Historical Society Journal* 9 (July 1916): 221-227.

Edwards, William. "Shiloh, the Counterstroke That Failed." *The Quartermaster Review* 15 (No. 4, 1936): 31-37, 74-75.

Eisenschiml, Otto. "The 55th Illinois at Shiloh." *The Journal of the Illinois State Historical Society* 56 (Summer 1963): 193-211.

———. "Shiloh—The Blunders and the Blame." *Civil War Times Illustrated* 2 (April 1963): 6-34.

Haskell, Fritz. (ed.). "Diary of Colonel William Camm, 1861-1865." *Illinois State Historical Society* 18 (January 1926): 853.

Houghton, Edgar. "History of Company I, Fourteenth Wisconsin Infantry, from October 15, 1861 to October 9, 1865." *The Wisconsin Magazine of History* 11 (September 1927) 26-49.

Houston, Sam Jr. "Shiloh Shadows." *The Southwestern Historical Quarterly* 34 (July 1930): 329-333.

Hurst, T. M. "Battle of Shiloh." *The American Historical Magazine and Tennessee Historical Society Quarterly* 7 (January 1902): 22-37.

Jackson, Alice F. and Bettina. (eds.). "Autobiography of James Albert Jackson, Sr., M. D.." *The Wisconsin Magazine of History* 28 (December 1944): 197-209.

Jackson, Luther. "A Prisoner of War." *Annals of Iowa* 19 (July 1933): 23-41.

Jordan, Phil and Charles Thomas. (eds.). "Reminiscences of an Ohio Volunteer." *The Ohio Archaeological and Historical Quarterly* 47 (October 1939): 304-323.

Jordan, Thomas. "The Battle of Shiloh." *Southern Historical Society Papers* 35 (January-December 1907): 204-230.

————. "The Campaign and Battle of Shiloh." *The United Service: A Monthly Review of Military and Naval Affairs* 12 (March-April 1885): 262-280, 393-403.

Kelly, Maud. "General John Herbert Kelly, The Boy General of the Confederacy." *The Alabama Quarterly* 9 (Spring 1947): 9-114.

McWhiney, Grady. "Braxton Bragg at Shiloh." *The Tennessee Historical Quarterly* 21 (March 1962): 19-30.

Mahon, John. (ed.). "The Civil War Letters of Samuel Mahon, Seventh Iowa Infantry."
The Iowa Journal of History 51 (July 1953): 233-236.

Mills, George. (ed.) "The Sharp Family Civil War Letters." *Annals of Iowa* 34 (January 1959): 481-532.

"Missourians." *The Missouri Historical Review* 37 (April 1943): 315-342.

Moore, Samuel A. "Ten Minutes With The Old Boys." *Third Reunion, Iowa Hornet's Nest Brigade Held at Newton, Iowa, Aug. 21 and 22, 1895* (Newton: Record Print, 1895).

Ness, George T. Jr. "Louisiana Officers of the Confederate Navy." *The Louisiana Historical Quarterly* 27 (April 1944) 476-486.

Parish, John. (ed.) "A Few Martial Memoirs." *The Palimpest* 1 (October 1920): 114-121.

Richardson, Frank. "War As I Saw It, 1861-65." *The Louisiana Historical Quarterly* 6 (January 1923): 89-106.

Romero, Sidney J. "Louisiana Clergy and the Confederate Army." *Louisiana History* 2 (Summer 1961): 287-291.

Ruff, Joseph. "Civil War Experiences of A German Emigrant As Told by the Late Joseph Ruff of Albion." *The Michigan History Magazine* 27 (Winter 1943): 271-301.

Salter, William. "Major-General John M. Corse." *Annals of Iowa* 2 (April 1895): 1-19.

Shoup, F. A. "The Art of War in '62 – Shiloh." *The United Service: A Monthly Review of Military and Naval Affairs* 11 (July 1884): 1-13.

Stephenson, W. H. and E. A. Davis. (eds.). "The Civil War Diary of Willie Micajah Barrow September 23, 1861-July 13, 1862." *The Louisiana Historical Quarterly* 17 (July-October 1934): 436-451, 712-731.

Terry, James G. "Record of the Alabama State Artilery From Its Organization in May 1836 to the Surrender in April 1865." *The Alabama Historical Quarterly* 20 (Summer 1958): 141-146.

Throne, Mildred. (ed.) "Erastus B. Sarpers' History of Company D, 12th Iowa Infantry 1861-1865." *Iowa Journal of History* 56 (April 1958): 153-187.

———. "Iowa and the Battle of Shiloh." *Iowa Journal of History* 55 (July 1957): 209-274.

———. "Iowans in Southern Prisons 1862." *Iowa Journal of History* 54 (January 1956): 67-88.

———. "Letters from Shiloh." *Iowa Journal of History* 52 (July 1954): 235-280.

Walker, Arthur L. "Three Alabama Baptist Chaplains, 1861-1865." *The Alabama Review* 16 (July 1963): 174-184.

General Accounts and Secondary Critiques

Adams George W. *Doctors in Blue: The Medical History of the Union Army in the Civil War.* New York: Henry Schuman, 1952.

Andrews, J. Cutler. *The North Reports the Civil War.* Pittsburgh: University of Pittsburgh Press, 1955.

Bearss, Edwin. Artillery Study Shiloh National Military Park, Project No. 17. Shiloh National Military Park: February, 1964, Unpublished paper, 52 pages, in the Shiloh National Military Park Library.

Black, Robert C., III. *Railroads of the Confederacy.* Chapel Hill: University of North Carolina Press, 1952.

Boatner, Mark Mayo. *Civil War Dictionary.* New York: David McKay Company: 1959.

Booth, Andrew. *Records of Louisiana Confederate Soldiers and Louisiana Confederate Commands.* 3 vols. New Orleans: n.p., 1920.

Brazelton, B. G. *A History of Hardin County, Tennessee.* Nashville: Cumberland Presbyterian Publishing House, 1885.

Brewer, W. *Alabama: Her History, Resources, War Record, and Public Men From 1540 to 1872.* Montgomery: Barrett and Brown, 1872.

Bryant, Thomas J. *Who Is Responsible For The Advance Of The Army Of The Tennessee Towards Corinth?* N.p.: N.p., 1885.

Byers, S. H. M. *Iowa In War Times.* Des Moines: W. D. Condit and Company, 1888.

Crozier, Emmet. *Yankee Reporters, 1861-1865.* New York: Oxford University Press, 1956.

Cunningham, O. Edward. Roster of Louisiana Units in the Confederate Army. Unpublished paper prepared for the Louisiana Civil War Centennial Commission, 1964.

Davis, Jefferson. *The Rise and Fall of the Confederate Government.* New York: D. Appleton and Company, 1881.

Devens, Richard Miller. *The Pictorial Book of Anecdotes and Incidents of the War of the Rebellion.* Hartford: Hartford Publishing Company, 1867.

Dillahunty, Albert. *Shiloh: National Military Park, Tennessee National Park Service Historical Handbook.* Washington: Government Printing Office, N.d.

Eaton, Clement. *History of the Southern Confederacy.* New York: The MacMillan Company, 1954.

Eisenschiml, Otto. *The Story of Shiloh.* Chicago: The Civil War Round Table, 1940.

Elson, Henry W. *The Civil War Through the Camera.* New York: McKiney, Stone and Mackenzie, Publishers, 1912.

Fiske, John. *The Mississippi Valley in the Civil War.* Boston: Houghton Mifflin Company, 1900.

Force, M. F. *From Fort Henry to Corinth.* New York: Scribers, 1881.

Fuller, Claude and Richard Steuart. *Firearms of the Confederacy.* Huntington: Standard Publications, Inc., 1944.

Gosnell, H. Allen. *Guns on the Western Waters: The Story of River Gunboats in the Civil War.* Baton Rouge: Louisiana State University Press, 1949.

Harper, Robert. *Ohio Hand Book of the Civil War.* Columbus: Ohio Historical Society, 1961.

Henry, Robert S. *The Story of the Mexican War.* New York: Frederick Ungar Publishing Company, 1961.

History of Tennessee from the Earliest Time to the Present. Nashville: Goodspeed Publishing Company, 1886.

Hoburt, Edwin. *The Truth About Shiloh.* Springfield: Illinois Register Publishing Company, 1909.

Hokanson, Nels. *Swedish Immigrants in Lincoln's Time.* London: Harper, 1942.

Howard, Samuel A. *The Illustrated Comarehensive History of the Great Battle of Shiloh. Kansas City: Franklin Hudson Publishing Company, 1921.*

Humes, Thomas. *The Loyal Mountaineers of Tennessee.* Knoxville: Ogden Brothers and Company, 1888.

Lindsey, T. J. *Ohio at Shiloh.* Cincinnati: C. J. Krehbiek and Company, 1903.

Lonn, Ella. *Foreigners in the Confederacy*. Chapel Hill: The University of North Carolina Press, 1940.

———. *Foreigners in the Union Army and Navy*. Baton Rouge: Louisiana State University Press, 1951.

Monaghan, Jay. *Civil War on the Western Border, 1854-1865*. Boston: Little, Brown and Company, 1955.

Murdock, Eugene. *Ohio's Bounty System in the Civil War*. Columbus: Ohio State University Press for the Ohio Historical Society, 1963.

Ninth Reunion of Iowa's Hornet's Nest Brigade, Held at Pittsburg Landing, April 6 and 7, 1912. Des Moines: Bisland Brothers, Printers, 1912.

Official Roster of the Soldiers of the State of Ohio in the War of the Rebellion, 1861-1865. 8 vols. Cincinnati: The Ohio Valley Press, 1888.

Paris, Comte de. *History of the Civil War in America*.4 vols. Philadelphia: Joseph H. Coates and Company, 1875.

Patton, James. *Unionism and Reconstruction in Tennessee 1860-1869*. Chapel Hill: The University of North Carolina Press, 1934.

Pitts, Charles. *Chaplains in Gray: The Confederate Chaplains Story*. Nashville: Broadman Press, 1957.

Polk, W. M. "Facts Connected With The Concentration of the Army of The Mississippi Before Shiloh, April, 1862." *Southern Historical Society Papers* 8 (January-December 1880).

Pollard, Edwin. *The First Year of the War*. Richmond: West and Johnston, 1862.

Reed, D. W. *The Battle of Shiloh and the Organizations Engaged*. Washington: Government Printing Office, 1902.

Roseboom, Eugene. *The History of the State of Ohio*. Columbus: Ohio Archaelogical and Historical Society, 1942.

Shotwell, Walter. *The Civil War in America*. New York: Longmans, Green and Company, 1923.

Steele, Matthew F. *American Campaigns*. 2 vols. Washington: Combat Press, 1951.

Swinton, William. *The Twelve Decisive Battles of the Civil War*. New York: Dick and Fitzgerald, 1867.

Temple, Oliver. *East Tennessee and the Civil War*. Cincinnati: The R. Clarke Company, 1899.

Thurston, Gates P. *The Antiquities of Tennessee and the Adjacent States*. Cincinnati: The Robert Clarke Company, 1897.

Tuttle, James M. "Brigade Report," *First Reunion of Iowa's Hornet's Nest Brigade Held at Des Moines Iowa, Wednesday and Thursday, October12 and 13, 1887*. Oskaloosa: 1887.

Webb, Willard. (ed.). *Crucial Moments of the Civil War*. New York: Bonanza Books, 1961.

Wiley, Bell. *The Life of Johnny Reb: The Common Soldier of the Confederacy.* Indiananapolis: The Bobbs-Merrill Company, 1943.

Williams, T. Harry. *Lincoln and His Generals.* New York: Grosset and Dunlap, 1952.

Winton, E. D. *Story of Pontotoc.* Pontotoc: Pontotoc Progress Printing, 1931.

Worthington, Thomas. *Colonel Worthington Vindicated: Sherman's Discreditable Record at Shiloh on His Own and Better Evidence.* Washington: F. McGill and Company, 1878.

———. *Shiloh; Or the Tennessee Campaign of 1862.* Washington: McGill and Witherow, 1872.

Victor, Orville. *Incidents and Anecdotes of the War.* New York: James D. Torrey, Publisher, 1862.

Unit Histories

Ambrose, D. Leib. *History of the Seventh Regiment Illinois Volunteer Infantry.* Springfield: Illinois Journal Company, 1868.

Belknap, William W. *History of the 15th Regiment Iowa Veteran Volunteer Infantry From October, 1861, to August, 1885.* Keokuk: R. B. Ogden and Son, 1887.

Bering, John and Thomas Montgomery. *History of the Forty-eighth Ohio Veteran Volunteer Infantry.* Hillsboro: The Higlhand News Office, 1880.

Briant, Charles C. *History of the Sixth Regiment Indiana Volunteer Infantry.* Indianapolis: W. B. Burford, 1891.

Buck, Irving. *Cleburne and His Command.* New York: The Neale Publishing Company, 1908.

Chamberlain, W. H. *History of the Eighty-first Regiment, Ohio Infantry Volunteers, During the War of the Rebellion.* Cincinnati: Gazette Printing House, 1865.

Connelly, T. W. *History of the Seventieth Ohio Regiment, From its Organization to its Mustering Out.* Cincinnati: Peak Brothers, 1902.

Cope, Alexis. *The Fifteenth Ohio Volunteers and Its Campaigns, War of 1861-65.* Columbus: Published by the author, 1916.

Duke, Basil. *A History of Morgan's Cavalry.* Bloomington: Indiana University Press, 1960.

Duke, John K. *History of the Fifty-third Ohio Volunteer Infantry, During the War of the Rebellion.* Portsmouth: The Blade Printing Company, 1900.

George, Henry. *History of the 3d, 7th, 8th, and 12th Kentucky, C. S. A.* Louisville: C. T. Dearing Printing Company, 1911.

Hancock, R. R. *Hancock's Diary or A History of the Second Tennessee Cavalry With Sketches of the First and Seventh Battalions.* Nashville: Brandon Printing Company, 1887.

Hannaford, Edwin. *The Story of A Regiment: A History of the Campaigns, and Associations in the Field, of the Sixth Regiment Ohio Volunteer Infantry.* Cincinnati: Published by the author, 1868.

Hart, Ephrain J. *History of the Fortieth Illinois Infantry.* Cincinnati: H. S. Bosworth, 1864.

Hartpence, William R. *History of the Fifty-first Indiana Veteran Volunteer Infantry.* Cincinnati: The Robert Clack Company, 1894.

Head, Thomas. *Campaigns and Battles of the Sixteenth Regiment Tennessee.* Nashville: Cumberland Presbyterian Publishing House, 1885.

Hinman, Wilbur. *The Story of the Sherman Brigade.* Alliance: Published by the author, 1897.

Horn, Stanley. *The Armies of Tennessee: A Military History.* New York: The Bobbs–Merrill Company, 1941.

Jones, Thomas. *Complete History of the 46th Regiment, Illinois Volunteer Infantry.* Freeport: W. H. Wagner eand Sons, 1907.

Keil, F. W. *Thirty-fifth Ohio: A Narrative of Service From August, 1861 to1864.* Fort Wayne: Housh and Company, 1894.

Kerwood, Asbury L. *Annals of the Fifty-seventh Regiment Indiana Volunteers.* Dayton: W. J. Shuey, 1868.

Kimbell, Charles Bell. *History of Battery "A" First Illinois Light Artillery Volunteers.* Chicago: Cushing Printing Company, 1899.

Kimberly, Robert and Ephrain Holloway. *The 41st Ohio Veteran Volunteer Infantry in the War of the Rebellion.* Cleveland: W. R. Smellie, 1897.

McElroy, Edith. *The Undying Procession: Iowa's Civil War Regiments.* The Iowa Civil War Centennial Commission, n.d.

McMurray, W. J. *History of the Twentieth Tennessee Regiment Volunteer Infantry. Nashville: The Publication Committee, 1904.*

Metcalf, Clyde. *A History of the United States Marine Corps.* New York: G. P. Putnams Sons, 1939.

Morrison, Marion. *A History of the Ninth Regiment Illinois Volunteer Infantry.* Monmouth: John S. Clark, 1864.

Payne, Edwin Waters. *History of the Thirty-fourth Regiment of Illinois Volunteer Infantry.* Clinton: Allen Printing Company, 1903.

Rennolds, Edwin. *A History of The Henry County Commands Which Served in the Confederate States Army.* The Continental Book Company, Kennesaw Georgia: 1961.

Renick, John H. *The 44th Indiana Volunteer Infantry.* LaGrange, Indiana: Published by the Author, 1880.

Rietti, J, C. *History of the Mississippi Rifles, 10th Mississippi Regiment.* Glasgow: W. Anderson Fadie, N .D.

———. *Military Annals of Mississippi.* N.p., N.p, N.d.

Robertson, John. *Michigan In The War.* Lansing: W. S. George and Company, 1862.

Rowland, Dunbar. *The Official and Statistical Register of the State of Mississippi.* Nashville: Press of the Brandon Printing Company, 1908.

Stevenson, Thomas. *History of the 78th Ohio Volunteer Infantry, From Its "Muster' in" to Its "Muster' Out."* Zanesville: Hugh Dunne, 1865.

The Story of the Fifty-fifth Regiment, Illinois Volunteer Infantry in the Civil War. Clinton: Privately printed by the author, 1887.

Tennesseans in the Civil War: A Military History of Confederate and Union Units with Available Rosters of Personnel. In 2 parts. Nashville: Published by the Civil War Centennial Commission, 1964.

Thompson, Edward. *History of the Orphan Brigade.* Louisville: Leslie Thompson, 1895.

Vaughan, A. J. *Personal Record of the Thirteenth Regiment, Tennessee Infantry.* Memphis: Press of C. S. Toof and Company, 1897.

Wood, D. W. *History of the 20th Ohio Volunteer Veteran Infantry Regiment, 1861-1865.* Columbus: Paul and Thrall Book and Job Printers, 1876.

Worsham, W. J. *The Old Nineteenth Tennessee.* Knoxville: Press of Paragon Printing Company, 1902.

Worthington, Thomas. *Brief History of the 46th Ohio Volunteers.* Washington: Privately printed, 1878.

Wright, Henry. *A History of the Sixth Iowa Infantry.* Iowa City: Torch Press, 1923.

Biographies

Ambrose, Stephen. *Halleck: Lincoln's Chief of Staff.* Baton Rouge: Louisiana State University Press, 1962.

Badeau, Adam. *Military History of Ulysses S. Grant, from April, 1861, to April, 1865.* New York: D. Appleton and Company, 1881.

Cassidy, Vincent. *Henry Watkins Allen of Louisiana.* Baton Rouge: Louisiana State University Press, 1964.

Catton, Bruce. *Grant Moves South.* Little, Brown and Company, 1960.

Cleaves, Freeman. *Rock of Chickamauga: The Life of General George H. Thomas.* Norman: University of Oklahoma Press, 1946.

Conger, A. L. *The Rise of U. S. Grant.* New York: Century Press, 1931.

Cortissoz, Royal. *The Life of Whitelaw Reid.* 2 vols. New York: Charles Scribner's Sons, 1921.

Dyer, John. *"Fightin' Joe" Wheeler.* Baton Rouge: Louisiana State University Press, 1941.

Elliott, Charles W. *Winfield Scott, the Soldier and the Man.* New York: The Macmillan Company, 1937.

Freeman, D. S. *R. E. Lee.* 4 vols. New York: Charles Scribner's Sons, 1934.

Fuller, J. F. C. *The Generalship of Ulysses S. Grant.* New York: Dodd, Mead and Company, 1929.

Henry, R. S. *As They Saw Forrest.* Jackson: McCowat-Mercer Press, 1956.

———. *"First With the Most" Forrest.* Indianapolis: Bobbs-Merrill Company, 1944.

Holland, Cecil. *Morgan and His Raiders: A Biography of the Confederate General.* New York: Macmillan Company, 1942.

Hoppin, J. *Life of Andrew Hull Foote, Rear-Admiral, United States Navy.* New York: Harper and Brothers, Publishers, 1874.

Hughes, Nathaniel C. *General William J. Hardee: Old Reliable.* Baton Rouge: Louisiana State University Press, 1965.

Johnston, William Preston. *Life of Gen. Albert Sidney Johnston.* New York: D. Appleton and Company, 1878.

Jordan, Thomas and Roger Pryor. *The Campaigns of Lieut-Gen. N. B. Forrest, and of Forrest's Cavalry.* New Orleans: Blelock and Company, 1868.

Kamm, Samuel R. *The Civil War Career of Thomas A. Scott.* Philadelphia: University of Pennsylvania Press, 1940.

King, Charles. *The True Ulysses S. Grant.* Philadelphia: J. B. Lippincott, 1914.

Lewis, Lloyd. *Sherman: Fighting Prophet.* New York: Harcourt, Brace and Company, 1958.

Liddell Hart, B. H. *Sherman, Soldier, Realist, American.* New York: Dodd, Meade and Company, 1930.

McKee, Irving. *"Ben-Hur" Wallace: The Life of General Lew Wallace.* Berkley: University of California Press, 1947.

Malone, Dumas and Harris Starr. (eds.) *Dictionary of American Biography.* 20 vols. and Supplement. New York: Charles Scribner's Sons, 1928-1944.

Myers, Raymond. *The Zollie Tree.* Louisville: The Filson Club, 1964.

Pickett, W. D. *Sketch of the Military Career of William J. Hardee, Lieutenant-General, C. S. A.* Lexington: James E. Hughes, Printer, n.d.

Richardson, Albert D. *A Personal History of Ulysses S. Grant.* Hartford: M. A. Winter and Hatch, 1885.

Roland, Charles. *Albert Sidney Johnston: Soldier of Three Republics.* Austin: University of Texas Press, 1964.

Roman, Alfred. *The Military Operations of General Beauregard in the War Between the States, 1861-1865.* 2 vols. New York: Harper, 1884.

Seitz, Don. *Braxton Bragg: General of the Confederacy.* Columbia: The State Company, 1924.

Sheppard, Eric. *Bedford Forrest: The Confederacy's Greatest Cavalryman.* New York: Dial Press, 1930.

A Soldier's Honor: With Reminiscences of Major-General Earl Van Dorn, By His Comrades. New York: Abbey Press, 1902.

Wallace, Isabel. *Life of General W. H. L. Wallace.* Chicago: R. R. Donnelley and Sons, 1909.

Warner, Ezra. *Generals in Blue.* Baton Rouge: Louisiana State University Press, 1964.

———. *Generals in Gray: Lives of the Confederate Commanders.* Baton Rouge: Louisiana State University Press, 1959.

Williams, Kenneth P. *Lincoln Finds A General.* 5 Vols. New York: The Macmillan Company, 1952.

Williams, T. Harry. *McClellan, Sherman and Grant.* New Brunswick: Rutgers University Press, 1962.

———. *P. G. T. Beauregard: Napoleon in Gray.* Baton Rouge: Louisiana State University Press, 1959.

Woodward, W. E. *Meet General Grant.* New York: Garden City Publishing Company, In, 1928.

Wyeth, John. *That Devil Forrest: Life of General Nathan Bedford Forrest.* New York: Harper and Brothers, 1959.

Post-1966 Bibliography Addendum

Allen, Stacy D. "Shiloh!: The Campaign and First Day's Battle." *Blue and Gray* 14, no. 3 (Winter 1997): entire issue.

———. "Shiloh!: The Second Day's Battle and Aftermath." *Blue and Gray* 14, no. 4 (Spring 1997): entire issue.

Ash, Steven V. *When the Yankees Came: Conflict and Chaos in the Occupied South, 1861-1865.* Chapel Hill: University of North Carolina Press, 1995.

Bearss, Edwin C. *Hardluck Ironclad: The Sinking and Salvage of the Cairo.* Baton Rouge: Louisiana State University Press, 1966.

Chaffin, Tom. *Pathfinder: John Charles Fremont and the Course of American Empire.* New York: Hill and Wang, 2002.

Cimprich, John. *Fort Pillow, A Civil War Massacre, And Public Memory.* Baton Rouge: Louisiana State University Press, 2005.

Clark, John E. *Railroads In The Civil War: The Impact Of Management On Victory And Defeat.* Baton Rouge: Louisiana State University Press, 2004.

Cooling, Benjamin F. *Forts Henry and Donelson: The Key to the Confederate Heartland.* Knoxville: University of Tennessee Press, 1987.

———. *Fort Donelson's Legacy: War and Society in Kentucky and Tennessee, 1862-1863.* Knoxville: University of Tennessee Press, 1997.

Daniel, Larry J. *Shiloh: The Battle That Changed the Civil War*. New York: Simon and Shuster, 1997.

————. *Days of Glory: The Army of the Cumberland, 1861-1865*. Baton Rouge: Louisiana State University Press, 2004.

———— and Lynn Bock. *Island No. 10: Struggle for the Mississippi Valley*. Tuscaloosa: University of Alabama Press, 1996.

Davis, William C. *Breckinridge: Statesman, Soldier, Symbol*. Baton Rouge: Louisiana State University, 1974.

Engle, Stephen D. *Don Carlos Buell: Most Promising of All*. Chapel Hill: The University of North Carolina Press, 1999.

Fahey, John H. "The Fighting Doctor: Bernard John Dowling Irwin in the Civil War." *North and South* 9, no. 1 (March 2006): 36-50.

Frank, Joseph Allan and George A. Reaves. *"Seeing the Elephant": Raw Recruits at the Battle of Shiloh*. Urbana: University of Illinois Press, 2003.

Gott, Kendall D. *Where the South Lost the War: An Analysis of the Fort Henry-Fort Donelson Campaign, Feb. 1862*. Mechanicsburg, 2003.

Hartje, Robert G. *Van Dorn: The Life and Times of a Confederate General*. Nashville: Vanderbilt University Press, 1967.

Hughes, Nathaniel Cheairs. Jr. *General William J. Hardee: Old Reliable*. Baton Rouge: Louisiana State University Press, 1965.

————. *The Battle of Belmont: Grant Strikes South*. Chapel Hill: The University of North Carolina Press, 1991.

———— and Roy P. Stonesifer, Jr. *The Life and Wars of Gideon J. Pillow*. Knoxville: University of North Carolina Press, 1993.

Flood, Charles Bracelen. *Grant and Sherman: The Friendship That Won the Civil War*. New York: Farrar, Straus and Giroux, 2005.

Kiper, Richard L. *Major General John Alexander McClernand: Politician in Uniform*. Kent: The Kent State University Press, 1999.

Lash, Jeffrey N. *A Politician Turned General: The Civil War Career of Stephen Augustus Hurlbut*. Kent: Kent State University Press, 2003.

Marszalek, John F. *Sherman: A Soldier's Passion for Order*. New York: Free Press, 1993.

————. *Commander of All Lincoln's Armies : A Life of General Henry W. Halleck*. Cambridge: Belknap Press, 2004.

McDonough, James Lee. *Shiloh: In Hell Before Night*. Knoxville: University of Tennessee Press, 1977.

McWhiney, Grady. *Braxton Bragg and Confederate Defeat: Vol. 1: Field Command*. New York: Columbia University Press, 1969.

Myers, Raymond E. *The Zollie Tree: General Felix K. Zollicoffer and the Battle of Mill Springs*. Louisville: Filson Club, 1964.

Pinnegar, Charles. *Brand of Infamy: A Biography of John Buchanan Floyd*. Westport: Greenwood Press, 2002.

Piston, William Garrett and Richard W. Hatcher, III. *Wilson's Creek: The Second Battle of the Civil War and the Men Who Fought It.* Chapel Hill: The University of North Carolina Press, 2000.

Prokopowicz, Gerald K. *All for the Regiment: The Army of the Ohio, 1861-1862.* Chapel Hill: University of North Carolina Press, 2001.

Rabb, James W. *Confederate General Lloyd Tilghman: A Biography.* Jefferson: McFarland and Company, 2006.

Shea, William L. and Earl J. Hess. *Pea Ridge: Civil War Campaign in the West.* Chapel Hill: The University of North Carolina Press, 1992.

Simpson, Brooks D. *Ulysses S. Grant: Triumph Over Adversity, 1822-1865.* Boston: Houghton Mifflin, 2000.

Smart, James G. ed. *A Radical View: The "Agate" Dispatches of Whitelaw Reid, 1861-1865.* 2 vols. Memphis: Memphis State University Press, 1976.

Smith, Timothy B. *This Great Battlefield of Shiloh: History, Memory, and the Establishment of a Civil War National Military Park.* (Knoxville: University of Tennessee Press, 2004).

———. *The Untold Story of Shiloh: The Battle and Battlefield.* Knoxville: University of Tennessee Press, 2006.

———. "Historians and the Battle of Shiloh: One Hundred and Forty Years of Controversy." *Tennessee Historical Quarterly* 63, (Winter 2003): 332-353.

———. "'Gallant and Invaluable Service:'" The U.S. Navy at the Battle of Shiloh. *West Tennessee Historical Society Papers*, vol. 58 (2004): 32-54.

———. "'A Siege From the Start:' The Spring 1862 Campaign against Corinth, Mississippi." *Journal of Mississippi History*, vol. 66, no. 4 (2004): 403-424.

———. "Myths of Shiloh." *America's Civil War* (May 2006): 30-36, 71.

Stickles, Arndt. *Simon Bolivar Buckner: Borderland Knight.* Chapel Hill: University of North Carolina Press, 2001.

Sword, Wiley. *Shiloh: Bloody April.* New York: William Marrow and Co., 1974.

Sword, Wiley. *Shiloh: Bloody April.* Revised Edition. Dayton, Ohio: Morningside Bookshop, 2001.

Symonds, Craig L. *Stonewall of the West: Patrick Cleburne and the Civil War.* Lawrence: University Press of Kansas, 1997.

Tucker, Spencer C. *Andrew Foote: Civil War Admiral on Western Waters.* Annapolis: Naval Institute Press, 2000.

Turner, George Edgar. *Victory Rode the Rails: The Strategic Place of the Railroads in the Civil War.* New York: Bobbs Merrill, 1963.

Wills, Brian Steel. *A Battle from the Start: The Life of Nathan Bedford Forrest.* New York: Harper Collins, 1992.

Woodworth, Steven E. *Nothing But Victory: The Army of the Tennessee.* New York: Knopf, 2005.

———. (ed.) *Grant's Lieutenants: From Cairo to Vicksburg.* Lawrence: University Press of Kansas, 2001.

INDEX